IN SEARCH
OF THE
LOST MOTHER
OF INFANCY

Lawrence E. Hedges, Ph.D.

JASON ARONSON INC.
Northvale, New Jersey
London

This book was set in 10 point Goudy by TechType of Upper Saddle River, New Jersey, and printed and bound by Haddon Craftsmen in Scranton, Pennsylvania.

Library of Congress Cataloging-in-Publication Data

Hedges, Lawrence E.
    In search of the lost mother of infancy / Lawrence E. Hedges.
      p. cm.
    Includes bibliographical references and index.
    ISBN 1-56821-274-7
    1. Object relations (Psychoanalysis)—Case studies.
2. Psychotherapy—Case studies. 3. Transference (Psychology)—Case
studies. 4. Mother and infant. 5. Personality development.
6. Psychotherapist and patient—Case studies. I. Title.
    [DNLM: 1. Psychoanalytic Therapy—methods—case studies.
2. Psychoanalytic Theory. 3. Mother–Child Relations.
4. Transference (Psychology) 5. Professional-Patient Relations.
6. Personality Development. WM 460.6 H453i 1994]
RC489.025H43 1994
616.89'17—dc20
DNLM/DLC
for Library of Congress   94-8092

Manufactured in the United States of America. Jason Aronson Inc. offers books and cassettes. For information and catalog write to Jason Aronson Inc., 230 Livingston Street, Northvale, New Jersey 07647.

To each person who has allowed me to grow

and to write about it

by deeply involving me in his or her life

In Memoriam

My long time friend and colleague Sandra Russell is a major contributor to the clinical and theoretical understandings of this book. One of the extended case studies was contributed by her, though for reasons of discretion her name is not directly associated with it. Sandy had been following my work on the organizing experience carefully for over ten years, posing penetrating questions and making vital suggestions at every juncture of its development. Perhaps more than anyone else Sandy understood the subtleties of the organizing experience and how they were to be understood and worked with. Before she could help me put together the final versions of *Working the Organizing Experience* and *In Search of the Lost Mother of Infancy*, Sandy succumbed to a sudden asthma attack while horseback riding with her husband, J. Michael Russell, and their son, James, in Yosemite, July 12, 1993. Sandy's death was a great loss to me and to the many who knew and loved her. Her theoretical and clinical contributions to psychoanalytic thought are celebrated and memorialized in this book in her case study, which those who knew her work will immediately recognize, and in the naming of the woman in the chapter "Sandy: The Development of a Transference Psychosis." None knew better than Sandra Russell the powerful human truths put forth by the analytic speaker in that chapter.

Contents

Acknowledgments

It was Hedda Bolgar who put me up to this work when I was preparing a lengthy lecture to be given at the California Graduate Institute in April of 1980. It has been my custom since the early 1970s to set up classes and to arrange lectures in order to motivate myself into focused reading and to create an occasion for pushing myself into thinking through sticky problems that were otherwise easier to muddle through.

By 1971 I had spent two years of full-time postdoctoral study in child psychoanalysis as a National Institute of Mental Health Fellow at the Reiss-Davis Child Study Center in Los Angeles when Heinz Kohut's (1971) remarkable monograph *The Analysis of the Self* first appeared. I continued studying at Reiss-Davis two additional years taking seminars with Marshall Wheeler, Rudolf Ekstein, and Itamar Yahalom while concluding my analytic training cases. In Marshall's seminar we read Kohut's book together aloud, line by line, marveling at its boldness, its breathtaking foray into a strange wilderness, and its innovative intricacies. It is difficult now to relate to others the challenge Kohut's book provided to the psychoanalytic community then. Shibboleths were shattered wholesale by this golden-tongued man who introduced a language of self transferences never heard before. Many still cannot abide his thoughts, but I doubt they have given him serious or careful study. Like Freud, Kohut is a genius whose mind cuts wide trails across well-established and sacred terrain, alienating high priests whose duty it is to protect against sacrilege.

Kohut was a Freudian scholar and teacher, and, like Freud, he was a philosopher and an epistemologist. I was particularly impressed with his 1959 essay, "Introspection, Empathy, and Psychoanalysis: An Examination of the Relationship Between Mode of Observation and Theory," which spelled out a newer, clearer philosophy of science for psychoanalysis. Kohut maintained that the field of psychoanalysis was effectively limited by the data of personal introspection and vicarious introspection on the part of the analyst, which he termed *empathy*. Psychoanalytic empathy was to be considered a tool for collecting data, analogous to extrospection in the physical sciences—nothing more and nothing less. I organized classes and lectures on Kohut's "Psychology Without Original Sin" (so titled because he had abandoned drive theory) in the early and mid-1970s that filled lecture halls to standing room only. Kohut's work was clearly of great interest to practicing clinicians. In the next few years I encountered Kohut myself, both formally and informally. I will never forget attending his last inspired talk given at Berkeley just four days before he died, a talk preserved on videocassette by Marion Solomon, who is also to be credited for bringing many teaching analysts to California.

For me, Kohut created an opening, an epistemological window, through which to view the richness of the psychoanalytic field, which extends far beyond the established theory and rituals. I remain an ardent fan of his work. I empathized with him when, at the 1979 UCLA Self Psychology Conference, after having heard many new papers delivered by diverse writers hailing themselves as "self psychologists," he declared that he felt he did not belong here. I found it particularly interesting to watch Kohut struggle with, on the one hand allowing himself to be used as the supportive and inspiring father figure that budding creativity always requires, and on the other hand, watching ideas he had painfully sculpted over a lifetime diluted and corrupted by less powerful, detracting, and competing ideas.

By the mid-1970s there appeared a series of important studies that were also ground breaking in their clearly thought out systematic approach to preoedipal personality issues; notable are the monographs by Mahler, Pine, and Bergman (1975), Blanck and Blanck (1974, 1979), Kernberg (1975, 1976), Kaplan (1978), Searles (1979), and Giovacchini (1979). Roy Schafer's (1976) *A New Language for Psychoanalysis*, in which he penetrated the terminology of psychoanalysis by his call for more sensible, down-to-earth formulating, rounded out the thought tools that I needed to go forward. Donald Spence's (1982) work on narrative truth followed close behind.

By January 1980 I was in advanced stages of preparation for my California Graduate Institute lecture on "Treating the Borderline Personality" when I feared my ideas might be too brash, that I might be going too far out on a dangerous limb. I consulted with someone whom I knew had been doing this kind of work for years, Hedda Bolgar. She had grown up in Vienna reading Freud as his books were coming out. In 1938 she had joined hands with Franz Alexander in a move to Chicago, and both of them later moved to Los Angeles. As a psychologist not allowed to call herself a psychoanalyst in this country, Hedda was often sent the "unanalyzable" patients, then called "depressed" and "borderline psychotic."

Hedda had carefully studied my sixty-page manuscript before I arrived. She began with, "See here now, surely you don't expect people to understand this as a lecture. What you have here is the outline for a book or a series of books." And so the project began. Hedda was wonderfully supportive of my approach and offered considerable case illustration. The lecture was another standing room only crowd of some 250 therapists, all of whom were keenly interested in the new work of Kernberg, Mahler, and others. I might add that the greatest times with Hedda were wonderful Friday afternoons with wine, cheese, and her cats—filled with stories of old Vienna and the great analysts as she painstakingly helped me sort through the many issues that my theorizing had stirred up.

Up until that time I was engaged in clinical practice and teaching and had not considered writing a book. But when Hedda hurled the challenge, I wrote *Listening Perspectives in Psychotherapy*. She remained immensely helpful in putting it together. But I can clearly recall envisioning as early as 1965 the need for a total reformulation of psychoanalysis. One day, when talking with my professor and mentor at the University of Iowa, Leonard Eron, I naively said, "The problem with psychoanalysis is not that its fundamental observations are wrong, but that its formulations are reified and vague, closed ended, and not sufficiently open to creative expansion and research. Someday I am going to rethink psychoanalysis and put it in terms that can be studied." Professor Eron was a kind and supportive man whose eyes did not roll up in response. But my memory vaguely recalls a slight smile crossing his face, accompanied by a mild hypertensive flushing. "What outlandish ambitions graduate students have," he must have thought. But perhaps he knew me well enough to wonder about it. He sent me a letter filled with pride and congratulations when I sent him a published copy of *Listening Perspectives*—the pride was accompanied by admonishment for still not having published the behavioral study I did for my dissertation!

When I so naively and brashly declared my intention to rethink psychoanalysis in 1965 I was envisioning the project from the standpoint of logical positivism, the philosophy of science arising through the nineteenth and early twentieth centuries. Little did I imagine then that I would have to do a research project into relativity, quantum mechanics, and chaos theory to be able finally to reformulate psychoanalysis along lines acceptable within the contemporary scientific community.

I have been pleased at the accomplishment that *Listening Perspectives* represents. With philosophical help from Gustav Bergman and J. Michael Russell I was able to formulate a revised philosophy of science and psychoanalytic epistemology that did indeed allow me to rethink and rearrange in a very curious and helpful way most of the field of psychoanalysis. My friend Jim Grotstein is persistent in reminding me that my work is not as strong as it might be if it were more Kleinian influenced. I'm certain he is right, but I have not been schooled sufficiently in Klein's work, or Jung's, or Reich's or Lowen's, or Adler's to be able to consistently and responsibly include them. All psychoanalytic perspectives are complex and comprehensive in themselves and not to be taken lightly. So I must leave an integration of those perspectives to others. But I have been pleased to see that the listening perspectives

I define have been found helpful organizers for many practitioners of these other schools of thought as well.

Though I had done supervision, in-service seminars, and ongoing case conference groups with therapists since 1970, it was not until September 1981 that our monthly Friday night reading group began in Newport. We started with D. M. Thomas's *The White Hotel* and ended that year's series in the spring of 1982 with an evening memorializing Heinz Kohut during which Charles Coverdale and I discussed Kohut's enduring contributions to psychoanalysis. And we viewed the videocassette of Kohut's last talk at Berkeley.

Times were changing in America and nonmedical practitioners with psychoanalytic training like myself were setting up national organizations, procedures for certifying training, and psychoanalytic institutes. William O. Erwin, Ray M. Calabrese, and I organized the Newport Psychoanalytic Institute in 1983, where I served as founding director for five years until it was time to step down and go back to writing. I still teach a class or case conference each year and serve as a supervising and training psychoanalyst. During my tenure as director at the Newport Psychoanalytic Institute, I was able to bring my favorite psychoanalytic writers to Newport to pick their brains: John Gedo, Robert Stolorow, Jay Martin, Ernst Praelinger, Jerome Oremland, Stuart Schneiderman, Gregario Kohon, André Green, Evelyn Schwaber, Joyce McDougall, Hedda Bolgar, James Grotstein, Rudolf Ekstein, and on numerous occasions, Christopher Bollas, who is a native son of Southern California and now somewhat of a patron saint. Frances Tustin and Margaret Little had to send regrets based on age and health. Roy Schafer, Donald Spence, Peter Giovacchini, Nina Coltart, and Harold Searles all indicated a willingness to visit, but our calendars never got together. Each of these people has affected me deeply and personally by his or her sincere and dedicated interest in reformulating and preserving an intellectual and clinical tradition in his or her own way. Each impresses me with a profound respect for the people with whom they work. And each believes in his or her own way that people long considered unanalyzable by classical psychoanalysis are indeed worthy of and capable of making rich use of the psychoanalytic dialogue.

From the outset, Jason Aronson has been an inspirational help and support and then later Joyce Aronson. When I sent him the *Listening Perspectives* manuscript he sent back a contract within three days and has rendered firm and prompt publishing support ever since. But it was not simply that he was willing to publish my works that meant so much to me. From the beginning Jay showed that he *understood* what I was up to, a feat most readers and reviewers have not been able to accomplish! Most know Dr. Aronson as a publisher but are not aware that he is also a psychoanalyst. Jay Aronson has also worked to keep me terminologically clean and conceptually as much as possible on the straight and narrow, recalling from his days at Columbia Psychoanalytic Institute the excellent and creative revisionistic work of Sandor Rado that has unfortunately largely dropped from view because he insisted on developing his own terminology rather than being willing or able to write originally from within the established tradition.

I have necessarily had to create a few new concepts and terms for my purposes, but each is thought through and has an explicit and powerful clinical utility. I have been pleased to eliminate or limit most highly specialized psychoanalytic terms that are not immediately useful in a listening context. I also work toward eliminating doctor–patient healing language because I believe psychoanalysis not to be fundamentally medical in its approach, but rather personal growth producing and consciousness raising. There are many legitimate and powerful medical applications of psychoanalysis, but I believe that medical language itself has limited severely how we think about and practice our discipline.

My chief support for the twenty-one years of her life has been my daughter, Breta Hedges, to whom *Listening Perspectives* is dedicated. Early on she came to respect my need for time to read and write. When she was old enough to ask and to want to understand what I do, we spent a summer thinking together. I wrote a series of "Letters to Breta" that describes what a psychoanalyst does in as straightforward a manner as possible. Later when Breta was old enough she began to work in my office. She then became editor-in-chief on the computer for the rest of the series, and helped organize the manuscripts of the books in this series.

Patti Lynn, Lynn Van Sweden, Ray Calabrese (for his background management of the entire project), Sandra Clinton, Jean Bourns, Gary Conway, and Jason Keyes have all helped with the manuscripts. Joan Carlson has contributed most of the transcriptions. Judy Cohen remains the professional editor fully behind my work at Jason Aronson Inc. in New Jersey, and she, Carol McKenna, and Elaine Lindenblatt have been involved in editorial production. Joyce Hulgus collaborated extensively with me on *Working the Organizing Experience* but for personal reasons had to decline actually co-authoring that book. Many of the clinical and theoretical notions that Joyce and I worked out there come into play in the present text, and I wish there were more ways to credit her for her many powerful contributions throughout.

Interpreting the Countertransference was dedicated to my longtime friend, partner, and emotional supporter, Ray Calabrese, who in every endeavor of my projects has stood by my side loyally, encouragingly, and enthusiastically.

Many colleagues from the Newport Psychoanalytic Institute and the Listening Perspective Study Center have been credited for their contributions to the development of ideas in *Working the Organizing Experience*, the companion volume to this casebook. Those whose influence is particularly important in the present book are Fred Baily, Marilyn Boettiger, Tony Brailow, Suzanne Buchanan, Carolyn Crawford, Jolyn Davidson, Kim Dhanes, Leslie Drozd, Kathryn Fields, Dee Fryling, Tim Gergen, Jacquelyn Gillespie, Lyda Hill, Robert Hilton, Virginia Wink Hilton, Ron Hirz, Jane Jackson, Sandra Jorgensen, Marc Kern, Kim Khazeni, Michael Kogutek, Alitta Kullman, Marlene Laping, Steve Lawrence, Jack Platt, Dolly Platt, Karen K.

Redding, Linda Reed, Jeanna Riley, Margot Robinson, Howard Rogers, Karyn Sandberg, Andrew Schwartz, Diana Seeb, Gayle Trenberth, Robert Van Sweden, Mary E. Walker, and William White.

The saga has required the help of many. In each book footnotes and bylines credit the many therapists and colleagues who in very real hands-on ways have been the living, breathing, vital center of these studies. It would be impossible to credit adequately those who have spent so much time on the couch and in the consulting room telling their stories to me and to others, amidst all this flurry of theorizing and writing activity. I wish to thank those mentioned throughout the books as well as the others who must go unnamed for their enthusiastic support and generous contributions to this project that, to me, has been the most fulfilling experience of my life.

Special Contributors

Special appreciation goes to the following colleagues, who have made major clinical contributions to this book: Bill Cone, Cecile Dillon, Francie Marais, Sandra Russell, Sabrina Salayz, Jackie Singer, Sean Stewart, Ruth Wimsatt, and Marina Young. For reasons of discretion their names are not directly attached to the casework they have provided. Appreciation is also expressed to their clients whose work appears here.

Introduction:
The Listening Perspective
Approach

T he present study is a casebook. Following an introduction to the "organizing experience," is a clinical account of some very interesting material illustrating organizing experience in psychotherapy, which has been contributed by Jackie Singer. This is followed by a case presentation illustrating a pervasive organizing experience. The central part of the book contains verbatim transcripts of study groups comprised of psychotherapists who meet weekly to share their most troubling cases with each other. The cases have been selected because they serve to illustrate theoretical and technical issues in working with the earliest of personality issues. The conferences have been edited for confidentiality and readability and have been abridged for the sake of brevity. Each conference affords the opportunity to discuss theoretical and technical issues in working with the organizing experience. The honest person-to-person sharing among group members is moving in itself. Their collective understanding of this level of work is truly remarkable. We can be grateful to the case presenters and to all of the contributing group members for their willingness to have their most uncertain consulting experiences opened to view.

For a year I obtained permission from ten study groups to let the tape recorder run as a matter of routine, promising confidentiality should case material be selected for research purposes. At the time, people were aware that I was primarily looking for case material for my book, *Interpreting the Countertransference*. I also knew I was looking for material for a casebook on organizing-level experience. By the time I stopped routine recording, several cases had emerged for possible inclusion in the present book. Subsequently, when the therapist elected to discuss work with one of those cases, the recorder was again turned on so that several cases are followed over a four- or five-year period. The level of trust among group members is, as you will see, sufficiently high so that the presence of the recorder seems not to have interfered with spontaneity. The presenting therapist took responsibility for the disguising and editing of the case material. For reasons of discretion, therapists' names are not directly associated with the cases that actually represent their work.

BRIEF ORIENTATION TO THE LISTENING
PERSPECTIVE APPROACH

Four features can be said to characterize my general listening perspective approach.

1. *Psychoanalytic concepts are viable and valuable insofar as they are formulated within a human listening context.* My point of departure for theorizing is always that of sitting in a chair in a consulting room, listening as carefully and fully as possible to what someone has to tell me. Insisting on beginning all psychoanalytic thinking with the listening task is derived from my conclusion that whatever the human mind may be, it is certainly so infinitely complex, elusive, and ever changing that comprehensive and objective studies remain, in principle, forever impossible. Nor can we hope to observe mental functioning with a video camera hidden somewhere "inside," the usual metaphor lurking behind the notion of introspection. We can only listen (in the broadest sense) in awe to the things that people tell us and hope to develop a way of speaking and thinking about our listening experience.

My epistemological approach has been heavily influenced by the philosophers Ryle, Wittgenstein, Gustav Bergman, and J. Michael Russell. But I also felt it necessary to explore quantum physics and chaos theory to find out how researchers from many disciplines have found a degree of comfort with studying the infinitely complex, perpetually vibrating, ultimately uncertain, and forever unknowable universe we now know we live in. Those thinkers and writers and the many methodological considerations I learned from them are dealt with in the section on quantum and chaos theory in *Interpreting the Countertransference.* The result of my excursions into philosophy, epistemology, and quantum and chaos physics has been an insistence on formulating psychoanalytic ideas (following Heisenberg) only according to what can be directly observed or inferred from the sensory data of each psychoanalytic hour. Purely objective science, long ago abandoned as a way of thinking and working by physicists, now gives way in psychoanalysis to systematic subjectivity; the search for historical truth gives way to formulating narrational truths; defining mythical beasts gives way to the formation of subjectively viable frames of reference, in psychoanalysis formulated as listening perspectives; and a presumptive, *a priori* frame for studying the psychoanalytic dialogue gives way to moment by moment variable techniques for sustaining and studying the meaningful interactions of that exchange. I know of no single review of my work that shows a grasp of the profound implications of this overall shift in thought. Reviewers have glimpsed the clinical importance of the way I organize and formulate thought but have not shown a recognition of the impact of a reformulated metapsychology and epistemology. We can no longer afford to imagine that our accumulated wisdom is anything other than a series of ways of thinking or a set of ideas to orient us to human listening situations. Psychoanalytic knowledge is not about a thing, the human mind, but a body of thought about how people can achieve a mutually enlivening consciousness-raising experience. To maximize experience, the terminology of psychoanalytic theory and technique is formulated throughout my work in terms of a viable and palpable context of human listening and relating.

2. *The systematic definition and elaboration of perspectives from which to listen (in the broadest sense) to the ways in which people experience and represent aspects of themselves (in words, images, actions, and interactions) in contrast to the ways in which they experience and represent aspects of others, holds considerable heuristic value for psychoanalytic listening.* Within a "self and other" psychological approach, it has become fashionable to conscript from studies of early child development metaphors describing various kinds of interactions between children and their caregivers. In this way it has become possible to define different types of emotional-relatedness exchanges that characterize children's interactions with significant others, and to study these possibilities in the psychoanalytic situation. In abstracting four distinctly different modes of interpersonal relatedness suggested by developmental metaphors, I have taken the developmental approach one step further by defining four distinctly different perspectives for listening and responding in the psychoanalytic encounter. This book addresses predominantly the perspective for listening to the infant's earliest organizing experiences. The perspectives themselves are discussed from different angles throughout my work but they first achieved definition in *Listening Perspectives in Psychotherapy.* Table 1 summarizes the features and applications of the four perspectives.

3. *In listening to people presenting personality features widely referred to as borderline or various types of character structures, it is helpful to think in terms of a metaphor of childhood symbiosis, so that the demands of a tightly intertwined mother–child bond can be called to the listener's mind for both passive and active transference interpretation.* Early mother–child experience has been conceptualized by Mahler as an internal character structuring called *symbiosis.* The concept of symbiosis has the advantage of focusing analytic attention on a series of overlearned interactive "Mommy and me" scenarios that regularly fill the consulting room and can be usefully considered transference replications of an interactive nature. Replicated interactive forms of transference stand in sharp contrast to those Kohut defines as selfobject or narcissistic transferences and to those Freud defines as oedipal triangular love object transferences.

The easily grasped kind of symbiotic transference interpretation that the listener

Table 1. Listening Perspectives: Modes of Psychoanalytic Inquiry

I. THE PERSONALITY IN ORGANIZATION: THE SEARCH FOR RELATEDNESS

Traditional diagnosis: Organizing personality/psychosis
Developmental metaphor: + or −4 months—focused attention vs. affective withdrawal
Affects: Connecting or disconnecting but often inconsistent or chaotic to an observer
Transference: Connection vs. discontinuity and disjunction
Resistance: To connections and consistent bonds
Listening mode: Connecting, intercepting, linking
Therapeutic modality: Focus on withdrawal/destruction of links—connecting as a result of mutual focus
Countertransference: Comforting vs. disruptive, confusing, or nonlinking

II. SYMBIOSIS AND SEPARATION: MUTUALLY DEPENDENT RELATEDNESS

Traditional diagnosis: Borderline personality organization
Developmental metaphor: 4–24 months—symbiosis and separation
Affects: Split "all good" and "all bad"—ambitendent
Transference: Replicated dyadic interactions
Resistance: To assume responsibility for differentiating
Listening mode: Interaction in replicated scenarios
Therapeutic modality: Replication and differentiation—reverberation
Countertransference: Reciprocal mother and infant positions—a "royal road" to understanding merger relatedness

III. THE EMERGENT SELF: UNILATERALLY DEPENDENT RELATEDNESS

Traditional diagnosis: Narcissistic personality organization
Developmental metaphor: 24–36 months—rapprochement
Affects: Dependent upon empathy of selfother
Transference: Selfothers (grandiose, twin, idealized)
Resistance: Shame and embarrassment over narcissism
Listening mode: Engagement with ebb and flow of self-experiences
Therapeutic modality: Empathic attunement to self-experiences—resonance
Countertransference: Boredom, drowsiness, irritation—facilitating

IV. SELF AND OTHER CONSTANCY: INDEPENDENT RELATEDNESS

Traditional diagnosis: Neurotic personality organization
Developmental metaphor: 36+ months—(oedipal) triangulation
Affects: Ambivalence; overstimulating affects repressed
Transference: Constant, ambivalently held self and others
Resistance: To the return of the repressed
Listening mode: Evenly hovering attention/free association
Therapeutic modality: Verbal—symbolic interpretation, reflection
Countertransference: Overstimulating—an impediment

---

might make use of is, "when I treat you in such and such a way, in your mind and in our interaction I become your mother making the same old demand on you." This interprets the passive replication of the internalized symbiosis in which the analytic speaker presents the child role for interpretation. The more difficult kind of interpretation of the replicated transference for the listener to learn is, "I hate the way you treat me, because it doesn't allow me breathing space in our relationship.

Now I truly know how all of your mother's stifling affected you because you are doing it to me. How are we going to find a way so that we don't repeat this dreaded aspect of your past in our relationship? And how will we find a way for you to relinquish this mode of emotional interaction elsewhere in your life as well?" This is an interpretation of the active replication of the symbiotic transference in that it involves Freud's mechanism of turning a passive trauma into an active victory.

Anna Freud speaks of identification with the aggressor. Melanie Klein speaks of projective identification. I speak of an interactive character scenario and of interpreting the countertransference in such a way as to speak for the child self of the analytic speaker. According to developmental thinking, the time during which the analytic speaker was overlearning (i.e., internalizing) the emotional interactive mode operative in this scenario was that of early symbiotic relating with significant others. The child had no words to protest and perhaps no right or possibility of refusing the devious or destructive emotional interactive mode that is now being refused by the analytic listener. The mode was experienced as intrusive and/or traumatizing and through mimicry or primary identification taken in whole so that it has come to function as a part of the person's character structure. That is, not only are self and other internally represented, but their characteristic interactions and their relationship were internalized as well and will reappear later for transference analysis.

This sketch of my contribution to analyzing early symbiotic features in personality is necessarily brief and simplistic. In a psychoanalytic listening context the set of scenarios would be complex, the emotions stirred up would be difficult ones to deal with, and the interpretations would likely be accomplished mostly in a nonverbal mode. The working through of emotional-relatedness modes retained from the symbiotic period of personal development may take many months, once somehow replicated in the psychoanalytic interaction and identified by the analytic listener through countertransference responsiveness. This entire process of interpretively "speaking the countertransference" as a way of analyzing the replicated transference from the symbiotic developmental period does not represent countertransference disclosure in the usual sense of that term and is the central subject of *Interpreting the Countertransference*. Another casebook of mine, *Strategic Emotional Involvement*, follows up my interpreting the countertransference technique with lengthy and in-depth illustrations of difficult and agonizing countertransference experiences contributed by colleagues whose work I respect.

4. *At the core of all personality functioning lie infantile experiences of environmental failure. The listening perspective approach provides a way of defining an entirely new variety of transference experience metaphorically conceptualized as arising from the infant's traumas and disappointments during the earliest months of life.* During the organizing period, which spans approximately four months before birth to four months after, the infant is searching, reaching out in various sensory/motor/affective ways, seeking to form reliable physical and psychological channels to environmental sources of nurturance, stimulation, comfort, and safety. When

an infant's reaching is met in a timely and pleasurable manner by the environment, that way of reaching out is tried again until it gradually becomes a reliable channel. But when, for whatever reason, the reaching is not met in a timely, satisfying manner, or is actively neglected or traumatized, it is as if a sign were posted in the nascent neurological system saying, "Never go there again."

The organizing experience and organizing transference is, therefore, conceptualized as universal since no early environmental situation ever perfectly meets the baby's needs in the completely desired manner. In later psychoanalytic listening situations the concept of organizing transference is useful in considering the foundational ways a person remains reluctant or internally forbidden to reach out for various forms of emotional relatedness with the analytic listener. All people present to a greater or lesser degree "pockets" of organizing experience that can be listened to as organizing transference.

However, many people experienced actively traumatic intrauterine or postnatal situations that have left them living pervasively organizing experiences because very early in life they became terrified of human emotional connectedness. Not only did they fail to bond with their mothering partner, but they also have remained outside the pale of interpersonal emotional relatedness. Many of these people develop actively psychotic pictures that betray something of the nature of the initial trauma as well as the early way in which the infant tried to solve the problem of not feeling free to fully enter human emotional life. Part I of this book presents two in-depth case studies that contrast limited and pervasive forms of organizing transferences and how therapists can "work the organizing experience."

The search for contact, for the comfort of a warm body is common to all mammals. Like characters out of Kafka, people continue to search for human contact. But, also like Kafka's characters, just at the moment when human contact is within reach "something happens" to make it ungraspable. This mysterious, nonpersonal force often represented by the subjective sense of "something just happening" is the manifestation of the organizing transference, the subtle, invisible overlearned way of avoiding or breaking off human contact, which was once found to be traumatic. According to this line of thought, on the basis of primary identification (mimicry—monkey see, monkey do) the person early on internalized the ways in which contact failed or was ruptured before it could be achieved or sustained. I have called the ways in which people continue to live out the rupture in subsequent failed contacts with others throughout their lives the *organizing* or *psychotic transference*. When considered in abstract, this form of transference experience precedes the process of projective identification. In practice, an infant passes through many experiences and an organizing transference may be entangled with other early psychic mechanisms.

Transference psychosis is a term loosely used by psychoanalysts and is analogous to Freud's term *transference neurosis*. I take *transference psychosis* to mean that the full emotional impact of a person's ruptured strivings for human contact in infancy has slowly come to reside within the transference experience of the psychoanalytic situation. The resistance to establishing the organizing or psychotic transference takes an endless variety of forms, all aimed at foreclosing the possibility of reexperiencing in transference the total terror of the infantile trauma and (in infancy) the realistic threat of breakdown and death because human contact was not available when it was desperately needed. All humans experience some fear when feeling vulnerable and dependent on another who might fail to come through in a needed way. But people who have experienced traumas in infancy have in various ways come to believe that survival is not possible if they allow themselves dependency on another human being. *Gradually allowing the full force of organizing desire and fear to be attached to the person of the analyst and the analytic relationship constitutes the formation of the transference psychosis.*

Interpreting the transference psychosis can only begin after many months or even years of attachment experience and basic trust building in which the true emotional availability of the analyst is tested in various ways and found to be suitable for the project. The interpretive process involves studying two phases of the contact moment as it appears and reappears momentarily in the analytic interaction. The first phase entails the analyst searching to discern moments in which, for an instant, the person is oriented for potential contact. Perhaps it is a laugh or a smile that gives the moment away. It might come each time the person in analysis tells a joke or reviews the plot of an interesting movie. But locating those moments of contact is difficult for therapists since the chatter of the hour or the content of the psychosis tends to clamor on, engaging the analyst in unproductive symptom watching and dynamics formulating.

Once the analyst sees the value of and becomes able to identify the contact moment, the next task is to study in detail how the person in analysis approaches for contact. Each person has a characteristic way of searching, approaching, and orienting him- or herself toward the person with whom contact is desired. This manner can gradually be identified so that the analyst is oriented for the next and most crucial task. Then the analyst begins seeing how the person cuts off, breaks, or ruptures the momentary sense of contact with talking, anger, tears, hallucinations, personality switching, food obsessions, or whatever. The most subtle forms of rupture tend to employ features of the therapist's personality or working style to accomplish disconnecting ends so that the therapist unwittingly colludes in the rupture. Finally, the analyst is lying in wait, actively shutting out all the distracting content of the hour as much as possible until the person approaches for contact and comes directly into place, into contact. The analyst responds instantly with appropriate attunement, remaining ready to "spring."

At the instant the inevitable rupture in contact occurs the analyst somehow reaches out emotionally. If he or she is feeling confident of the moment there may be a token physical reaching as well—an inviting hand extended, perhaps. What is then communicated in any way possible is the same basic interpretation appropriate to the moment: "Wait, don't go away! You were here with me for just a moment. We were laughing, joking, or thinking together about things that interest us—just when you changed the subject or looked away (just when the rageful personality appeared or the hallucination or food obsession began). Can you stay here with me just a moment longer? Can we share being together with each other on a personal, emotional plane for a bit longer? I know you have been taught early in life and that you must pull away now. BUT IT ISN'T TRUE. YOU CAN STAY WITH ME. You are no longer an infant and the agonizing fear that you experience when allowing yourself to be with me is a fear you can learn to bear. Bear with me and tell me in any way you can what it feels like right now. What body sensation or experience now attests to your current state of fear and confusion?"

Little of this can actually be said at that moment because the person is living in a space devoid of words and threatened with internal terrors. The moment is absolutely concrete, the delusion so absolutely real, and reality appreciation so absent that the analyst must be very creative and cautious in this reaching-out and holding process. It will only be a brief moment that such contact can be sustained at first. Gradually, over repeated contact moments, the two will learn to remain together longer. Whatever coaxing serves to gently prolong the moment *is* the interpretation, given at a critical moment in time in a concrete (generally non-verbal) way, that allows the person a glimpse into that primordial place of terror while being held by the listener. Sometimes this nonverbal process of finding ways and time to contact extends over weeks and months. The ever-present danger is that the therapist will invite contact, which is then prematurely made, so that the terror of the initial contact trauma is stimulated and, in transference, the therapist inadvertently become experienced as the original perpetrator of the trauma.

When the analyst has successfully learned to track the person's emotional appearances and disappearances during the session, and when the analyst has found a way of inserting him- or herself directly and fully into the moment of contact rupture, the most surprising thing occurs. The analytic speaker's[1] eyes become big as saucers—in surprise or almost in shock. No one has ever invited or insisted that he or she stay present. No one has ever said at such moments, "I want you here, I desire your presence. We can only learn to be fully human with each other if you can find a way through your fear to remain connected with me. Human life is about being emotionally connected." There may at first be only blank or surprised stares without otherwise visible response. But over time the person perks up and sees the point of it. People then begin to communicate the sense of how "right on" this maneuver is and begin excitedly bringing to session instances from elsewhere in which they watched themselves breaking and then struggling to reachieve contact. Two then begin to study how they come together and what happens to spoil it. Real two-person relating begins. The working through of the

---

[1]Wherever possible in this text the social role designations of doctor–patient, analyst–analysand, counselor–client have been abandoned in favor of the more functional designations of listener and speaker.

transference psychosis or organizing transference then consists of two people coming to form what Searles has called a *therapeutic symbiosis* from which each can later individuate to become more fully human. Whether the organizing experience takes limited or pervasive forms in the person's life, those areas of creativity, originality, and spontaneity that have been cut off since infancy have an opportunity to come to life first *within* the actual relationship with the analyst.

Much of the time this organizing-level transference interpreting probably cannot be done without somehow involving actual physical touch in the interpretative moment—so concrete is mental functioning at these delicate moments that token touch or some other strong form of sensory contact (auditory, visual) may be required as an interpretation that serves to hold the person present, thereby overriding the delusion that one must fight, freeze, or flee. I do not endorse physical contact in psychotherapy for any other purpose—not for comfort, for reassurance, for humanness, or for filling in developmental deficits. However, I find we can talk all we want about how the analyst can "hold" through empathy, voice tone, eyes, and so forth. And I believe a well-trained therapist can hold in many nonphysical ways. But this does not mean that in a moment of deep body regression the client is at all capable of feeling the power of that holding. At that moment there is only terror and no capacity for higher forms of thought, reality testing, perception, or judgment. So we have a deluded therapist believing he or she has the power to hold with words and a fragmenting traumatized person who not only has no words, but no capacity for rudimentary perception of voice tones or facial expressions. In my experience, a hand invitingly extended at such a moment provides an option for the person that could not be provided in any other way. If the person reaches and holds on, it is like electricity flowing through two bodies. The message is "this is your trauma, we feel it right now together. And as we feel the warmth, the firmness, and the pulsing of one another's heart blood we know we are in this together and are going to find a way through."

In my book *Working the Organizing Experience*, there are numerous case examples of different kinds of organizing processes along with discussions of theoretical, technical, empathic, and management issues, which amplify and clarify the kinds of applications these ideas lend themselves to.

The present casebook serves as a guide in the difficult experience of learning how to identify and interpret the organizing transference or transference psychosis. With this brief preparation the reader has a general, if sketchy, sense of the overall backdrop required to conceptualize this approach to organizing or psychotic experience. The case material that follows centers on identifying and moving toward interpretation of the transference psychosis.

Another book of mine, *Remembering, Repeating, and Working Through Childhood Trauma*, focuses on the problem of memory as it has been studied in psychoanalysis. The psychoanalytic view of recovered memory is distinctly different from the Hollywood versions touted currently in the public press. The book urges therapists to take memories recovered in therapy and analysis seriously rather than literally, and considers the problem of technique involved in studying early trauma as manifest in later clinical pictures involving incest, molest, multiple personality, eating disorders, addictions, abductions, and other forms of splitting and dissociation. The distinctly different forms of memory that can be expected in each of the four developmentally based listening perspectives are defined and illustrated. How therapists can address infantile strain trauma as it reappears in transference and how therapists can avoid colluding with the acting out of resistance through accusation of real and imagined perpetrators emerges loudly and clearly from applying the listening perspectives approach to studying childhood trauma. It is my belief that most of the "recovered memories" as they are emerging in clinical practice today, have their roots in the organizing period of development.

These studies are a tribute to many people who have over many years worked diligently to bring to light the darkest recesses of the human soul. At times the work contained herein is difficult to read and grasp. But at other times it is light, fascinating, refreshing, and moving. I hope you find a way to encounter it deeply and to enjoy it.

I

THE ORGANIZING EXPERIENCE: THE STRUCTURAL FOUNDATION OF PERSONALITY

Madness Unmasked:
An Introduction to the
Organizing Experience

The history of psychoanalysis records the progressive discovery of how the various loves of our childhood have left their mark on our personalities and are manifest in our current living and loving. In Freud's study of himself he located the origins of human symbolic life in the triangular love affairs of the 5-year-old. Kohut understood the formation of the self through the influence of selfothers, the loves of the 2- or 3-year-old who confirms who he or she is through mirroring, twinning, and idealizing. Those who have studied our basic character structures note that the strong molding effect of the early (4- to 24-month) human bonding experiences is accomplished through loving interactions between (m)other and the very young child.

Each of these human developmental phases marks where a certain kind of love once was—before it became constricted and/or transformed into later versions. The living record of lost loves Freud called "transference love," the reappearance in the present of loving possibilities retained from the past. Freud noted that our resistance to experiencing our full capacities for love relates to painful experiences of loves lost and to our fears of reexperiencing those pains in present significant relationships. The psychoanalytic study of transference and resistance has been essentially the study of the history of our loves and of love lost.

The present study moves to consider our earliest potential psychological love that was prematurely foreclosed, stopped in its tracks, not allowed to come into full psychological existence. We each had a mother with whom we once shared body chemistry and bodily rhythms—primordial "love," as it were. Our very existence was dependent upon hers. By the time we were born we had already established a certain somatopsychic existence with her and with the surrounding others whose influence on her affected us. After birth most of us experienced significant physical continuity with mother's body. Those who lose their mothers at birth have a major shift to make that leaves its history in their personalities. But for all of us, the first few months of life were filled with stretching and reaching activities involving all of our developing senses and capabilities.

In the beginning our initiations held an infinite variety of possibilities for personal development, depending on the ways our reaching was or was not met by the human environment that surrounded us. Our possibilities for enjoying warmth, nurturance, comfort, sensory stimulation, muscular contractions, muscular relaxations, and organismic balance were global and totalistic at first. These inborn "essential potentials" (Jorgenson 1993) make up the human, genetically given essence from which love arises—Venus fully formed and fresh from the foam of the sea. Waking time was always a questing, and sleeping time was a replenishing and a time for mentally reprocessing waking experiences.

If our development went well in terms of carving out channels, of successfully finding ways to connect with the psychic life and rhythms of our mother and other mothering persons—for pleasure, nurturance, and stimulation—then the first bond that characterizes human psychic love gradually forms. A dance begins in which mother and child offer to and take from each other in turn and according to mutually agreed upon signals and rituals. Mahler's (1968) term for the infant's *internalized* way of experiencing the reliable aspects of this bonding dance with the (m)other is *symbiosis*. Borrowed from biology and social ecology, the term *symbiosis* connotes a mutual need-fulfilling relationship—that primordial form of merged love for which we are forever searching in one way or another throughout our lives.

Much has been studied about the symbiotic phase of development and its enduring impact on the structure of our body and character. Our early symbiotic experience records a series of styles or modes of searching, of relating, and of loving that come to characterize the way we live our daily lives and form our relationships. The set of emotionally charged scenarios we come to live with others are derived from our early symbiotic exchanges. As pieces of history, our symbiotic scenarios reappear in psychoanalysis as replicated transference modes of interacting that pervade our character and body structures. Their analysis can be secured through studying replicated emotional interactions as they emerge in the analytic relationship in forms of transference/resistance and countertransference/counter-resistance. But the story of the symbiosis and the ways of bringing forth its love dimensions for analysis has already been told, at least in its broadest dimensions by many (see Hedges 1992). For us to go "where love once was" is to focus our study on the yet earlier "organizing" period—the few months immediately before and after birth during which channels to the human psyche are and are not being established.

Of the myriad possibilities for connecting to the human emotional environment, each mother–infant dyad is able to develop only a limited number due to the nature of each and the possibilities afforded each by the environment. It is as if the infant sends out thousands of invisible tendrils reaching, searching for how he or she can best find response, can best connect to the other. The ways that succeed form the paths to the symbiotic dance. But what about the fate of the child's many other creative possibilities—the reaching, the questing, the spontaneous gestures that do not find their marks in human responsiveness? Infant research suggests that of the many attempts to connect, mother and child succeed only about 30 percent of the time (Tronick and Cohn 1988). That is, the rich endowment of each human infant encompasses countless possibilities, numberless reachings that fail. Venus may arrive fully formed with endless potentials, but in the imperfect world of humans she is likely to be only partially received.

How does it happen that loving human extension is not met and is thereby allowed to wither and die? And what is the nature of the internalized experience of the infant when a sought for connection cannot be made, or when a connection once made cannot be remade or sustained with the partner? These are the questions that fuel our study of the organizing experience as it is given for us to know in its later manifestations as organizing transference and resistance.

My thesis is that a living record of failed connection remains imprinted on our psyche. When joyful loving is not found or refound, or when painful neglect or rejection is experienced in infancy, an important potential for love and development is arrested, blocked, foreclosed from further development. In psychoanalysis these failures and ruptures in contact are regularly revived aspects of earliest transference love. But until recently we have not known how to frame them for analysis.

Green (1986) speaks of the "dead mother" who is known through sensual pleasure and then, when she fails to appear when needed, becomes internalized as lost or dead. Green holds that the dead mother interject remains as a blank or empty place in our psyche where love and desire once held forth. He shows how we then search the world for the rest of our lives for the lost mother of infancy. But, as Green so aptly points out, although we may search for her "out there" in the world, where love once was, she is not there. She for whom we search is inside ourselves, and she is dead. Her love and her loss have left its mark as an emptiness, a lack, a desire that we search to fill. I identify this set of early formed structures as the organizing transference—the blocks set up in the psyche to reaching out for love that was painfully not met. Some people's early extensions were massively ignored, rejected, or perhaps refused for reasons not of the parent's making. There are many reasons why an infant may not organize, the bottom line being that no mothering person can be found with whom he or she can organize.

All people, regardless of how well they were able to connect and proceed to other levels of development and phases of loving, suffered repeated failures and ruptures in the early connecting task. Contemporary life-styles of working parents increase the risk that in the early months of life crucial connections will not be made at the time and in the ways that the infant needs them to be made, thus giving rise to more internalized experiences of failed and ruptured connections, of "dead mothers." Venus with all her myriad possibilities and potentialities may have been present at birth or at least shortly prior to birth. But the riches of love and creative expression with which we were born rapidly diminish, leaving only memory traces, scars where love once was, but is no more.

In psychoanalysis we have learned to search psyche for lost loves of later eras. Now it is time to search for the lost love of infancy. Like loves from the oedipal, the selfother, and the symbiotic periods, lost love from the organizing period has left its own definite and indelible mark on personality. It is the therapist's task to learn how to identify and elucidate primordial love through the ways it is manifest in the resistances and transferences of the analytic relationship.

This book follows therapists and clients on their journey to where love once was, in search of the lost mother of infancy. The ways in which the presence of early ruptures in love can be defined are studied. Many ways in which the organizing-level transference can be framed are shown in the casework presented here. The many ways in which resistance to reexperiencing intense early psychic agony and physical pain can be unraveled and endured are demonstrated by the therapists who have offered their work here for us to study. Psychotic and organizing constellations long considered to be unanalyzable by psychological means are broken down and transformed before our very eyes. Delusional beliefs melt. The long-standing and much dreaded specter of human madness stands here unmasked and demythologized. We now know the origins of madness and how to frame it for transference and resistance analysis.

The Path to Organizing Infantile Experience

TRANSFERENCE AND RESISTANCE MEMORIES

A convenient metaphor for conceptualizing how primordial organizing experiences are retained in psyche is to follow an imaginary path along which an infant might extend herself in search of the nurturing and holding environment. The channels for connection *in utero* are primarily physiological. After birth the somatopsychic extensions and contractions take physical form at first, only gradually shifting to more psychic connections. At issue with human infants, as with all mammals, is survival, followed by safety, comfort, and stimulation. Sufficiently hospitable environmental conditions are afforded most infants so that psychological paths can become organized to needed features in the human environment. These paths can develop and become organized into mutually satisfying scenarios, interpersonal dances that lead to emotional bonding with the mothering partner(s) and to the intrapsychic experiences referred to by Mahler (1968) as symbiosis. But the frustrating experience of reaching and not finding is universal and the impact of failed extension leaves its mark on our character in various ways.

Often strain, if not more considerable trauma, is experienced by infants in their efforts to organize and to sustain reliable channels. We can observe in any mammal the terrified frenzy that results when the warm body and nurturance of the maternal body cannot be found. We assume that some sort of genetically based "survival instinct" operates that gives rise to frantic gross bodily reactions when the ongoing continuity of life seems threatened. When needful and desirous extensions are not met in a satisfactory or timely manner, or are met with abuse, we observe what Fraiberg (1982) calls the predefensive reactions of fight, flight, or freeze, which are common to all mammals. Human babies are no exception. Predefensive reactions to painful or frightening experiences set up memory barriers along paths of possible connection so that these paths are not selected again or are employed only with trepidation and caution.

In psychoanalytic situations of later life, these predefensive reactions can be studied as organizing or psychotic transferences and as resistance to establishing basic love, dependency, or trust in relationships. Where love once was or might have been is now blocked. The person in analysis moves in search of the lost mother of infancy. Reviving the somatopsychic memories or blocks to reaching out for love necessarily entails reliving primitive agonizing experiences in the here-and-now relationship with the analyst. For years the experiences that are bound to emerge as this early developmental period comes into focus in the transference were deemed unanalyzable because they were so enigmatic and did not yield to estab-lished psychoanalytic or psychotherapeutic understanding or technique. Negative therapeutic reactions arising from transference psychosis have been repeatedly reported with puzzlement, dismay, and pessimism in our literature. Only now are the conceptual tools gradually emerging that allow framing these organizing experiences for analysis.

What follows is a consideration of some expectable experiences that might be thought to characterize the infant's path toward connection with and disconnec-tion from the maternal presence. From the standpoint of psychoanalytic listening, these issues along the organizing path serve to prepare the analyst for the kinds of experiences he or she may encounter when working the organizing experience as revived in transference, resistance, and countertransference memories.

THE QUEST FOR RELIABLE CONNECTION

Living in a world of humans but not quite feeling human is the fate of many people who pervasively live organizing experiences in their daily lives. Kosinski's protag-onist in *Being There* (1970), Suskind's hero in *Perfume* (1986), and the character played by Meryl Streep in the film of David Hare's play *Plenty* (1983) further depict the longing, the quest, the search for the mother of primordial love who cannot be found. In living out organizing experience people search the world and analysis for connections that, no sooner than they are perceived, vanish in midair, leaving only yearning in their place. The organizing experience is, to a greater or lesser extent, universal because all babies record in memory quests that reaped failure. All babies erect blocks to kinds of human yearning and connection that they have experi-enced as painful. In transference these unresponded to, denied, or abused quests reemerge. How can the analytic listener frame them for systematic study? The path to organizing experience begins and continues seemingly endlessly with a search for what cannot be found.

THE EXPERIENCE OF THE REFLEXIVE WORLD

Freud's earliest theory of the mind (1900, Chapter VII) envisions primordial mental functioning as "reflexive" in nature, so that distinctions between subject and object and inside and outside cannot be made. The gradual buildup of memory gives rise to cause-and-effect reactions and thought, to a reflex arc that proceeds from sensory perception to motor response. But prior to the establishment of memory traces that render the reflex arc of mental functioning unidirectional, sensory and motor experiences are bidirectional, reflexive in nature. Not only do sensations give rise to motoric response, but random motor activities give rise to sensory experiences that possess a hallucinatory vividness. Dreams and memories that refer back to infantile experience are likely to possess this same sense of hallucinatory vividness, and are likely to loom large as especially real. Flashbacks that emerge and come to possess this same sense of vividness can be thought of as primary-process constructions like dreams.

From a listening standpoint this element of hallucinatory vividness points to the experience at hand as having a significant root in early infantile experience of a traumatic nature – traumatic or painful because favorable environmental responsiveness to infantile strivings opens pleasurable channels that then become progressively worked and reworked into later experience and therefore lose the quality of memory. But thwarted searching and reaching causes psychic pain along pathways that are then marked and blocked (Freud 1895a). It is the study of such early somatopsychic blockages that working the organizing experience addresses. The listener must be prepared for the *content* of the analytic hour to be reflexive in nature – that is, not truly cause and effect or secondary process in nature, but experience that is fundamentally unorganized and passes with hallucinatory vividness into and out of awareness. Considering the content of organizing experiences as reflexive in nature allows the listener to focus attention on the structure of the relatedness experiencing itself, not on the psychotic or organizing content per se. By relinquishing his or her usual concern with the content of the analytical hour and focusing on the structure of the search for contact and the habitual way contact is foreclosed, ruptured, or not sustained, the organizing transference can be framed for analysis.

THE IDIOSYNCRATIC USE OF SYMBOLS

The imagery or so-called symbols, whether in florid forms or more subtle forms, invariably captivate the attention of observers. But repeated attempts over many years by analytic listeners to decode psychotic symbols or to live in the psychotic world have ended in therapeutic failure. What finally becomes clear is that psychotic symbols are not symbols as we ordinarily consider them. The world of the psychotic is not something another person can enter. We can only be empathetic to the fact that another person has organized his or her somatopsychic experiences in unusual or idiosyncratic ways. We cannot know that personal way of experiencing. We can only know *about* it and that knowledge is of limited value in analyzing transference and resistance structures.

The usual route for understanding symbols is to begin from some conception of a cultural and linguistic code regarding the possible meanings and uses of a given symbol, and then on the basis of some consensual understanding of the symbol to determine how the individual employs the meaning in his or her personal discourse. For example, in Freud's theory for the treatment of psychoneurosis, the symbol is believed to be employed by the oedipal-age child for the purpose of repressing unwanted, internally generated stimulation of a sexual or aggressive nature. Following an analysis of dreams, slips, sexuality, and other primary-process derivatives, the original repressed meaning of the symbol is inferred and verbally interpreted by the analyst so as to permit a return of the repressed. Preoedipal symbols are generally referred to as representations because the motive for the use of these symbols is not disguise (as in oedipal neurosis) but rather representation of characteristic configurations of self and other experience [cf. Kohut's (1991) comments on self state dreams, and Stolorow and Atwood's (1982) work on the phenomenology of dreams]. Experience teaches us that we cannot listen to organizing level symbols in any of these ways. The motive force is expressive rather than repressive or representational.

Understanding psychotic or organizing symbols does not begin with reference to the consensual code of symbolic meanings. The infantile experience to be studied was structured in somatopsychic constrictions and blockages long before there was any ordered awareness of the social world or its codes. The experience is on the level of the body, in the register of the real—not of the imaginary or the symbolic. Rather, our understanding begins by noting and observing the ways in which the individual living out organizing experience in analysis approaches interpersonal contact, potential engagement, and the ways in which the person prevents or ruptures emotional contact and, therefore, the possibility of human emotional bonding. Once the details of the transference and resistance movements can be defined for the individual, it can then be seen that he or she has conscripted some image or symbol from social discourse and pressed it into personal idiosyncratic expressive service, which is not at all derived from the consensual system of symbol formation and usage. The psychotic symbol then can be seen as failing to operate in the usual or expected way by condensation or displacement of personal meaning through use of metaphor or metonymy. Instead, the organizing or psychotic symbol *expresses* (rather than symbolizes, substitutes, or represents) the idiosyncratic vicissitudes of contact search and contact rupture, the foundational structures of human relatedness.

In a case provided by Frances Tustin (Hedges 1994a), an autistic child, Peter, enthusiastically rolls a banana around on his tongue and swallows it in greedy gulps, only to appear immediately physically and emotionally depleted. The banana does not symbolize or represent anything. Rather, Peter expresses to Tustin the voraciousness and pleasant mouth sensations he feels when masticating and savoring the banana. But when the sensuous experience caused by the banana and his mouth movements ends, Peter becomes immediately forlorn and lonely without the "lovely mouth sensation of having mother's nipple as a part of his mouth rather than separate from it."

Tustin demonstrates during the hour with Peter how many ways his ring of keys, his missing milk teeth, and "boiler" are all idiosyncratic symbols made up to express an experience. But the symbols cannot be decoded in ordinary ways.

Listening for the approach to contact and the rupture of contact, and, more subtly, listening for the myriad ways in which the manner of the approach for contact itself already contains the assurance that contact cannot or will not be made, allows the highly personalized meanings of organizing symbols to emerge. This way of considering symbols stands in sharp contrast to the usual therapeutic methods of decoding meanings and offers an avenue to understanding critical memories from the organizing period.

NONHUMAN IMAGERY, PHYSICAL SENSATIONS, AND ORIENTATION IN TIME AND SPACE

The listener hoping to gain understanding and definition of organizing experience must be prepared to encounter an endless flow of images that refer to nonhuman elements and forces, of physical sensations that express structured fears, and of an array of confusions in temporal and spatial orientation. The organizing experience occurs before human bonding is established and serves to make boundaries impossible. When such early experience is expressed there will be a preponderance of elements referring to the nonhuman environment (Searles 1960) because the person has not become initiated (partly or wholly) into human relatedness life.

The organizing experience is also prepsychological, so somatic experiences, preoccupation, and images will predominate (McDougall 1989). Freud (1911) maintains that somatic sensitivity (hypochondriasis) bears the same relation to psychosis that anxiety bears to neurosis—it is foundational and no theory or technique relating to psychosis is complete without significant reference to somatic experience. Stimulation from the environment is received and experienced by the body. But without mental processes that have emotionally bonded to the human world of thought and experience the stimuli cannot be integrated smoothly from soma into psyche.

Ekstein and Motto (1966) write of psychotic children who live in a subjective world of action and impulse with time and space whirling around them. Organizing experience is derived from a phase in our lives that was not attached to consensual or experiential-based notions of time and space. As a result, most organizing experiences contain elements of confusion or disorientation with regard to these ordinary dimensions. A person who may be oriented in time and space on the basis of mimicry becomes easily lost and confused. Analytic listeners have often dismissed these variations as symptomatic without knowing quite how to contextualize them in the world of infancy, which is often experienced with peculiar regards for time and space. Studying orientation in time and space often sheds crucial light on the nature of connection and disconnection.

TRANSFORMATION THROUGH CONNECTION

Bollas (1979) holds that the infant's first experience of mother is one of state transformations. The infant experiences some desire or need, and shortly that state undergoes a transformation that later can be attributed to the activities of mother. Bollas points out that Freud unwittingly and forgivably arranged an acting out of the transformational situation of infancy in his creation of the analytic situation. As contact is made with the transformational environment an intelligence operates that functions to alter physical and psychological sensations. Once contact is made and can be sustained there is room to begin considering splitting and projective identification (M. Klein 1952, 1957). But organizing experience that is retained in personality and that appears in transference and resistance occurs prior to the time when contact can be reliably made and sustained.

In Genesis we are told that while God created the other animals, he breathed the breath of life into Adam. On the ceiling of the Sistine Chapel Michelangelo portrays the conveyance of Divine spirit from God to Adam through motivated extension and touch. In Madonna paintings the spirit of the Divine on earth is nurtured through swaddling, holding, suckling, and tender attentiveness. A recently published interdisciplinary symposium entitled *Touch: The Foundation of Experience* (Brazelton and Barnard 1990) explores in depth the meaning and impact of touch in human life. Several of the philosophical contributors to this symposium trace the study of touch from Plato and Aristotle through twentieth century commentators. The general consensus of opinion corroborates the Michelangelo conclusion that the human sense of Logos is passed down the generations through touch. Whether touch or laying on of hands is actual, proximal, or metaphoric, what is consistently seen to be of importance is the desire or intention on the part of the initiated in human spirit to reach out and touch the uninitiated.

Traditional analytic approaches have eschewed physical contact of any type as being a violation of the fundamental stance of analytic neutrality practiced so rigorously in the treatment of neurosis. Heinz Kohut's (1981) deathbed legacy to us involves not only a vignette in which he extended his fingers for a desperate (clearly preneurotic) woman to hold on to, but a commentary on the need to study the development of the human faculty of empathy from concrete physical forms to more abstract mental forms.

A problem with the traditional "frame technique" is that it is imbued with a set of moral imperatives about how analysis of neurosis should proceed. Frame morality developed while studying neurosis has been uncritically extended to analytic therapy with preneurotic people, with limited success. The "no touching" rule seems to have proven itself basically useful and valid—at least until we consider responding to the organizing experience of internalized terror of contact, after which another set of questions arises.

We now know that without involved and attentive human touch babies die of marasmus. We are now equally clear that quite apart from genetic and biological considerations, functional psychotic conditions are directly attributable to missing, defective, erratic, inappropriate, ill-timed, or intrusive physical contact early in life. From studies of childhood psychosis and psychotherapy with psychotic states in adolescents and adults, we are also clear that human contact, often manifest in some form of at least token physical touch, is requisite to transforming reflexive mental states into symbiotic bonding patterns. The foundation of human related-ness experience is now understood to be related to actual human contact, to touch in some form by another who is well motivated to achieve and to sustain the contact in a safe and enlivening manner. It is yet unknown whether transforma-tional work with organizing states can be accomplished without some limited, token, or concrete interpretive physical contact. There are obviously many legal and ethical as well as psychodynamic issues involved when we consider what kinds of contact may be appropriate or necessary. But our understanding of how concretely these organizing experiences inevitably present themselves points to a reconsideration of the possible meanings and uses of interpretive touching.

Case illustrations and additional theoretical and practical considerations are in Hedges (1994a). Later in this book I raise this set of issues again in context. An informed consent form that may be appropriate to consider appears in the Appendix. I recommend that whenever psychotic transference is to be worked that a third-party case monitor be involved for the protection of the therapist when the psychotic transference emerges as well as for the client's protection in regard to continuity of care. Considerations for a case monitor are detailed in Hedges (1994a). The term *interpretive touching* is a highly technical notion to be used with great care. It will be clarified later in the context of case illustration.

Basic organizational aspects of personality are not thought to be readily acces-sible for analytic study via the usual verbal-symbolic, introspective modes of investigation that have characterized the analysis of neurosis. Nor are organiza-tional issues available for analysis through the mode that Kohut has called self to selfobject resonance. Nor are they available through interactive modes of investi-gation or systematic countertransference studies commonly used in understanding the symbiotic and postsymbiotic replicated transference encountered in borderline personality organization. The investigative mode par excellence for listening to organizing aspects of personality necessarily becomes that of interpretive contact and interception (Hedges 1983b, 1994a).

Organizing features must be concretely met, intercepted, or contacted during discrete moments of sensorimotor or cognitive-affective extension in order for the impact of the inconstant configurations of the part-other to be experienced and registered in the emerging personality formation, along with various contrasting experiences of part-selves. Overtly psychotic phenomena represent abortive attempts at self-stabilization or self-nurturing stimulation and/or soothing, which only seldom include representations favorable for realistic relatedness to others.

THE CONTACT MOMENT

No mothering situation can provide the baby with timely and empathic responsiveness to her perpetual extensions all the time. Winnicott (1953) came to speak of "good enough" mothering to indicate that a certain minimal kind of responsiveness is required for ordinary development. Others have spoken of such things as the "average expectable environment." But whether by accident, fiat, or parental intention, many infant sensorimotor or cognitive-affective extensions inevitably go unresponded to. We do not know the exact effect of occasional lapses in attention or minor deviations in maternal preoccupation, but clinical studies of psychotic states demonstrate clearly the effects of chronically and/or traumatically failing contact, whether due to some shortcoming in the environment or attributable to some inborn factor in the infant that precludes experiences of contact that might stimulate object relations development. We can only assume that lesser failings have a lesser, but no less real effect.

Failed contact is a universal human experience that has been neglected in considering internalized emotional responses to not being connected with in the analytic encounter, particularly during periods when people are remembering by living out organizing experiences.

Thus far in our examination of the issues that baby encounters on the path to connection we have seen what appears to be natural, instinctually determined extensions that have been met and thereby reinforced by someone in the environment who was attuned to the subtleties of baby's physical and psychological existence. The path that is met by an attentive, enlivening other becomes circular so that baby is reaching, exploring, finding, and creating satisfying and stimulating transformational experiences for herself. "Look, now she's smiling, now she's reaching to me, now she's concentrating on her bowels—she's becoming a real person!"

The central thesis of this book is that the organizing experience revolves around the contact moment. The analytic listener's first task is to sort through the often complex and confusing reflexive content to determine where potential points of real interpersonal (affective) contact may be possible. Then the analyst learns to track the person's movement toward contact moments that seem as inevitable as any mammal searching for a breast. But somewhere just before, during, or immediately after contact "something happens" to make contact or sustained contact impossible. It is the specificity of the contact-rupturing experience that must be framed for analytic study. The person's internal, idiosyncratic way of rupturing contact is understood as the organizing or psychotic transference and can be fruitfully studied in the psychoanalytic setting. Resistance will come to be understood as the person's all-out efforts to avoid dealing with (a) the contact experience itself and (b) the traumatic life-and-death transference issues that terrifyingly must be relived if one is to sustain the contact.

As resistance and transference analysis proceed, the transference psychosis will gradually become established. This is a complex state of affairs in the analytic relationship in which the earliest mother–child relationship that prevented the person from developing further is being lived out. This same listening tool is as useful for people living pervasive organizing experiences as for people who may be much better developed in many or most ways, but who need to explore some aspect of early organizing experience in their analysis.

Freud's fundamental concept of cure in psychoneurosis is the establishment of the transference neurosis, meaning the full and conscious establishment of the triangular oedipal-incestual attitudes of childhood, in the here-and-now psychoanalytic relationship. That is, neurotic attitudes are created through repressive maneuvers of a young child. The analysis of defense and resistance allows for the full return of the repressed in the present (adult) relationship. Life's instincts, long held captive by repression, are now liberated and their first natural target is the analyst for allowing the experience of full being. The analyst's task ends with the full establishment of the neurotic attitudes in the analytic relationship – that is when the ordinary neurosis is replaced by the transference neurosis. There is nothing further to resolve, work through, or strengthen. The parts of the self that had been subject to repression have been liberated; the repressed (sexuality and aggression) has returned in full force to contemporary experiencing by the mind of a conscious adult in full light of day. (For an elaboration of Freud's notions of the curative value of the transference neurosis see Hedges [1983b, Chapter 4].) Many analysts after Freud have desired a happier ending, with the Oedipus complex being worked through or resolved. But Freud spoke of the "waning" of the Oedipus complex – a slow, lifelong diminishing of its unconscious power in subsequent relationships.

However, in preneurotic, preoedipal states more than merely experiencing a return of the repressed in the analytic relationship is required for personality transformation. Kohut speaks of processes or experiences of resonating understanding and of the benefits of human empathy (beyond mere observation of another). Psychoanalysts who write about borderline and symbiotic states, in one way or another, speak of shifts in the ego to accommodate new modes of relatedness. At the organizing level the establishment of the transference psychosis has often been seen as the ultimate place that the treatment may go, but it has never been considered curative in itself, as has transference neurosis. The reason is clear: the establishment of the transference psychosis marks the appearance of the "unthought known" (Bollas 1987) in the analytic relationship. Early environmental failures and traumas cannot simply fade harmlessly into the past unless something in the present replaces them or fills in the gap left by empty, failed, or traumatized experiences.

The transference attitude that is brought forth for analysis relates to the way contact has been ruptured traumatically in the past. But the effect of the infant's internalizing and subsequently continuing to live out the rupture experience is that personality fails to develop in significant ways. We might think that in the wake of the dissolution of a psychotic transference attitude, the person is ready to learn a new skill—that of sustained relating. But in practice it never works quite this way because the person has been so terrified of failed contact that the psychotic manifestation, the organizing transference, does not yield completely to analytic work unless and until the analytic speaker feels clearly that he or she can indeed safely connect with the real person of the analyst and safely use the analyst's being to organize around. For this kind of work to succeed, Kohut imagines that the patient would have to be willing and able to sustain long periods of pre-psychological chaos alternating with long periods of borrowing heavily from the personality of the analyst (Kohut 1984). The organizing experience that is internalized can only be fully brought for analytic scrutiny when there is enough belief established that other ways of surviving the internalized infantile trauma are possible and available within the analytic relationship. It is only within the context of reliable analytic holding that a person dares reexperience the life-threatening infantile trauma of the organizing period, which is still silently alive in the personality. Only as the analyst offers a new and better way of relating in the here and now can the ancient disconnecting traumas be relived and actively relinquished in favor of actualizing in the analytic relationship more complex and flexible relatedness modes.

With all the effort and devotion focused on the quest for human contact, how is it that the person living organizing issues is so often unable to find or to create ways of establishing the required connections? Every organizing issue or pattern that a person retains and actively lives on a daily basis is held firmly intact by a psychotic transference structure. Every organizing mode, regardless of its presumed cause, its thematic variety, or its pervasiveness in the person's life, owes its entrenched futility to a learned pattern of withdrawal from or avoidance of all or specially selected contact situations. The person has come to live in terror of the pain that in earlier life experiences was associated with contact and/or contact failures.

This fear of contact situations contrasts sharply with the fear of abandonment long familiar to analysts working with people living symbiotic or borderline interaction patterns or scenarios. At the earlier organizing level the fear is of contact, while after the establishment of a firm holding and mutual cuing process (of whatever character) becomes established, the fear is of separation, loss, or abandonment of the other. But what exactly is meant by "psychotic transference" and how can the problem be analytically approached?

The pathway to becoming initiated and integrated into the psychological structures that characterize human cultural life as we think of it passes through the symbiotic bonding experience. The feeling of being real, of being human like other people, of sensing an aliveness and cultural attunement with the human race is cultivated and achieved by two in a mutually engaging symbiotic exchange where each learns how to relate to the humanness of the other. When the young child has an opportunity to feel, to experience, to know about, to cultivate, and to live out her physical and instinctual endowment within a human-relatedness pattern governed by considerations derived from the human cultural and linguistic community into which she is born, she has the opportunity to feel real, alive, and human.

Depending on the degree to which a person was deprived of this opportunity for organizing a self in tune with environmental, cultural, and linguistic possibilities due to biological or environmental factors, her daily living will remain restricted to prehuman or nonhuman relatedness capabilities. The efforts that the person made in infancy to reach out, to seek human contact and bonding were somehow ineffectual. Perhaps baby's efforts were inadequate to draw the needed attention from caregivers. Perhaps her overtures fell on deaf ears, or worse, were met with sadistic, erratic, inappropriate, or traumatizing intrusions that caused her to withdraw from emotional-relatedness situations of a certain variety or from human contact situations altogether. What is learned and overlearned by virtue of its primacy in experience or its intensity of deprivation or abuse, is, "Never go there again." Freud (1895a) accounts for this absolute withdrawal in terms of the operation of the Psi system.

IDENTIFYING ORGANIZING TRANSFERENCE

Identifying transference experience from this level of development begins with the assumption that if psychological attachment, the bonding dance, has not occurred or has only partially occurred, there is a reason. And whatever the reason, it occurred historically in the earliest months of life. Evidence of closed-off psychic channels for human connection and somatic constrictions that make extensions painful are retained in the personality and in the body structure in ways that can be observed in later life as the organizing or psychotic transference. This earliest of transferences represents learning experiences of the infant that occurred whenever she emotionally extended or reached out and was somehow turned away, not met, or negatively greeted. The questing activity was met with environmental response that taught the infant not to strive in that way again. The "never go there again" experience effectively marks organizing experiences that later can be identified as transference.

Psychoanalytic work has been characterized from its inception by its focus on bringing into consciousness previously learned, "automatic" or unconscious emotional responsiveness patterns. Psychoanalytic studies have aptly demonstrated how earlier emotional-relatedness experience can be observed as structured modes of relatedness that become transferred into later interpersonal interactions. Psychoanalysts ask, "What is keeping this person rigidly held within a certain almost compulsive way of being, of experiencing, and of relating to others?" With people living organizing experiences, the transference structure can be seen as systematically functioning to limit or to prevent sustained human emotional contact. The person learned as an infant that emotional contact is dangerous, frightening, traumatic, and/or life threatening. Relatedness learning during the earliest months of life becomes organized around limiting the extension or reaching out experience and preventing all forms of contact felt to be frightening, unsatisfying, or unsafe.

In sharp contrast to (borderline) people living out later developed internalized symbiotic relatedness modes and terrified of rejection and abandonment, people living organizing experiences are terrified of interpersonal connection. At every moment of longed for and sought for contact, some (psychosomatic) image or experience of a traumatizing other suddenly intervenes to make sustained contact impossible. This is why the working-through process in analysis is accompanied by such intense physical pain. It is as though the minute the infant puts mouth around nipple and starts sucking, terror or poison was the experienced result. Overlearned aversion reappears later as transference. A person may be terrified of any human contact that is likely to cause him or her to reexperience that early massive and very painful trauma. What follows are three examples of how an organizing experience can appear and how we as listeners can gain some grasp of the organizing transference experience.

TRANSFERENCE ILLUSTRATION 1:
RAGING AT THE THERAPIST

A woman therapist has been treating a female client twice a week for three years. An intense therapeutic relationship has developed. The client is a very bright and sophisticated professional. She lives in the world very comfortably in regard to everyday matters, but she suffers privately from having a multiple personality. The most troubling switch is when she, without apparent reason, goes into a rageful self. Her therapist sought consultation in a crisis after she got a telephone call from the client following their last session saying, "I'm not coming in any more because there's something wrong with our relationship." The therapist inquired about the nature of the problem. The client responded, "I can tell you feel there's something wrong with my relationship with Naomi." Naomi is a lesbian woman the client has developed an intimate relationship with. She continued, "You don't think that it's right, or you think there's something wrong with Naomi. There's no point in our going any further so long as you think that way." She was angry, shouting at her therapist, and then she listed a number of other things. "You don't listen this way . . . and you're not that way . . . ," a tirade of angry complaints and accusations leveled at the person and the practice of the therapist that the therapist had never heard before.

The therapist is in a state of shock, feeling she may never see the client again. She is not even clear about what might have been said to upset the client. She cannot link her abrupt disruption to anything. The therapist asked the client, "What makes you think I don't like Naomi? I've always been supportive of your relationship with Naomi." But the client is certain the therapist disapproves of Naomi and of the relationship. So far as the consultant could ascertain, the therapist has no such negative feelings about the relationship and has no personal biases against lesbianism. In fact, the therapist seems glad her client has found a friend.

The therapist is in crisis because she has been able to schedule a telephone appointment with the client but is anxious about how it may go. She tells the consultant that her client is basically not a lesbian. She has had three or four relationships with women but they have been relationships in which she is looking for soothing contact with a woman, possibly in order to feel mothered. She cannot develop relationships with men because she does not know how to relate to men. She is confused and frightened by men. She has talked at various times about how even though she is having a sexual relationship with a woman, she does not feel that she is a lesbian. She does not feel like other lesbians. The client feels certain she is really not a lesbian. At one point the therapist had said, "I really don't think you're a lesbian either." It occurs to the consultant that this could be where the organizing transference became attached, that is, in the therapist's attitude that the client is not lesbian. The consultant asks, "How have you developed your view? From all you have told me of her relatedness capacities, she's emotionally 3 months old. We have no idea what lesbianism means to her, and we have no idea what her future may be. She has developed no real sexual identification yet and therefore no stable gender identity." The therapist immediately resonates with that. It seems the client is experiencing some breach in empathy. She has determined that her therapist has an attitude that the client is not really a lesbian. Now she claims the therapist disapproves of Naomi and of her relationship with Naomi.

The therapist has learned how to work the organizing experience very skillfully. For many months the two have worked over many connecting and disconnecting experiences in other relationships, although the client has not been able to work the organizing transference directly with her therapist—at least not until now. In a series of parallel transferences the two have been studying the ways the client connects and disconnects daily with people. She says, "I *feel* fully connected with people. I see people. I talk to people. I move in a social world. Superficially I do very well, but at some other level I know I'm not connected." She has the conviction that her mother "gave me away" in the seventh or eighth month *in utero*. And what she has been striving for ever since is to be bodily reconnected to mother, to be sustained in a physical relationship. The suggestion is that there was once a connection, but that mother broke the connection. The analytic speaker has no idea how to make or to sustain mental connections.

She has presented one critical traumatic memory. When she was perhaps 2 or 3, she and her mother lived in quite poor circumstances—in maybe one room with a bathroom down the hall. Her mother would often take her to the bathroom with her. When the mother was pregnant and had a miscarriage, the child witnessed her mother pull out the bloody fetus and flush the unborn baby down the toilet. It was a vivid memory. The consultant asks the therapist, "Do you suppose her mother also tried to abort her, because that seems to be what's coming up in the transference? I remember one man who had an endlessly recurring dream desperately hanging onto the edge of a cliff, clinging to one root, about to fall to his death at any moment. His mother later confirmed that she had used a coat hanger several times in an attempt to abort him during the pregnancy. His struggle to stay alive was vividly represented in the recurring dream. Do you suppose her memory is a screen memory? Or is it something she actually witnessed? My hunch is that the memory stands out so vividly because she believes 'that's what mother did to me. Mother flushed me down the toilet. Mother broke the contact and flushed me down the toilet in the same way.' Perhaps that's what she experiences you are doing to her right now. She has somehow succeeded in experiencing in transference that you are aborting her. She is using something in your demeanor toward her friend Naomi in order to project the organizing transference wish to abort her into the therapeutic relationship."

The deceptive thing, and the reason this example is clear, is that when a therapist first starts tracking these organizing experiences in transference they frequently look like symbiotic (abandonment) material. The speaker says, "I'm leaving you because you failed me. You abandoned me and I'm never coming back." Yet, upon closer examination, we realize that as the organizing transference begins to fit into place, the person waits for a moment in which she can re-create the organizing rupture in the relating.

This client re-created it by screaming accusations at her therapist about her attitudes and how bad she is as a therapist. Her intensity and abruptness as well as her departure from ordinary reality appreciation has left the therapist shaken. She says, "I've never been this shaken with this client before. I'm worried I'll never see her again. I'm worried she'll never come back." It is not too difficult to infer, under the circumstances, that an unconscious fantasy may exist on the therapist's part of getting rid of her. She then says, "Oh, you know, there's another thing. I have been delaying all week returning her phone calls. She called me. I think to myself, 'I've got ten minutes and I can call her. No, no, no. If I call her tomorrow I'll have fifteen, so I'll call her tomorrow.'" So the therapist is aware she is pushing the client away. The therapist also says she had the fantasy of, "Well, you know, she's threatening to be very difficult lately, and the truth of the matter is, if she didn't come back I suppose it wouldn't be the worst thing in the world for me." The client may have picked up some ambivalence in the countertransference that she reads as abortion fantasies or miscarriage fantasies. This is her way of accomplishing the disconnection, first inside herself and then with her therapist.

There are two ways we can study the presence of the organizing transference "rupture in relating": in its passively repeated form and in its actively mimicked form. In the present example we might first infer that when the baby needed something, mother attempted in some reasonable way to give the baby what she needed but it was not right. Mother's attempts failed somehow. So the baby began screaming. We then picture this mother, who, with limited resources, did not know how to respond to the baby's screaming. Maybe the child had an earache. Not being able to bear the tension, the mother leaves the scene so the child learns "when I scream mother leaves." So the analytic speaker now screams at her therapist with the expectation that she too will leave her. Her way of accomplishing the rupture is to scream. When the consultant suggested this to the therapist she quickly reviewed every relationship the client has had with a man. At the point in the relationship at which the client begins to feel connected to the man, suddenly she switches into another personality, which is a "screaming bitch," and starts screaming and yelling obscenities and accusations at the man, and so the man does not stay around. She accomplishes the break by screaming accusations.

But the activity of actually accomplishing the break belonged to mother and so is somehow identified with, mimicked. Following this line of inference, did mother scream at the baby for misunderstanding her needs in the relationship, for not being responsive to mother's attempts to care for her? We do not know exactly how the primary identification with the mother who broke the contact operates from this limited material but it provides clues to future analytic understanding. The therapist is still left worrying, "What am I going to do with this disconnection?" Since the therapist has been traumatized, like the mother may have been with the child's needs, she too seems almost ready to flush her down the toilet.

An alternative formulation might use Fraiberg's (1982) notion of "pre-defense." In observing interactions of neglected and abused children with their parents, Fraiberg noticed three almost biological reactions that serve to (defensively) control the stimulation: flight (aversion), fight, and freeze. This client's screaming at men and at her therapist might be considered a fight response in the face of the anticipated abusive overstimulation and contact rupture that the organizing transference threatens to generate. (The following two transference illustrations describe the flight and freeze reactions.)

These interpretive hunches connect immediately with the therapist. Then she is ready to discuss it with her client. The consultant warns, "Don't rush into this material because one thing we know is that when people are in organizing states they cannot handle much at any given moment that is abstract, that is verbal. Just be with her for now. You have learned from her rantings. You have seen the small window to her soul from your own shocked experience, which no doubt in some way represents her trauma as an infant. But if you start to talk about it too soon, you will be introducing ego functioning into space where ego does not belong, which may have been her mother's worst empathic error. If so, then you become her psychotic mother by trying to be too helpful!"

The therapist says, "I just never know what to expect from these organizing people. I've been really gearing up for the worst." The consultant responds, "Well, maybe you will have a difficult experience with her when you talk with her on the phone. These people have a way of making it very hard on us." The therapist says, "But it also occurs to me that maybe when I call her, at the other end, there will just be this still, quiet little voice that says, 'Hi, I've missed you.' "

The following week the therapist reports exactly that. She was able to stay with the client and help her feel how awful it was to think that her therapist in some way might disapprove of Naomi or think that a lesbian relationship was not right for her. The rupture had been repaired, the connection remade so she could continue to stay in therapy. But the crucial transference experience that appeared is by no means understood or worked through. This episode represents her first tentative foray into working the organizing transference directly with her therapist. Now the heat is temporarily off and the therapist has a clearer view of the nature of her disconnecting transference replication. The organizing transference seems to be worked through in a series of waves or episodes. The therapist will be more prepared to act quickly next time. The interpretation will perhaps be possible in the non- or preverbal way the therapist stays with the client in her rageful self and invites her (perhaps with extended hand) to stay connected and to live out together her terror of being with the therapist rather than to disconnect or rupture the connection with rage.

TRANSFERENCE ILLUSTRATION 2: FLIGHT FROM THE THERAPIST

A woman therapist has been treating a female client for three or four years. This client has been driving an hour and a half each week to see her therapist. The therapist says, "So there's a long umbilicus." The client has presented as tenuous in her ability to maintain relationships. In the last six months she has talked frequently about terminating therapy because of money and distance. She canceled her sessions in bad weather and during the winter holidays. On several occasions the therapist has empathically said, "Well, okay, I can understand how busy you are and how far it is. You have accomplished a number of things in therapy, so if you want to consider termination we can talk about that." She even suggested helping her find a therapist who was closer. But that was all rejected. The client talked about termination, but the therapist was forbidden to.

On the occasion in question the client called during the Christmas holidays and without any warning canceled all future appointments. Her therapist made several phone calls in unsuccessfully attempting to reach her. She sent a Christmas card.

She did everything she could to reach out to her. The therapist thought, "Well, maybe it is best that she stop and this is her way of stopping. Maybe I shouldn't be pursuing her." This *laissèz-faire* attitude may be appropriate for listening to more-differentiated forms of personality organization, but it is clearly not empathic when working an organizing transference in which the client cannot initiate or sustain connection. This therapist is an empathic and intuitive woman and so remained persistent in her attempts to restore the connection. They finally did connect by phone and the therapist found out what happened. The client said, "In the last session I was telling you about my friend Valerie and you turned away. Then I knew you didn't care for me so there wasn't any point in my coming back."

As the incident was discussed in consultation, the consultant encouraged the therapist to attempt a review of events to try to recall some content about what was being talked about with Valerie. Concrete images about contact ruptures serve us well in understanding organizing experiences. It is often important to ascertain exactly what was being talked about, and why turning away to pick up a cup of tea was seen as a rejection. The client has been slowly backing away, but not letting the therapist back away. The therapist cannot talk about termination but the client was waiting for the moment when the therapist turns at a critical moment so that the rupture of the organizing transference can be attached to the therapist's turning away. The consultant says, "She has found a way to live out the organizing transference of mother disconnecting. This is the window to the organizing experience we are waiting for. We wait for the moment in which the reenactment of the turning away, the breaking of contact, the rupture of experience happens in the transference."

This episode might be mistaken for a symbiotic-relating scenario or narcissistic breach in empathy—"just when I needed affirmation from you, just when I need something from you, you turned away." It could be seen as splitting, or as abandonment, or as selfobject failure. But the consultant had heard developments in the case several times before, enough to realize that there was a deep organizing component. In response to the consultant considering the rupture as disconnecting transference, the therapist said, "She's been married for twenty years. So I had always thought of her as basically symbiotic or borderline in her object relations. But now I recall a number of instances with her husband in which she must have been in an organizing pocket and experienced her husband as the psychotic mother." But now the rupture of relating had actually been re-created with the therapist. The therapist says, "It's funny, during this time period she had moved. She called my answering machine to leave her new phone number on it. And I did not take the phone number off the machine before I erased the message." So the analytic listener is ready in some sense to let her die, too.

The therapist was fired up with these ideas because they seem to make sense and to organize in her mind many past incidents. She was ready to talk to her client about all of this. The consultant cautioned her not to rush, and explained why. The therapist tuned in quickly and said, "I feel like, where we're at right now, is we're both lying down in a playpen and I have to wait for her to come to me." The consultant reminded her the baby has to be allowed to find the breast. The transference to the psychotic mother will be reenacted again and again so there will be ample time to interpret. But she can use her new understanding to be with her client in new ways. The therapist was reminded of what she already knew from her studies of the organizing experience, that abstract verbal interpretations per se will not touch this very early transference.

Interpretation at the organizing level must be a concrete activity, often manifest in physical gesture or interpretive touch at the specific moment when the analytic speaker is in the act of pulling away from contact, of (transferentially) creating a rupture. Viable interpretation of the organizing transference involves an actual, physical, concrete reaching out of one person toward another in such a way as to communicate, "I know you believe you must break off our personal engagement in this way now. But it is not true. You have, as an adult, the ability to stay here now with me and experience your long-standing terror of connectedness. How can you manage not to leave me now? Can we manage to remain in contact for just a few more minutes?"

Clients often deliberately and perhaps wisely conduct the early phases of therapy at quite some distance from the therapist by spacing appointments far apart or arranging long and difficult drives. They know that closeness can only be experienced by them as traumatic.

The therapist had arranged this consultation because she was concerned about her own anger. In the midst of all the client's coming and not coming, calling and canceling, connecting and disconnecting, the therapist had become enraged and said she was "just ready to kill her." She even made a slip and said, "I have an appointment with her on Saturday," when the appointment was on Thursday. She is an excellent therapist and she really does want to connect, but it is easy to understand the countertransference ambivalence. The ruptures in relating that organizing transferences necessarily entail stir up organizing experiences in the therapist.

TRANSFERENCE ILLUSTRATION 3:
FROZEN IN IMPOTENT RAGE

This example is from a much later working-through period of analysis and occurs in a personality much more capable of verbal abstractions than the previous two. An emerging theme of an otherwise very well-developed woman in therapy with a male therapist has been related to the organizing period. The woman's mother, during the baby's first few months of life, was afraid to pick up her baby for fear of "breaking" her. It has been discovered through several years of intensive psychotherapy that there were many strengths the mother was able to stimulate in the child, but at the deepest psychic level there are connecting difficulties.

The emergent theme over several weeks was the analytic speaker's rage that occurs on a fairly regular basis in social situations when she knows that the person she is interacting with can indeed do more for her, and be more there for her, but somehow flakes out. In short, her rage is mobilized at people when they have more to offer than in fact they are actively giving in the current relationship.

In a key session she develops the theme further. Early in her marriage, her husband was far more warm, far more giving, and far more available than he is now, and she is angry that he is not more available when she knows he can be. She becomes exasperated to the point of feeling utterly helpless and frozen.

Similarly, she indicates that what attracted her to a close friend was that the friend has so much to give. She is well traveled and well read, alive, active, versatile, a good conversationalist, and much more. But when her friend recently had a bit of the flu and refused to get out of bed to go to the client's son's first baseball game, "then I don't see her any longer as what she could be or might be for me. And I become angry and disillusioned with her. Now I know what has been bothering me so much lately about her in our relationship. Too often she cancels, flakes out, or blobs out when I know she doesn't have to, when I know she has far more to give but is choosing not to. I become completely immobilized in impotent rage."

In the discussion of various examples that have occurred with her husband and her friend, she said, "Now I'm finding that when I'm enraged at the other person for not living up to their potential not only do I not get what they have to offer me, but also I am totally unable to take in, to get, to make use of what they can in fact offer me."

She referenced some examples from previous transference experiences in therapy where she, in complaining bitterly about the therapist's seemingly endless unavailability over holidays and weekends, was so preoccupied in her hours leading up to the holidays that she was unable to make use of whatever good experiences might be possible in the sessions. Her comment is, "Something always happens." The emphasis here is on the subjective statement of the disconnecting experience being impersonal. It's not, "I'm disappointed with the other," or "The other lets me down," or "The other fails to live up to their potential." Rather, it is, "We're interacting and then *something happens* and the potential that is there isn't being lived out, and I fall into a lost state of sadness and grief, which is usually manifest in instantaneous but frozen rage."

At this point in the session the client realizes she has lost or repressed a further insight regarding her husband and friend that she was very excited about only a moment before when she connected to it. But just as quickly as the insight came, it fled and she was very disturbed for some time about having lost it.

Late in the session she provides another example of some neighbors whom, when she first began to get to know them, she experienced as somewhat available. Now she experiences them more as users than givers. And while, she acknowledges, this latter is no doubt also true in ways, she cites several instances in the beginning of their relationship in which the neighbors were very supportive, very helpful, very outgoing. But the man in the couple began on occasion to have other things that kept him unavailable. And the woman was not able to have lunch with the client as often or visit over coffee. Before too long there were enough gaps in the relationship that it became unbearable to her. She says, "It's easy to say they aren't meeting my needs. I'll have to go elsewhere." But she realizes that this is not entirely the case. They do have some things to offer, but because they are not offering all that they can, she feels that "mysterious unbearable pain" again.

After a few thoughtful moments she said, "It sounds like a reason to break contact." The therapist quickly replied, "No, it's the *way* you break contact." She then said excitedly, "That's exactly what I lost. I was trying to formulate the problem with my husband and my friend in terms of how I break contact but I could not quite get there. If I'm always living in what a person could give me but isn't, then several things happen: One, I have reason not to relate to them. Two, I'm not relating to them at all but I'm relating rather to my fantasy. And, three, they do have something to give or I wouldn't be relating to them, but in my distress and frozen anger I'm completely missing what they have to give to me. I break the contact by being sad and enraged, complaining about what I'm not getting."

At this point she slowed down and indicated that she was emoting very deeply, that she felt she has reached a very profound point. "I know somehow that this can change my life if I can finally get hold of it. If I can find some way of fully knowing about this, I will be able to change many things." Her therapist said, "It seems as though you have located the mechanism regarding how the contact is broken and how it relates to the early experiences of your mother who, much of the time, was there so that you knew full well what things she could provide. But when she was preoccupied, or not able to give, or frightened about how she might harm the baby, she bowed out leaving you stuck, knowing that she could give more but not giving it. No wonder she reports that you were such a good baby and slept a lot!" The content of the transference is, "You could be giving me more but you're not."

Then the client said, "Now I know why my daughter seems to be left out of this dynamic. You know how I've always said with her it's somewhat different? Well, the difference is that I'm not expecting to be given to by her. I understand that her role isn't to give to me and so I'm much freer to relate to her without this pain coming up. The few instances in which I do lose it with her, I may feel that she's not giving me her full cooperation as freely and fully as I know that she can. But, in fact, I am able to take a great deal from her by simply being with her—by being present while she is losing her teeth, or brushing her hair. I go to softball league with her and I receive through just watching." The therapist said, "You do take what she has to offer." She responded, "Yes, but it's often very indirectly, just by enjoying being with her. Whatever she does is so wonderful and beautiful that it's a very rich experience just being by her side."

She then commented about last week's session. "I was concerned that you didn't know about my feelings of caring for you and how grateful I feel to you for just being here with me. I get a lot from you by just being with you even if you don't have a lot to give on a certain day. (The therapist had a serious eye infection on that day and his spirits were a little off. It was something she detected and expressed concern about within the session.)

"Now," she continued, "I find I'm a little scared about knowing all of this. Things keep clicking in my mind—more and more examples. It's like my whole life is built on this single mechanism. No wonder I wasn't happy when John, my supervisor, failed to tune into me completely when I knew he could. If I finally identify this, I may be able to change. I am excited, but I think I'm mostly very scared. I think the scare is that I won't remember this, I won't be able to take hold of it. I won't be able to make it my own."

The therapist said, "No. The scary thing is that you will remember it. You are in the process of deep change and as you are changing you are coming face to face with a terror you have avoided all your life. The terror of having to encounter a real live person who has some good things to offer but who may not, for a variety of reasons, be willing or able to give fully in all areas. Sooner or later in every relationship you encounter this situation and it brings back the sad and rageful reactions you had to your mother during your earliest months of life. So you have been unable to continue relating or you have given up the relating when the conditions are not met right. What you are scared of is actually allowing yourself to negotiate the uncertainties of relationships and to survive the positive possibilities as well as the painful disappointments that are bound to be a frightening and powerful consequence of fully knowing and living out what you are now discovering."

Each of these three illustrations shows how the rupture of the organizing experience is repeated in transference. In each instance multiple interpretive possibilities exist. The decisive moment of organizing transference interpretation is not visible in any of these examples—in the first two because the relationship had not yet arrived there, and in the third because the *in vivo* interpretations had already begun and the client was in a later stage of "owning" the interpretative work, although she expresses fear of losing it. Examples of the actual interpretive and working-through process are provided in a later chapter.

The presence of Fraiberg's (1982) three "pre-defenses" of aversion, freezing, and fighting is suggested in the three case vignettes and may be seen as the clients' ways of achieving a rupture in contact that, due to transference projections, is threatening to become overstimulating.

THE ORGANIZING THEMES TO BE CONSIDERED IN THIS BOOK

Private Madness Is Universal

Throughout time and in all cultures people have developed a variety of ideas and prejudices about madness. The general tendency that is echoed in our own culture has been to see madness as separate from ourselves and mad people as fundamentally different from ourselves. The human tendency has been to externalize and persecute our own sense of uncertainty—our own private madness—which is basic to the foundations of the psyche.

As psychological sophistication increases, we are better able to discern the nature of the basic organizing processes and to perceive blocked-off channels for interpersonal relating as they occur in all people. What has heretofore been referred to as a universal core or kernel of psychosis, I will discuss as *enclaves, pockets* or *layerings of organizing experience* as they necessarily exist in all people by virtue of the conditions of early child-rearing. With optimal experiences in early life, the occasional parental failure to attune with the needed supply in a timely fashion is generally overshadowed by favorable experience so that only small areas of functioning may be closed off. However, many individuals experienced their earliest yearnings for human contact so traumatizing that they have withdrawn in a variety of ways from the world of social consensus, from the world of ordinary interpersonal-relatedness possibilities. Their organizing experience is pervasive and governs all aspects of daily life. We might think of a spectrum based upon the degree of pervasiveness, intensity, and the urgency with which people's lives are colored by aspects of organizing experience.

Terror of Contact Is Central to the Organizing Experience

Unlike the so-called borderline states where the theme of abandonment is central, in organizing (and psychotic) states the fear of interpersonal (affective) contact is central. At the beginning of an analytic experience it is not at all clear why a given individual failed to bond, failed to enter into a reciprocal symbiotic dance with some parental figure. But for reasons that emerge in the course of analytic relating, the person living in an organizing state must avoid interpersonal contact at all cost. Contact is traumatic because it is either over- or understimulating, and so-called psychotic symptoms clearly serve to ward off interpersonal contact.

The Organizing Transference Functions to Prevent Bonding

Transference in organizing states exists as a memory of the way the infant (for whatever reason) became frightened of connection to the primary nurturing other, usually the biological mother. Conceptualizing the organizing or psychotic transference as "the moment of emergence of the (internalized) psychotic mother" helps to identify the intrapsychic experience that compels a breaking off of contact. That is, in terms of the infant's urgent need systems, the inference is that it was not possible for the responsiveness of the mothering person to be sufficiently attuned to the infant's immediate reality.

From the infant's perspective the mothering process was crazy or psychotic and is retained in memory as such. The clarifying notion is that developmentally—for whatever reason—the other who might have been turned to for providing nurturance, contact, stimulation, comfort, and an ordering of experience that would permit the evolution of personal spontaneity and creative potential within an interpersonal context, was somehow experienced as traumatizing due to over- or understimulation or to a failure to organize the infant's experience into smooth and efficient relatedness patterns.

The "psychotic mother" is here used as a theoretical construct and is not seen as necessarily related to any real person as objectively perceived, but is rather the internalized representation of the other who was experienced as traumatizing to connecting possibilities. For example, even the best parenting cannot provide perfect attunement and responsiveness to a child in pain due to some birth defect, childhood anomaly, or disease. The technical problem is how to grasp, from the infant's point of view, the fault with the mothering processes without faulting the real mother. By speaking of the appearance of the psychotic mother we are able to point to the internal representation of the other that appears at moments of potential human contact as psychotic or organizing transference that can be secured for analysis.

Resistance Is to the Emergence of the Psychotic Mother Transference

The resistance in the psychoanalysis of organizing states is to making or sustaining certain forms of contact that are bound by virtue of internalized experience to be traumatic. To attempt to sustain personal contact is to raise the threat of the reappearance of the traumatizing other who is so internalized and integral to experiencing that terror and pain accompany any possible emotional linking. Resistance to the organizing transference appears in many forms to ward off human contact experiences that threaten a reexperiencing of transference terror.

Interpretation of the Organizing Transference Is Concrete and Paraverbal

The organizing experience is related to some primary blocking of experience during earliest infancy. Contact with organizing states is necessarily paraverbal and concrete in nature. Interpretation of the appearance of the psychotic mother transference is almost invariably accomplished by some form of physical (concrete) touching. Touch, which serves to interpret inhibiting organizing structures, like all interpretation, is very specific in nature and timing. Concrete interpretive touch is accomplished and timed in such a way as to communicate paraverbally to the person in analysis, "You have achieved contact with me right now and we both feel it. I know that you believe you now must flee, break contact, withdraw emotionally because contact in your history is dreaded. But you are no longer an infant and you have the ability as an adult to stay in contact with me. You can maintain contact. The pain and fear you now feel is left over from infancy. We can find ways for you to hold on to me safely. You do not have to break away. We can experience your traumatic history together. We can share your fear and pain and come to understand its nature. We can grow together." The touching advocated in this technique must be aimed at these purposes and offered in such a way and at such a time that the person feels safe and willing to receive these messages, or it will be intrusive, wrong, and potentially overwhelming and dangerous.

Countertransference Brings Its Own Madness

There are several kinds of countertransference to organizing states that can be expected by listeners working the organizing experience.

1. *Denial of human potential.* The most common form of countertransference has seen organizing personalities as witches, evildoers, hopelessly psychotic, and in other ways not quite human. In this attitude is a denial of human potential and a denial of the possibility of being able to stimulate desire in such a way as to reawaken it and to analyze blocks to human relating. We hear: "I can't reach you, you are too sick. You are untreatable so we will lock you up or give you drugs to sedate or pacify you."

2. *Fear of primitive energy.* When an analytic listener invites the organizing experience into a transference relationship, he or she is asking that the full impact of primitive aggressive and sexual energies of the analytic speaker be directed squarely at the person of the listener. Listeners fear the power of this experience because it can be quite disorienting and, if not carefully assessed and monitored, potentially dangerous. But fear of basic human affectivity is irrational and we now have at our disposal many rational ways of inviting and managing the organizing level affects and energies. The key technical consideration is not whether the person on the basis of *a priori* criteria is treatable, but whether the listener has sufficient holding and supportive resources available to make the pursuit of treatment practical and safe for all concerned.

3. *Encountering our own organizing experiences.* When we as listeners invest ourselves emotionally in reaching out again and again to an analytic speaker only to be repeatedly abandoned or refused, it stimulates our own most primitive experiences of reaching out to our own mothers during our organizing developmental period, hoping for a response and feeling traumatized when the desired response was not forthcoming. Our own "psychotic mother" transference can reappear projected onto the analytic speaker as we attempt to provide systematic

and sustained connection for people living organizing states. How each of us as individual practitioners develops staying power is the crucial question. Our own therapy is essential as is consultation with colleagues during trying phases of this work. Attempting to work the organizing experience without adequate resource and backup support is like a single mother trying to manage a difficult or sick baby while holding down a job to support herself, caring for several other children, and trying to live some life of her own. We need support to do this very taxing kind of work.

4. *Empathy leading to breaks in contact.* After the preliminary phases are well under way—that is, after the listener and speaker have established basic working rhythms that are comfortable and safe, and after the listener has been able to discern and bring up for discussion the specific ways in which the speaker engages in and searches for contact and then cuts off contact—we notice the speaker begins excitedly to see in outside contacts as well as in the analytic hour how the breaking of contact is being regularly accomplished. Speakers in analysis are often excited by the therapeutic process at this point because for the first time in their lives something is finally making sense about themselves. They begin a valiant struggle to maintain contact nearly everywhere they go, especially with the listener. Then we notice a tendency on the part of the analytic listener to begin withdrawing into inattentiveness, preoccupation, or even drowsiness. This type of countertransference activity, which tends to occur only well into the treatment process, represents the listener's empathy for the terror that contact provides for the speaker. That is, the speaker, for the first time in his or her life, feels hot on the trail of something that promises human satisfaction—sustained contact. But in the person's enthusiasm to achieve as much contact as possible as fast as possible, it is the listener who senses the internalized danger and in some way is deliberately (consciously or unconsciously) slowing things down a bit. This countertransference reaction can be spoken to the speaker so that two may gain a fuller appreciation of the joys and dangers of human contact.

All Organizing States Are Transformable

Our clinical work over the last decade suggests that all functional (as opposed to organic) states that are due to traumatically interrupted channelings in infancy are, in principle, transformable. That is, we have encountered no reason that, given the proper conditions, organizing experience cannot be brought into an analytic relationship for analysis so that channels once closed off can be analyzed, thereby opening them to human contact and further development.

In practice, however, the question of whether or not a given person can be worked with revolves around the resources required for physical and psychological containment during the analytic process. For example, a person with psychotic, homicidal rage cannot be safely treated once or twice a week in a private practice outpatient setting. Likewise, a person whose channels have left him or her with severe limitations in learning capacity may require parallel tutoring or other support along the way. A person whose organizing experience pervades his or her entire existence may require almost daily contact over long periods of time in order to fully engage in the transformational process. A person who was repeatedly assaulted (physically or sexually) in infancy will develop a persecutory psychotic transference and the therapist practicing without auxiliary help in case management may be in for a false malpractice suit. The emergence of a psychotic transference is, after all, what is being promoted in order to analyze the organizing experience. This means that at the moment a person is subjectively experiencing the psychotic or organizing transference, the therapist is perceived as the psychotic mother and an ordinary sense of reality testing will not be fully present. Part of the ongoing assessment procedure with organizing states is to begin imagining what the experience of the psychotic mother looks like to each person and to be sure the actual practical dimensions of the treatment setting can tolerate the emergence of such a transference. There are many psychotic transferences that clearly are not safe for the therapist in independent practice to take on. Risky psychotic transference should be treated in public or private nonprofit clinics or residential settings where there is wider support for the work and lowered risk of legal consequences to the actual therapist or treatment team. Many psychotic transferences may require a secured residential facility and the availability of medication and/or physical restraint.

The Backdrop of Sustained Contact

The basic rule of free association was developed by Freud in order to promote the analysis of neurotic states. Over time, following the command to "say everything that comes to mind" has come to be thought of as neither desirable nor possible, in principle. But the notion or ideal of feeling completely free in the presence of an analytic listener to let one's mind ramble uninhibitedly still serves as a valuable backdrop against which to perceive whatever actually does happen. Suddenly one's thoughts are interrupted by something, or one's mind goes blank, or one forgets a thought in the middle of a sentence. The analytic investigator is interested in each event. Why at that moment was free association interrupted? The ideal of free association points a direction, sets a pace, defines a ground for a psychic figure (of transference or resistance) to be seen against.

Likewise, in working the organizing experience, the ideal of sustained interpersonal contact serves as a backdrop against which to see the ways in which an analytic speaker approaches contact, reaches for it, momentarily lights up with affect, and then just as quickly darts away—sometimes obviously, sometimes not so perceptibly. In this book the ideal of sustained human contact in working the organizing experience is analogous to the ideal of free association in the analysis of neurosis—both serve as backdrops against which transference experiences can appear and be secured by two for psychoanalytic transformation.

SUMMARY

As this book unfolds the reader will encounter a number of different kinds of organizing experiences from very different kinds of people. I hope to show that what has been shunned for ages as madness can now be understood as a universal human experience traceable to the earliest psychic experience of becoming disorganized or traumatized in face of failed contact. The hallmark of the organizing transference is a terror or horror of interpersonal affective linking or contact. The dread of contact relates to one's personal history of reaching out affectively as an infant and being received in such a way as to have been traumatized to the point of refusing to reach out that way ever again.

The organizing transference is conceptualized here as a memory formation of the experience of the traumatizing other whom I have chosen to label the "psychotic mother," an internalized representation of the failure of environmental responsiveness to be fully attuned to the infant's real and immediate need states. Resistance is to reexperiencing the transferential trauma which results from opening up the long-closed channels of potential experience. Interpretation is necessarily paraverbal and concrete—usually simply a timely being with or an interpretive touch that communicates the analytic listener's awareness of the present contact and the urge to flee—along with the coaxing to stay, to remain open to contact, and the invitation to share together the sense of trauma and physical pain that necessarily accompanies the opening of blocked channels.

Countertransference may deny the person's basic humanity or raise a fear in the analytic listener of the opening up of primitive energies that are bound to be directed at the person of the listener. Working the organizing experience is bound to stir up the analytic listener's own terrifying organizing experiences or manifest itself as some form of withdrawing, seen as empathy with the speaker's terror of contact.

Only practical considerations place limits on working with organizing states, not the nature of the experience itself. The overlearned or internalized tendency to repeatedly break off contact according to a style once experienced in the primordial past (and often seen as psychotic symptoms in the present) can best be perceived against a background that promotes sustained contact between analytic speaker and listener. While it might seem that learning to sustain contact is the aim of this kind of work, that cannot be true. If it were, we would need only good teachers or reparenting specialists, not analysts. The goal is to analyze, to break down, the primordial organizing structures that still manifest themselves as the psychotic transference accompanied by powerful resistance.

Organizing structures can be brought into the light of day and relinquished by a dedicated speaker who is determined over time to learn not to retreat from developing contact with the analytic listener, even in the face of terror and pain. The analytic listener who has developed staying power through his or her own analytic work and who is willing to be sustained by ongoing support from colleagues is in a position to coax the contact and, in the process, to frame for analysis the structures that emerge to block interpersonal affective exchange. Human bonding requires that two people be free to live a true spontaneous, and very real life with each other, despite whatever limitations and restrictions reality may place upon them. Analyzing the organizing transference and resistance structures clears the way for human bonding or for what Searles (1979) has called the development of a therapeutic symbiosis.

CONTRASTING LIMITED ORGANIZING EXPERIENCE WITH PERVASIVE ORGANIZING EXPERIENCE: BART AND EDDIE

3

The Emergence of a Subtle Organizing Transference[1]

A Clinical Contribution by Jackie Singer

GETTING TO KNOW BART'S EXPERIENCES

Bart had broken up with his girlfriend of two years because she had wanted a commitment but he was not able to give her one. He began therapy one week later. He said that he had no friends and he wanted more social life. Bart described his time alone, that he so dreaded, as "dead time." He said he wanted to know himself better, to learn to make "choices," and to stop getting involved in relationships just to avoid being alone.

Bart initially described himself as having a strong sense of responsibility with many "shoulds." He felt he was a good listener although he felt that few people listened to him. He rarely said no to people even though he often wanted to. Bart reported that he used to feel angry that he was like this, but that the anger is now either well contained or has melted away. He is simply not satisfied with life.

Bart is a well-functioning person who has been employed in the same company for fifteen years. He has achieved an important management position as well as a financially comfortable life-style. He has a grown child who lives in another state, a cat he is fond of, and many hobbies he actively participates in and enjoys. He had been in once-weekly psychoanalytically oriented psychotherapy for two and a half years when most of the incidents to be described took place.

---

[1]The case material presented in this chapter was audio recorded and transcribed for supervision purposes so that a verbatim process of the actual therapy hours is possible. Excerpted portions of the transcription have been edited for clarity and readability.

A series of themes gradually emerged in Bart's work that had implications for the developing organizing transference.

"My Blood Is Running Cold"

An early clue about Bart's "organizing pocket" was the remarkable ability he developed to describe physical sensations in session. Although he had talked about physical sensations outside the office, it was a year into therapy when he first allowed himself to feel body sensations in session.

5/26/88

Bart: Last session you asked me about why I "numbed out." I was surprised. I said, "because I didn't want to deal with life threatening issues." Boom. I made a note to bring that up later. I got to thinking about that. That's a pretty stout statement. I don't know if it's literally true but I think so. I've somehow associated intense feeling, intense deep feelings, with harm. I think that may be part of the reason for the numbness. That's the word we used, I think. That's quite right. Seems to be. I'm thinking about where those feelings came from. I know when I've been upset about a failed relationship the feelings do seem life threatening. Really. That may be a reason. But anyway that's what came up. It somehow seems insightful. It just popped out.

Jackie: (Bart's therapist is a woman.) Sometimes things just pop out.

Bart: Yeah, boom. That one just jumped right out.

Jackie: Can you tell me more about that life-threatening sense?

Bart: Well, uh, mmm. I'm not quite sure how. It just seems so. It . . . in the back of my mind . . . now this sounds peculiar, but part of me believes this. That, mmmm, I won't die naturally. That somehow or other I'll get overwhelmed by feeling. And that will be the end of me. My blood's running cold right now. It's a weird feeling.

Jackie: Would you tell me more about that?

Bart: I'm just physically feeling that feeling right now. Just, I don't know. Whatever that feeling is. Dealing with something. I don't know. I can't explain it. Just blood running cold. I can feel it right through my arms especially.

Jackie: Right now, as you talk about it?

Bart: Yes, I can physically feel that sensation. And part of me believes that. It's like background.

Jackie: Background?

Bart: It's like a major piece. It's part of a structure. A structural piece of beliefs.

Comment

As I reviewed the session, I realized I had made the mistake, at the end of this excerpt, of focusing on the content of what he was saying about "background," "unnatural death," and so forth, instead of trying to help him sustain the physical sensations to see where they took us. I had a hunch that the blood running cold was indicative of some rupture of contact. But because I got lost in the content, I had failed to grasp the intimacy that had been generated between us by his telling me about intense feelings being life and death propositions and about the body sensations stirred up by his sharing that with me. I should have encouraged the physical sensations to occur in session and had him tell me about them. I might have seen how they emerged to break the interpersonal contact just achieved as he stammeringly described how feelings were a life-threatening matter to him, especially those related to loss of a relationship. Only later did I realize that if I could hold him through this sensate experience, the necessity for ruptured contact might lose its power. Or at least by sustaining the contact we could hope to study exactly what had happened to him earlier in life when intimate contact was a possibility. I knew that when he experienced such feelings again, my goal would be to keep him with the experience.

Before, when he had spoken of various puzzling sensations in connection with being with girlfriends, I could not quite grasp their context or possible meanings. Now the physical sensations had occurred in session with the possibility of our understanding them as transference memories. We now had the possibility of studying them together in a relational context as they were happening. During the ensuing months there were more brief flashes of sensation during our time together, but I was not able to hold him through the experiencing. Eleven months later I had the opportunity to at least be able to talk about what needed to happen between us with fairly astonishing results.

"There's a Hole in My Back"

Blood running cold was not the only physical sensation that Bart experienced in relation to our therapy. In another session, he reported having a very powerful sensation as he left the office following a particularly good session.

6/8/88

Bart: Oh boy, oh boy, oh boy. I don't know if I want to get into this right now or not, but I'll relate it anyway. I had an unusual experience leaving here last week. It was really an odd sensation leaving and I thought, "let's pay attention here now a little bit." The first thing I noticed was I had my back covered with one of my hands. When I get ill or feel I'm getting ill, my lower back and kidney areas get really cold. I don't know how to convey this other than to say that it feels like there's a hole—where sickness can enter and leave—Chinese medicine or something like that, you know. But anyway, they'll get really cold. I'm always very aware of that because I've learned that I'm very vulnerable then to illness. This lower back area gets cold and I'll keep it warm and covered. It's just something I pay attention to. So I noticed I involuntarily did that.

Jackie: Put your hand back there?

Bart: Yeah, I was just walking down the hall leaving here and I had my hand behind my back, right on that spot. The other thing that happened was, I was aware of being very reluctant to leave here and that's never happened before. Usually I just meander out. You know, I'm thinking about things. But last week I took a long time leaving. I ambled down the hall and I think I stopped at the rest room. It just dawned on me. I had the same image just now—it crossed me then—it's like a little kid going off to school and not wanting to, so he's stopping and looking at everything. You know, whatever distraction there is to keep you from moving on. I felt very childlike and it took fifteen minutes for me to get out to the car. Then I sat in the car for awhile. I guess I was umm, I'm not sure, reluctant to re-enter the world, you know. We had talked a little about time out and time in, that sort of thing. I don't know what happened, but the thing that was noticeable was I felt very childlike.

Jackie: Describe that childlike feeling for me. Is that like . . . childlike feeling young, feeling protected, feeling scared?

Bart: I think it was probably more vulnerable, more exposed. And I think that was one of the reasons I was reluctant to leave here. It just kind of evolved, I mean by the end of the hall it was a lot different than the beginning of the hall. It was really strange. I don't think I wanted to get on the

freeway and get back into things, you know. So I was feeling umm, afraid, but that's not quite the right word. Uh, I felt like I needed to be comforted a little bit. I just felt real, well I guess . . . I keep coming back to afraid. But that doesn't sound quite like the right word. It's kind of hard to explain. I remember sitting there in the car for awhile. I watched the trees blow in the wind just to neutralize a little bit, because I didn't know what else to do. I didn't particularly want to go yet. I waited until I got around to the point where I could function again. I was really not ready to function in the real world again—drive, shift, you know. It just didn't feel real. If felt very different. And during the latter part of that period I remembered back to . . . for some reason it crossed my mind that it felt good to be in this spot. It felt good to be experiencing this childlike mode. It seems to me that I used to be able to be in that mode a lot and it was fun. College days and earlier life, it seems to me. I really felt like I was being childlike. It felt good. But at the same time it was distressing. I mean it was kind of startling or a little distressing, but at the same time I felt a little happy.

Jackie: As you say that was a happy experience, a word that comes to my mind is "innocence." There's an innocence with children. "I can just be who I am and it's okay. I don't have to do adult monitoring to make sure I'm being 'appropriate.'"

Bart: Not as much as I used to. Yeah, I'd say that's fair. I was kind of happy about it in a way. When I went out of here I was just going to pay attention to myself. This hallway for some reason is like a transitional thing. I slipped into this sensation and was able to stay with it without a lot of editing or controlling.

Jackie: Just letting things come up . . .

Bart: Seemed like it, but it was real odd – just really ambling. I was just not ready to leave. It was not so much sad that I was leaving here as opposed to reluctant to go on. So it was an extension of our time together. On that transitional thing I was able to stretch it out and then fell into something different – a pleasant reverie that I seldom allow myself. It was good, I thought.

Comment

In context, Bart's increased willingness to observe his physical sensations allowed him to notice some new things following a therapy session that he had enjoyed. The discussion that followed centered around his awareness of the possibility of staying connected with his enjoyment of our being together and not having to break the connection so fast.

We were also able to explore further the recurrent feelings of coldness. Here the sense was that as he left the session his lower back and kidneys were cold, as though leaving made a hole in his body's defenses, making him vulnerable to illness. We discussed it in terms of his body shutting down its circulatory functioning when it experienced fear, like when Mom might "drop" him. He then described Mom, in general, as being rather cool. It was not clear at this time if the aimless dawdling was a reluctance to leave the warm feelings he experienced with the therapist (Mom), or possibly his being able to make a transition away from warm connections gradually and safely by dawdling.

OF VOICE TONES, FEELINGS, AND PUNISHMENT

6-8-88 (Continued)

Bart: I'm going to jump to something else now. I had another notion, I don't know how well I can even talk about it. But in terms of relationships, the way I disconnect with people, which is generally pretty abrupt, there is the word *punishment*. I don't know if I can go beyond that. I'm getting that blood running cold feeling right now again. Of punishing someone I care about – someone I'm in relationship with . . . of showing them . . . it's old though. I've just had wisps of it this week and that's why I wanted to get it out. Punishment has some history, pattern, or design. Like, "I'm not going to call that person anymore because we don't get along," or whatever. But that's not the real reason. The real reason is because I want to punish them. I had glimpses of that punishing attitude this week after we had such a warm last session. Like I'm going through this complex rationale, but just beneath the surface this punishment idea is coming through. It has before. But I think I never admitted it. Whew! So, it kind of popped up a few times this week and I wanted to get it out.

Jackie: I wonder if at some point punishment may come up here?

Bart: Uh, I've had . . . I'm going to talk in terms of "voices." That's interesting. I just lost your question. Did you ask, "Has it happened?" Or "Could it happen?"

Jackie: Either one.

Bart: Oh. I don't know. What I started to say was I've had a fantasy not based in real fact . . . of . . . I almost forgot what I was going to say. I had to really stay with that one. I don't know if it's punishment or not I've thought of, but anger. I think it's more anger. I don't think it's punishment, but thinking about being angry here and how that works. And it's really weird. Right now I'm getting this, I want to say "righteous indignation" feeling, a real sense of being angry with a purpose, now I'm losing track. Anyway. Whenever I think of that, I think not so much in terms of pictures, but in terms of voice, of tone.

Jackie: Yours?

Bart: Mine. But I don't think so much in terms of visuals, which is what I usually think in. For some reason on this kind of thing I think in terms of tone.

Jackie: What would it sound like?

Bart: Oh. Well, different tones. I think I alluded to that very obliquely last time or the time before when I said "growling" or there was some word, I can't remember now.

Jackie: I think it was "growl." You said it for one of the voices, the hostile voice.

Bart: I get these tones, I think of them in tones.

Jackie: So you have a "voice picture" in mind of being here and feeling this angry feeling.

Bart: Yes, I think so.

Jackie: And it comes out in a head voice as well as in your own real voice?

Bart: Yeah, I sense emotions through voice more than anything. But, it's like separating different voices I guess. I'm saying tones because I don't want to say voices. They're like different voices. That's how I have a sense of these groups of feelings by tones or voices. I guess I can identify— I haven't really taken it this far before—this set of feelings I'm dealing with by the way they're spoken, in tone. Huh. That's more formalized than I've said it before. It's all been at a distance. Like I identify groups of feelings by tones that I hear. These tones are in my head but also enter my voice.

Comment

It was not until much later in therapy that we were able to make sense of how the notion of punishment related to his early organizing period. His intent to punish was a mimicry derived from a primary identification he had made with his mother's reaction to her narcissistic injury when she felt not needed by the baby. She broke the connection by putting him down—something he experienced as a sort of punishment for his not fulfilling her. Had she been holding him with her hand warming his lower back and kidneys when she put him down, leaving him feeling cold and vulnerable?

In this session Bart links the physical sensation of being cold and vulnerable with the positive connection that had been made the previous hour. However, by slowing to watch himself in the ways he and his therapist had frequently discussed, he transitioned more smoothly. But in the days that followed the warm session he flashed on punishment and "righteous indignation," which were only later related to mother "dropping" him. These were tones in his head and voices containing sets of feelings. Only last session he had alluded to growling, angry tones that carried his sense of anger at his therapist. But anger for what? It was clearly a "warm and good" session. Why would he feel anger?

He becomes momentarily disoriented in session while telling his therapist that he believes he experienced the angry growling tone toward her. And that the tones carry a quality of righteous indignation and anger with a purpose. From the information available we might surmise that the growling tone of righteous indignation was in response to his therapist's dropping him at the end of the session. The repetition he expressed appears to have been righteous indignation that her narcissistic needs were no longer being met and she dismissed him. His association of punishment contains either his fantasy as to why he was passively being dropped or punishment as an active identification on his part to push her away—a thought that momentarily confuses him as he shares it with her. But the more subtle possibility that only becomes clarified much later in therapy is that her crime is connecting successfully, warmly, intimately with him. Connection stirs deep terrors and generates confusion, like what he experienced when she asked about his anger toward her.

4/13/89

Jackie: In our relating we do a lot more fluctuating than in your other relationships, between getting closeness and distance, closeness and distance. So the skill, the ability to monitor yourself gets an opportunity to work a lot here.

Bart: Yes. Probably so. But fluctuations aren't the goal. That's not the objective. It's like the wrong muscles get exercised. Yeah. That's kind of an observation I've had recently.

Jackie: What can we do to limit the distancing disconnection?

Bart: That's the sixty-four thousand dollar question. I've wondered how to break out somehow. I was hoping you had an idea.

Jackie: What if we talk about it when it happens here with us and see if we can stop the distancing as it's actually happening?

Bart: That would be very hard, I think. Well, I don't know if it would be or not. The thing that . . . [he fades out]. I'm getting apprehensive now. Which is good. But at the same time, it's real unnerving.

Jackie: Can you talk about that?

Bart: I just felt for a moment there like a cornered cat. Or a little cornered animal. I was kind of getting that real apprehensive feeling.

Jackie: And . . .?

Bart: I didn't know what we . . . [hems and haws] . . . I didn't have a

clear idea of what was going to happen, but it felt threatening. [He's really
fading in and out and looking for
words.] And . . . so I was kind of
scared.

Jackie: Something's getting out of
control?

Bart: Umm . . . Well, I guess that's
it, although that doesn't sound right,
exactly. But that's probably what it
is . . .

Jackie: . . . Increased intensity?

Bart: Probably. Maybe so. [He's
fading out and I'm trying to keep
him here.] Yeah. I don't know. Something like that. I just . . . It's peculiar.
I felt . . . this is the . . . oh, this is
the same sensation I've described before.

Jackie: Blood running cold?

Bart: Yes. Or just real . . . those
kinds of things. I'm kind of glad we got
in touch with it real quick, but at the
same time, geez. It's . . . [lapses into
silence].

Jackie: Can you talk more about it?
Because this is a moment where we
could shut off or keep going.

Bart: Yes. Okay. It's just . . . what is
it? I'm not sure if it's a fear of you
learning something about me. Or if it's
a fear of me learning something about
me . . . I think it's more . . . I'm not
sure. At first I thought, "Well,
mmmmmmmmm, we're really going to
get into things I don't want to get
into . . . although I don't think it's a
fear of you learning something.
There's kind of a surface shell at that
level. But it seems more like . . . it's
just a real kind of undefined . . . I can't
really attach it to anything. I'm struggling right now to go away from it. It's
a fear of . . . I'm not sure. Maybe of

exposure. Uhhh. And I'm not sure if
it's exposure to you or to me. It's like a
real fear of going into an area that
either   I   don't   know   anything
about . . . Because what started it was
I wasn't quite sure where we were
going to go together . . .

Jackie: And . . .?

Bart: Mmmm. [Thinking and gone]
Well, we were addressing [pausing]
what we had to do in our work together. And, so it was like . . . like I
gotta get a shot tomorrow and I don't
want to do that but I gotta do it. But
it's on a much bigger scale than that,
you know. We gotta do this. Sooner or
later we gotta do this. You know. We
can keep going on this way avoiding
things for a long time, but sooner or
later you gotta do it. And so it's kind
of like real straight talk. Facing things.
And I still am . . . I don't know what
all that's about. I can get evasive about
it because . . .

Jackie: I let you.

Bart: Well, sure. That's true.

Jackie: I don't know quite how to
push you into where you need to go.

Bart: Well . . .

Jackie: I truly don't know what to
do or say. Like, "Bart, if you've got it,
come on. Let's talk about it." I don't
know how to help you feel safe enough
to do what you know you sooner or
later have to do.

Bart: Yeah! [Enthusiastically – obviously, safety is an issue]

Jackie: I'm not clear on exactly what
the fear is. So I don't know how I
might help make things feel more safe
for you to have the kind of exposure
experience here you need to have.

Bart: Exactly! But I'm not sure what
the fear is either. It's amazing how

basic it feels. I mean really basic. And that's why I had this animal cornered thing. It was a real basic fear. Not one of necessarily fighting your way out. Although, it's kind of like, my abilities break down. My abilities to evade or manipulate, steer, or escape are kind of neutralized and I don't know what to do.

Jackie: Are you still there now?

Bart: Yeah. It seems like it will be really emotionally wrenching and I don't want to do that. I mean I do and I don't. I think that's where . . . I'm not sure where the fear comes from. It's really physical. I feel it. I don't recoil or anything but I am physically really feeling it a lot.

Jackie: Where are you feeling it?

Bart: In the stomach, the pit. And cold.

Jackie: Cold everywhere? Can you pinpoint it?

Bart: A circulatory kind of cold.

Jackie: Does it stay with you the whole time we're talking?

Bart: No. It's really intense and then kind of subsides, but it's real . . . It's like falling off a building.

Jackie: It happens for a split second?

Bart: A little longer than that. Uhhhhh. And maybe I lost track of things for a bit, I think. That's where the abilities aren't there and that's where I get . . . I don't know if losing track is . . . it's hard to follow you. When I most feel you reaching out to me I have a hard time making sense of what you're saying. And maybe that's

what started it. Maybe I was feeling real threatened . . . not like I was going to get harmed . . . mmmmmmm . . .

Jackie: It sounds big.

Bart: Ohhh yeah. Well said. [He is clearly welling up with sensations.]

Jackie: It sounds like it's a core. We've gotten rid of all the other stuff and that is where we are now, at the physical center of things. We've talked about everything. We've done that, been there.

Bart: Yeah, I know. [Laughs] What's next. We need to get back to this, I agree. Because that was my feeling. We're not getting anywhere. Well, that's primarily my fault, I think. We need to get somewhere. I just don't know what the heck the safe . . . maybe safe isn't the right word, maybe it is. I don't know. What the mechanisms will be. How to do this. I'm trying to go back in the conversation. What was making me afraid, making me feel cold? I think you were addressing facts, like "We've got to do this." I don't know what it was.

Jackie: I think we were addressing how, after a time when we've gotten fairly close to some things in our relationship, the intensity gets real strong. Then all of the sudden you feel cold and afraid and our relating stops. It sounds like you lose me, lose your thoughts. This is similar to what you say happens with your girlfriends—you "vague out," "numb out."

Bart: Right. And it's scary as hell and very confusing.

Comment

Bart clearly now had the idea of where we had to go—to reexperience his body sensations in the context of our relationship. In the sessions that followed Bart began to get very good at trying to stay with his physical experiences. I got better at anticipating when we were approaching these memories of physical sensation and was ready in an instant to help him track their course. Then together we could begin to decipher their meaning in our context. One day he reported a unique event.

5/4/89

Bart: Something else. Uhh. It's interesting that I'm still having some phenomena with memory. I've been trying to think of early experiences and it's really kind of funny because instead of having memories, I'll get shudders. It's not so much a memory picture per se. Or if there are pictures they'll be very very brief . . . they'll almost be like . . . not colors, but blurs. There's not an image I can see, but there's more of a physical sensation, which is interesting. But it's very startling. It's hard to stay with it because it's startling and kind of unnerving. The whole experience. It's extraordinary. It's not a normal sensation. It's really powerful! Almost like lightning bolts. It's really strange. It's kind of, I don't know what to think of it. They're awfully strong. And it's only happened a couple of times. It happened on the way down here today as a matter of fact.

Jackie: On the way here today . . .?

Bart: Well, I was trying to do a recollection of what early memories I have and I have kind of standard ones. Ones that I've had for a long time. Ones that I've always remembered. I was going through that and would just get this bbbzzztttt sensation. There's some sort of context within it, but it's so quick I can't see it enough to tell you what it is. They're like sensations but they seem very packed, condensed,

and quick. And I don't know whether I'd want to sustain one anyway.

And the other thing is, boy, how do I say this, a couple of nights ago, Thursday night, I was playing some music, I really like music a lot. And so I was kind of boppin' along to this music. I was walking through the hallway to the back part of the house. I don't know how I got started doing it, but I started doing these little facial expressions. I know what it was, yeah, I was making an expression and then I'd make another one. I was doing it to the music, you know, only it got kind of carried away and it really surprised me. And so I kind of just went with it as I was walking down the hall. It was this whoosh of . . . it's hard to explain . . . but I kept doing it. I was going faster and faster and it felt very, very, very releasing. I started to say freeing but it was a sense of being released. A lot of expression. Damn. I wish I could explain it better. And then I stopped. I had to stop all of a sudden because I was going to lose control and . . . I didn't know what. And it happened just in a period of four or five paces. Kind of wow!! [Demonstrates the upward movement of intense sensation through his body and its powerful effects.] It felt really good.

Jackie: The sensation was toward your face?

Bart: Well, I was moving my whole body, too. It was physical movement and a release through that. But it was more than just physical. Boy, I want to use terms like, well, "really in touch with a vein." It felt really creative, really fresh, and extremely spontaneous. Extremely. It was really neat. It was just kind of an experience.

Jackie: And then it had to stop?

Bart: Well, yeah. Because it was so strong. The strength is what I think really . . . and very quick and very fast. It was like a real burst of energy. But it was more . . . a burst. That's it. [Makes a sound—boom] It wasn't sustainable. It wasn't slow enough to draw it out. And it was so strong. It was like a spike. It was just like that [Gestures a spike]. It couldn't keep going vertical. It was really interesting. And it harked back to . . . I just remembered I used to do that. I'd completely forgotten about that until just now. It wasn't as intense as it used to be. But . . . it's almost like dance but it's not . . . It's like being physical . . . it's an expression. I don't know. I just used to do goofy things like that.

Jackie: So it's a whole physical thing, not just energy in your head or face?

Bart: It's a whole movement thing. It's like emotion. It's like a dance I guess. Just kind of bursting.

Jackie: So you used to have these kinds of experiences.

Bart: Yes. When I was in my twenties. During that period. I'd forgotten about that. I felt happy too. I thought, "That was *nice*." It was a little surprising, but I felt good about it. So, those were two things. [Laughs] I don't know what to say other than that. I would class them both as, I guess, good things. It's experiencing intensity for real short periods of time, so maybe that's practice or warm up or something, but that's what it is.

Comment

It seemed clear that our experiences together were permitting the beginning emergence of strong body memories. Prior to this description, the sensations he reported outside sessions and those he had with me had been more ominous, frightening, terrifying, mysterious, and associated with some kind of (emotional?) death. On this day he reports some startling sensations on the way to his therapy session in connection with trying to recall some early memories. By now Bart realizes that what he is searching for must be very early infantile experiences. The memory flashes are not exactly colors, or blurs, or images, but total, unnerving, generalized powerful body sensations that are like a shudder, like a lightning bolt. The recollections are sensations that are packed, condensed, and quick.

He relates an experience from the previous Thursday night when he was enjoying music and dancing in his house by himself. During four or five paces down the hall he abandons himself to a series of facial expressions that he describes as joyful and releasing. He identifies the feelings as "not normal," but says, "It's like being in touch with a vein—really creative, really fresh, and extremely spontaneous." But just as quickly as the pleasurable body experience spiked, "I had to stop all of a sudden because I was going to lose control . . ." Bart says, "It's a whole movement thing. It's like emotion. It's like dance, I guess, just kind of bursting." Bart spontaneously remembers that during his twenties he used to do similar "goofy" things that he remembers as happy, nice, and good. He interprets these short bursts of intensity as some kind of practice or warmup. This interpretation reflects his awareness that he is on a journey toward the recovery of lost body sensations that recur in relation to his therapist. It is interesting to note that the first sensations he recovers are numbness, vagueness, and "blood running cold." As Bart now allows joyful feelings and physical release to emerge, he says it's like being in touch with a vein. It would seem from this report that excitement and joy are associated with blood rushing upward in his veins, which is accompanied by a sudden need to gain control over the sensations of pleasure.

BART'S SENSATION OF SIZE DISTORTION

7/6/89

Bart experienced another sensation in one of the therapy sessions right after we had discussed his reluctance to move into the initiator role in relationships. We are discussing "us" and he starts to lose track and then relates the sensation.

Jackie: If you kept coming in here, holding your hand out and pouring your heart out, and got nothing back, and I didn't reach out to you and relate, how long would you come in?

Bart: That's a good question. [Long pause] It makes sense. [Pause] Well, there certainly seems to be some sort of more noticeable dissatisfaction, but as far as moving into an active role, I don't know. I don't know about that bridge.

Jackie: Let's think about how it is in here. Because we have gone from time to time with you not bringing things up, maybe waiting for me to bring them up or waiting for them to just happen. And there have also been times when you've really brought

something in, like the time you told me how much you enjoyed when I gave you the framework and theory that I was working from; I would have never known that you wanted that.

Bart: Okay.

Jackie: Now you ended up getting it and responding and saying you liked it, but I had no way of knowing.

Bart: Yeah.

Jackie: And I wonder if while here, when you initiate, do you get met and what happens versus when you come in here and respond and do just what you think you're supposed to do?

Bart: I think as far as the latter goes, I've kind of tried to be more in touch with what's really going on—not really having an agenda. It's kind of like I don't think about an agenda but how I feel about things. So, in that sense, I think that I've been more and more real. I guess. I lost my train of thought again. It's sort of going on a little bit.

Jackie: Is there something going on at another level where you're kind of talking on the outside and something else is going on?

Bart: No, I just forgot. I hate that. It's weird. It just slips away. What did you ask?

Jackie: I was asking about the difference between when you take an active role here versus a more passive role.

Bart: I don't know if I can tell the difference. I'm trying to think of examples. I don't know. [Pause] I can't seem to make much out of this.

Jackie: I'm thinking in terms of reaching out and wanting something versus wanting it and not reaching for it, and how different that might be.

Bart: I suspect it would be better.

Jackie: And what that means to your life and how you see who you're going to be.

Bart: Yeah. I can think of lots of instances of how delighted I would be when people would do or say something that I wanted them to.

Jackie: And they never knew. They maybe just did a bunch of things and just hit on one.

Bart: Yeah. And it would be like . . . I used to be. I'm having the oddest old physical sensation. I haven't had it in quite a while.

Jackie: Tell me.

Bart: It's really hard to explain. Shoo. I don't know how to tell you. It's a thing I've had as long as I can remember, as a kid even. Of things getting much bigger. And it still bothers me in my hands. I still get physical sensations in my hands. Things are growing. The sensation is of everything getting really really huge.

Jackie: Where are you?

Bart: I'm still right here.

Jackie: Are you getting big now?

Bart: I am, especially my hands. It's really odd. The tactile sensations are real, real pronounced. Whew. Man. It's the oddest thing. I have this vague kind of picture . . . but I can't explain it. It's almost like looking at something microscopic. Now I have this sensation of letters. I keep thinking of the letter "A" for some reason. I can feel my fingers on my hands touching my legs. The pores on these pants feel like they're this big [Gestures].

Jackie: What's happened to everything else in the room? Do other things change in their size dimension too?

Bart: No. It's a physical sensation that changes. And there's this background kind of blackness with these huge letters rolling through. I've had it before. It used to wake me up when I was a kid. It would get so intense that it would just keep expanding and getting bigger and bigger. It is really incredibly physically uncomfortable. [Talks a little more about it and the session is over.]

Comment

The sensation reported here as extremely uncomfortable is also recalled from childhood almost as a recurring nightmare that would disturb his sleep. Based upon these and other comments he has made, the suggestion is that though Bart may have had to clamp down on physical sensations during infancy, at times during childhood his tactile sense would break out of control and loom super-large. In those moments he only senses the discomfort of physical sensation. The background of the world is only "blackness with these huge letters rolling through." As Bart experiences this tactile sensation with me, are the pores in his pants which are so large that he can feel his hands touching his leg memories of infantile skin sensations? Are they memories of touching the pores of mother's skin? Are the large letters rolling though the background blackness the awareness of the world of adults ("A") and restrictions? Is there the possibility that the "A" is a dreamy reference to Hawthorne's *The Scarlet Letter* and therefore to forbidden sexual thoughts?

TWO LEARNING TO HOLD ON TO THE CONNECTION

A month later I was able for the first time to hold Bart in contact with me for a very crucial part of our interaction.

8/3/89

Bart begins talking about how important his sessions are becoming to him and how hopeful he is feeling about change for himself.

Jackie: Maybe one of the things you could concentrate on in here is how good it feels to be here enjoying yourself with me. You keep coming. I know you don't like working on some of the things that come up, but I think as far as being here and our being together you are increasingly able to enjoy yourself with me.

Bart: Yes. It's my great hope—to be able to enjoy myself with people all the time.

Jackie: It's as though you are wanting to say, "I like being with you. Time with you is really great. I don't like leaving when I have to. When the session ends, it's like I want more from you." If you really let yourself resonate with how you do feel being with me, I wonder what kind of picture would show up for you?

Bart: I can try. [Hesitant] I don't know what that is. It seems hard to

attach what I know and can say with how I feel. To hook onto those words or to let them hook onto me. [He's very quiet here.] It's interesting what's happening right now though. When you said those things I was with you and then I started to vague out for a moment but I've let myself be here and realize that I do enjoy being with you. Not long ago if you had said what you just said I wouldn't have heard a word of it.

Jackie: How so?

Bart: Because it's talking really straight, real directly and I think . . . it seems to me that sometimes the vagueness or the confusion occurs when there's more direct talk. Like when you're saying directly how you feel. Or just now when you said directly what we both know I feel. That's when the confusion begins.

Jackie: It's almost always when it's about us.

Bart: Yeah. Right. Does that prove to be the case in your notes?

Jackie: As a matter of fact, yes. Only the other day I was reviewing one of the first times when you became really vague here. We were talking about us.

Bart: Making some kind of connection with you made me very uncom- fortable in some sense and I would disassociate.

Jackie: You stayed here today.

Bart: Congratulations! [Both laugh.]

Jackie: I got to keep you with me. How nice!

Bart: That's super. Yeah. That's great. Yeah. I like that [very pleased with himself].

Comment

Two weeks after this session Bart had an extraordinarily intense session in which he did not disconnect or go vague at all. My final line was "And I got to be with you the whole session!" We were both pleased, knowing what an achievement this was for him.

BART'S SENSE OF VAGUENESS AND THE INTERNAL COLLAPSE OF THOUGHT

The physical sensations of Bart's blood running cold, the coldness in his back, the enlarging hands, and the tones were not the only kinds of sensations that Bart described. There were much more subtle ones that were very much a part of the sessions but ones I could not easily detect. Bart was so adept at hiding them that a good percentage of the time I was unaware of their presence. We would be talking about something and at some point Bart would get a bit vague. On the outside, he appeared to be thinking and working through a thought or feeling and would be telling me about it. Not wanting to interrupt him or to intrude by calling him on it (especially because I couldn't really tell for sure that anything different was happening), I would just listen to what he was trying to say. I might even do some reflective listening in the hopes of deepening his disclosures. I thought often that I was with him and that we were connected and resonating. But I slowly came to realize that we often were experiencing false relating or pretend situations. We were living out together an imitation of a meaningful conversation. The inner experi- ence that he only later became able to describe was that during such moments he became lost and confused. So while our conversation appeared to be an inter- change of two people connecting, it was more of a way he had learned simply to be. Bart could mimic what was socially appropriate. But that was far from the dynamics of two people engaging in any intimate verbal interaction. On several occasions, Bart gave extremely graphic descriptions of what was going on for him on the inside.

5/19/88

Jackie: You're saying that it's okay for us to just be here together?

Bart: Right. I think so.

Jackie: And not to have to have something that we focus on away from us to look at. To simply see what comes up with the two of us sitting here together?

Bart: Whew, um, yeah, interesting. There isn't anything going on right now. I want to be real quiet. I don't want to say anything.

Jackie: Okay.

Bart: [Immediately] I jumped out of that real quick because it's the same thing. The need for quiet is a mechanism too. Because I felt real nervous when we were talking about just being here together now and not having an agenda. And I didn't know what to do, so I wanted to close up and be real quiet. I've had that before—not knowing what to say and being absolutely baffled like sometimes when I used to fight with Candy. I would get to the point where I didn't have anything to say. And it was the same mechanism. It felt like going incommunicado.

Jackie: So being quiet is a shutting down rather than saying, "I just want to be here with you and just be quiet and that's okay."

Bart: It could be . . . I don't know. I didn't know what to think of it, so I associated it with the mechanism I use to "get by."

Jackie: "I don't know how to respond so I'll just go into quiet." What happens when you're in quiet?

Bart: Let's see. I'll have to work through this. I don't know exactly. I started to say I get hyper-alert, but at the same time, I mean it's almost like a control. I'm very aware of what's going on around me to start with, but then there's confusion. I've had this happen a couple of times where I'll get confused in here. I'll lose my train of thought and get confused and I don't hear you for a little bit.

Jackie: There was a time last week when you were saying something and I was trying to follow it. When I relistened to the tape recording, I found myself thinking, "Here I am trying to 'get it,' and what I should have been paying attention to is that something else is going on inside of Bart that I can't quite get hold of."

Bart: Yes, exactly.

Jackie: You were saying words and appeared to be talking to me. But for a period of time you were off somewhere else.

Bart: Yes. That happens sometimes. I'll lose my train of thought, or I'll lose where we're at. Often it's when you're saying something important to me, or you're summarizing things, or giving me one of your observations. I'm trying to think what will trigger it. Sometimes a thought will carry me off. That's why I have a difficult time outside trying to remember what you said about me. Because I don't remember, or I don't hear it, or something else was going on. It's this shutting down, like narcolepsy. This momentary falling asleep. You just, boom . . . What happened? I go somewhere. It started to happen just a moment ago.

Jackie: I was talking about our being together here.

Bart: Right. Right. I'm not surprised. So I guess it's related to intimacy. There's a paralysis and an inability to convey my thoughts. That's where I was getting confused—still being aware of what's going on, of what I wanted to say, but not being able to get it out. Geez, now that I think of it, it doesn't sound real good. They're momentary lapses of consciousness. I'm still conscious of my surroundings, but I get confused and lose track. . . . It's a complete distraction or a complete diversion of attention away. In arguments with Candy which were high emotional moments I would get really confused at times. And it was even more maddening because she would get this icy coldness about her and then I'd get completely lost. It would get to a point where I simply couldn't speak. The two things would get hooked up together. I would get lost. I'd come back. I wouldn't know what the heck was going on, and then I couldn't say anything at all.

Comment

What was Bart describing for me? Clearly some form of threat of interpersonal engagement set off the "vague" reaction. Is losing immediate consciousness or attention to the moment a way of preventing or rupturing contact? Is the inability to speak simply the result of momentarily losing track of the conversation or the train of thought and not wanting to reveal the lapse to the other? Or is the thought disruption and the speech dysfunction an expression of the nature of the organizing-level trauma that is being remembered in the present moment of threatened contact? He elaborates the experience on other occasions.

6/2/88

Bart: I got to a point where again, I wasn't really able to communicate. It's similar to what happens at the end of sessions. Or at times of hearing but not being able to react. It's hearing but being hazy.

Jackie: Those are the experiences you've described that occur when I'm talking to you or something important is occurring between us?

Bart: Exactly. I remember not being able to speak very intelligently. It was just a seizing up—it was a "seizure," I'll use that word. In a sense it was a seizure, like an engine seizes up, freezes, stops functioning.

Jackie: An emotional seizure.

Bart: That's a good way to put it. I wanted to be able to respond but I was unable to respond. Emotionally I couldn't get anything out other than gibberish.

Jackie: And those moments as they come up in here are some of the ones we really want to look at.

Bart: Yes.

Jackie: When we find one, we can go back and see what we were talking about that may have set off the emotional seizure.

Bart: How do we get the seizures to occur here? See, that's the thing. I'm afraid of getting into those. I got a real sophisticated mechanism that keeps me out of those places.

Jackie: And I have a real sophisticated mechanism to put you into them! [Both laugh]

Bart: Well, yeah, to put me into them. [Laughs; sudden change in voice tone]. I don't understand. To put me into them?

Jackie: To keep you from getting away from them.

Bart: I'm getting confused right now.

Jackie: Something's happening right now.

Bart: Absolutely. I can't make out what you're saying. I lost track of thought. Sometimes I feel like, "Where are we?" [Bart's words are all jumbled here.] I lost track of the logic of the conversation.

Comment

The actual moment that the contact was ruptured was when we were playing and laughing spontaneously about his having a sophisticated mechanism for avoiding emotional seizures and my having a sophisticated mechanism for putting him into them. The focused clarity of what we were saying to each other and the intimacy in play allowing us to laugh and joke about something so deep and significant to our relationship moved us into immediate and deep personal contact. This contact moment then was instantly ruptured by the emergence of an internalized state of vagueness and confusion. He suddenly lost track of the logic of our thoughts; he couldn't make out what I was saying, and he wondered "where are we?" This could not be a clearer example of how Bart gets lost, has emotional seizures, and loses his speech whenever a moment of intimate contact in an important relationship occurs.

7/14/88

Bart: It was the mechanism again. I knew when I told you about it, you would ask, "What has just happened?" For a period of time, it was like I went into a kind of mental paralysis. I would try to push my way out or to explore what I was feeling right now. I'm trying to get in touch with myself so I can intervene in the operation of the mechanism. But I couldn't do it. It was like a paralysis. It was like being in shock and tied to the same panic I felt when I was so cruelly rejected by Mary Jones when I was 13. Shocked into

paralysis. I couldn't speak other than just minimally and I couldn't think clearly either. I would try to regain my composure but would not be able to, not at all. It was really strong. Familiar, but I hadn't experienced it so intensely in a long time.

Jackie: You are telling me about the vague feeling where you go into confusion?

Bart: There was part of that there. That inability to think straight. It was like a sudden clash of a bunch of stuff at once. It was this tremendous confusion of thoughts, pieces of this, pieces of that, like different thoughts slammed together and shattered for a moment. I was not able to express myself because it seemed like the whole thing sank very deeply. It was not able to come out in anger or surprise, or in just plain curiosity or addressing the situation. It was just this abyss and the sensation was strong. I kept trying to get a handle on it, but the sensation was very chaotic, troublesome, and frightening. It had to do with sensations of being hurt in that first Mary Jones rejection episode. That rush of realization that people do not care about you like you thought they did. That things can change. That people can shift their affections. That what I have relied on isn't always going to be there.

Comment

Bart had described his interaction with Mary Jones as the first important intimate relationship he consciously remembered in which he entrusted his feelings and became vulnerable. He proceeded in the relationship as though everything was fine (perhaps in a state of reverie) only to find that she "dropped" him with no apparent concern for his feelings (perhaps the way his mother had "dropped" him).

Bart initially believed that his reluctance to relate stemmed from this rejection, which he experienced as cruel and uncaring. He presented it as the point at which he became acutely aware of his traumatic seizures of functioning.

I believe that this is merely a screen memory for his ruptured contact with his mother, which is now replicated in current relationships and which keeps him from allowing full intimate contact.

People living organizing pockets often perceive rejection or abandonment from the other when it is they who have become traumatized by contact and must emotionally flee.

4/20/89

Bart: I don't know if I can consciously control myself. I ask myself that. So what's the fear? Why won't I let go? I don't have a good answer for that. That's the odd thing. Like last week when I got scared. I don't know why I was. I don't have an explanation.

Jackie: I was thinking about "blood running cold" and how when we are scared, our system does clamp down. So I'm not surprised that there's a physical coldness.

Bart: Yeah. It's a physical reaction. Definitely. I'm still trying to grasp what it was on my way down here today. There's a loss of control. One of the things I sense is I don't always know how to react. I get tripped up somewhere and don't have a reaction. Then there's a panic. I'm not sure what to do. I'm not sure what to say. There's this thing going on because there's a trip up in the reaction process. Then I'll lose track of what you are saying.

It's almost like I can't hear you or it doesn't make any sense. I hear you but at the same time there's this other thing going on—this panic that prevents the words from getting through or making sense. I can't interpret them anymore, so I get lost. It's like walking into a room and the door suddenly closes behind you. And you go, "Oh, man, I've walked into something I can't get out of." Then boom, something just collapses or something jumps up and this whole confusing process starts. Panic dissolves into losing track of what's going on.

Jackie: It's difficult trying to make sense of the world after your thought processes have collapsed.

Bart: Yes. It's definitely something like that because it's really disorienting. I'll be talking to someone and the subject will shift to light chat. Then it will be shifted to a serious subject by the other person. I will try to maintain this light chat to the point where I almost wind up just babbling. Or just dribbling off into something nonsensical. It's a way of maintaining distant talk. I know what they're talking about, but I'm trying to talk about, "What a beautiful blue sky." Somebody's talking to you seriously about something . . .

Jackie: And trying to connect with you.

Bart: And I'm going zzzzzpppp. I'm aware of what they're doing but my mouth's stuck babbling.

Jackie: Do you know what your insides are doing?

Bart: They are doing a fast regroup. Trying to determine how to maintain.

Jackie: You said you don't do it in here with me, but my guess is that you do do it sometimes.

Bart: Yes. But, it's not to such extremes. It's like the conversation is going along like this. I'm conversing and then the person will turn a little this way [gestures] and I'll just keep going off that way [gestures]. All of the sudden there's this gap that's real apparent. Sometimes I can cover it up quickly and regroup, and come back to the conversation. But sometimes I dribble off.

Jackie: If I caught such a moment and asked you about it, could you recognize it?

Bart: Sure.

Jackie: Would you be able to say, "Yes, it's happening right now."

Bart: I think so. I'll admit to most anything. But I won't bring it up. There's this whole conversation that just crossed my mind of making talk when there isn't anything to say. It's the same thing. It's this "appropriate" thing to do. It's like good manners. I'm associating that with my mom right now. She's very good at not missing a beat and being right in tune with what's going on. And probably controlling it, now that I think about it. She's very "appropriate." I have this image of genteel society or parlor conversations that are all very proper. You don't talk with swear words or say certain things. There is this structure of what you do and don't do. If you break out of that, you're being really rude, crude, or in some way violating the rules. So with my mom there is this conversation in which she cannot tolerate incongruities and she'll fill in gaps when there are gaps. She keeps things moving, no matter what.

Jackie: And that's what you do?

Bart: I feel compelled to try. I'm realizing as I'm speaking that I've learned that really well. I too can keep things moving, no matter what.

Jackie: You are saying that it's not real connecting. It's not us really being here together.

Bart: No. Definitely not. People say things in a tender way, or in an angry way, or in a real emotional way. Then there's this pause, so I fill it in with something. Kind of color it in, and gloss it over, or bridge away from it. But I'm trying more now when those moments occur to be quiet and let myself be present in the moment, to let myself be internally reactive to what is happening. It's not my responsibility to make things nice or easy for the other person. And that's a lot of what it is. It's being very polite. It's extraordinary politeness which appears to fill in a gap but in fact creates an emotional gap. That's what my mom does—fills in for people if they make a boo boo. She glosses it over it or . . . "boo boo" [laughs]. That cracks me up. [Laughs]

Jackie: That comes from a very young place?

Bart: I think so. "Boo boo!" That just cracks me up. [Laughs loudly again.]

Jackie: I wonder what boo boos Mom glossed over?

Bart: I don't know. That's not a word I use every day, I'll tell you. [Still laughing] That's insightful right there. There's this conversational fixing, or bridging, or glossing over. It's a real tool for controlling the situation. I'm just realizing how much it has been used. On the surface it kept things "proper." I'm not sure if it served to keeps things simply superficial, or more emotionally distant, or both.

Jackie: It doesn't sound like filling in, bridging, or glossing over allows for much realness, for much interpersonal connecting.

Bart: It doesn't.

Jackie: You might have other more real kinds of feelings or emotions you want to express, but it's not proper—better to gloss over things and not have to relate.

Bart: Right. Yeah. That's exactly what it is. It's like this parlor talk. This level of polite chitchat and you really never say much to each other or ever really get into it.

Jackie: Let's catch ourselves if we do it in here. I don't want to do parlor talk with you. I want to get into things. I want to be here with you. I want to relate to you in all the richness we can.

Comment

I noted that it will be interesting to watch exactly how the glossing, bridging, or fixing of conversation operates on an internalized basis for Bart. That is, he reports a sense of internal collapse. When does it occur? And what is the function of the bridging? Is he simply covering a dysfunctional moment as he suggests, a moment when he can't quite make sense of things. Or is the bridging, covering, glossing mechanism a way of breaking or preventing emotional contact or of securing distance? At this point it seems that the threat of interpersonal contact or intimacy triggers a transferential collapse of thought. The superficial, false, polite bridging may be the way Mother created the original trauma. And on the basis of mimicry or primary identification this internalized mechanism of bridging parlor chat now serves to continuously re-create the rupture of interpersonal contact.

NARCISSISM IN THE COUNTERTRANSFERENCE

By April 1989 we were partially able to construct a narrative picture of what Bart's experience might have looked like when he was a baby, but we were not yet able to gain an understanding of where Mom was in the relationship with infant Bart that made connecting incomplete or traumatic. Bart described his mother as "a nice lady." He had fond childhood memories of family activities such as May Day celebrations and family outings, and there was no evidence of pronounced trauma other than the stern restriction to be well behaved. I thought that if perhaps we could discover this missing piece, we could know what it was about the mother–child relationship that seemed to keep him from having active, enjoyable relationships to rely on for his social life. Those relationships Bart did engage in seemed prohibited somehow from realizing their full potential.

Some fascinating information came during a session where I really had to struggle with a very strong countertransference response.

4/13/89

Bart: I spoke of this once before, I think, of a kind of giving up, of simply not trying. There seems to be so much disappointment. I get to feeling I can't weather much more. I think that's maybe another reason why I get evasive. Because I've taken the real hard feelings, the real intense ones, and moved them out to the edge of the thinking circle. Maybe that's why I get real frightened when you talk about having to eventually get to those things here with you.

Jackie: What's it been like to feel here with me?

Bart: Well, [pause] I think I keep it pretty well leveled so I don't necessarily let myself feel a very wide range with you. So in that sense, I don't think it's much different here from on the outside. My relationship with you is pretty much the same as many others.

Jackie: So people in your life can't ever get close enough to feel they've made an impact?

Comment

As I thought about it, I realized this last comment came from my feeling angry and wounded during this session by being lumped by Bart with all of the disappointing relationships of the world! Through consultation, I was able to identify and analyze a number of feelings that came from this interaction where Bart told me he didn't feel much more in our sessions than he felt elsewhere.

First, I felt very unimportant to Bart and I felt like he could easily leave me. I felt a coldness and distance from him that I didn't always feel. I felt like he didn't need me in my function as therapist, and I felt that he was really discounting me as a person as well as our time together. I felt like he was dropping me. I felt I wasn't doing things in the right way so I could keep him interested in our work. I also felt a twinge of wanting to say to him, "Fine, if this isn't a special enough place, and I'm not an important person to you then you can just leave."

As I reflected on my feelings, I realized that they bore a remarkable similarity to the "punishment" and "righteous indignation" feelings that Bart had described earlier. Was it possible that I was feeling like Mom might have felt? I had made the initial connection with the baby and had done the appropriate mother things (feeding, burping, changing, and so forth). I had functioned. I perhaps felt then that my job was over. I wasn't needed to be functioning anymore. Why should I just hold the baby while he appears to be paying no attention to me? He is seemingly absent. He purposelessly gazes and dozes, absorbed in his own world, unaware of my presence. Perhaps she didn't know, or couldn't accept, that he couldn't really see her. All he could feel was her warmth and his wholeness right then. Perhaps she didn't realize that part of her importance for her infant was to just be there for him and to let him feel her presence. Perhaps her own narcissism (like mine) had gotten in her way when he wasn't responding in a way that fulfilled her. Perhaps she would then put him down. According to Bart's recurrent sensation of coldness and lower back vulnerability, we might surmise that the baby's experience was that of being put down or dropped. Perhaps when her needs in the relationship weren't being met she would abruptly put him into his crib, making him feel like he was falling from a secure place to a place of aloneness where his blood might run cold, where he would feel an insecure hole in his back where her warm hand had held him. Perhaps the infant felt a sudden sense of confusion and disorientation as he tried to regain his sense of reality in drastically altered circumstances without a mother to organize around.

The discovery of what Bart's early experience might have looked like and felt like pointed to some possibilities regarding what may be restricting Bart's relational life. What terrifying images might Bart unknowingly reexperience internally when he would begin to feel connection happening or perceive its imminence that would cause him to have bodily sensations of blood running cold and plummet him into a world of confusion, vagueness, disorientation, and loss? The conceptualization of this picture also made other things Bart had mentioned previously take on added significance and helped us focus on what needed to be done with the organizing material in order for him to make a shift.

I provided the word *reverie* for the valuable time that Mom and baby might have simply enjoyed each other's presence in a dreamlike state. Since it appears that this mutually pleasuring experience is not what Bart was able to internalize, it left him without any experiential knowledge to use in enjoying his current relationships. This absence of reverie time seemed to be replicated in many of these relationships. One woman even told him that he was very good at starting relationships but he could not sustain them. When he reflected on this, he realized that about six months after a relationship started, he began to get "antsy" that something had to be done. He had internalized his mother's attitude that it was not enough just to be present with the person. Something worthwhile, proper, or productive had to be kept going. Simple enjoyment of each other was not a possibility. Emotionally connecting was somehow dangerous and had to be prevented.

Another girlfriend told him, "You get women interested and you are interested, but at a certain point, the relating stops." Bart realized that he created his own sense of obligation in a relationship. The other person would finally irritate him. He would then wait for something to legitimize his anger and he would leave. As he began to reflect back on these ideas, it all started to make sense.

Comment

Here Bart finds other rationalizations for why relationships don't work. But by now, he has a rudimentary sense that he is doing something to spoil them. He can't quite formulate yet how he begins engineering a way out when the relating pressure moves toward intimate interpersonal contact.

4/27/89

Jackie: In relationships with women, you say you go to a certain point. It seems that although you establish the relationship so that you can enjoy others, somehow people are always dropped, let go of.

Bart: Yes. [Quiet] That well could be. They get dropped. But I don't understand how, if that happened to me and caused me so much pain and agony, why I would do it to them?

Jackie: Because you learned both sides of the relationship with your mother. The Mary Jones rejection when you were 13 replicated the hope of relating and the agony of abandonment. In learning how to relate to your mother you took in both sides of the relationship including the trauma of Mom dropping you.

Bart: You mean I took in and now live out the whole of what happened to me?

Jackie: Exactly. You then can play

both parts. Sometimes you're the one who gets dropped and sometimes you may create that same emotional experience for others.

Bart: I see.

Jackie: You function well as a partner in a relationship.

Bart: I know that.

Jackie: It's that reverie part of just enjoying each other that poses a challenge. Mom may have wondered, "What does he want with me? I can't feed him more, I can't do any more for him. It must be time to put him down." My guess is that some of the women in your life have wanted just to be with you. Just to enjoy your company. And not be doing anything. Just be with you. Or perhaps they have wanted to have other kinds of emotional contact with you. But you don't know how to do that part. You didn't get any experience with that part of relating. Mom cut that off. She didn't know that you just wanted to gaze at her and have another little gulp of milk and maybe fall asleep and wake up. If you've ever watched a baby do that, they're just perfectly happy. It's the quiet transitional time and space where creativity, spontaneity, and thoughts begin.

Bart: Yes. I see that. I'm trying to see if that fits. I'm trying it on. I'm trying to see the part that plays in the development of a relationship. When and where it comes in. Because it's not right away. It takes awhile.

Jackie: You're busy functioning as a partner . . .

Bart: Setting up frameworks, activities, escalating, developing—that's the right word. And then it gets to a point. If you put a time frame on it, it falls about six months, I've noticed.

Jackie: So after the framework for basic relating is all set up, after you come to know each other's patterns, after you've got all the basics down . . .

Bart: Right.

Jackie: Now it's the time for close interactions, for being together emotionally and intimately.

Bart: It's happening with Melinda right now. I want to examine what's going on, but I don't have any sense of how to go further. If I look at my relationships, I understand the path to this point, but I don't have any point of reference about what relating might look like beyond that place because I've never been further.

Jackie: "I know you're my baby, I know I'm your mom. You're fed and warm but I don't know what else to do with you so I'll put you down and busy myself elsewhere." You do to others what was done to you.

Bart: This is a convincing road map.

Comment

At this point I began to realize that Bart had been telling me about the disorientation he experienced when being "dropped." But I hadn't been able to formulate it very well. I went back in my notes and found the following entry on 5/19/88 right after his telling me about one of his girlfriends breaking up with him.

5/19/88

Bart: It was just this dismissal. Then it got real intense. I mean it was pretty intense up to then, but after that the grief of the situation was surprising. All that stuff just got incredibly overwhelming and I had a period of time there that I was very shaky. It was grief, or extraordinary emotion. It was the flip side of the coin. The unpleasant side. I remember the surprise and the intense emotion. I got confused. [Bart at this time also talked about the feeling of "falling," which we were able to correlate to the feeling of being "dropped."]

Jackie: You said it was like falling from a building?

Bart: I was talking about the sensation of my stomach moving.

Jackie: You seem to be describing the sensation of being dropped or put down.

Bart: I was just thinking that.

Jackie: I wonder if you were dropped. Many babies are dropped or left unsupported and it's very traumatic.

Bart: It's possible. [At this point Bart twitched or convulsed noticeably and I commented on it. His response was that he was still with me and that he was okay.] I can recall falling out of bed when I was a really little kid and then having dreams and nightmares about that. But that's not early enough. I used to have terrific nightmares or recurring nightmares, two of them. Maybe they were tied together. They used to wake me up to where I couldn't speak. My voice was gone. I had to pound on the wall.

Jackie: When was this?

Bart: As young as I can remember.

Jackie: Do you remember the nightmares?

Bart: Yeah. Kind of. Two things, one was like an Arab in the sense of very dark. I don't remember the action. I only remember the person. Like a hooded monk or a hooded Arab. I said Arab because they wear the cape and hood and are dark. I can't remember what happened. The other thing I remember is the silver knife.

Jackie: And these were both nightmares?

Bart: They used to wake me up and they were extremely powerful. I would wake up absolutely terrified to the point I lost my voice. I couldn't speak. I remember that.

Jackie: "I wasn't able to call for Mom."

Comment

The construction of this picture also lent credence to Bart's mention about his inability to extend, in this case vocal extension. The dreams suggested the terror of the forbidden, terrifying, injuring oedipal father. They are remembered from that time period of his life (probably age 4 or 5). In this context they suggest a fear of relating to father's emotionality (the Arab) and to whatever personal damage the silver knife must have meant to him. Being unable to sustain contact to Mother, how could he possibly make safe contact with Father?

4/13/89

Bart: I just had a flash about extending. I will not extend. But I will react to someone extending fine. Because if I extend I don't know whether they're going to touch back. I had this image of touching. So there's this unsureness about that. But if they do extend toward me, then they want to be in contact, so it's fine.

Jackie: Our research shows that when babies reach out and Mom meets them they learn to extend and to reach out freely.

Bart: Yeah. And I don't do that.

Jackie: We can assume the reception wasn't satisfying in some way. "Mom, you didn't come when I needed you to, so now I'm going to do it on my own time or not at all."

Bart: That's definitely how it works for me.

Jackie: So what happens if you reach out to me and you are not met?

Bart: I won't do it. That's the whole point. It's not even a matter of taking a chance. That's the scary part. I get this feeling of, "Ooohhh I'm stepping off somewhere and I don't know where it's at." So I actively stop all reaching, all venturing toward others. I wait for them to reach toward me so I can respond, but even that eventually becomes scary and is cut off.

Comment

Had I not been able to use my countertransference feelings, I might have missed being involved in the experience of Bart's infancy and thereby missed the opportunity to deeply and personally understand his story. It may be of interest that the last statement above of Bart's was inadvertently attributed to me in my process notes. The first formulation possible, according to my supervisor, was that I was feeling in the countertransference the unavailability of my own mother, and is derived from the listening perspective for the organizing developmental level. The second formulation, that in the countertransference I was feeling treated by Bart in the neglectful way he was treated by his mother, is derived from the perspective for listening to symbiotic, merger, or borderline developmental experiences.

LISTENING TO BART FROM THE SYMBIOTIC OR MERGER LISTENING PERSPECTIVE

The case material thus far presented has focused on some subtle themes that can be isolated for consideration by listening from the perspective of the early personality in organization. But most of the time Bart's work concerned various higher or more complex levels of personality integration, so that other perspectives for listening were more helpful in appreciating his material. To illustrate the contrast, some of that work is presented now.

In listening to Bart's descriptions about relationships throughout his life, I kept watching for the moment of "disconnect" that might give me a clue as to why he wasn't able to develop stable, fulfilling relationships. We talked about this often. One day Bart wondered if "connecting" ever happened with him at all. I asked him if he thought we had ever connected. (I felt we had because we had known each other for quite a long time, we enjoyed our time together even when there was difficult material, and we talked about things (in depth.) Bart said he wasn't really sure we had ever truly and personally connected. His response gave me cause to ponder about our relationship. I then began to realize that much of our relationship could be listened to as a replication of Bart's symbiotic "Mommy and me" scenario. This merger or borderline listening perspective highlights characteristic modes of engaging the other that are interpersonally engaging but ultimately inimical to ongoing self development.

It is usually easy for me to discern "Mommy and me" symbiotic scenarios when they are enacted as a struggle with the client, for example, a power struggle, a limit-setting struggle, or a feeling of, "I can't be who you want me to be." But with Bart, it wasn't until late in therapy that I understood the very comfortable and compatible way we interacted was fundamentally a replication from the symbiotic period of his early development. Our interaction was amiable, pleasant, polite, and courteous. The majority of his other interactions were similar. Bart is a pleasant and likable guy to be with. What I could interpret from this was that pleasantness and niceness was the form his connection with Mom took. He was a "good boy" engaging others within the narrow band of emotional relatedness that could be received by Mom. But this limited mode of relating left most aspects of Bart such as intense emotional expression, creativity, or thinking about himself (versus pleasing/helping others) largely undeveloped. Mom couldn't receive these parts of him.

He remembered as a little boy accompanying his parents to antique shops and having to be ever so careful not to bump into things or to disturb anything. He remembered sometimes sitting perfectly still and being well behaved with his hands in his lap. We came to label this the "good boy syndrome." He saw clearly how these behaviors, considered appropriate and reasonable at the time by his mother, had become his adult way of being in the world. This style necessitated considerable denial, or at least suppression of any intense emotion or confrontational action, and created a narrow range of relational possibilities with others. Later we came to call these internalized restrictions his "governors," devices "installed" in childhood to limit his levels of excitability.

Having some preliminary notion of what Bart's symbiotic or borderline scenarios might look like, I began watching for moments that might be telling. I knew that somehow we would need to go outside the "governors" to expand Bart's possibilities of relating, but I wasn't sure just how that was going to be accomplished. The session of 9/8/88 started us on course with something I did quite spontaneously and unconsciously. Partway through the session, the tape in the recorder needed turning over. Instead of going around my chair like I usually do, I sort of stepped or almost leaped over the corner of the coffee table closest to me in a rather ungraceful way. Bart gave a hearty laugh in response to that. I momentarily experienced some embarrassment at what felt like a faux pas, but was quickly able to have a good laugh with him. I was surprised that I chose that route to the tape recorder. Retrospectively I have to wonder if I unconsciously knew that I had to go "outside the governors" of appropriateness characteristic of our sessions.

Immediately after my ungraceful moment, Bart began talking about being more comfortable and relaxed. I took the opportunity to highlight the interaction saying, "So you got more comfortable and relaxed when I leaped over the end of the table." We had connected in laughter at that moment and it was a different kind of interaction than we ordinarily shared. We laughed and enjoyed the moment together. It was as though unconsciously I had confronted the politeness scenario by refusing the "good boy syndrome" for myself. My out-of-decorum enactment represented my breaking free of the restraints that prim and proper governors provide. We both enjoyed how "unladylike" and "inappropriate" my behavior had been while enjoying a spontaneous "leap."

9/8/88

Jackie: Did you get more comfortable and relaxed when I did that thing with the coffee table? Because we really connected then. That was a different kind of thing we did together. We laughed and enjoyed the moment together.

Bart: Yes. That may have been part of it. It seemed like it. It was great! Yes, I think that sometimes I want to make this process different between us, more alive.

Comment

Bart felt the difference in our interaction. He agreed with me that we needed to do more things like this. A few weeks later about halfway through a session he told me that his grandmother had died since I had last seen him. He told me fairly dispassionately and described how his family had responded to it.

9/22/88

Bart: We really hardly talked about it. There wasn't any grief shown. The family actually had a really good time when we came together. But it's not a close group in the sense of saying or showing things directly. The feelings are there but it's very reserved. I don't know what to think about all that. I'm really torn, because the sharing that is done has value, and yet it really makes me mad that there isn't more spontaneous feeling and openness. I don't know what the exact story is. Are we hiding ourselves from each other? Are we afraid? If so, of what? I have some turmoil about all of that. We talked about my grandmother and all that. How bad are you supposed to feel? She was 92. It's not like someone died at 38 all of a sudden. It's completely different.

Jackie: But you still lost someone who has been important to you. And your mother lost her mother.

Bart: Yes, and she's the one who won't show much in the way of feelings. My dad will show a little more. But she's the one I took the cue from. It's becoming real apparent now that we just don't show things. Maybe in ways we don't even feel them.

Jackie: She plays it really close to the chest. Which is what you do in relationships. Then the other person has no idea about how you feel. Remember what I said was going to be hardest for me in this new phase we are in is that I wasn't going to know, and maybe I never did, when you silently and invisibly left the room while I thought you were still here.

Bart: I expect people to just know things, to tap into how I feel. But they're not mind readers. This business of picking up cues is so subtle. I can tell things with my mother, but you've got to be watching things really close to know what's going on. I guess I'm a little angry about why it has to be so subtle. It's all tied up in a lot of weird protocol and manners of just the way we are and the way my grandmother is. And my mother's that way because her mother was. There's this whole heritage of control.

Comment

I sensed Bart wanted to talk about his grandmother and encouraged it by the way I was with him. As he did, he began to cry, at moments almost uncontrollably. My sitting quietly with him enabled him to feel and to show the emotions that had been bottled up for so long. He was allowing himself to venture outside the limits of his emotional governors and to relate in a way that I sensed he had been deprived of for so long. As he experienced this process, he was able to confront the fact that his family had been unable to live with emotions that make life complete and how that has affected him. Some people might refer to such an episode as a corrective emotional experience with my giving permission for, or validating his feelings. But much more seemed involved for him to be able to shift so completely out of a lifelong mode of relating. I was actively standing against, refusing the polite and appropriate "Mommy and me" scenario, in favor of inviting his more spontaneous true self to come to life—at this moment around the issue of grief, a few weeks earlier around shared enjoyment.

Bart: We shouldn't have to be alone like this. I don't know why our family can't share their feelings in this way with each other. It upsets me. I don't think it's right. I was taught how not to share myself in relationships. [Crying] It's a shame. The heck of it is that there's a lot of good in that group. I don't know how it got that way. They're not malicious, but there's an element missing.

At the end of the session, I highlighted that by being willing and able to share this moment with me, he had given me the gift of his relating in a very significant way. When I said, "See you next week," he responded with, "You bet," like he wasn't going to deny himself this kind of relating again. He was finally getting a sense of what it was to fully emotionally relate to and resonate spontaneously with another human being.

It was interesting to see how the whole family culture was laden with restraint, the kind that produced his constricting governors. But at the same time I could see how an infant raised in such restraint might not simply become a passive recipient of the family culture. Bart's organizing-level transferences had suggested to me that long before this restrained exchange had been assimilated, he had learned actively to disconnect—primarily it seemed because Mother wasn't often emotionally there when he reached out. And secondarily, his disconnections mimicked through primary identification her distancing, "punishing" demeanor or her "righteous indignation" (that the baby had needs). Bart did learn later to engage in the suppressed family style, but before that he had learned many modes of disconnecting that then dovetailed with later learned patterns of restrained relating.

I had begun to stand against the stylized restrictions that the governors had put on his relating. From this point on there were a number of other things that happened that also served to confront his internalized scenarios. Bart described the good boy syndrome on several occasions.

11/10/88

Bart: It's not fair because it's not normal to be like this. It's rather like being a straight line. I sort of distill out goodness. And people know it's not right. I know it's not right. Because I'll be nice, nice, nice, but there's a part of me you can't get to because I won't let you. There's a certain percentage of me people can get in touch with and another percent they're not in touch with at all because I don't want to get into it. So I'm this nice guy with a part missing or closed off.

Jackie: People can sense that?

Bart: I'm sure of it.

Jackie: So you're telling me that there's something you're not doing with me?

Bart: There's a part that I keep in check.

Jackie: So all of Bart doesn't get to live.

Bart: No.

Comment

Bart began reporting several changes that were taking place. For instance, he was feeling and showing anger toward a relative whom he had previously ignored. He was also feeling upset in his current relationship because his girlfriend was not accepting of any show of anger on his part. He was protesting, saying that anger was one of the colors on the palette of human emotion. This was a stance he had never taken before. He was not liking the restrictions she was stipulating for his anger. He also was able to arrange a clean breakup with his last girlfriend in a straightforward way. Previously, he would wait for a catalyst and then use that as his way out, but he dealt with this one directly and felt very good about himself for it. He was becoming increasingly aware of how restrained he was in relationships. These episodes predicted a period of anger in the transference relationship that would parallel his breakthroughs in the areas of experiencing joy and grief with his therapist.

5/11/89

Bart: This is an odd thing. This week has been some more recollective things. I had an eye exam at noon. I'm doing the peripheral vision test sitting erect as she was giving me instructions. I had this mental picture all of a sudden while I was receiving the instructions. I felt like a little boy. It was really weird. I got this flash. I'm following the instructions getting ready to take a test and there was this kind of alertness. I had this flash of being a little kid. The posture's what triggered it. I was forced by this contraption to sit erect. I thought this was odd. The way I was sitting there all prim and proper, like a little kid being formal.

Jackie: Being good?

Bart: Exactly. It was really odd. Didn't feel bad, but I was aware of it and it lasted a little bit.

Comment

I recalled other formulations that Bart and I were working with that also suggested the symbiotic, merger, or borderline listening perspective. The characteristic style of relating from the false self or good boy syndrome that necessitated denial, or at least suppression of any intense emotion or confrontational action created a very narrow range of relational possibilities with others. This certainly characterized that narrow band of relatedness he could engage in with Mom as well as other people in his life.

2/9/89

Jackie: The expression "be alive together" came to me as we were talking. I was thinking about what we've been talking about, the mechanisms, the walls, the closing down. I was thinking that what we're talking about is your not being fully alive with people. Not allowing that. Almost like your whole life has a "governor" on it.

Bart: That's good.

Jackie: Like speed governors people put on their cars so if they exceed a preset limit an alarm will sound.

Bart: That's a good word, a fitting concept.

Jackie: And I was thinking, "Bart is living his life with a governor."

Bart: Yes. That's undoubtedly true.

Jackie: The "good boy syndrome" keeps you from fully experiencing things.

Bart: "Governor," "governor." That's a good word. I think it probably goes into more areas of my life than I realize. I think it's real pervasive. I'm wondering now where my natural controls end and the programmed governors begin? Or are they the same thing? I used to take real pride in being able to be in control of myself and being able to control a situation. Risk situations and that sort of thing. But I think my controls too often go to the point where they become restrictive. Whereas before, that wasn't the idea. The idea was to be in control so you could do something rather than not do something. To have control of your skills in a skill-demanding situation—what we used to talk about in auto racing—is essential. You also had to control fear and tension—things that could get in your way and cause problems. You had to gain emotional control over things and then you could be fully attuned to what you were doing.

Jackie: That's in line with what I'm thinking because if you do that you can be more fully alive to yourself and to what surrounds you. Control by an automatic governor doesn't allow critical feedback from the environment to be taken into account. A governor prevents you from being fully alive in relationships.

Bart: Yes. I think so. A blind emotional governor in relationships works in a way that's not beneficial. I'm becoming more aware of how controlled I've been in this relationship with Melinda. And to an extent in all relationships right now. I don't feel nearly as open and giving as I could be at all. I was talking last week about being tired or whatever. But the reluctance seems to be somewhat different. I don't know if wariness is the right word. Just reluctance.

Jackie: Do you have any sense of what that's about?

Bart: Well, not clearly. The thing I've been afraid of is that it seems there's been a crystallization over time of the control mechanisms, a kind of a refinement of this whole governor thing. But it feels so comfortable or natural—almost as though over time the regulators have come to make sense, to be the acceptable ways of being.

Jackie: The way things are just supposed to be?

Bart: Yes. But it also disturbs me. I don't know if it's just Melinda. But there seems to be a real reluctance to extend.

Comment

By now I had deliberately cultivated an open and spontaneous attitude toward Bart in sessions, realizing that promoting full emotional relating served to confront his governor scenario. In one session I found myself in the countertransference being unduly subdued so I discussed it with Bart. I usually have cut flowers from my garden in my office and on that occasion there were some particularly spectacular new roses.

2/9/89

Jackie: I was thinking how when you are here, there's a part of me that wants to behave differently. I feel thrilled when I know you're coming in.

Bart: Is that right?

Jackie: Yes. I look forward to our sessions and to our being together. I think of things that are fun to talk about and I feel a certain excitement anticipating our time together. But sometimes when you come in, I find myself going into a different mode of experiencing you. I become careful about what I say, and I modulate myself in the same way you have described that you learned to do as a child. I think that our extraneous banter is sometimes in the service of a force of modulation or regulation that arises from you or me or from both of us when we come together. I don't know how this happens to us. Like when you came in tonight what I really wanted to say was, "Bart, look at these great new roses!" They've just opened and they are so wonderful I was bursting with enthusiasm to point them out to you. But I didn't. As you were talking about choosing to live within the governor, I thought, "I wonder if I'm letting Bart make that choice for me too because I really didn't relate to him as spontaneously and enthusiastically as I wanted to."

Bart: That's an interesting phenomenon I've noticed before. I think I truly do affect the way others relate to me. Somehow or other, I set it up. I don't know how it happens. I remarked recently to you about this. About how I set the emotional tone not only for myself but for others. Like I act so as to force others into some way of reacting to me. Not all of them. But I've often had people tell me, "You always seem so in control of things." I think it affects the situation. I know after awhile I can put an atmosphere into the relationship. I don't know if that's good. I used to be a lot more ecstatic . . . I still am at times.

Jackie: You come in lots of times really excited. I remember one night I noticed you were really playful and we sort of toyed with that idea. My all-time favorite moment with you was when I nearly leaped over the end of the coffee table. You lost it laughing at me. I thought, "Wow, that was fun!"

Bart: Yes, that really was. I understand what you're saying. That somehow I create an atmosphere which is more or less controlled according to something in me.

Jackie: And that I am truly responsive to that. Almost as though I'm controlled by your governors as well. You're mothering me the way she mothered you!

Comment

Bart often spoke of parlor conversation to designate the kind of superficial and controlling talk he believed his mother did. At times he came to admonish me for perpetuating this meaningless kind of relating and challenged me to help him do it differently.

6/29/89

Bart: Then there's this whole conversation we've had about making talk when there isn't any. Like it's this "appropriate" thing to do. It's like really good manners. I'm associating that with my mom right now. She's very good at not missing a beat and being right in tune with what's going on and controlling it. She's very appropriate. It's crafty. It's well enough done. And I've learned her skill of keeping things moving so well! If I'm in the right mood, I'll fill in and give the right word and keep it moving. But it's all on a superficial level. I hate it.

Jackie: You're saying, "It's not the real stuff. It's not the real connecting. It's not us really being here together."

Comment

Bart reported a dream in which we were together in an office or living room setting talking and then we began sort of playfully kicking at one another's feet, like kids sometimes do in fun. I asked him to show me how this kicking of feet looked and this led into a conversation about the silly things kids do when playing with each other, like making faces. We began to make some faces, playing, and reminiscing together. We enjoyed wonderful eye contact and laughter in this.

I continued to stand against the borderline scenario by being as emotionally spontaneous as I could, and by speaking the words of protest over control that needed to be spoken by him when he was too small to protest himself. I was saying that we were both too narrow in our relating and that I wanted to relate in a more fulfilling and mutual way. I stood fast on the point that I didn't want to be a "good little boy" any more. In one session Bart even told me to "loosen up!"

As our relating relaxed we continued to toy with facial expressions, ear wiggling, and storytelling. I found it important to stop worrying so much about doing therapy or being productive in favor of simply relating in enjoyable and spontaneous ways with Bart, thus providing a nonverbal confrontation of his good boy scenario with a kind of experience Bart had never had with anyone in his life. We were pushing the bounds of his emotional governors of the symbiotic scenarios and beginning to feel some real life and relatedness between us.

LISTENING TO BART FROM THE SELFOTHER
OR NARCISSISTIC LISTENING PERSPECTIVE

Another interesting development occurred recently when I was able to interpret from the narcissistic or selfother (selfobject) listening perspective. Earlier in therapy Bart had experienced difficulties in accepting compliments of any kind. As he began to be more open and I continued to explore ways of confronting the limiting symbiotic scenario, I realized that if I ventured now toward allowing myself some extension into a higher level of relatedness (that is, his need for narcissism or self consolidation), I would also be further challenging the governor scenario. But if he could not relate with me at the selfother level I would be risking a regressive, organizing level disconnection. But our work was going well at that time and I reasoned that if my risking didn't go well, we at least by now had many ways of talking about it and of recovering.

In one session, I told him some very positive things that I thought about him and our relationship. In doing so, I was able to allow some of my authentic emotions to show through. I wasn't completely sure at the time if he would be able to take the experience in. Later in the week, he called asking if he could read the transcript from that session, that there were some things that interested him. Unfortunately, the tape had not recorded that week, so I was unable to send him the requested transcript of our interaction. I too was disappointed because several features of the session were new for us.

A couple of sessions later, he confessed that he hadn't told the whole truth about why he wanted the transcription. Bart said that after the session he thought about what I had said. But he couldn't trust his memory on whether I had really said those positive things about him or not. I told him his memory had served him well, and I (continuing to press the selfother resonance) reviewed for him how much he as a person had touched me, my way of doing therapy, and my life. It was not uncomfortable on this occasion for me to let him see the emotion I felt relating to him in this way. He was able to overcome his narcissistic shame and to stay with me for affirmation and confirmation of his personality, of himself. This way of tolerating relating was entirely new for him. Upon reflection he found he wanted more. It felt good to be seen and admired by an empathic eye, to feel the maternal pride in his accomplishments, and to feel himself confirmed as a strong and attractive man whose power in the world of relationships is growing. Even as he had enjoyed idealizing me, he enjoyed this appropriate aggrandizement of his self.

He had wanted to read the transcript to enjoy the swell of self-pride that he had so long denied himself. He was especially pleased that, although he retreated momentarily to a more subdued position, he had not disconnected, and that he had been able to move to a position of enjoying self-affirmation and confirmation, as well as feeling inspired by his idealizing relation to me. This new position vis-à-vis me as his selfother had become possible after we had analyzed his frequent tendency to disconnect emotionally and after we had analyzed the emotional modulation imposed by his internal governors. This new movement was stretching his emotional relatedness (1) from early forms of avoidance of traumatic connection, (2) through his characteristic modes of moderating emotional relationships, (3) to selfother confirmations, and (4) toward more complex forms of symbolic interpersonal relating.

3/25/90

In the ensuing months of Bart's work, we continued to analyze the complexities of the ways in which we related, but I could tell that while Bart was feeling closer to me, he also held himself back, not fully admitting the importance of our relationship. A major breakthrough occurred after Bart had been unemployed for a couple of months, having taken a voluntary layoff. I received a message from him one evening. He wanted to tell me while it was clear in his mind, that he had been "hiding" the last few sessions in parlor talk and needed to talk about our relationship or he was afraid he was going to distance and he didn't want to do that. I returned his call promptly because I thought this was a huge reach he was making and I wanted him to be met in a favorable and timely way. We scheduled an appointment for two days later. During this session, he said that while unemployed—without the distraction of the busy-ness of work, and interaction with his acquaintances there, he was able to realize the importance of our relationship. This frightened him because he didn't want to be dependent on the relationship, but on the other hand, he couldn't think about leaving it either. I comforted him by reemphasizing that I would keep the appropriate boundaries and that ultimately he would be able to leave because he would "take me with him" in the internal representation of our relationship, and that he wouldn't need me to be with him physically. This was a big step. Bart was able to initiate a contact, maintain the contact throughout the session, and, while talking about the power of the emotions connected with the relationship, he was able to stay with the feeling and not break the connection.

As Bart continues to make progress, it is fascinating to watch how powerful the earliest layering of organizing experience is in determining how later developed parts of his personality function on a daily basis.

4

Playing Peekaboo
with Sunglasses

Matt: The man I am going to talk about in our conference today is like my baby that I have birthed and brought up through the first four months of life. Having my own child has been helpful in getting a perspective on my work with this man and with the organizing experience in general.

Larry: Your own child is quickly outgrowing the organizing phase.

Matt: Yes, and as she does, it makes the concept *organizing* take on a whole new perspective. I now see what early life is like and how it develops into pattycake, peekaboo, and the very real sense of symbiotic connectedness.

Larry: Many of the people you see in your practice never quite made it through to those kinds of reliable connectedness.

Matt: No, they didn't. And you can feel it. There is so much to be said

about the subjective, phenomenological understanding of being with a child that can never, in my mind at least, be articulated. Likewise, I find it almost impossible to describe what the feeling is like of just being with somebody who is disconnected or of describing what it feels like to participate in the development of a real sense of connectedness. The feeling of watching the process is awesome. I have learned so much from my own child. And what she has taught me has put a different perspective on everybody I work with, especially people living life at the organizing level.

The person I will present today I have been working with for four years, the longest I have ever worked professionally with anybody. Every year in this person's therapy with me has been like a month in my daughter's development. To give you a bit of a picture of him, Eddie is 48. He is Hispanic and grew up in New Mexico. He came to me diagnosed as "chronic schizophrenia, paranoid type." That's about as psychotic as a person can be. And he was. In our first session Eddie was having active hallucinations, seeing little green men coming out of the wall. He was hearing voices saying that he should kill himself and what a piece of shit he was. Eddie arrived in an old orange T-shirt, battered pants, red tennis shoes, with hair sticking out all over, and a strong body smell clearly related to poor hygiene. He presented a stereotyped "paranoid schizophrenic" feel. Four years ago I was at the beginning of my clinical experiences and certainly did not know a lot about anything. In just trying to be with people I was flying by the seat of my pants. As I look back at where Eddie was then and as I look at my new daughter, I can put all of this together with a new sense of meaning.

In hindsight, I was like a mother who has always been told what having a baby was going to be like. But then when the actual baby arrives, that first month you find out you don't know what to do! You're not even prepared. Some mothers are prepared by observing their mother and their grandmothers. Many mothers are not prepared at all. Teenage mothers, for instance, who get pregnant at 16 and have a kid can't possibly be ready to be with that child emotionally as it sends out silent tendrils to be connected with. That's what starting with Eddie felt like.

All of a sudden I have this person in my office who is telling me about – you know, in training you always hear about people seeing little green men. But here is Eddie, larger than life, saying he is seeing little green men coming out of the wall in my office and is very serious about it. He really sees little green men! But Eddie doesn't give you a sense of, you know, that spooky paranoid schizophrenic feeling when you're in the room, like feeling the lighting goes down a degree. It's not scary or unsettling being with him like it is with some folks. He's not violent. This man would not hurt a fly. He is sweet. He is gentle. He is kind. Violence is not in him in any way. I've always felt that, from the very first. I've always told my colleagues that. But it's never really been believed. In the very beginning my supervisors didn't think I knew anything. That was valid because at that point, I didn't! But it always felt safe to be with Eddie. That's what's been nice about him. To be in a room with him feels safe, yet it's like opening a door in that movie *Poltergeist* when you see everything flying around. Like so much is going on in the room at the same time. You can feel it.

So as I am with Eddie the first year, it's like a teenage mother being with an infant she has no idea what to do with. She learns to change the diaper by just doing it. She has seen it on TV so knows what to do. That's what it felt like to be with him the first year. It was the same way being with my daughter the first month. The first year with Eddie and the first month with my daughter are analogous. Not really knowing what to do. This child doesn't even know you're in the room.

You're just doing things to and for it. There is no real sense of connectedness at all. And I'm just flying by the seat of my pants like with my daughter the first month.

The second year and the second month were difficult. The first year I saw Eddie I was at a clinic where the supervision really wasn't sensitive to Eddie's needs. It was somewhat abusive for me, that whole training experience of being at that clinic my first year. Mine was probably not all that different from most internship-type experiences. And then to have this man there who I'm not really knowing what I'm doing with at all. Then the supervisors telling me, "This man is dangerous, we need to change the locks on the door, how did you ever take a person like this on? He's going to steal things from us." I mean my supervisor went into a paranoid state. "This man is going to come and rummage through our computer and take all of our records. He is out to get us now. We've got to be careful."

Part of me is thinking, "Okay, what do I know?" But part of me is sensing this is just not a valid reading of Eddie, that violence, crime, boundary violation is simply not here with this person at all. I left this setting and moved with Eddie to my present clinic to continue my supervised training. It was a lot better in terms of supervision. The emphasis was more on connectedness. The whole perspective was different. As I changed clinics and took Eddie with me, the supervisory perception of him changed from "somebody we have to be afraid of who is going to torch the office," to "somebody who is deeply hurting and you need to find a way to connect with him and see what his world is about." So as the supervisory perspective changed that second year I could develop a sensible frame to work in. This was like the second month of being with my daughter. It's difficult being attentive to everything all the time but you just get used to it.

All of a sudden there was a settledness I felt with Eddie with our being used to each other and being in a different clinic with more compassionate and enlightened supervision. I don't really know the impact on Eddie of my inviting him to move clinics with me. My attitude was, "Mother knows best, come along now." And he did. I don't know that anyone had ever invited Eddie to come along with them before. So it was bound to have had an impact. Of course, I was still flying by the seat of my pants, not really knowing what I was doing. But there was a settledness. Somehow we were becoming used to each other. We had had a year to sit in a chaotic room together and get used to each other. He was still not really aware of me, that I was a person in the room with him, just like my daughter at 2 months was not really aware of me. But she was used to me and I was used to her and there was this settledness in our ritual of relating. It felt very much the same way with Eddie.

In the third month with my daughter things were getting more and more settled, but there was a certain awareness she had developed. She could see me, hear me, feel my touch, my presence. She was watching, listening, noticing when I was in the room.

It was not the mutual, interactive connectedness you feel in games like peekaboo and pattycake, but in the third month with my daughter it was very clear that she knew I was there. She was interested in me and gestured toward me in ever so many ways—clearly a movement toward me without quite knowing how to spontaneously engage me in play.

In the third year with Eddie it became clear that he began to see and know that I was there. All of a sudden I'm a living presence in the room to be reckoned with. It's not quite an interpersonal connectedness though, but he knows I'm there. There was a mutual welcoming familiarity we both could sense. A lot of it can't be articulated. You have to feel it. It was the same thing with my daughter. You can just feel that she knows I'm here and that I'm playing with her and doing things for her. And yet as I would try peekaboo, it was like I might as well be doing it to a watermelon. I mean she seemed aware that this person was doing something, but she was not really engaging with me in the game. It was the same with Eddie. Both seemed wide eyed in amazement and interest without knowing quite how to respond to me. I felt well received but not engaged yet.

Larry: Tell me more about your experience during that third month. I would appreciate hearing about your feelings of what it's like to be there trying to relate. What was that like for you?

Matt: With Eddie or my daughter?

Larry: Either—both.

Matt: There is something that happens with the other person. When they begin to get some sense of awareness that you are there, all of a sudden you get more of an awareness in yourself that they are there. I don't know which comes first, the chicken or the egg, your awareness or their awareness. But when they become aware of you—this is what it feels like to me—all of a sudden they are more real. When I walked into the room and my daughter's head turned at 3 months, I knew she was there, that she was a person, that she was oriented toward me. With Eddie, when I would walk into the room and Eddie would look at me rather than looking at the ground or at the little green men coming out of the wall I knew he was coming alive. He would look at me and make momentary eye contact. There is something about his knowing that I'm in the room with him that makes him more real to me. It's not yet a sense of psychological connectedness. It's mutual awareness and mutual regard of some sort.

Larry: This is a fascinating set of experiences you're comparing. I'm wondering how the human sense of agency evolves. How exactly does the sense of "I" (ego) that Freud thought was crucial and unique to human life make its appearance in that third month/third year when there arrives a sense of mutual awareness? Eddie was seemingly suddenly aware that you are aware of him and you are aware that he is aware of you.

Matt: Right. And that's it. That happens somehow. That sense seemed to evolve in one session. It's that quick. The session before it wasn't there. He walked into one session during that third year and suddenly he's somehow present in a new way. It's like one day you walk into your daughter's room and she looks at you. You feel she knows you somehow, feels your importance to her.

Larry: You know she is looking, regarding you differently.

Matt: Right. You feel it. All of a sudden something is different forever. Something is changed forever that is never going to be the same. Some form of personhood has arrived, almost magically. You feel an aliveness in your body and an aliveness in them. It's not a symbiotic connectedness yet, but the bridge for connections has been laid down. You still can't play peekaboo, really. You can do it and she'll know you are there, and perhaps be amused, but you are playing peekaboo at a different level now. At the first month you're playing peekaboo and you might as well be watching TV. The child just doesn't demonstrate an awareness that you are especially doing anything. Although her body reacts, her visible psyche doesn't. There is a difference.

Now you play peekaboo with this child or this client and they are trying to figure out at least what are you doing. There seems to be a questioning awareness, "You are here, what are you doing now? What is your purpose?" It feels that way. But it's not like in the fourth or sixth month where you can play peekaboo or run out of the room and run back into the room and they lighten up and they coo and there is this whole exchange going on that's based on mutual cuing,

clearly the beginning of the internalized state of symbiosis. That is psychic interconnectedness. When you develop that symbiotic mutually engaged kind of connectedness, it's the same type of connectedness as this early form, but it grows; it has a life of its own. There is a difference between that advanced mutually engaged symbiotic-level awareness and the third month when you are first experienced as an active presence in the room and you become aware of that experience.

From this sudden beginning, symbiotic connectedness just seems to grow. It's a strange experience to try to describe. I've been struggling with articulating a lot of my feelings during all of this because everything is felt in the countertransference. It has to be explained through that. It can't be explained any other way. As I was struggling with trying to articulate these things, I thought if you could all climb into my body right now and take a whiff of what I'm feeling, it would be clear. But words are hard. It gets very difficult to talk about in the way I want to communicate it.

In the fourth month, all of a sudden with my daughter and me there emerged clear and reciprocal connectedness. You just feel it. One day in the fourth month you go in the room, you play peekaboo with her, and she is playing back. Something happens that's inarticulate, but it's there. And all of a sudden there is another level of aliveness. It just gives you so much energy that you want to engage this child more and more. You are thinking of different games. Everything becomes a way of connecting now, everything becomes a game, from food and feeding, to changing the diapers, to rocking and going to sleep. It draws you out and it brings an aliveness that's incredible and that aliveness grows until the sixth month where she is now. It's just incredible. I mean I just can't explain the connectedness you feel as compared to earlier months.

EDDIE APPROACHES SYMBIOSIS

Matt: Now with Eddie in the fourth year, here is what's happening. It's not like what happened with my daughter. It's all of a sudden he is aware in the room. Like in the third year he is aware of me and we are moving toward connectedness, but something begins to happen in the fourth year that I notice. My daughter and I developed a symbiosis, if you will. It feels that way, at least for me. And I can see it happening with Chelsea, my wife, we're sure. I mean it's there. What you don't feel in yourself you will see in the interaction with your wife. With Eddie though, what began to happen in the fourth year is different.

Eddie's mother died at the beginning of our fourth year together. One day he walks into the room wearing dark sunglasses. And every session since he always has these dark glasses on. Right away that puts a block between us. All of a sudden—just when we were beginning to make headway with mutual awareness, with the beginnings of connectedness—we can't get any closer to each other. There's an invisible blockage. And I notice in the countertransference I'm daydreaming. I cannot stay connected with him at even the sense of mutual awareness and enlivenment we had before. In some sessions I can, but there is so much effort involved trying to stay with him. I find myself four out of five sessions almost completely daydream-ing most of the time while he talks on about one thing and another. I couldn't quite sustain my former interest in following Eddie.

Now I wouldn't say we had regressed or gone back in time, it's just like we reached something that happens in the fourth month that I felt with my daughter and I've read about in your books that takes place. There is that special mutually engaged emotional connectedness and then all of a sudden the world changes and you begin to grow on a different plane, on a psychic plane. Relating suddenly becomes fuller. With Eddie we established in our third year the awareness that we are in the room together and that we are doing something worthwhile together. But as we move toward connection all of a sudden something just falls apart. We don't go back in our relationship, it's more like we're suspended in time. We're not going forward either. We have been stuck in the fourth month for almost a year now, not really going anyplace, stuck, barely clinging to the sense of life that does exist between us, but not able to become fully alive and vibrant with each other.

Mike: This sunglasses thing happened right after Mother died?

Matt: Right after Mother died. The day his mom died he wore dark sunglasses into the room. Her death seemed uncanny in its timing, like some sort of synchronicity. It follows the Kleinian metaphor of the beginning of the fourth month as the beginning of the "depressive position." I understand the depressive position to mean that the infant now realizes that he or she is not fully in control of the comings and goings of significant others, especially of Mother. That is, the sense of infantile omnipotence takes a dive. Mother, whose body brought me pleasure, and who was virtually indistinguishable from me, dies at the fourth month. And the infant acutely feels her loss. But then too come the pleasure in finding ways to connect.

Larry: Which we might surmise is historically when Eddie's mother died for him psychologically. André Green in his paper, "The Dead Mother," formulates that the earliest mother of the "purified pleasure ego," the nascent sense of "I," is constructed by the infant around experiences of sensual pleasure. As the infant develops an awareness of Mother's other emotional preoccupations (with the father, with the primal scene, with others, with herself) he or she decathects this mother of primary pleasure, leaving a gaping hole in psyche. The psychic space of primordial pleasure that mother first occupied is encapsulated but left empty. Human desire arises in an attempt to fill in the gap where mother once was, the lack. Where love once was becomes a lifelong search for the lost mother of infancy. But when the sensual bridge to mother's psyche has never been laid down, has never been comfortably and safely traversed, the extended tendrils of potential human connectedness withdraw. The infant learns not to reach out, not to

connect, not to expect reciprocal engagement. And this learned internalized structure, which I call "the emergence of the psychotic mother," serves to perennially foreclose the possibility of achieving mutual connectedness.

Just as you describe with Eddie, the channels of awareness that might conceivably be utilized in the service of interpersonal connections that would foster psychic growth wither and become functionally dead. Those nurturing, pleasuring infantile modes of experiencing that once represented mother, nascent love as it were, have died. And with the death of the mother of primary pleasure comes the death of the infant self and the loss of the hope that achieving human connectedness will ever be possible.

We infer from Eddie's chronic state that his mother died for him by the fourth month. And now uncannily as he reexperiences an awakening of hope with his new mother, Matt, his real mother actually dies. I have observed this before. I don't know how to account for such seemingly mysterious psychic events but they always seem more than coincidental. Perhaps the quantum physicists are right when they declare that we are all interconnected in ways we have yet to dream of. That there are only "six degrees of separation" between one human being and another, and perhaps much less between a mother and her offspring. In any event she dies and Eddie places a dark glass barrier that obscures the previously developed sense of aliveness between you two. He now sees you "through a glass darkly."

Matt: Yes. As he wears the dark sunglasses, right away that in itself introduces a disconnection. He can see me darkly, but now I can't see him. I feel completely disconnected. Part of me says, "Whew, good"—you know, relieved. Part of me says, "No this is something important. He is grieving and that's obvious. But what else is going on?"

Howard: Did he live with his mother?

Matt: No, he didn't live with his mother. He was raised in a small town in New Mexico.

I was looking back through my notes over the first two years with Eddie. The two words that stand out are *connectedness* and *disconnectedness*. The themes. And this is before I had even read *Listening Perspectives* (Hedges 1983b). Everything is naturally revolving around my feeling connected and him disconnecting. When I entered this group at the beginning of the third year of working with Eddie about a year and a half ago, that is when we started to connect more. The emphasis in our group here and in *Listening Perspectives*—what we do in here, the way we talk about organizing people—the emphasis becomes working toward connectedness. I started to get the perspective from this group in the third year when we started to have that awareness of each other. So everything has fit together really interestingly in each of our lives.

Marilyn: And what about his relationship with his mother?

Matt: His relationship with his mother? Eddie has five brothers and sisters, all from different fathers. His mother, the way he describes her, sounds paranoid schizophrenic, too.

Larry: Where is he in the birth order?

Matt: He's the second to the youngest. So he's number four and then there is one brother after him.

Larry: Are they fairly close together in age?

Matt: Yes, they are fairly close together. Less than a year I believe. Maybe only nine months! Getting details from this man and getting a sense of where things are is really hard. "Where are you Eddie? When were you born? What happened until you were ten?" Answers simply aren't available. You have to kind of take in what you get, breathe it in over the years and get a sense of where things are for him. Mom feels paranoid schizophrenic, too. She always told Eddie he was just like his father, "a no good piece of shit." Which is interesting since that is what the voices tell him. That he will never make anything of himself. His mother never had time for him. He talks about his mother as never being connected with him in any way, shape, or form, ever.

Marilyn: This man is on medication?

Matt: He's been on many medications. He's had many psychiatric consultations from his numerous hospitalizations over the years. You can't get clear information from him by asking direct questions like, "Eddie, how many times have you been hospitalized? Three?" You don't get information like that.

Larry: Memories don't operate the same way with these people who live at the organizing level as they do for the rest of us. Our personalities are organized according to our relatedness experiences. Human memory is organized around personal and meaningful relatedness experiences, not impersonal and meaningless events. This means that when a person has developed few reliable relatedness possibilities that little can be remembered with consistency, conviction, and certainty.

Marilyn: Most people don't attempt psychotherapy with these functionally psychotic people. I mean you are really a maverick in that regard.

Matt: Well, I can see why they don't. [Group laughs.]

Larry: Why do you say that?

Matt: Because you don't get improvement every ten sessions, or you don't get a sense of feeling like you're accomplishing anything very often. Setting up treatment plans and goals makes no sense when working with a person like this. Defining dimensions of improvement makes no sense. It is something entirely different we are tuning in to.

Mike: Have you read any of Harold Searles's papers? You get the feeling that he waits ten years for one of his patients to say, "Hi." "Wow that was a great session," he says, and then goes on for another five years! I'm sure it's not so bad as all that, but this work requires time, persistence, and patience.

Matt: It's not like working with a borderline person where you get more of a sense that you can see things moving, you can feel what's happening in the interaction, where you can watch transference developments. You have to deal with so much of your own stuff working with organizing people. I have had to deal more with my countertransference than anything to do with him—just to be able to stay with him and not interfere is a slow, delicate, and almost invisible process.

Larry: In what ways have you studied yourself with Eddie?

Matt: Well, number one, feeling that you're alone in the room with yourself for a year and pretending that you're doing "therapy" with him when you're simply waiting for the little green men to diminish in number and intensity as he finds I am not going to intrude or try to force him in any way. You're thinking about how you're feeling yourself. Strange thoughts are coming up in your mind. All of a sudden I found myself having paranoid thoughts at times with him. I have never seen a hallucination, but I have found myself imagining his little green men on the wall. I've tried to stay with him but it's taxing.

Mike: It really opens up the opportunity for you to get into that primitive organizing part of yourself when you work with these people.

Larry: What was it like being with him the day his mother died? What was that session like?

Matt: Okay. Somewhere in my notes I have it, but I'm not going to go look for it now. I have to talk about the session before because that session was a positive session. I look at my notes, "Eddie is planning." He is always planning on going to school; he never goes of course. All of these plans of doing this and that, but there was more of a sense that we felt connected

because there was more of an exchange. There is usually a lot of that
sense of falseness in connectedness
that Larry talks about, but in the session before his mother died it felt more
real that day than usual. Then he
comes in the next session. There is
something interesting that happened
too when his mother died that I need
to talk about.

Since I've been working with Eddie
the last four years life has gotten
steadily better for him. He's not on
nearly the amount of medications he
was on when I first started working
with him. We have slowly cleaned that
up. His health was completely
breaking down when he first came in.
His body is not breaking down any
more. He went from living in a series
of mental institutions to board and
care homes and now he is living inde-
pendently in a room and board house
and has applied to HUD for housing.

Karen: Wow! [Group expresses
amazement.]

Matt: Life has gotten better. Outside therapy life is definitely better. He
used to take a bus to my office. But just
before his mother died, he starts to
bring in with him a man who is also a
schizophrenic who was sitting in the
waiting room while Eddie came in for
his session. This man gives him a ride
to therapy and is a friend of his whom
he has known for years. But, you
know, you never get a sense of "how
did you meet." That's why it's hard to
be with him, you never get a firmness
on things. You just get a feeling that
you have to, over years, put it together
as best as possible. His friend is completely paranoid schizophrenic, too.

He's on heavy medications. But there
is more of a connected feeling with
him. He is, once again, one of these
safe types, though. The people Eddie
hangs around with are very safe,
harmless people. This man with him
sits in the waiting room and reads the
Bible. Over the last year before Eddie's
mother died I had gotten to know his
friend and he actually wanted to come
into the session with Eddie. And
Eddie wants him to come into the
sessions. So I've let his friend sit in on
a session.

The day Eddie's mother died, Eddie
came in with dark glasses. I was trying
to get a sense of what was happening
inside of his world that day. But the
way that he had the glasses on I felt
disconnected from him and I felt like I
couldn't get inside. There was that
barrier. I couldn't see his eyes with the
glasses. He wasn't looking at me, anyway. He was looking at the ground in
this real psychotic state, talking about
how his mother was dead and having
associations about women in his life
whom he has never felt connected
with. He desperately wants a relationship with a woman. His goal in life is to
have a relationship with a woman.
More than any man or anything else,
this is what he wants. On that day
there was just a rambling, a real psy-
chotic-type place where his associations were loose. They were not word
salad or anything like that but sentences didn't fit together. But it was all
about mother never being with him,
how he never had a relationship with
a woman. He was married at one time
for seven years but never related and
that ended in disaster. Now he needs

to get a relationship with a woman. A lot of guilt with the voices talking. When he first came to me the voices were clear and audible, but after a while he heard only mumbling. Now the voices don't get through with any words, they are all mumumum mumum mumm. He can hear this all the time in sessions. That day the voices had returned and were saying he killed his mother, what a piece of shit he was, and that he was going to die because of that.

Larry: So if the other leaves it's because he killed her. What about the voices?

Matt: He always calls the voices "demons." He was connected at one point with a very fundamentalist church. At the church they all joined him in calling the voices demons. "These are demons and they are going to get you." It was a real hard time for him after his mother died and it was real hard for me, too. There was not that sense of being in a room with somebody who is grieving and they're crying and you're with them in their grief and they're telling you how they miss their mother. Or like you may spend months in a grieving process together, but it has a beginning, a middle, and an end. This has not been that way. There was sudden grief, chaos, psychosis, self blame. It was hard watching this man who had begun to coalesce himself with me break down into a psychotic mess with demon voices persecuting him again. I think the glasses may also have been a way of blocking out hallucinations, too.

My being with Eddie then was like seeing a baby in dirty diapers and my being disabled, not being able to do anything to help. I felt this with my daughter, too. It was interesting; I can't change my daughter's diapers because of my disability [the therapist has a body paralysis and moves in a wheelchair]. I can't move my fingers. So when she's a mess and I want to do something and I can't, I feel just terrible. The same feeling often comes up with Eddie. I wanted to do something to help him, but there was not a damn thing I could do. It's hard.

Larry: You're moving your hands now, what are you wanting to do?

Matt: Well, with the infant, I am wanting to stand up, take the diaper off, clean this infant up, put powder on, get her to smile, and dress her up in a clean diaper. With this man it's the same thing. I have the feeling that I want to get out of my chair, I want to give him a shower, clean him up, dress him up, put some cologne on him, sit him down, and take away the psychosis. I want to have him grieve and have him talk to me like somebody who is on a higher developmental level.

Larry: If you weren't in a wheelchair and had mobility of your hands, how do you suppose that would translate into an actual reaction with him? I hear the fantasy, you want to shower him and so forth, but what would be your fantasy of what you might actually be doing?

Matt: I think if my body were more active, I wouldn't touch him. I know that. He is not a man I would want to risk touching for some reason. Certainly not now. My position would be different. I would take on a different posture that would somehow sit me up more. I'm always trying to adjust my chair trying to get in front of him, I'm always going back and forth and fidgeting. If I were walking around, especially in this session, I would maybe get up, pull my chair closer, get in that position where I would be in a thinking or feeling body posture that says, "I want to be with you." To communicate something somehow through my body with him, which I can't do because of my disability. My communication with him seems somewhat shut down because I can't communicate with my body the way I want to with him. I can feel it and it's frustrating. I would take on a body position with a proximity that would at least somehow unconsciously permeate the psychosis. I would say, "Here I am for you when you're ready." I think at least if I were expressing myself in ways I felt might generate connections, then that would give me more of a sense of patience to wait.

Larry: Is that something that you could bring up with him? Could you simply tell him what you just told us?

Matt: You know, I've shared with him my frustrations over the years. But this is where I'm at with him. Things I say just don't go in. Interpretations. My sharing the countertransference. He goes, "Oh yeah, yeah." And then he's off. You can feel it. It just doesn't go in.

Larry: You may be more expressive with your body than you think you are but the communication just doesn't seem to get through.

Matt: That's probably true.

Larry: I'm wondering if at a given moment when you feel you want to do more with your body, if you might speak that. "Eddie, I'm having a sense that I want to be closer to you. I wish I didn't have this wheelchair in the way."

Matt: I haven't spoken it in that way.

Larry: I don't know if that would get through to him or not, but I was wondering if it would be worth a try.

Matt: Anything is worth a try with Eddie. You can't mess up with this person. I've tried it all. I've talked to the voices. I've done it all, "Let's draw." There's not a therapy technique devised I haven't at one time or another attempted in order to make connection.

Karen: And you haven't given up. That's what's striking to me.

Matt: This is a person who's going to be with me for the rest of my life! I can feel it. [Laughter.]

Larry: Don't be too sure. He may surprise you and get better! [Group laughs.] I'm interested in your saying that you are aware that your body is wanting to move in closer.

Matt: My body is wanting to do more, and that's related to the daydreaming this last year. As my daughter has moved to the fifth and sixth months I can feel the connectedness that is so neat to have. And then I feel the disconnectedness I have with Eddie. I want to say, "Okay, Eddie, we are in the fourth month. We are supposed to start *doing* something now." It's just not happening, and I can feel myself daydreaming in the sessions. During the session before Eddie's I am feeling symbiotically connected to a borderline person. After Eddie I see a person who is as close to neurosis as I'll probably ever see. There's such a difference in the sessions. I can be with these other people. Eddie walks in and I'm thinking, "What am I going to do for lunch?" Then I think, "Knock that off." I cannot consistently stay with him. My daydreaming takes over. It's only by volitional will that every part of my being pulls together to stay focused on what he's rambling about.

Larry: One of the things you and I have talked about, Matt, in terms of countertransference with organizing states is the tendency to do exactly that, to let your mind wander, to be drowsy. That is, we have discussed mental activity on the part of the therapist which serves to re-create a sense of disconnection. Here I'm very interested because you're making the analogy to the fourth month in the fourth year of therapy and right at the outset, at the point where connection is beginning, he is bringing in his friend. Just when he's starting to connect to you he wants his friend to come into sessions with him. Then his mother dies and I'm questioning whether the timing of that event is altogether coincidental. But at that moment he starts the disconnection with his sunglasses and you start the disconnection with your mental wandering.

According to the theory we've been pursuing with people like this, at the point where connection begins, that's where both parties, therapist and client, are doing their very best to replicate the psychotic transference of disconnection. The client, because

connection is terrifying, and the therapist, either because it stimulates his own primitive organizing experiences, or because, out of empathy, he or she understands how terrifying connection is for the client and consciously or unconsciously the therapist waters down the connectedness through inattentiveness.

Matt: I am painfully aware of what you're saying.

Larry: What did the mother die of?

Matt: She was older and she sounded quite psychotic. These severely unorganized people, their bodies start to break down at around 30 and continue to deteriorate. She got to a place where she was 60 and her kidneys were going, her body went. She didn't die of cancer or a heart attack. But over the years her internal systems gradually broke down. Without coherent, goal-directed psychic activity the soma doesn't thrive either.

Madeline: Did he experience that as unexpected?

Matt: He experienced it as unexpected. But it was very clear that it was happening. From what he was telling me I was saying to myself, "She is going to be dead soon." I would ask him about it. But that wasn't his conscious reality. His reality was she is going to be around long enough until we (Mommy and I) can do something in the future. The fantasy remained that "we" are always going to have time to get our relationship back on track, to get it together somehow. That's not the way it was at all.

Larry: I'm wondering if that's part of the "delusional process" for him.

"My mother isn't here, my mother is dying on me. But in my own mind I don't believe she's dying. And furthermore I believe that somewhere in the future she will be able to connect with me. I will be able to go to school." There's a whole future thing that seems to work to deny the fact that she is perennially not present, dead for him. And she has been since his fourth month.

Matt: And then when she does die it's really upsetting. He had this sense that Mom was going to be around forever.

Marilyn: I'm wondering how he experiences Mom such that he is able to experience the loss of her. This guy to me sounds mentally retarded in addition to being paranoid schizophrenic.

Matt: I've never given him an IQ test but he certainly is not terribly bright. But he can read fine, and I can have an intelligent conversation with him. He's probably "dull normal" in his intellect, but I wouldn't say mentally retarded. I wouldn't even say he was borderline intellectual functioning. It's just that his psychosis has dulled his intellect so much.

Larry: That's one of the standard findings in the history of intelligence testing. The psychotic process encroaches so that the functioning you observe is "scattered." For example, you may get the vocabulary responses scored all the way up to 36 items. But you are going to find items 2, 4, 8, and 12 missing. Very simple items. As you examine the content of those you begin to find that it's the psychotic process that has encroached. The typical finding with schizophrenia is someone who is able to give many significantly higher correct answers than their overall IQ score would predict. Because there are so many gaps, there is so much scatter in their responsiveness. I'm thinking what Marilyn is saying is that if you were to give Eddie an IQ test, no doubt you would find scatter leading to a depressed IQ score. But in interacting with him what you pick up is that capacity for much higher possibilities.

Matt: It's true what Marilyn says. In thinking about him and in reading my notes, he does sound mildly retarded, but I'm convinced he is not.

Karen: Tell us what you want from us.

Matt: I want to know how not to daydream in the room with this guy! (Laughter!)

Mike: Have you talked to him about the sunglasses and how you react to the sunglasses?

Matt: I have talked to him about the sunglasses. I've asked him what his thoughts are. "Eddie, you are grieving the loss of Mom." I want to know how he experiences that and want to know more about his ideas of what's happening. He says, "The light hurts my eyes."

Mike: Have you ever asked him to take them off?

Matt: No.

Karen: How would you feel about telling him how difficult that is for you relating to him?

Matt: I would feel okay about doing it. I don't know why I haven't done it, now that you guys are bringing it up. But as we're talking I suddenly realize that as much as I really do want to connect with Eddie, there is a part of me at the same time that doesn't want to connect. And when I think of asking him to take off his sunglasses I can feel my resistance to working more directly on the connection again. But at this moment when I take a deep breath I realize I would feel good about saying, "Eddie, take off your glasses. It's hard for me."

Larry: Why do you suppose you haven't? He's been wearing them for a long time. It's a super-obvious thing to say. Why haven't you said it before now? "Why don't you take off your sunglasses?"

Matt: You know what, the amazing thing is I haven't even thought about saying it. I know if other people would come into the room I wouldn't hesitate to say, "Take off your sunglasses."

Larry: So you're protecting something?

Matt: I feel that if I did that with him it would hurt him.

Larry: And about yourself?

Matt: That I would be hurting somebody. It feels like if I said, "Eddie, take off your sunglasses," that would be an intrusion for him, that would be very hurtful for him. I would feel like I'm hurting him.

Larry: What would be the hurt, and why would he be hurt by taking off the sunglasses?

Matt: I don't know. It seems somehow, as it keeps me disconnected from him, it keeps him contained somehow. It keeps him safe.

Larry: Safe from the psychotic mother transference?

Matt: Yes. That's clear

Larry: We are always looking for that moment when there is contact,

touch. That's when we expect the psychotic mother to reappear to break the contact. So it sounds like since the sunglasses have gone on what you both have been doing is flirting with the touch, doing your best in some ways to make contact, but both of you know that contacting each other, interacting emotionally is terrifying. And so your mind wanders, you don't ask the super-obvious question. He would be hurt if you did. I think the hurt would occur when you reached out and touched him by saying, "Please take off your sunglasses, I want to see you." At that moment something terrifying would happen to him. Peekaboo would begin. I think you both know that. But I think that feared moment has got to be carefully studied, analyzed, and eventually broken through.

Matt: I'm amazed right now. The question of "take off your sunglasses" never even entered my mind!

Larry: My hypothesis is that the reason it didn't is because you knew that he couldn't yet, or that if he does he is going to encounter that schizophrenic mother. And he's afraid of what she's going to do to him. I was wondering about the death of Mother and the sunglasses. If, as you say, he was never that close to his mother, the loss has to be not so much of the actual mother, but more the loss of the fantasy of some day being held by the good, the present, the nurturing mother. A Kafka-esque fantasy— "someday I'll find a way to the Castle, to that nipple on the hill." I was also wondering if the loss of Eddie's mother at such a critical time in your developing relationship might make the emotional danger of really connecting with you much more real? And if the sunglasses were a way of forestalling that danger?

Matt: I'm sure you're right, now that I reflect on it.

Larry: I think you should wear sunglasses to the next session! You should play sunglasses games like peekaboo games. (Group laughter).

Karen: What would your fear be about that?

Matt: Of wearing sunglasses? I love it. But of course I worry that it might be misunderstood and be seen as humiliating to him or as making fun of him.

Karen: Even if you put words to it?

Matt: Yes. He's very concrete you know.

Larry: (Humorously) "You wear sunglasses so I can't see your eyes, so I thought today I would wear sunglasses so you can't see my eyes." (Laughter)

Matt: Maybe I will try that. We might both get a good laugh!

Larry: Well, don't rush into it. I find in these matters you have to trust your intuition. What you've said is, you are blocked at the point of beginning to play peekaboo-type games. It's interesting that you chose peekaboo as a descriptive metaphor because we're talking sunglasses.

Matt: It is funny because I play peekaboo with my daughter with my sunglasses.

Larry: It sounds like you are almost ready to play peekaboo with Eddie. You are stuck not being able to move to the "now I see you, now I don't" level of relating, which is manifest in

peekaboo. Our theory tells us that the reason you cannot is that just at the moment when his mother might have started playing peekaboo games with him, something happened. Did she slap him? Did she throw him down? Did she walk away? Did she go psychotic at the baby's need for connection? Just when he was reaching out, reaching for her eyes, reaching for her face, what did she do or fail to do?

You've said there was another baby born only nine months after him who had a different father. Was she losing his father, forming a new relationship, discovering she was pregnant again for the fifth time? Not that we'll ever know any of these answers with any degree of confidence. But considering the kinds of things that might have contributed to his developmental arrest may be helpful in studying transference and resistance possibilities. But the fact that you have been reluctant to be more forthright with the sunglasses tells us that you empathize with what pain and confusion he may need to go through next. Or your reluctance may say that you were more comfortable or safe daydreaming with your own organizing mother babbling than you were with whatever happened when you went after a connection with her.

Mike: That's when Eddie's mother died for him, just when he was planning, wanting to learn, going to school, hoping to reach out, hoping to find her, wanting to find the good life in connection with her. But it feels very much like in this safe, nice, warmhearted kind of a retarded-looking guy, there is terror, deep terror of his crazy mother. At least when she was down in New Mexico she was safely tucked out of the way. But now with her wandering around Heaven or wherever, she just might show up to haunt him most any time now!

Larry: I'm thinking of his friend he brings to your office. Organizing people have a way of finding one another in this world, like he has found this man. I've supervised a number of therapists who work with married couples, two organizing people who have found one another. Of course it's really interesting watching two organizing people have a relationship, let alone trying to keep life moving forward with three children. Especially when nobody in the family can move to the level of peekaboo. It seems more like a family of bears cooperatively and competitively occupying a cave together. We learn whose territory is which corner of the cave and who sleeps with whom and all of those basic mimical things. It's cohabiting on the basis of instincts. But what you have described so beautifully earlier with your own daughter, whatever it is that makes for two human beings, two agents, you and me, playing and laughing with our sunglasses—that doesn't happen in these families of organizing people.

Matt: Whatever that is is the key and the answer is somehow bottling it up and using it. It's where I'm stuck.

Larry: The analytic process here entails trying to discover what *prevents* Eddie from connecting, from relating, from bonding with you. With your own baby you said very clearly, you walked in one day and she was able to

engage you. Eddie cannot do that. Something is preventing him from being there in the way that Stacy was there one day.

Marilyn: But don't you think in part that's biological? Are you assuming that with enough therapy he can be helped to reach that place?

Larry: I don't know what to assume about a man like this. The general assumption of the past is that psychosis is biochemical, it's genetic, it's irremediable. And whether its origins are constitutional or not, over time there are many biochemical implications. These people develop poor health as Matt has indicated. But I have actually watched a number of people like this transform their relatedness potentials, their creative energies, and totally change their lives. So I am not pessimistic about what possibilities lie ahead for Eddie, especially not with someone so doggedly and devotedly trying to connect as Matt! I don't know that we have any cause to be overly optimistic either except that some interesting and hopeful processes have been set in motion that have encountered a block somewhere in the distant past.

Here we see four years of two people trying to do something together. Two people *wanting* to play peekaboo. I am inferring Eddie's desire from the fact that he comes regularly and his despair over his mother dying and with that his despair over what appeared to him the one hope of ever connecting he had before Matt came along. He and Matt have found some way to insure being together, and they both seem motivated toward experiencing each other. Even the sunglasses seem like a dynamic communication to me—and at a critical moment. "My mother dies and I block out the light of the world. It hurts me."

Madeline: He has kept coming back and so have you. There's something important in that alone.

Larry: The etiological question has always been, Do we have a genetic factor determining the schizophrenic inability to connect to mother? Or do we have a baby who is adequately genetically endowed, but because of whatever early failure there has been to form connections with the human environment, all sorts of psychological and biological sequelae occur? That has been the central question of research on psychosis for years—What is the relative contribution of biological and environmental influences to the development of psychotic life styles? The available medications are truly miracle drugs in terms of allowing a diminution of symptoms that cause trouble for these people in the world. But the enigma of psychosis remains. The history of our psychotherapeutic success rate is dismal because we haven't broadened our approach to these people. And we don't know if there are hard biological variables we may be working against, or if and to what extent psychic transformations may permit biological transformations to occur. We have just heard that this man's overall biological deterioration has been reversed during the course of psychotherapeutic contact and that his living conditions have remarkably improved.

Matt: I tend to think that a lot has

to do, at least in Eddie's case, with a mother he couldn't connect with because the therapy has made a significant difference in his overall health picture. But we are at this point where we seem stuck and haven't found a way to go any further. Things in Eddie's life are better. His medication has been reduced dramatically. He is no longer on lithium and he needed lithium for the first two years. He is only on one antipsychotic and he takes one other medication to reduce its side effects. From the beginning of therapy he has gradually been able to cut down on the number and the quantity of medication. I think it's because of therapy. I really do. So I can take heart in that, even if I can't ask him to give up his sunglasses!

Mike: I do, too. If you read Rosenfeld, Searles, Giovacchini, Tustin, Grotstein, Ogden, and Eigen, people who have worked for years with psychotics, it's all laid out in the work that they do, how they do it, and the progress that is made—slowly but surely.

Marilyn: But I think if we had a biologically oriented psychiatrist in here, we would hear a whole different viewpoint.

Larry: I'm sure we would.

Stuart: I worked with a psychotic man several years ago who had been functioning on a fairly good level for quite a while, an electronics engineer. He had a psychotic break at work and became completely paranoid schizophrenic. He thought that all the people at work were androids and that there were wires in his house and in his head and everything. I worked with this guy for four years and brought him from this psychosis. It was very interesting. He came from an organized paranoid psychotic state to an organizing level, to a borderline level, to a narcissistic level, and then to considering himself and others as independent people. After four years of therapy he came in one day and said, "I feel like walking down the street and saying to everybody, 'Look at me,'" which was really a developmental step for him. He is fine now. This guy, he's back at work, he's got friends and I know it was because of the therapy. True, he started off a lot better off than your guy did. But a failure to connect is a failure to connect and it simply isn't healthy for human beings.

Matt: Eddie is making improvements and, you know, it's terror that keeps him from connecting more to me. Now I want to know what do I do next?

Larry: I'll tell you! [Group laughs.] I think you're focused in the right place. You're focused on the interface between two potential agents, two human beings developing a life together: between his becoming aware of your agency, your "I," and your becoming aware of his agency, his "I," and the two I's finding some way to meaningfully interact. Somehow in this last year you've become stuck at that interface. Undoubtedly the death of his mother has been a setback. I think the sky's the limit in terms of ways that you and he might try to pay attention to each other, to come to know one another. We talked about peekaboo games as a metaphor for

mutually engaged emotional interaction. I've noticed some therapists begin to do various kinds of art therapy, or card games, board games, jigsaw puzzles, riddles, joking games — you know, anything to begin the I/thou sense of affective interaction.

The direction of your work with Eddie is to promote moments of connection so that the disconnect mode can be discerned and analyzed. Connection per se isn't the point of working in this way. The person stuck partially or, like your man, almost completely at the organizing level cannot move into relatedness with people because of some invisible terror we can trace to some prebonding mother–child trauma. The entire history of the study of psychosis is marked by the repeated failure on the part of most investigators to locate the point of disconnect and to find a way of studying it.

We have numerous records of therapists who have spent laborious years with psychotics attempting to decode psychotic symbols, to enter the psychotic world, and to provide new realities through more effective holding — all to little avail. The discovery made possible by self and other psychology extended developmentally downward is that organization of mental activity proceeds through human contact and that the psyche and the human memory are structured according to the object relations experiences that were historically possible for the individual.

When someone like Eddie lives outside the place of human love relations, there is a reason for it. In my experience the reason is rarely a biological reason. Even retarded children and children with severe birth defects can come to know human connection and love. Some inner force in Eddie, some psychological internalization from the earliest months of life, prevents him from having human contact that might allow him to grow, to expand his consciousness of himself and others. Our task is to create an interpersonal atmosphere in which the reasons for his failure to bond can come to light in transference and resistance analysis. We are now learning how that ambience can be created and finding ways to discern the connect and disconnect modes and to work them for transformational possibilities.

Psychoanalytic knowledge has never been about the nature of the mind or of human truth. Rather, what we have painstakingly learned over time is how to create an interpersonal situation that can serve to bring to conscious focus various unconscious and nonconscious patterns that serve to limit individual human lives.

Matt: This picture he drew to show what disconnectedness for him is like. The clouds up above he says are Mother and that's what keeps him from connecting to everything. [picture of clouds/mother is passed around.]

Marilyn: It's very fluid, isn't it? Nothing is very solid.

Larry: No.

Karen: When I think back to the example that you gave, Stuart, and I think of some things that Searles has done with people who have been crazy, the successful clinicians have basically gotten to that person's level somehow.

Larry: We do that when we play peekaboo with a baby when it's ready. We are aware that the baby has a certain capacity to track certain kinds of activity at various stages of development. So we engage in an activity that the baby can track. That's what I'm saying. I think the sky's the limit in terms of promoting activities that two can track together. Since the major countertransference problem you are experiencing right now is your mind wandering, perhaps you need to try to attend to that one first. What would keep you in the room more effectively? What sort of thing might you be able to introduce into the room that would keep you more present?

Matt: I know if he took off his sunglasses, and I could see his eyes, that would keep me more present.

Larry: So begin there. Now I wouldn't just ask him to take off his sunglasses, I'd begin a dialogue about it.

Matt: Right.

Larry: And the dialogue might involve your putting your sunglasses on, or your trying to say, I'll lower mine a little bit, if you lower yours a little bit! Who knows what kind of peekaboo you could get going!

Matt: If he were to walk in and I had my sunglasses on he would just start laughing. I could see him doing that.

Larry: You could begin to play with him?

Matt: Yeah, I could.

Marilyn: I'm struck by your saying the sky's the limit and in this picture the clouds obscuring the sky are Mother.

Larry: That's Eddie's limit, the internalized psychotic mother.

Karen: The mother is the limit, and if you can stretch beyond mother then . . .

Larry: That's it. Kafka's characters are always searching, always hoping. There is a way up to the castle on the hill, to the breast, but every route gets blocked, every possible connection always somehow collapses. With a new baby it's different. Babies don't have to be taught to connect. When your baby was ready she knew how to connect, you didn't have to teach her connection, you just had to be there, available for connection. She did the rest.

What we have to study is what Eddie is doing to prevent the connection, because that's the one point where we have transference. There is the transference constellation to a crazy mother that is somehow internalized and prevents the connection. The clouds are the limit. Mother stops him. And the only way we can study what it is that prevents his connecting to people is by trying to foster and promote connection and then to see what happens to foreclose it. So anything you can possibly begin to promote back-and-forth exchange, any slight movement, any slight animation, is going to begin to give you the opportunity to say, "Well, we were enjoying this game of rummy until something happened and then what?" or "I was sitting here and I was watching you draw," or "We were playing the sunglasses game and when we wore that out things kind of fizzled here between us. What was that like for you?" Because it is that point of disconnection that provides the focus for the analytic project.

Matt: Well, I'm going to start some new things. Talking with you all has given me a new sense of life with Eddie. "Let's do something with the sunglasses" or "Let's play a game" doesn't become obvious when you're struggling to be with a person like this. Like I never even thought of the glasses.

Larry: I think it's often more a question of how you are going to survive the hour. Under those conditions it's difficult to be maximally creative.

Matt: Yes.

Larry: Just to break through drowsiness or your mind wandering is beside the point. It's rather to pay attention to breaking through and notice as you begin to let a little more break through, does he clamp the sunglasses on more tightly? What happens in this interface between two agents? Why can't there be two agents in the room interacting, enjoying each other? That's the question that has to fuel our work. Why can't there be? He is saying, by virtue of his whole life experience, "There can't be. My mother and I cannot interact. We cannot play peekaboo." Your question to him, in any one of a thousand ways, is, "Why not? We'll let's just play a little bit of peekaboo and see where we go. Let's see what comes up to make it so intolerable, that makes it frightening, that makes it boring. Let's see what's happening when one or the other of us begins to flake out, how can we understand that?" These are the questions that fuel the analytic process at the organizing level.

I think also, Matt, you may be letting yourself feel too confined by your chair. You are not a confined man mentally or emotionally. You filled this room with yourself today. You are very expressive, your body is expressive. And when you're with your clients it's the same way I'm sure. No doubt there are people who experience being tied to their wheelchairs, who are slaves to the handicap. You own your wheelchair. It's a part of you, but you also extend well beyond it. So I think you may not be aware of how many ways you in fact are able to reach out to this man. It's just that his internalized organizing state prevents him from responding beyond a certain point. Then he puts up the sun shades. In his picture the clouds, which he calls Mother, obscure the sun—but it's peeking out up here in the corner!

Madeline: Your reaction has been not to step forward at times because you feel like it's going to be intrusive.

Matt: Intrusive, yes. Like it's going to hurt him. Like the light of day is too strong.

Karen: My hunch is that when he and Mom at four months or whenever were about ready to connect, rather than her running off, like you had suggested, that she intruded and he had to develop a barrier to protect himself. Now that barrier is his internalized mother who shades him from reality.

Larry: That may well be the problem. You are certainly afraid of intruding here.

Matt: I've never thought of it that way.

Karen: Because that's what you're resisting doing.

Matt: Somehow he was intruded upon in a way that was damaging.

Larry: And you protect him by daydreaming, shading him from your full animation.

Matt: I appreciate the help today because I feel like now I have more track to go out on, whereas before I was feeling like I didn't have any track. It feels good to have it, so thank you.

Larry: Thanks, Matt. [Group thanks Matt.]

CONSCIOUSNESS BEGINS FOR EDDIE: EIGHT MONTHS LATER

Matt: Today I want to focus on my last session with Eddie. I know the session was important, that he was communicating a lot to me, not only verbally, but by the way we were relating to each other. So as soon as he left I recorded my thoughts. I wanted to put everything into words. I didn't try to think about it. I didn't try to make interpretations. Sometimes when I begin to think too much about a session, or what's happening, I start to interpret and then it clouds how I present it. It changes it.

But first I need to back up and talk about a few things. I finally began to get Eddie to take off his sunglasses. That was a really important experience. As soon as I got him to take off his sunglasses and established a kind of peekaboo relating with him, he began insisting on wanting to bring in his friend John to our sessions. John is the friend who brings him to my office. I was really resisting that. I kept saying, "Eddie, we need to keep these sessions for ourselves." But then what began to happen is that our sessions changed to his talking only about John. [Group laughter.]

Larry: He is not going to let the internalized psychotic mother come alive without a fight. So now we have resistance analysis to do.

Matt: It was really clear that Eddie wasn't going to get off the topic of John. John was going through one crisis after another, so finally, giving in, I said, "Okay, bring him in." [Group laughs.] This all happened immediately after I had him take off his dark sunglasses, which he wore for months in sessions. There was something so instantaneously nice about his taking off his sunglasses that it felt really great. At the same time, it felt something was really upsetting for both of us in that. Then he wanted to bring John in, and I began to allow John to come in. Over a series of several sessions I found myself drawn into working mostly with John. And in one session, Eddie actually fell asleep on his chair! [Group laughs.] His sunglasses are off but now his eyes are shut, he's asleep. And I'm

dealing with this other guy. [Group laughs.]

Madeline: He drew you into the system.

Larry: He is going to keep you one step removed from having to experience that demonic mother.

Karen: What I found fascinating about last time you presented him was that here we have this absolutely brilliant therapist blinded because of the relationship to this really obvious thing, that they are not connecting because of the dark glasses between them!

Matt: It was only four years! [Group laughs.]

Karen: Since then I've thought about you so many times when I'm stuck with somebody. "Okay, what am I not seeing?" It probably isn't going to be as obvious as dark glasses, but . . .

Larry: A lot of times it is.

Karen: It may be. "What am I not seeing here?" It's a metaphor I will never forget, I mean really. When we get drawn into these intense projective relationships how can we be anything but blinded?

Matt: It had been put to me that these are glasses he needed to see and read with, and yet, at the same time they kept us completely disconnected. It turns out he didn't need them as much as I was led to believe. The glasses came off, and as I said in my notes, "It's a peekaboo experience for both of us." That's exactly what it was like. We joked about them and played with our sunglasses a bit. But then he insists on bringing in John. They're both living in a boarding house. I thought, "Okay, he's trying to tell me something through having John come here." Someone here questioned last time about his family and his younger brother. We got a little mileage out of that. Eddie began to talk about how his younger brother would always get in the way of him and his mother. But the bottom line is, though I can make interpretations about this and how this may relate to what's happening now, John is still in the room and Eddie is asleep! [Group laughs.]

Larry: So much for interpretations!

Marilyn: He brought his brother in for you.

Matt: And his brother took mother away.

Larry: And sure enough, his brother was more engaging. [Group laughs.]

Matt: So then I begin to think, "We've got to get John out of here." So over several sessions, I began to talk with Eddie and John about how important my work was with Eddie and how we had to keep the integrity of the individual sessions, that I didn't have room for John in my schedule, but there is a men's group in our agency led by good therapists that would be a great place for John to be. So I'm saying, "Let's get you in the group." I'm making arrangements with the therapist, I'm having John call the therapist and having the therapist call John to get him in—all that to get John out of our sessions! [Laughter.] With these organizing people you just don't say, "Hey look. This isn't working. John, you're on your way! Eddie, let's get back to our individual sessions." It just doesn't work that way. These two

can barely function in the world, why would I expect they can follow straightforward instructions?

Marilyn: You got off too easy having him take the dark glasses off. This is all part of the same psychotic transference deal. [Laughter.]

Matt: In my fantasies I was hoping it would work that way, but I struggled for some time. I even had individual sessions with Larry. "How do I get this man out of here and get back with Eddie?" In the midst of this Eddie and John went out and got an apartment. So Eddie has now gone from living on the street, homeless, to a series of mental institutions, to board and care homes, to room and board, and finally to his own apartment with a roommate! It was working out really well for him. Something healthy is happening as he moves into an apartment, getting away from these multipsychotic people that lived in the room and board home. Eddie feels like he has some privacy and for the first time he has his own room, even though I feel he's temporarily somewhat disconnected from me. Finally I get things arranged with the group. John has talked with the therapist, and things are looking good for both of them. The week before John is supposed to begin group I'm looking forward to returning to my individual sessions with Eddie, and I'm in the process of moving my office. That was bound to be disruptive for Eddie. That week John's brother dies—he overdoses on drugs and alcohol. So Eddie comes back and we have this session in which all he talks about is how much pain John is in. John is out in the waiting room in pain, his Thorazine has been doubled. I'm feeling like I'm punishing everybody because I won't let John come in. But I was taking courage in feeling that I had succeeded in drawing some boundaries.

Now Eddie knows I'm moving my office. I've alerted him that things will be very different there. I have all new furnishings for my new office. So he asks what's happening to the old office furniture since his apartment has no furniture. I said I was going to give it to Goodwill. Eddie kept talking about not having furniture for his new apartment. Almost in exasperation I finally said, "Eddie, is there anything in here that you'd like for your new place?" He said, "Yeah, everything." So much for drawing boundaries! [Laughter.]

Karen: Perfect. "You two move in with me!"

Matt: I gave him my couch, my chair, and all the pictures. So through December he would come with John, who would bring his truck. [Laughter]. John would wait in the waiting room. Eddie would come into session. [Laughter.]

Karen: And leave with part of you! This is very funny. [Laughter.]

Marilyn: What great transitional objects. I've heard of a client taking a pillow or something from the therapist's office before . . . but this? [Laughter.]

Matt: I wasn't very comfortable with it, but it seemed the only way to go. Then Eddie began to tell me how his room looks just like my office. He arranged it exactly like I had my office. John liked this, too. John felt like he could be with me this way too. It was

starting to feel real strange. It didn't seem right somehow, but it also didn't seem right to dispose of things Eddie genuinely needed to renew his life.

So there I was feeling somewhat un-therapist-like. And magically, Eddie began to talk as never before. "We have a lot to talk about. I've been playing a clown. Part of me is out here (in front) but the real me is back here (inside). I want to lay my cards on the table, but I'm not going to be able to do it until we get settled in, until we get into your new office and I get used to it. There is so much I want to tell you about my experience." Experience is the word he actually began using. I was bowled over by it all. "My experience." "People don't want to know what my experience is. People want to misinterpret me and I want to tell you what my experience of myself is." He began to talk about when he was a child he would see these beasts. He said that they were real and he thinks they were part of the spiritual world. He was saying it in a captivating way. It really felt clear to him. He described when his mother and brother would leave him alone in the house and he would see monsters and spiritual things.

Marilyn: Where the wild things are.

Matt: He says they were real and psychiatrists and doctors have never believed him. He hasn't talked much about them because people always misinterpret him. I am listening and saying, "I hear you. This feels very real for you. People haven't understood how real they were for you." He replied excitedly, "Yes, that's it." And then it felt like he pulled back, "But we can't really go any further yet, I have so much to say. I want to lay my cards on the table." He said that a lot. "But not until we're settled in." And then he would leave with another picture. [Laughter.]

Larry: The instant he excitedly connects he immediately retreats, blocks the possibility of a two-way connection.

Matt: I moved into my new office. In the meantime Eddie got a real job at a homeless shelter as a caretaker! [Group expressions of amazement] It's the first job he's had for years. He's been living on disability. As caretaker at this shelter for the homeless he does most everything—cooking, managing, clean-up. He's kind of a Renaissance man at the homeless shelter now. He has a lot of different jobs and responsibilities taking care of all these homeless people. It's really interesting. He gets minimum wage. He will lose his SSI benefits because of it, but he wants the job more, which I found interesting. Now he has this job where he does everything from janitorial work, to locking the doors, to counting the people at night, to cooking, and managing.

Madeline: What a tremendous responsibility for a guy with his history.

Matt: Yes. And he loves it. And he's doing a good job, too.

Larry: He has become a "caretaker?"

Matt: That's what he calls it.

Larry: He has required so much care for so many years and suddenly he has identified with the caretaking role.

Madeline: He is able to give back some of what he has gotten.

Larry: And just after he's filled up his apartment with artifacts from his own caretaker!

Matt: Let me read some notes from our first session in my new office. "Eddie looks the best I have ever seen him. As he sits in the office he considers his prospects as caretaker in a homeless shelter." He already had the job at that point. "This is not only a minimum-wage job, but provides living expenses as well. It's hard for him to leave the people he is in the apartment with, especially John, and move on." This is a real struggle for him because they basically want him to live at the place. He finds it really difficult, so what he has essentially done is he's got this job and they've given him this room, but he is also keeping the apartment and John is over in the apartment with a couple of other psychotic people. I don't know how else to describe them, because that's just what they are. They all share this apartment together and pay rent. So he has two places. I don't know if he's going to transition over and stay at the homeless shelter or go back to the apartment, but he has kind of both in the air for now.

Marilyn: Where is your furniture?

Matt: At the apartment. He has it all in one room, set up just the way I had it set up. John has finally got into group and he's loving it. This is a good group for him because he needs to be with some better-developed people. Eddie and I are now having individual sessions. Now, what I want to talk about is the most recent session last Monday.

Larry: So, here he is in your new

office, a man with a responsible job presenting himself without sunglasses, without a sidekick, looking the best he ever has and ready to lay his cards on the table on Valentine's Day?

Matt: Yes. It was very different. The first thing I notice is that John is nowhere in sight. Eddie comes in and asks if he could borrow some money. I'm thinking, "All right, what are the rules?" "Okay Eddie, what do you need?" I am always vacillating on what to do with this man. He said, "Well, not much." He owed John some gas money so he needs to borrow $20. I said, "I only have $10." I looked in my ledger book trying to justify giving him the money. He had a credit balance, so I was basically giving him some of the money back he had already paid in advance. I gave him $10. He then notices his mouth is dry and he wants something to drink. I have no drinking fountain in my new office. Eddie is on a medication that always makes his mouth dry. I suggested he might go next door to McDonald's and get a drink. I know that if I don't allow him to get something to drink all we are going to be talking about the whole session is how dry his mouth is. He came back with a tall drink and a Big Mac too. [Group laughs.] He said, "Is it okay if I eat?" I say, "Go ahead."

Marilyn: "How far can I go?" [Group laughs.]

Matt: After Eddie finishes his Big Mac he proceeds to tell me three dreams. The first dream he had two days ago. This is the first dream he had ever shared with me and this is our fifth year. In the dream he is out in this mountainous area eating different col-

ored wafers and surrounded by rocks. Colored wafers. Orange, black, red, you name it, every color. And as he is eating the wafers there is a black and white snake that is lurking around the rocks to bite him, to poison him. I purposely didn't make any interpretations, not wanting to spoil the effect of his telling me a dream. I just tried to ask him questions about the dream elements.

That was dream number one. It's a running joke with us—about ten minutes into the session either he'll catch himself with his glasses on and start laughing, and then take them off, and I'll start laughing. Or I'll say, "Eddie, your glasses." And he'll start laughing and take them off. Up to this point in the session he still had his glasses on and neither of us had made notice of it. I was so startled that he was bringing me a dream that the last thing I was thinking about was that his glasses were on.

After he shares that first dream, he recalls a dream he had in 1958. This is a "prophetic dream," as he says. It predicts the future. In this dream he is walking along the beach with a light-colored woman and there is a bamboo hut on the beach, or a shack with snakes in it, pythons he says. He then recalls that he was actually in Venice Beach later, in the '60s, and that there was actually a bamboo shack that had snakes in it.

The third dream he had in 1975. This is another prophetic dream. In this third dream he recalls helicopters over his house and police surrounding him. He then experiences this when he is married to his ex-wife in the '70s. He comes home one night and there are helicopters above his house. Actually they were going for the neighbor's house, but they were so close. He recalled, "Oh, I dreamed this." You know, prophesying. Those are the three dreams he shares. As I end the session I tell him that I will digest and think about our session, feeling it was very important. I was trying to validate that he is communicating important things to me. By the second dream, I noticed he has his glasses on and I say, "Eddie, your glasses." He laughs and he takes his glasses off and sets them down by my tissues. He comes back about three minutes later to retrieve his glasses. He has never left his glasses in my office. These are the things he can't see without, supposedly.

Larry: He left his defense, his resistance to contact with you?

Matt: Yes. So I am very much interested in everybody's thoughts.

Larry: What's coming up for you?

Matt: It felt like he revealed something to me that is startling and in trying to think about it I am trying not to wreck this startling feeling he left me with. In the first dream, he is in a mountainous area surrounded by rocks. He is eating different colored wafers, orange, black, and red. There is a snake there, black and white, around the rocks getting ready to bite him. He feels it also to be poisonous. It feels to me like the disconnectedness, the black and white splitting, is lurking. As we are together in the midst of our sessions, it feels like we are both always waiting for something to, at any moment, enter to disrupt us.

Something is going to poison the session and wreck the relating.

Larry: In the dream he is eating wafers (communion?) with others near mountains (breasts?). He gets you to give him something that is rightfully his to pay John for gas (energy). He feeds himself with what you have given him, gives you three dreams and leaves his sunglasses (defenses, resistance) with you. My association is that in some way or another in his life, as a result of his connection with you he has been able to take in many things. Whatever these colors mean, whether they are the people he is surrounding himself with, or colors in your furniture and pictures of your new office, which I am sure is quite colorful, or whatever—Eddie's affects have been stimulated. And he is taking in nourishment.

Mike: There is something that's happening here I want to comment on. The first part of what I heard is that he took a lot of you in. He took your furniture and pictures. He connected with you. He sort of incorporated you. The next thing I hear is that he makes a statement to you that he is starting to have insights into his own process. "I've been clowning with you. There is a false me and there is a real me." Then he says, "I am going to tell you about some of this." And he starts telling you hallucinations and dreams. In the dream there is a stream of consciousness that for this man I find remarkable. There is a snake in the first dream. That makes him think of the snake in the second dream. That second dream is a prophecy that makes him think of another dream he had that was a prophecy. It's almost like the apparatus of consciousness is being . . .

Larry: Actually formed in the moment.

Karen: Birthed.

Mike: Right. Like a development or achievement he is actually making by being with you in the moment. This has a quality very different from the ritualized stories he's tended to tell you.

Matt: Yes, this session was very different.

Marilyn: I'm reminded of an experience I had as a mother of my first child. I remember the first time, almost eighteen years ago, when he was probably 4 or 5 months old that I took him to the doctor for a well-baby visit. I remember the doctor took him and was examining him, so that he was physically separate from me. I can remember how protective I felt of him and not liking the doctor picking him apart. I mean that's what the doctor is supposed to do, to find out if anything is wrong, are the reflexes okay, and so on. But I can remember how protective I was. "Don't analyze this. Don't pick this beautiful child apart." I feel really protective of your client here, Matt. He's presented you with some absolutely beautiful things. It's like, I don't know that I want to get into picking this apart, to analyzing something that for now stands to simply be appreciated as something beautiful, spontaneous, and human. We've waited a long time for this baby to reach, to feed, to enjoy you and to be enjoyed by you. You have him "eating out of your hand" now, this very

frightened and confused man — at last. That's my association to your experience. I can literally still vividly remember him being taken from me and handed to the doctor and the doctor examining the child and my feeling, "Let me have him back. He's okay."

Larry: I'm glad you said that. I think we are all feeling protective of Eddie and very pleased for Matt and Eddie that something exciting is happening, that he is feeding, that multiple affects are being enjoyed, even though there is the background threat of going back to the poisonous black and white of affect splitting. But I am also responding to a difference in what we hear about Eddie and the story of your protectiveness with your son. Your boy was young, healthy, and innocent. Eddie is neither young nor innocent. And Eddie has been made psychotic, as far as we can tell, by invasive infantile trauma. We celebrate that he is saying to Matt, "I am now wanting to feed. My affects are now being released in a variety of ways. I am now telling you about my monsters as a child that no one has ever believed. And I have wonderful dreams." But lurking in the background is the danger of the psychotic process — the splitting. So in this case what we want to be protective of is not merely all of us taking him apart, analyzing Eddie, but of the poison within, which is the psychotic transference, which to Eddie, is far more dangerous than our taking him apart. I think your protective instinct is really what we are all feeling.

Marilyn: Right.

Larry: The threat of the psychotic

mother, the poisonous mother, the mother responsible for black and white splits, the mother whose abandonment set monsters running in his soul, is ever present, even though he is in a feeding position maybe for the first time since infancy. So you are hopefully feeling now the position that Marilyn describes, the nursing mother who just wants to let the baby suckle in peace. It would be easy to interfere with this very delicate process.

Karen: There are many symbols. While he's feeding he is dreaming of being in the (breast) mountains. Wafers are certainly used in Christian ritual, a taking in of the body and life of Christ. Even the snake, not merely a symbol of evil but of transformation, of healing that may well be experienced as a threat for Eddie.

Howard: The snake is what tempted us from Paradise.

Larry: But also the Kundalini energy that provides the organization of the life force.

Karen: As you said Kundalini energy, my whole body had a chill. I'm wondering in what ways he expresses what's happening to him physically. Because I think that's the level that this is imprinted on. One of the reasons I think you're resisting thinking about it, is that this kind of memory is stored physically, not in thought.

Marilyn: It's primordial.

Matt: In our first two years together, Eddie's body was still breaking down. He had all manner of physical symptoms and was always going to doctors. Psychotic deterioration is an understatement. Not only was he floridly psychotic, but his body was "paining." Arthritis everywhere, his whole body would just stiffen up, his back, his teeth—most of his teeth have been pulled. Recently he went to this dentist who wanted to pull out the rest of his teeth without really any reason and then not give him bridges. I mean I'm not a dentist, but I don't think he needs his teeth pulled out for no reason. Nor does Eddie and for the first time ever he is resisting—protesting mistreatment at last. Yes, the first two years were filled with pains, real and hypochondriacal.

Larry: As rudimentary relatedness has formed, thinking of the sunglasses play as a representation, the focus has shifted away from concerns with body parts and into developing consciousness, or a knowing together. We think of the serpent in Eden tempting us toward "the tree of the knowledge of good and evil." Once having tasted that fruit, primal paradise, Eden is lost and we live in a real world with real serpentine temptations.

Matt: Nor is he physically deteriorating like he was. He was in a clear degenerative process.

Larry: One of the things we see as we look at the organizing experience, in terms of the evolution of consciousness as we ordinarily think of it, is that the emphasis on the body parts, the deterioration, the pain, the arthritic pain, the emphasis of those begins to shift as consciousness shifts, as consciousness builds. The infant can only be hypochondriacal, body centered. The infant can only be aware of body sensations, but at some point, when the connection to the mother begins to become experienced, the focus changes and consciousness, which in Greek means "knowing together," begins as the mother–child connection begins. So the focus on body parts is slowly relinquished for the symbiotic connection. Freud (1911) in discussion of the Schreber case of psychosis says that hypochondriasis stands in the same relation to psychosis as anxiety to neurosis—as fundamental. I think what we are seeing is the beginning of consciousness, the beginning of the symbiotic connection, and your very deep concern about how delicate it is.

Karen: I was thinking how beautiful it was that you simply heard the thirst, and let him go right then. I had a client who lost his wallet and he was having trouble settling down for the session. Finally I said, "Go and try to find your wallet." That was the beginning of trust with us, after a year of seeing this guy.

Larry: You have a body need.

Karen: You have a body need and you go for it.

Marilyn: But the fear of taking in poisonous food is ever present, especially since we thought last time that his original trauma probably resulted from overintrusive and ill-timed mothering.

Larry: Yes. The transference danger is that the psychotic formation from the past will, in some way or another, be projected into Matt, or will be acted out by Eddie in some way or another. It's not a matter of, "Are we going to run into trouble?" It's a matter of when, what kind, and can we stem the tide together. Eddie's only hope of having his life's emotional burden lightened lies in living out the transference experience with Matt as the psychotic mother. And how will all of that transpire?

Matt: Well, I have a fantasy and a fear that he's going to die on me. I have this fear like I'm going to come in next week and tell you all that he was killed.

Madeline: This stuff is powerful.

Larry: When we begin to achieve contact, the fear that he might die or something like that usually represents our awareness of the tenuousness of the contact and how easily lost it is. And our empathy for the lethal power of contact in this man's history. I think it's very important to try to speak your concerns to Eddie, to process your feelings with him so you both can keep the danger of a significant breach in contact always before you. So that you both can work on understanding things when his internalized psychotic mother appears in the room to wreck the relating. We are dealing with mental phenomena that are not well understood. We do know that people do die in psychotherapy from various causes. I think perhaps to begin to express to him that, on the one hand how wonderful it is that something good is happening, but on the other hand you are aware of a bit of agitation, as perhaps he is, from indications in his dream. It might be good to talk about all the meaning that black and white snake might have, and that you are worried about him just as he is worried about himself. And that right now, while he is trying something new with you, he needs to be very careful with himself. I think that often people need to hear this.

With our borderline patients we run into this risk when they are succeeding in letting go of the borderline scenario. Suicidal thoughts seem to come from nowhere to represent the old self suiciding, being killed off. A new self is being formed, but right at that point there is a great danger to these people because of the agitation and grief over the loss of the old, familiar self. They know they are "suiciding," killing off the old self. And accidents do happen.

But in the context of organizing issues the fear of dying is more likely to be related to the anticipated breakdown of mental processes as the organizing transference comes into place. The monsters he told you about that have been very real to him his whole life are now being brought into the light of day. So let's not minimize the potential of realistic danger. I think it's good to alert him to that fact and say, "You know a lot of what you're beginning to do with me is the direction you've been wanting to go for a long time. And yet, when people begin to make major shifts like this they are often not quite themselves for awhile and they can be in danger in simple situations like walking across the street, cutting with knives, working with machines, or simply tripping or bumping into doors. So keep that in mind, Eddie, this week and take very good care of yourself." And the same

might be true for you. Being in close contact with an organizing experience can be disorganizing for us as well.

Matt: Well, yeah, I've developed an attunement with Eddie because he was one of my first clients. So we've really developed together and we've developed an attunement together. I remember my first session with this man. Boy, something's been developed in each of us. This has been a unique opportunity to grow together that somehow has solidified something in both of us.

Larry: You may find yourself wanting to say that to him as well— how exciting it is that he's showing you he has benefited from the relationship and you hope that he is well aware that you've benefited from it, too. I think that kind of thing can be shared. Thank you, Matt.

Marilyn: Wonderful!

Karen: Great material!

Matt: It's good to have a place to speak freely about this taxing work. I don't know where else I could share in this way and grow and leave feeling so good about our relationship as I'm feeling.

Larry: Great!

Marilyn: It feels perfect!

Mike: Carry on!

POSTSCRIPT

As of mid-1994, Matt continues to treat Eddie and they are approaching almost seven years together. Eddie is moving forward in terms of his social development and physical health, and he is functioning in the world at a satisfactory level. He dates women, manages a homeless shelter, and owns and drives his own car. Of course there are occasional major as well as minor setbacks related to his primary organizing constellation. Yet, Eddie and Matt march on and are well into tackling the frontier of bonding or borderline states and issues. Though Eddie's fundamental progress is all well and good, for Matt the most exciting phenomena to observe and participate in are the manifestation of Eddie's consciousness and his growing ability to think, or, as Eddie would put it, "reasoning." Eddie is now able to conceive and hold thoughts that are like stories in that they have an aim with a lucid beginning, middle, and end. He is able to remember, forget, have associations, dream, and use his thoughts as objects that can be shared, examined, explored, felt, and transformed for more sophisticated uses. This relatively new ego space and ego function have given him a greater capacity to work the organizing transference and therefore a more optimistic potential for true bonding and relatedness possibilities.

WORKING THE CONTACT MOMENT

5

Capitalizing on the Contact Moment

Listening for transference experiencing always presupposes the development of a certain perspective. The following case conference is presented to illustrate one way the organizing transference might be observable in clinical practice. Here the primary listening task is to sort through the myriad personal concerns that the analytic speaker presents and to note how she approaches her therapist searching for personal contact. Then the task is to discover at exactly what moment in the sequence the speaker manages to foreclose the possibility of contact or succeeds in rupturing whatever contact might have been momentarily achieved. That is, in sustained interpersonal relatedness, emotional contact and interaction between two people is achieved. In order for an infant or an older person in therapy to achieve interpersonal emotional bonding, the two involved must learn to cue off of each other's personality. When a person has never achieved an interpersonal bond or when parts of a person's personality have never been included in a bonded relationship, the moment of potential contact takes on a special importance. Here we see an empathic therapist struggling over time to sort through a set of frenzied concerns in order to find a way to be helpful to her client.

Heather: The person I want to talk about today is a woman in her mid-forties whom I met three years ago. She called because she heard I was doing parent groups. She was about to get remarried and she wanted to come in by herself for premarital counseling because of difficulties with the children that each was bringing to the new marriage. I explained that I usually see both people together for at least the first session. She said that wouldn't be a good idea. I said, "Is there a problem? Does your fiancé not want to come?" "Oh, no. He's willing to come, you know, all in good time. But I would like to have three or four appointments for myself first." Not to give up too easily, I said, "It's usually better if the three of us meet together first. Then we can agree on how to go from there." "No, no, you'll understand after I meet you myself." I said, "It's not how I usually proceed but we'll begin as you suggest."

She came in very friendly and curled up on the couch in a very girlish way. She took off her shoes, put her legs up, curled up with three pillows around her, and proceeded without prompting to tell me her history, beginning with her relationship with her parents. So the first few sessions that's exactly how it was, her telling me about herself and her past. After her divorce she had met the daughter of this new man through her work and they became really good friends. The daughter said, "Oh, you ought to meet my father." One thing led to another. The two of them got together, hit it off well, and quickly became a couple. The relationship was progressing nicely. They supported two homes. She has teenage children. There were no pressing issues with her children.

This new man was everything that her husband wasn't. He was a very stable person with a secure job. They were getting along fine. He was willing to take care of many of her household needs because her job required her to be out of town every three or four days. When she was going to be out of town, he would stay with her children.

No problems, everything was going well. He lived close by with his grown son. She never stayed at his home because it was such a mess. She couldn't understand how they could have TV dinners in front of the television, put them down when finished, enjoy the show, and go to bed without even picking things up. It was just a mess. But it wasn't her home, so that was all right. She would get upset with her own children who were not picking up. It sounded to me like they were being typical teenagers. She would get into yelling matches with them, racing up and down stairs, screaming and yelling, running after them, giving them a piece of her mind. After a blowout she would usually go into her room to take time out to recover. Then she would come out and apologize. Then everything would be okay for a while.

When she first began seeing me she was concerned about how her fiancé would react to her style because this man was calm, cool, and collected. He never got angry. He got along with her children even better than she did. She could never get him into an argument because there was nothing really to argue about. If she showed signs of anger he wouldn't fight but would just freeze and withdraw. She didn't know how it was going to work out. There was some anxiety about how they were going to live together. How are they going to share a bedroom and a bathroom? How is he going to feel seeing her with curlers in her hair? Will she be able to take care of him in terms of cooking the foods he likes? Will he still like her without makeup?

She reported that he didn't see any problems. The fourth session she said, "Okay, now he can come in."

Larry: Tell us your understanding so far. She just wanted to lay all this out before you met him?

Heather: I think she wanted to prepare me for how difficult the situation is.

Linda: For her?

Heather: For her, yes. She didn't want to waste his time listening to all this, you know, the curlers, the bathroom, the laundry. It seemed to me she didn't want to criticize him in front of me. You know, saying what a sloppy house he has. She wanted to give me his history of being married to a schizophrenic woman who had died leaving her kid screwed up. She wanted to give me all that without his being there. He basically raised the boy because his wife was repeatedly hospitalized for long periods before she died.

I saw them for couples work about three months before the wedding. It was basically management of, "How are we going to do this together? What type of house are we going to find? What type of carpeting? Who is going to have what space? What are the rules of the house?" Then they worried about the honeymoon. It was a lot for them to consider. "How are we going to arrange everything together?" We intellectualized and we laid out plans because nobody really knew how it would all work out or how they might feel about it all. They invited me to the wedding. I didn't go. I left them with, "Go, have a good honeymoon, and finish out the summer. Enjoy yourself,

come back in three or four months and let's see how things are. We'll get together for a kind of 'check up' session." At the end of October, she called. It wasn't a check-up session though, it was a crisis.

Carolyn: They got through the choice of carpet decisions and now it was something heavy at last!

Heather: Their house was gorgeous. They got all new furniture. It was great. Everything was wonderful. In terms of the children, she did not appreciate their response. That was the upsetting thing. His son lives in separate quarters. He has his own entrance so that he really doesn't have to be involved in their space. The problem is that nobody's taking care of anything. She complains that she's the one who has to take care of everything. And she's the only one who knows how to do anything right. They do have a housekeeper who comes in once a week. But there's a lot of housekeeping to be done during the week. According to her, nobody knows how to cook. Nobody knows how to paint, to clean, and so forth. She's the only one who knows how to do anything and she does it all. Then there were long-distance trips, pressing business, and the upcoming Christmas holidays, all of which detracted attention from the crisis and our sessions were soon temporarily suspended.

She returned in February. We worked on how she is managing her life. She has a high-functioning job entailing a lot of computer work and writing leading to intense, time-consuming projects. Then it's just a crazy time, lots of overtime plus being involved in other projects. Then she comes home and everything has to be perfect at home. I was trying to work with her to realize how she extends herself and how she lets herself get so overtired that she barks at everybody because she is so resentful that nobody helps her, nobody takes care of her. But, if anybody does try to take care of her, she barks at them for doing it because it's not right.

One thing we were working on was to get her to come home and take some rest before getting into evening activities. We tried to devise ways of establishing a comfortable transition from the pressures of work to life at home. We had to establish that she didn't have to take care of the homework for the children because they're old enough. They can take care of themselves. They were good students and were not really problem children at that time. The older son was going to a local college. The father couldn't care less if he ever graduated. He was not very concerned if he was getting C's, B's, or A's. She was invested in, "How come that kid is not producing, how come he's not doing his work, how come he's coming home drunk at three o'clock in the morning? How come he's not helping around the house?" We worked on, "Get away from that. Don't worry about his bedroom being a mess. Detach yourself from that. Detach from how messy your children's bedrooms are. Let's worry about you."

A typical evening would begin with her announcing to everyone, "Heather told me I should rest." Her husband would say, "Go rest awhile, I'll start dinner." So he would start dinner. She

would come down from her rest half an hour later. I bet she watched the clock and timed it, and said to herself, "Heather said I should do half an hour rest. Okay, time is up now." So she comes down the stairs into the kitchen and she sees her husband working on the dinner. But she would notice that he didn't cut tomatoes the way she thought they should be cut. Or maybe the celery was not chopped finely enough. Something minor, totally irrelevant, and totally unimportant for most people would regularly set her off. Then, she would go into the family room and fester. She might not say a word but would be getting more and more upset.

She is soon picking an argument with her husband or with the children. Initially, her husband had incredible tolerance for her outbursts, but after a while he could be provoked into an argument. Now that they are arguing, the problem is that she vents and then is fine, but he's becoming chronically angry and less communicative. He's not responding to her any more; he's withdrawing and the more he withdraws, the more insecure she becomes. She complains of rejection and abandonment. Then she feels he doesn't love her anymore. The more she feels insecure, the more she becomes angry at him. Now she's saying, "Obviously there's a good reason for me to be angry at him." Then they get into a second level of argument about his not arguing with her. He would say, "Oh her, there's no way I'm going to leave her. She just gets me so angry. I don't know."

So for some time we went over

these kinds of concerns every week. Each session exists almost as a separate session in itself. It's basically the same kinds of material over and over. Somehow the meanings and the implications of the whole relationship cycle don't register, though she is an intelligent woman. She's very well put together as a package. She takes good care of herself; she looks good, she speaks well, she comes off as competent and intelligent. But our talks just don't sink in. Each session is, "Heather, please help me! I feel totally helpless and confused. If he would only change, if he would just do things that make me happy, if only he would . . ."

But if he does take care of her needs, ninety percent of the time it's not good enough because he failed in some regard. He says, "It's out of my character to be outgoing, to share my feelings, to discuss things with you, so when I do it, it's hard work for me but I try. So if I don't do it a hundred percent of the time, or a hundred percent right, I'm sorry. But if it's even coming eighty percent of the time, it's really hard work for me." She says, "If it's not a hundred percent of the time, too bad. It's not good enough." Then there were a series of family problems and our sessions were interrupted.

When she came again, her husband came with her. This time he really gave it to her. "You're mean to the kids. No wonder the kids don't have any respect for you." He is totally lined up with the children. She says, "You're not supporting me." He says, "I cannot support you because you are unreasonable, you don't make any sense,

you make demands that are totally irrational. No wonder they talk back to you, no wonder they don't listen to you." She felt hurt. She could not believe that his son took her sister out for dinner but he never takes her out. There's no acknowledgment, nobody's paying attention to her.

Last weekend was the sixteenth birthday of her daughter. She and her husband were supposed to go shopping, do laundry, and prepare dinner. He said, "Gee, I'm tired. Can I lie down for a while before we go?" She got pissed. She said, "Fine, you go and take a nap. I'll go for a walk". She walked and didn't go home. She walked seven miles down to the beach and realized she didn't know where she was for a moment. She got into a telephone booth, called a friend, and said, "I'm not going home!" Her friend said, "You ought to at least call to let them know where you are." So she called her husband and said, "Come and pick me up," which he did. She took two days off from work, Monday and Tuesday. She called me Monday morning, frantic, "I have to see you. This is an emergency." I was able to see her Tuesday. She said, "I'm not going to work the rest of the week. I feel like a kid playing hooky. I'm not going back to work, and nobody can make me! I told them I'm sick. I have a doctor's appointment. You're a doctor, aren't you? So I have a doctor's appointment. And that's that. I don't know what's happening with me. Heather, you have to help me. I don't know what I'm doing. I'm ruining my marriage."

I'm sitting there thinking I don't

know what to do. I feel we cover the same things over and over again. She says her mother was a complainer and a nag. Her husband gets to her by saying, "You're turning into your mother aren't you?" And she just goes berserk. She doesn't want to be like her mother.

Larry: Did her mother kill herself? Is there a suicide danger?

Heather: No, I'm not picking up suicide.

Larry: Is she wanting to go to the hospital like her mother?

Heather: No.

Bill: I was wondering what kind of a connection drew the present husband to her.

Larry: His first wife was schizophrenic.

Bill: Yes. I was wondering what his way of choosing women was and what he connected to in her.

Larry: Chaos and frenzy I would think.

Heather: Yes, for sure. He provided acceptance for her. She would organize all the vacations, all the trips, all the weekends, what they were going to do, and how they were going to do it. As a social organizer, she's excellent. She's the one in the family who does all the nurturing. All the holidays are remembered. She always has to have a party for everybody in the family. She exerts herself and then complains because nobody's helping her. So he doesn't have to do anything in the relationship because she takes such good care of everything.

Mariana: I know she's got kids. Is she really relating to anybody in all of this?

Heather: That's a good question. She's doing a lot of things. She's busy, busy, busy.

Mariana: But . . . any personal emotional relating at all?

Heather: She reports that when she's with her husband, alone, on vacation, or away from the home, everything is wonderful. But I don't know exactly what that means. Recently they were in Hawaii for a week by themselves and everything was wonderful, wonderful. Then they came back and it was a disaster. Something good apparently happens when they are alone together. He pays attention to her, they make love, and she feels secure. She needs that reassurance from him. When she doesn't feel supported by him, she just loses it. I think she used to be close with the children when they were young, but right now she's not because all of her energies are focused on her husband. Of course the children are older now. Her boy has a girlfriend so he's into his world and his college. The daughter is busy with her friends. Once a week she used to have dinner with the daughter and then with the son. It was the "What are you doing?" type of contact. But now, for the last couple of years the interest has not been there with either of the kids at home. She claims she just doesn't have the time but I think she simply couldn't relate to them as people after they became old enough that they weren't exclusively tied to her.

Carolyn: Has she gotten angry with you at all for not helping or is it more like a chronic pleading for help?

Heather: I haven't picked up anger yet. I can call a spade a spade with her and we can chuckle and have a bit of fun together when we're alone.

Carolyn: But she feels kind of helpless and . . .

Heather: Yes, she feels helpless and it's "Heather, you've got to help me." She went and saw her doctor. He prescribed Xanax. Perhaps that will help, she thought.

Bill: It appears to me that the way she fails to relate is what happened to her, a child with a schizophrenic mother. Does it feel like there's any symbiotic relating going on?

Heather: I can't tell for sure.

Carolyn: Because you said you feel helpless in a sense. You're lost in the relationship so is there some sort of "lost" scenario happening? Or is it more that your woman simply can't feed, that she can't really take anything in because she can't stay oriented to nurturance?

Heather: It's more like she can't make use of anything I offer.

Carolyn: That's what it sounds like.

Larry: We're very hard pressed to point to anything you've said that resembles a reliable bonding process or a symbiotic scenario. There could be ways in which the frenzy and chaos have a certain style, but that's not clear. I was trying to get inside her shoes. If we were to write her story, it would be very Kafka-esque. From one seeming nightmare to the next with a few resting spots between. The world doesn't cooperate. This doesn't happen, that doesn't happen. There is only an endless cycle of work, ritual, work, ritual, but no connections to herself or to others, no interpersonal meanings, no consistency of related-

ness style, no real pattern unless there is some unseen structure in the frenzy and disorganized chaos. We can hear no real method to the madness like we are used to hearing in borderline symbiotic scenarios.

Heather: There is a certain constant element of complaining about "not having enough for myself." But when you go through some reasonable way she might get more for herself, because with their financial resources there are all kinds of possibilities, she isn't able to tap into anything because for one reason or another it won't do or it's not good enough.

Larry: What's not good enough?

Heather: If she gets a housekeeper she's not doing good enough housekeeping. If she gets somebody to drive the kids to wherever they are going to go it's not good enough. If she doesn't do homework with the children, well, she's a bad mother. If she's not available to be at home for so many hours, she's not a good wife. I asked her, "What do you need to do to be successful at work?" "To kill myself." "Okay, are you hearing what you're saying?" "Yes. My job is very demanding," and I believe it is. She gave me the statistics of how few women this huge national company has who are vice presidents and she's right up there in a very small percentage, so she's highly competent in her work.

Steve: You're saying it doesn't feel like you get through to her. It's like she talks about whatever concerns her but as far as what you're presenting to her or helping her with, it's like she doesn't get it. Yet she's bright enough.

Heather: That's it, exactly.

Steve: You're talking about the Kafka quality, Larry. When I hear her talk about some of this family interaction it sounds a little more developed. Does that still seem organizing level to you?

Larry: Yes. Because I don't hear anything truly human in her world. She speaks as if the people in her world are all defective robots rather than people to relate to. Her activities are intelligent but somehow rote and ritualistic rather than human, emotional, or relational. We don't hear of her love for her children, how she needs them and how they need and love her. We don't hear how individuals in this particular family constellation relate in order to acknowledge the personal existence of each other or where anyone else may be coming from emotionally. We don't hear anything in the material that suggests that there's one shred of human relationship anywhere in her life. The best she is able to come up with in relation to Heather is, "Please, help me."

Heather: And she never speaks as if there are any relationships inside her.

Larry: It's all stereotypical, mechanical, and basically nonhuman.

Steve: How about the husband?

Larry: My guess is that he had a schizophrenic mother or an organizing mother as well because of his incredible tolerance for nonrelatedness. Both of his wives have been at that level. So he has some kind of an affinity for or perhaps a kind of symbiosis with frenzied, chaotic states that he's managed to find some kind of internal balance with.

Heather: It's familiar to him.

Larry: Right. At the beginning she worried he wouldn't be able to put up with her chaos. But he managed well. Now after two years he's become identified as one of the children striving to survive in the midst of a crazy mother/wife. He's found a family in which he can be a child once again with a crazy mother. We know that there are many people who live on this organizing level and who can function very well in the corporate world, even at very high levels. When you don't have to worry about object relations, you can accomplish a lot in business and corporate life. [Group laughs.]

Carolyn: Not much stands in your way!

Heather: She's the type who cannot go to bed unless every pillow downstairs is put in the proper place. And if you change this pillow and put it over here, wow! She cannot even go to bed unless everything's exactly in order. She's a true compulsive [sarcastic tone in her voice].

Larry: You seem angry with her.

Heather: I don't believe I'm angry with her.

Larry: Just a little?

Heather: Do you think I'm angry with her?

Larry: You're making fun of her with the pillows and the perfectionism.

Heather: I think it's ridiculous.

Linda: Yes. But are you able to be empathic with her extreme need for rituals and perfectionism? What is all of that for her?

Heather: It seems like I'm able to be very empathic with her because in session I seem to be able to say exactly what she needs to hear to calm her down. "You're right, Heather. That's exactly how it is." I seem to be able to understand her in that way.

Larry: Or at least to give the words she wants to hear. But you're also exasperated with her because you go over and over important things and she doesn't seem to get them. Nothing takes . . .

Heather: Nothing changes . . .

Linda: The milk seems to go in but it leaks out somewhere! She doesn't spit it up but she doesn't take it in either.

Heather: Yes, she may, at that particular moment, feel understood. And then she wants her husband or her kids to understand her in that way and to respond accordingly!

Linda: Can she feel any understanding of herself?

Heather: No. Not at all.

Larry: I think you're exasperated in your relationship with her because she's unable to take anything from you.

Heather: That sounds like more where I'm at.

Larry: She doesn't know how to feed. She cannot keep her mouth around the nipple to take anything in that would give her nourishment. I think you're exasperated because she just keeps coming and ventilating but she can't take anything in you have to offer. The countertransference may remind you of your experience with your own mother in infancy who just wouldn't respond in a way that assured you that you were alive and well.

Heather: I think so. I don't feel that

we're any further along than we were when we started.

Larry: That's the exasperation.

Bill: What else about her compulsions and rituals?

Heather: She's very much aware that if things are not ABC, she cannot function. She has three or four different plans. We have plan A. If something goes wrong, we have ready plan B, plan C, and plan D. So one of those plans is going to work. She has a perfect way of getting to work and if there is, for whatever reason, some obstacle, she has alternative route B, to get to work, and route C. It's very specific and planned, a lot of energy goes into it.

Larry: Her mind is involved in external forms and rituals but she hasn't developed an internal life to guide her.

Carolyn: It doesn't have spontaneity.

Heather: I got tired of listening to all her preparation for Christmas celebration.

Larry: These people always love Christmas because there are so many things to do. And it's so clear what you're supposed to do.

Steve: How are you thinking about the countertransference?

Larry: The countertransference is basically helplessness and exasperation. That's because there is no linking, because there are no interpersonal connections. There is no way at present that Heather can offer anything to this woman. Or that this woman can take something in and process it and then give something back to Heather. So it has the same quality that parents feel so often in the first couple of months of life with their baby. Like the parents of an infant, Heather is getting fatigued and when her ministrations don't work she becomes exasperated with the colicky baby. There may also be a countertransference fear of how it will be for Heather if her client finally does succeed in directing her full instinctual energy toward Heather. If a transference psychosis can be established what might it look like? We hear her rantings and irrational expectations and rage at home. Is Heather ready to draw all of that energy toward herself in the transference?

Heather: The only thing she gives back to me is, at that particular moment in the session when she smiles and says, "That's exactly how I feel."

Larry: So she can be a good baby. And when she's with you, most of the time she smiles at you! She's a pleasant baby!

Heather: The pleasant attention is there much of the time.

Mariana: She says, "Yes, you're guessing right. This is right. You're attuned to me." But are you? Is she really feeling understood or is she simply relieved that she can speak with someone about her concerns without having to actually interact with them?

Heather: Yes. I think you're right. Her pleasure is only for that moment. But that's the beginning and the end of it. Nothing takes, nothing sticks.

Larry: I'm going to venture a speculation that at the very moments in which she's busy saying, "That's exactly right," and smiling so pleasantly, that she's taking leave of you. There

might have been a brief flash of connection, but she's off and running away with a smile. Or she may have only sensed the threat of connection and knows how to forestall it with an agreeable smile. I'm speculating that the contact is broken at that moment when it most seems like she is present.

Steve: Is contact intolerable?

Larry: Yes. She had a crazy mother. And the way she could avoid further traumatic or overstimulating contact was to smile contentedly and hope to be left alone. This is the flip side of raging because every detail isn't just right. But when she says, "Oh, that's just right." The smile throws everybody off—it appears like a connection but I'm guessing it's a flight from contact. I'm always amazed at the skill and ingenuity people use to "pass" as normal, or to create the impression that relating is occurring when in fact the person is in flight. These people have been fleeing connections since infancy and have established skillful and deceptive ways of creating an illusion that they are interacting when they're not. It's very sophisticated mimicry.

Steve: There may be a feeling if she stays connected?

Larry: Perhaps. But the problem for her is much greater than simply avoiding a feeling. Let me step back two or three steps and show you where I'm going with all of this. When we talk about this organizing level of psychic development there's a crucial event we always want to watch—the moment in which the person seeks and finds a connection, and the following instant in which that connection is, through some means or another, ruptured, let go of, or broken off. The reason this contact moment is so critical is because connection holds out the possibility not only for nurturance but for relationship that can promote growth of all kinds. A satisfying connection leads the way toward the mutual cuing processes that permit bonding and symbiotic psychic structuring that make a person feel alive, worthwhile, and human.

When I was writing "The Organizing Personality" chapter for *Listening Perspectives* I asked a group of people working with organizing personalities to meet one year for a brainstorming seminar. What to me was a very important day came when we had been studying one particular woman for a long time. The session being reported began with the client asking for "a treatment," which meant acupressure, a technique she knew her therapist had studied and used in a few previous sessions at the client's request. The therapist, however, had been backing off from any physical contact with the client because she felt it was overstimulating and confusing to this very chaotic woman. The therapist had carefully explained her concerns to the client on several occasions. This particular therapist was especially good at connecting to symbiotically organized people. As our study group listened to the notes of the session we heard this very empathic therapist speak empathically about her concern that "a treatment" might not be the best thing today. We heard a skillfully managed empathic connection take place. We then heard that at that moment the heavens opened up with glorious angels singing from the throne of God. And there were great golden clouds billowing up, filling the heavens with light. God's jeweled sword lowered onto the therapist's head signifying that this indeed was the perfect therapist for this client.

Mariana: A blissful kind of a moment with two people feeling a warm and beautiful connection.

Larry: Seemingly so. But Dolly Platt showed us quickly that at that moment of potential or seemingly wonderful connection, the woman had in fact broken contact through a hallucinatory event. Linda Reed, the therapist, had succeeded in making contact with her client by demonstrating her caring in not being willing to touch her unless it would be usable touch. It was an intolerable contact for her client and the hallucination signaled the breaking of it. This woman actively hallucinated a lot. She refused to take medication. She loved her hallucinations and moved in an esoteric religious community where she could use them freely in order not to be in realistic contact with anyone. Therapists treating multiple personalities report this contact rupturing all the time. Just when an empathic connection is made between the therapist and client, the personality switches in a tempting sidetrack to avoid the transferentially based internal trauma that must be relived when meaningful emotional connections are made.

I'm thinking that being this conforming, placid baby is your client's way of not having the contact. It's a way of, what is it that they say in England, of "fobbing you off"? Of giving you something to make you go away. If she smiles and gives you "wonderful, wonderful," that makes you happy and gets you off her case to connect. What better way to derail a schizophrenic mother who bugs you until she can be comforted by your smile? She doesn't have to deal with you anymore then.

Heather: Then she comes at me with, "Heather, I need help! Please help me!"

Larry: Do you feel she's connected in that moment?

Heather: For a second, perhaps.

Larry: I think the helpless ploy is another way to set you floundering so you don't have to have a meaningful interaction. She can only function on the basis of sophisticated mimicry or complex ritual—sequences, plan A, plan B, plan C, clean house, neat pillows, and so forth. It's the external ritual, the house, the job, the Xanax, all these external trappings that hold the mind. We know that evocative memory only develops through object relations. Most less-developed people don't have evocative memory in the beginning phases of treatment. They can't remember what their therapist's face looks like from week to week. They can't remember what the therapist said or what her voice sounds like. As object relations move forward, the complexities of human memory can be organized around relatedness. It's not unusual for such people to have few or no effective memories of childhood because the relationships that organize human memory are lacking. Cumulative strain trauma in infancy leaves its imprint that can be remem-

bered in such things as frenzy, chaos, and massive anxiety that the person is desperate to control. When the person later attempts to get to the bottom of what went wrong, the early strain trauma can only be remembered and studied as transference re-creations—here her frenzy, her tension-relieving smile, and her pleading for help that she cannot make use of.

Heather: I have that sense about her from the little that she's been able to give me by way of a cut-and-dried narrative of the past. It didn't seem to belong to her.

Larry: As therapy proceeds, people can begin to remember what you sound like, remember some of the things you've said, and remember what you look like between sessions. It often takes three or more years to begin establishing the object relations wherein memory can develop, which organizes the mind and permits internal structure and further growth through connection. This woman doesn't have any of that. Everything is body memory and ritual. She's bound to be a fantastic worker because so much of corporate life is based upon reliance on form and the performance of a ritual. [Group laughter]

Bill: You really have to do the thinking for your baby!

Larry: But people stuck with organizing level blockages break the interpersonal connection before the thoughts can be taken back in, before the sensation can be perceived by the mother/other, digested, and recycled in terms of response.

Wilfred Bion, a British psychoanalyst, spent a lifetime considering the question, "How is it that one monkey thinks and none of the others do?" His theoretical answer is complex. His formulations utilize a metaphor of "the container and the contained." This metaphor is highly abstract and does not simply refer to a mother holding a baby. Bion reasons that when an infant is born into the world, it is capable of having sensations, which he calls "beta elements." The question is, how do those sensations begin to get organized into thought? With your client they're organized in terms of sequencing, ritual, timing, and the other elements of perfection. A human infant can be lifted from the primate level of ritual and mimicry. A human baby has sensations and the mother, as you just said, does the thinking. She thinks about what those sensations and their visible manifestation might mean. Based on her thoughts she does various things, she shifts the environment in such a way that the infant's states change. By processes of classical conditioning, sensations become associated with movements that serve communication. Mother first participates in some thought process, does something of intelligence to alter the sensation state. Before too long the child begins to show an understanding of the cause and effect of that cycle as he or she associates more complex elements with it. That is, the child begins linking sensations with maternal activities that result in an alteration of states.

Bollas (1979) carries the idea a step further when he says that the first way the child knows mother is as the trans-formational other. Grotstein speaks of the earliest mother as the background selfobject. States are transformed, and that is the first experience of mother. We don't have any sense that this woman is able to make use of external thought to transform her body states. The exasperation you're feeling is that she has not been able to relate to you in such a way that when she says, "Heather, now what should I do?," you're able to maneuver the world in any way so that she is able to experience a transformation. It's as though she has the sensations. She says, "Help, help!" and she looks to you. You say, "Well, how about ABC?" At that point, rather than being able to take in and utilize what you have to offer that might transform her, she says "Yes, yes, wonderful, wonderful." I'm betting as you study this sequence more closely you will find that this is how she blocks the contact, thereby foreclosing the possibility of receiving anything that could offer a transformation.

Heather: Let me give you another element. I'm realizing she spends the whole session telling me how terrible things are. Along the way I say, or make a comment, "No wonder," or something like that. For an instant there is a flash of connection but she goes immediately to tell me some more of how terrible things are. Then I make a quick empathic comment like, "Of course you hate your children . . ." Again an instant of connection and she's off again to something else. Finally, toward the end of the session, and she's very prompt with ending the session of course, she looks at the clock and it's three minutes before the session is over. Then comes the "Help me, what should I do?" At that moment it's like, "What am I?" But I think that's where I'm failing her because at that moment I'm supposed to come in and say, "OK, do ABCD . . ." But of course I don't have the time, and at such a moment I don't have the plan either.

Larry: Exactly. The plea is delivered so as to make connection impossible, and perhaps to leave you in a state of self-doubt. If there is a thread of symbiotic connecting here it's probably in this. I think your focus needs to be on where in the hour there is a moment of connection you can capitalize on and sustain so as to hold her a bit longer in relation to yourself. There are two questions to ask yourself. One, how is it that she may let you contact her? And two, how is it that she fends off the contact once achieved?

Heather: Possibly she's more available when she's telling me how terrible things are for her, how people are horrible to her, or how her circumstances are awful.

Larry: "I have hunger in my life."

Heather: And I can acknowledge that I've heard her hurt and hunger.

Steve: Wait a minute. What's the transference here?

Larry: The one element that is transference, that is internalized as early object relatedness, is the way contact is broken off. That maneuver is a memory—a memory of how she had to fend her mother's intrusions off. Or of how her mother fended off her attempts to have her needs met very early on.

Heather: Her biggest complaint is that her husband doesn't empathize. When she comes to him and says, "Look what the children have done. They ruined my sofa." He replies, "Ah, children are children, don't concern yourself with it."

Larry: He can tolerate craziness but has no way to be in contact with it.

Heather: And she goes into a frenzy, he doesn't.

Larry: He's fine, he's got a good symbiosis going. (Group laughs.)

Heather: It drives her crazy.

Mariana: But to go back to that train of thought where she's complaining, "I'm hungry" and you say, "Of course you're hungry, I can understand that."

Heather: "You haven't eaten for three days, no wonder you're hungry."

Larry: At that moment she's got her mouth open, and there's a breast ready, but she turns away.

Heather: "Let me tell you, I am also tired."

Linda: "I'm also needy."

Heather: "What will I do? You've got to help me."

Larry: I believe that instant is the instant to capitalize on. That one instant contains the organizing transference. I think the critical element is the way in which she turns away from the nipple. If you can begin in any way, shape, or form, to point to that moment. "Stop just a minute. I think just a moment ago you were telling me this, this, and this, and you were needing something from me. I told you I understood it. But I think it's difficult for you to just let us be together and to appreciate that understanding, to enjoy our being together. Because immediately you turned to something else. Do you have any understanding of why it's hard for us to remain together and in contact?" Now, she won't be able to give you anything at first. At the present time you just want to begin marking the key event. Noting that she turns away and wondering what there may be to understand about her action. As you begin to notice it more, you will notice certain styles or certain patterns that characterize her approach and her manner of rupturing contact once attained.

Often I find that the mode of rupture is already implicit in the way the person makes an approach. That is, it's not infrequent that the very manner of approaching for contact contains the anticipated or required rupture before the other person even has time to flinch. One man persisted in telling me he was sure that I would not be able to believe what he had to tell me. As he related one bizarre fantasy and happening after another he could be certain that any person in his right mind would immediately declare him crazy. Or at least raise some skepticism about the tall tale. I drove him crazy by refusing the bait, by asking why it mattered that his mother didn't see the alien saucer and the iridescent blue light and called him crazy. I wanted to know what it mattered what she or anybody else thought. It was his experience, wasn't that good enough? He knew beforehand that the stories he was telling me would cause me to shut him out by calling or thinking him crazy.

Your patient will catch on to the contact moment very quickly after you point it out a few times. After a while she will begin noting it too. I have written about a woman who actually turned her back when her therapist was able to make an empathic, connecting comment.

Heather: Now I know why she comes back again and again.

Larry: She wants to be fed.

Heather: Yes, but she doesn't turn away at that moment physically. It's more like this, she's demonstrative, she comes forward.

Larry: And she says, "Yes, yes, wonderful, wonderful."

Heather: "Now, let me tell you other things."

Larry: I think that's her way of not taking in what you just spoke to her about, and of not making use of the potential contact that was just there. If, as I believe, there is a transference moment here, then we have the hope of studying some aspect of remembered early relatedness, which is retained in her personality functioning. I know at these lower levels it seems strange to call it transference, because what is internally structured in psyche is of such a very different nature than what we have been accustomed to thinking of as neurotic or narcissistic transference. But there is an internalized pattern that prevents contact which would otherwise lead toward emotional bonding, toward symbiosis. This is her way of not letting the milk come in. She brightens up and says, "What a wonderful mother you are. I'm so glad I'm here." Meanwhile she has surreptitiously spit out the milk or at least she certainly hasn't taken it in. That's the moment when you say, "I so appreciate the kind thing you just said to me, it was so nice. But I have the sense that you moved so quickly away from that, that you were unable to enjoy that we had a moment of contact together about how much you hate your children."

Heather: That's her whole life-style. She goes from one thing, to the next, to the next, never really processing anything.

Larry: Nothing is digested. Let me see if I can say this another way. We know about oedipal transferences, and how they form. We know about the selfobject, narcissistic transferences. We can talk about borderline or symbiotic transferences in which the replication of the scenario, the replication of the bonding pattern must be lived out somehow in the transference relationship and then finally confronted in the therapeutic situation. At this organizing level the sole event that contains an internalization that provides us with a transformational lever is the movement toward the contact followed by the movement to break or prevent that contact. Those movements repeat early object relations. Frances Tustin turned me on to this. In her beautiful clinical work with autistic children she listens to the content and expressions, but she also listens for a representation of the contact mode and moment. She listens to content only because those are the child's metaphors and she wants to be able to be in tune with them so as to focus on the point at which "you wish the nipple were a part of your mouth. And because it isn't, you have to pull back."

That's the interpretation for your patient.

Heather: Because if she enjoys the nipple, then something will happen in the transference experience that will be traumatic somehow. Better not to connect.

Larry: We have to find a way of getting her to elaborate, to represent somehow what she fears will happen. The only way I know to promote this is to slow things down when the contact moment is hot.

Steve: I was thinking this patient is totally narcissistic. It goes way, way back.

Larry: Yes, she's narcissistic in the earliest Freudian sense of psychotic, primary narcissism. But not the Kohut or Kernberg sense of later or secondary narcissism involving the formation of an organized grandiose self. Rather, this has been referred to as primary narcissism where the world and I are the same, or ought to be—infantile omnipotence Winnicott calls it. It frustrates her to have to deal with an imperfect world that is not herself, not under her control.

Heather: What about the rituals?

Larry: Autistic children live their lives on the basis of rituals. I'm concluding that if she stops her perfectionistic rituals, she may find herself regressing and maybe needing hospitalization containment.

Steve: So she's holding herself in some ways, but there isn't an object relations pattern that sustains her.

Larry: That's right. Her life is based on mimicry, on ritual. All primates live on the basis of mimicry and ritual. And she has superior intellectual potential so she can function in the human world very well. But she will be the first to tell you that she doesn't feel human. I recently read Carlos Castaneda's latest book, *The Power of Silence*. He defines what he calls "silent knowledge," reflexive animal knowledge, without reflective thought. There's knowledgeable awareness of the world, a fine-tuned awareness. Humans have lost the knack of living on the basis of silent knowledge because they are given to reflective thought, which interferes with silent knowledge. As a result, Castaneda maintains, human beings are warped, contorted, distorted, and crippled in contrast to other animals that simply know. They are instantly and exquisitely responsive to everything around them, because their minds exist in relation to the environment, not in relation to an internalized thought system they have taken into their heads. According to this view, the function of animal gray matter is to keep them at all times knowing, to maintain heightened awareness of everything around them—silent knowledge. He says human beings create clamorous knowledge, reflective thought knowledge that gets in the way of living in the world.

This woman lives closer to silent knowledge. Her words tell us little about her. In some sense you might be better off if you never listened to what she says because she is not connected with her words in the way most of us are. But in another sense we can expect her content to point toward or represent idiosyncratically her being in the world. Human beings do develop an internalized system based upon reflections from human culture,

and the linguistic system. Human psyche arises on the basis of our collective reflective processes, which this woman has not learned to access. I have the impression that the vast majority of people since the beginning of time and still throughout much of the world today live on the basis of a primate colony symbiosis. Most people in the world today live in symbiotic cultures, reactive to their elders and perpetuating age-old cultural-relatedness patterns.

In Western civilization a few hundred years ago, the idea of "self" began to take hold. The notion of a self has been present in the educated and ruling classes since antiquity. But the idea that every man, woman, and child can have a self is a product of the French Revolution. Or perhaps it would be more accurate to say that the French Revolution was the product of humankind's growing belief that people have "selves." The self is a cultural convention. I often liken the agreement about everyone having a self to the chess move of castling, a convention that adds interest and complexity to the game of life. We may think in terms of independent selves, but many people we meet in our clinical practices, like the majority of people living in the world today, do not experience a self. I was surprised when learning Portuguese for a trip to Brazil that this modern language does not even have a word for self other than soul. So your patient, competent as she is to live in the world, has not yet entered the realm of human relatedness.

Heather: It's even hard for me to convince her to come for regular sessions, to show her that continuity is important in our relationship—or for that matter to get her to acknowledge in more than an intellectual way that we even have a relationship!

Larry: You don't need to work so hard. If you are simply there and watch for moments when you can reflect back to her how much she wants to relate to you and how impossible that seems to her—that's enough.

Heather: Yes, but what's the "treatment plan?" [Group laughs.]

Larry: You can't do "therapy" yet— she's essentially an infant who needs to be seduced, attracted into interpersonal relating. She's not there yet. You have to make friends first, to learn to be together comfortably.

Carolyn: My managed care coordinator would say, "Now, what's your treatment plan, lady?" [Group laughs.]

Larry: It's enough for now for her to begin to flirt with the nipple, to begin just imagining being present and comfortable with a satisfying breast. Maybe from time to time, she'll take a little nip. The more often you can see her, the better. And an hour is probably much too hard for you and for her to endure. Frequent half-hour sessions will do the trick for the time being and some scheduled phone contact can be added later.

Heather: I've begun to find ways to have fun with her.

Larry: More power to you. That's definitely the right way to go with her, but her inability to make use of you is exasperating, I know.

I believe that the therapeutic action here is twofold. First, by studying the methods of approach and avoidance of contact you begin analyzing the psychotic or organizing transference. Second, by continuing to invite her to collaborate with you in noticing and discussing contact moments you are *de facto* sustaining useful contact for longer than she is accustomed. It is these moments of being together and establishing a dialogue, a dance, an emotional interaction that leads into the establishment of the therapeutic symbiosis that Searles (1979) speaks about.

With presymbiotic personality organization the treatment plan calls for finding some way to establish a symbiotic relationship with the therapist that can later be differentiated and separated from. The mother of the psychotic transference, which must be analyzed, will not make a clear appearance until you are able to achieve some reliable sense of contact or movement toward it. On the one hand the therapeutic symbiosis is the leading edge of her psychic development. All humans, as Kafka teaches us, are always searching for contact, yearning for symbiotic ties. But on the other hand, the psychoanalytic task is to bring to light and dismantle whatever internal structures persistently crop up to prevent a complete bonding dance. I say, "Hang in there, Heather." She clearly wants to relate and has the intellectual, social, and financial resources required to stay in therapy long enough to analyze the psychotic structure and begin building a new world based on object relations.

Heather: Thanks. This clarifies where I'm going with her.

6

A Fear of Amputees

Michelle had been seeing her therapist Cecilia twice weekly for a number of months because she was phobic about amputees. Whenever she left the house she would somehow manage to run into people who were missing limbs so that she had become reluctant to leave home. Her parents had both died several years before, leaving her a modest inheritance. She had held a steady job in a business firm for many years, but since her parents died she has been living off the inheritance. She supports a man who is not as successful as she, whom she married seven years ago. Michelle had a sum of cash in the bank from her inheritance with which he has opened a small franchise business.

Cecilia had to commute a distance to arrive at her office in time to see Michelle and was a few minutes late on several occasions. One day it was raining heavily and the therapist was later than usual. Michelle had almost given up on her and was leaving as Cecilia arrived. Michelle reproached Cecilia for not being responsible on her job and told her how responsible she herself is. Michelle called later to cancel all further appointments. Cecilia spoke of Michelle to the case conference group she belongs to and was encouraged by group members to make every possible effort to bring this very shy and phobic woman back into therapy. After a number of calls and notes Michelle agreed to see Cecilia, but seemed distant and was not willing to resume her twice-weekly schedule. Her verbalizations seemed sparse, impoverished, and superficial to the group, and were seen as possibly a testimony to how extensive the phobic qualities in her personality were. With her therapy restored, suddenly things got better for her. She became intrigued with the therapy process and resumed her twice-weekly appointments. Several weeks later the following conference occurred.

THE EMERGENCE OF AUTISTIC THEMES

Cecilia: I now see Michelle on Tuesdays and Thursdays for an hour each time and I'm happy about it. We're making some headway into her phobia because it was her request that I help her deal with her fear of amputees. She wants to get rid of it, especially because she's going on a trip with her daughter to Pennsylvania. Just the two of them are going, so there is no other adult she can hide behind or who can save her when she gets anxious in case she sees an amputee. The threat of seeing one is always there.

When she first started, it was hard to even talk about amputees. Her fear was absolutely overwhelming. But recently she was able to stand on the balcony and look down on one. She was happy about that so I complimented her. [Reading from process notes] Michelle says, "Yes but *they* didn't really see me. I can see them from the balcony but they didn't see me." She is afraid that they can see her as well. Michelle continued, "I'm not eating, I've lost my appetite. I no longer care if I don't eat ice cream." So we talk about some eating factors. She pursued her request, "How can you get me over my phobia? I can't have it. I want it gone." I said, "Tell me more about what happens to you with this fear. What is it? "When I see an amputee I think that I'm them." I said, "Oh really? What part of you is cut off?" "My mind is cut off." "Who cut it off?" She said, "It was my father, men." "Well what happened? How did he cut it off? How old were you?" "I was real young, maybe four." "Can you tell me more about it?" She had a mask-like

expression and said flatly, "It's hopeless. I'm hopeless." I asked, "How does it feel?" She looked at me, "My mind is cut off."

From the stiffness present I could tell she was daring to say something to me that she had never before expressed to anyone and could not verbalize in a feeling state. I asked, "What have you experienced?" Then she was able to continue. "Well, I've never been able to think anything through." As she said that I was really taken aback because she changed and spoke as if reciting an intricately detailed, well-memorized piece of material. I was too shocked by her style to write it all down. She claims she has never been able to think anything through like other people can and yet, in telling this, she has obviously thought it through. It was fascinating!

Larry: So there was a brief opening where you two were connected and then she broke it off quickly with a recital. What happened next?

Cecilia: She said, "I feel like they're out after me." I said, "That's a good thought, we need to develop that, I want to know more about it. It's very important to me." She took a deep breath and said, "You know I haven't done things, I haven't done things like other people. I'm afraid." Then she referred back to what we had previously discussed about connecting and she said, "I'm afraid to connect. I don't know how. I'm scared I might die. If I depend on someone, they're gone." I said, "What about me? Do you think if you depend on me that I'll be gone?" She said, "Yes." She was very upset about this. This was not a light issue at all. So I reassured her that I would do my best to be there for her. Then I reminded her, "I've told you about my study group. These people know of you and if anything ever did happen to me, you could call them and they would be able to help you." That was a tremendous relief for her. Tremendous relief. She started smiling. She really liked this idea.

Larry: So there's safety in her knowing about us?

Cecilia: Yes. I assured her, "There are several people there and any one of them could help you continue."

Bonnie: You told her that you had connections.

Cecilia: Yes.

Bonnie: She knows she can't make connections but you have them so she feels safe. That's really interesting.

Cecilia: If anything happens to me she'll be all right. However, later on she worried that if she connects to me, something is going to happen to her.

Larry: Yes, ordinarily that's what you would expect to hear, "If I connect with you I will dissolve. *I* won't be here anymore."

Cecilia: But here she's also saying, "If I connect with you, *you* won't be there. It's very frighting to her. I think the fear was holding her back from being freer with me. It was not long ago after she first found out that the group was here that she was very up and intrigued by the idea of therapy. I had asked her permission to discuss her here. That was when she resumed biweekly sessions. It was a little safer.

Larry: When she found out that there were others, substitute Cecilias,

she felt safe enough to resume her regular sessions?

Cecilia: That's right.

Larry: Recall the Frances Tustin videotape (1985) we watched together, in which she addresses some of these issues with her autistic children. She made the point that some people had interpreted her earlier writings as saying that autistic children had no objects. She makes clear that she never said that. Rather, she formulates that in a satisfactory intrauterine experience the child has no need to distinguish between his or her body and that of the mother. Following birth the mother's attentive, soothing efforts attempt to bridge the gap, to make good the loss of the uterine environment. If the mother is unavailable or depressed, she is not able to make a satisfactory bridge through body sensuousness and the infant is precociously forced to deal with the problem of the separateness of mother's body. Children who become autistic remain concretely connected to mother's body and are unable to make the connection to mother's psychological presence. If mother's body disappears it is part of the child that becomes lost.

Later, Tustin believes, this loss is represented by autistic children as the "black hole" where mother once was but is no more. Children are afraid of falling into the black hole of relatedness because of the pain of finding the other unreliable or traumatizing in some way. Instead, they become preoccupied with manipulating the more controllable sensorium. Autosensuous objects are used to produce autosensuous shapes on the sensory receptors, which can be controlled—since the comings and goings of the maternal body and her psychological presence cannot. They are afraid of connecting with a needed presence over which there is no control. So when it comes to caregivers they are often more or less interchangeable because there is essentially little or no personal connection to one special mother.

I thought for Michelle the problem might be that she is terrified that if she does connect with you, she will experience you as a part of her body—a part that can disappear against her will and leave her a mental amputee again. Just when she was beginning to feel comfortable with the regular rhythm of her sessions, you turned up late on several occasions. This had the effect of reminding her that the real Cecilia is not a part of or a function of her body or mind but an external person who has a separate and uncontrollable existence. Just as she was beginning to experience her need for you, her connection to you, we see the appearance of the organizing transference to the over- or understimulating, psychotic mother. According to this way of thinking, your lateness permitted the emergence of transference to the maternal body, which was unreliable and frighteningly not under her control.

I thought when you told her about your consultation group she heard you saying, "Don't worry, if the real Cecilia, who is separate and unreliable, fails you, if something happens to her, there are substitute Cecilias," substitutes for the sense of safety that she feels in the presence of continuity of

experience—metaphorically, of the reliable maternal body. "Don't worry, my friends know about you and will make certain that you don't lose the part of me that you need to keep as a part of your personal and ongoing sense of continuity and safety."

According to this way of thinking, when you weren't there for your appointment exactly on time, when she desired you, she had to deal with your reality as a separate person—the reality that you have a separate life, that something else, some preoccupation in your life made you late. That you are not a part of her. At that point she became terrified because she could not tolerate relating to you as a separate and therefore, in her mind, uncontrollable, person. In her work with you it seems that she needs to reexperience that point in her early life when she and the maternal body were united, very early on and perhaps even *in utero*. As you two work with the transferential unreliable maternal body, you will be *de facto* helping her bridge to more psychological relating, to learn to sustain contact with a separate psychological being who comes and goes but remains psychologically connected and nurturing. It seems she can only relate to you now as a longed-for but potentially failing maternal body.

Cecilia: She wants us to absorb into each other then?

Larry: Yes, and you reassured her, "Don't worry the maternal body will not go away. I have friends who will not fail you if I disappear." It will be interesting to see if this formulation holds up for her. There is not a sense that, "I have a special irreplaceable mother," but rather that the maternal functions can be readily replaced.

Mike: In other words, she lives in Melanie Klein's "paranoid-schizoid position." What she will be doing when she separates is moving to the "depressive position."

Larry: According to Klein, the depressive position begins by the third or fourth month of life when mother's body is clearly recognized as separate from my body and not subject to my control.

Howard: That's the source of bodily separateness?

Larry: Yes. But don't confuse physical separateness with the sense of psychological separateness, which occurs much later, after the symbiotic relationship has formed and is being relinquished. Michelle's version of the paranoid-schizoid position is based on fear. She is afraid of losing you as a part of her body, the mind or thinking part, represented by her phobia of amputees. Only much later can she fear loss of you as a significant person that she values who has her own mind. When Michelle worries that if she connects to you, you won't be there, what can she be telling you? Possibly that for her as soon as there is the hope of continuity it disappears, dissolves, is cut off. We can't be certain yet.

At this point we might consider the advantages of the Listening Perspective approach for being tuned in to this woman as opposed to many traditional objectivist theoretical approaches. The theories of Melanie Klein, for example, are fascinating and lead us to look for "things," things I like to call "mythical beasts," like the paranoid-schizoid position, projective identifications, bad objects, and so forth.

Mike: I can study and understand her positions and mechanisms as ideas. But it's hard for me to tap into them and to deal with them while I'm in the consulting room actually working with someone. I sit there asking myself, "How do I get the paranoid-schizoid position out into the open today and try turning it into the depressive?" Meanwhile, I have to keep talking, interacting, scrutinizing fifty transactions for the paranoid, the schizoid, and the depressive and try to figure out what to do with them.

Larry: To my way of thinking, Klein's contribution was not so much in naming mythical beasts that roam our rooms, but in describing positions or postures that we as humans once experienced in infancy and still continue to live out in various ways in our daily lives. For me, these are not best viewed as pathological positions or maneuvers, but as aspects of human nature that are troubling when in later life they continue to be lived out consistently or in the extreme. To my way of thinking, it's not like there is anything to change or to be cured, but much to be understood, to be represented in words, pictures, emotions. body states, and interactions.

When we follow the model for Newtonian science with a medical coloring, we tend to look for real things like splitting, the hysteric, or the paranoid position. Traditional scientific thinking is based on the belief that there is a more-or-less fixed reality out there that we can know about, define, and manipulate. But the more mythical beasts we create in the scientific, objectivist mode, and the more laws governing them we invent, the further we are from the experience of the consulting room. It is easy for us to get caught up in archaic "scientific" thought modes instead of permitting ourselves the enlightenment that relativity, operationism, the quantum principle of uncertainty, and the chaos universality principle offer us. "Thing" concepts categorizing people and their "mechanisms" are not only far from human experience but they lead us into unrealistic thought modes. Traditional scientific thought can now be seen as its own kind of almost group-supported psychosis—it has sought to define delusional realities, that is, to see things that are not necessarily there. Quantum physics makes clear the elusive nature of the infinitely complex and contradictory realities that surround us.

Our concepts need to be ones that help us sit in our consulting room chairs and continue to be intrigued by the narrative, the story, the images, the mythical themes that emerge to represent the personal truths of the person with us. Our theoretical concepts need to help us attend to the narrational engagement, as though we two are on a journey together experiencing life and each other in an ongoing and progressively richer saga. Our concepts need to be able to help us deal imaginatively with what comes up for each of us as we go along.

With people who are living ad-vanced oedipal (or neurotic) relatedness patterns, their life is already embedded in the cultural mythology, in the flow of the Logos, the demands of the linguistic and cultural system. But with people who live preoedipal relatedness modes their personal embeddedness in cultural mythology is idiosyncratically limited. Each person has his or her own personal idiomatic narration and modes of interpersonal experiencing that are unique and not fully embedded within culturally determined forms or mythologies.

Our task is to be with each person who comes to our consulting room in such a way that their main relatedness habits, their private and personal narrational interactions and somatic states, can be mirrored back to them in representations that serve to give them additional degrees of freedom from the original relating patterns learned in infancy and early childhood. Only with oedipal relatedness (metaphorically derived from the 4- to 7-year-old age period) can this be effectively done in words and culturally derived symbols. The narcissistic (3-year-old) mode requires living out overlearned patterns of finding self to selfother resonance that Kohut taught us to discern as selfobject transferences. With symbiotic (4- to 24-month-old) modes of self and other emotional engagement, listening entails waiting until the interactions or scenarios established during the early bonding period reemerge in replicated forms in the therapeutic relationship so that they can be confronted and relinquished.

When the focus is on basic orienting or organizing patterns (modes established in the months immediately preceding and following birth), as seems to be the case with Michelle, we listen for the person's way of moving toward connecting with us and then how they regularly achieve a rupture or disconnect. That is, we listen for ways of observing and interpreting the disconnect mode, the appearance of the under- or overstimulating mother transference that forces a break, a breach that forecloses emotional bonding possibilities as it appears to have done with Michelle.

The content or reflexive material of Michelle's sessions is of little importance to us except for maintaining empathy. Cecilia tells us Michelle's story was like a rehearsed recital, a story developed to account for what she feels is wrong with her. But, as you saw, not only was the story unconvincing, but her clicking into recital mode assured her that there would be no sustained personal engagement or connection with Cecilia. This kind of work is often hard on our narcissism! We like to believe we are being personally responded to and specifically valued for how wonderful we are. But when the organizing relatedness level is active we might as well be machines, robots, or the forces of nature or fate. Michelle is reassured by the idea that you are replaceable. Remember our reading last year Searles's *The Nonhuman Environment* (1960)? Well, though Michelle somehow knows how to recognize you, at this point it is the function you serve that is important

and if one of us could perform that same safety producing, soothing function as well, bye, bye Cecilia! [Group laughs.]

Cecilia: Shall I continue with the hour? Michelle explains, "I don't have family; they're gone; they're all gone. I wasn't a good daughter; I was jealous. I fought with my brother." I said, "What did your mother have to say about that?" "My mom, she didn't care. I never apologized for the way I was. I should have. I might be a street person. My mother said I should have gone. I should have left because I wasn't good. I might have been a street person. I have always had such thoughts. I have a dream that I live in a big underground room with closed curtains and I'm trying to get out of this jumbled, messed up room."

Mike: The dream image is a fantastic one of being encapsulated, feeling closed in, and struggling to get out.

Larry: Frances Tustin talks about two varieties of autistic children. One she calls "encapsulated" where the children live in their own world closed off from interactions with others. These children tend to literally close themselves into small spaces. She distinguishes encapsulated autism from "entangled" or "confusional" autism where the children haven't completely withdrawn from the maternal body, but in various ways are entangled and confused with it. Such children may appear to relate more readily to others in the environment but their relations are not realistic because the inside (self) and the outside (other) are hopelessly and delusionally fused or entangled.

In Michelle's dream there are curtained windows and a jumbled up mess she's trying to escape from. It's as though she has at one time had contact with the outside world because she knows it's out there. There is potential for contact with the outside world, but she has retreated underground and closed the curtains. She knows it's a jumbled-up mess inside. Entangled or confusional autism implies that there is more awareness of and a delusional entanglement with the outside world.

Cecilia: But more than being just a dream, that's pretty much how Michelle lives. There are weeks now when she only leaves her house to come to our sessions. Then she talked about Father. He used to kill chickens, cut off their heads, and then hang the bodies. This occurred, as she remembered, during preschool. She remembered at the end of the session that her godparents raised a lot of chicks.

Larry: Here's another amputation of sorts. And she mentions it following a moment when she was contacting you through talking about her mother saying how bad she was, her fear of being a street person, and her telling dream. In moving to Father and his killing chickens is she cutting off the connection she just established with you or is she furthering it by letting you know why she must hole up underground? "There are dismemberments and killings out there." Are those closed curtains for amputating the world, for amputating the part of her mind that might have connected

to a physically separate mother, to a world of relatedness that could enable her to grow, but instead proved dangerous and amputating? I think that the fear is that you too will become an amputated part if she connects to you. While the memory is dated at about 4 years, and while it is the father (or godfather) chopping off chicken heads, it's probably safe to assume that the dynamics come from a much earlier age. But at age 4 she came to represent in these vivid telescoped or screen memories that somehow her head was also chopped off. At age 4 she already knew something was painfully or frighteningly wrong with her.

Freud speaks of screen memories that condense a whole emotional atmosphere of a period of childhood. Kohut extends Freud's thinking with the notion of a telescoped memory, one that uses images from one developmental period to collapse or telescope similar emotional issues that may span many years. The memory seems to say, "I am frightened by these chickens with their heads cut off hanging around. It makes me realize that there is a force much larger than myself that has the power to cut off important (mind) parts of me." She may have attempted a psychological tie with mother, but it was somehow blocked or cut off. And it appears she holds herself responsible for the cutting off because curtains close from the inside. It's not that there are shutters that somebody has closed or that someone has boarded the room up. Her fear is that she will let you in and then discover you are a separate person. Then the part of her mind that is connected to you is in danger of being cut off, because you have a mind of your own, because your mind is not her mind. Then she will have to close you out like she almost succeeded in doing at the beginning.

Mike: So everything is part-object to her? I mean that's how she sees Cecilia and that's the transference?

Larry: You might say it that way. But "part-object" theoretical language doesn't describe adequately anybody's actual subjective experience. It's abstract and experience-distant. The experience is, "I am bound to experience you as me, your body is part of my body. If I allow this connection to you, you will disappear, and part of me will then disappear with you." The infant has no sense of full differentiation from the uterus. An exception is possibly when there are alien chemical or other noxious factors present. Sometimes we trace the transference experience to the intrauterine environment where the awareness of otherness is prematurely forced upon the fetus by alcohol, drugs, anoxia, nutrient shortage, an Rh factor or something else that traumatizes the fetus. It's the premature forcing into the child's awareness of the mother's separateness that's frightening. If the mother is depressed or unresponsive, or the child for whatever reason is not able to use environmental support, the child is forced prematurely to realize that she has a mind of her own. Michelle's mother was once known but then the curtains were closed, and "part of my mind is cut off, amputated." She fears having to reexperience in transference the trauma of desire being cut off. Her

encapsulation and closed curtains represent her flight from traumatic connections. So we have some explanation for the phobia! This is beautifully illuminating material.

Cecilia: Next time she comes in and says, "Sometimes I wake up screaming. Or when somebody wakes me up, I hit, I strike out, I start yelling out awful things: 'Get the fuck away from me, you bastard.' I didn't know I did that until with my first husband. I told him to wake me up in the middle of the night for sex. And that's how I woke up." She didn't know about the screaming until he told her. She says, "I still do it." "It sounds like you're protecting yourself. Maybe the child is protecting herself." She says, "I didn't know those words as a child." So we explored it but that's all she could give me. There were no further memories around that.

Larry: My interpretation would be that she's following up on things from the previous hour. She's talking about what her reaction is when her autistic state is disturbed by an outsider. Her bodily needs are being taken care of by sleep. And even though she told her husband to wake her up for sex, when the autistic state is disturbed by an outsider there may be tremendous rage. Rage that the other is separate, that the other is not in her autistic capsule, that her capsule is being invaded. Rage at you for being late because at that moment you were not in her autistic capsule and she cuts you off, closes you out, for weeks. She only agrees to see you again when you persist. The rage she is telling you about in the middle of the night I believe is the transference rage at you for your past crimes of being late, and who knows how else you have failed her.

Cecilia: The next session is lighter. She says, "I talked on the phone to my friend." We discussed several of her conversations with friends. I comment, "It looks like you're really trying to connect." "Yes I really want to connect. I have to get rid of this phobia. I'm a bigot." She frequently will berate herself for various kinds of discrimination. She can't understand it, because she was out marching for the blacks in the 1960s, and she is still in many ways a social activist and a hippie.

Larry: She hates amputees also. You might reassure her with, "I understand you think you're a bigot. But I think that when you accuse yourself of being a bigot, you stop looking at your feelings and thereby limit our understanding of what is really behind the amputee theme." I find in working with preoedipal issues, if people berate themselves for being, say, depressed, sick, crazy, or a bigot, then they succeed in avoiding any real consideration of what may be happening. I tend to encourage people not to criticize or judge puzzling things about themselves as the judgment gets in the way of noticing what's going on. If she only attacks herself for being a bigot, saying she's bad and has to change, then she doesn't get a chance to see the full implications of her bigotry. She only repeats her mother's criticism of her. She's closing off her analytic investigation by saying, "This is bad. I've got to change it."

Paradoxically people do their best to close off the possibility of exploring themselves by making contracts to change. Whatever useful happens in psychotherapy doesn't come from mandated or contractual change. It comes from letting a cascade of representations of self and other come out into the open until one's horror is aroused. Then people begin to get a full sense of who they are and what this nightmare is all about. Only then is there a possibility of some sort of transformation. But she amputates herself with judgments before the work of consciousness raising can even begin.

Cecilia: She says, "I want to be free. I haven't left home since I was here last time." Then there's a pause. She spontaneously starts talking about this memory. "When I was about 9, between 9 and 11, I was skating. I was going to skate at the ice pond, at the recreational center. There was a girl with an amputated arm eating." Michelle remembers standing a little above the pond on a snow mound. She started yelling names at this girl. Just real vicious. "The girl was about the same age as me. It looked like the arm had been lost in an accident." She says, "I can tell how an arm is lost by the way it hangs. So I started yelling at her. I was fat and they made fun of me. So she was worse than me. So I felt superior and I was making fun of her."

Larry: I'm thinking about how children do such cruel things to each other or to the handicapped. There's something in us that when we see someone who is handicapped or maimed in some way or another that wants to deny or to attack it. Children often attack defects, usually out of hatred of perceived defects in themselves. In her memory she sees herself standing "above," feeling superior to the girl. She makes clear that she turns the passive trauma of being humiliated into active victory.

One of my child analytic training cases was a 7-year-old boy who used to physically attack me. The way my room was set up the play table had two small chairs at ninety-degree angles that we sat in. He repeatedly wanted to play with Lincoln Logs and would start to build something, instructing me what I was to do. Then he would drop one of the green roof slats on the floor, demanding that I pick it up. As I would reach over to pick it up he would whop me on the side of the neck with one of those green roof slats! I was weary of being hit but I didn't understand what he was doing until my supervisor pointed out that I had a visible scar on my neck where he was hitting me. He was commanding me to expose my vulnerability and then attacking my deformity. He was telling me that other children attack him because they can tell something is wrong with him. So when Michelle screams, or hates, or is bigoted toward minorities, or the handicapped or deformed people, she may be identifying with what's "wrong" with her because she hates the amputation of her mind. Recall that Freud (1900) interpreted racial or minority references in dreams as the downward displacement of hatred that could not be directed upward (to Father) because of fear of retaliation or castration.

Howard: The material is so much richer than it was a while back. How long has it been since you reported on her? About six to eight weeks?

Cecilia: Yes it has. "So the girl yelled back and threatened me. I was afraid." Then she started again berating herself. She carried on for a long time. "I was so ashamed. I can't believe I did such a horrible thing to someone. I was wrong. It has to be one of the worst things I've ever done. It seemed as though she was going to get me." It was after this she began hiding. That day they missed the train going back home because she ran and hid in the bathroom. It was at this point that the fear of amputees became a big part in her life. I said, "You're expressing a lot." She was really crying. "You were expressing a lot of rage that you felt because this girl represented something you hated in yourself. You used her to work out that rage. The fear and rage you have within you, you attached to the amputee." It was about that point that her phobia flared up again.

Larry: It appears that this emotional breakthrough in sharing her shame with you caused her to once again fear that you could be cut off from her. The fear moves her to a displaced, and therefore less real, plane of reality in relation to you, thereby successfully closing you out, the minute she had succeeded in opening her curtains for a moment. Interesting that the two memories—of beheaded chickens and the ice skater with a missing arm—are assigned to age periods we often associate with a flourishing of childhood desire—infantile and adolescent sexuality.

Cecilia: I said, "You need to forgive yourself," and, "I forgive you."

Larry: Sorry, we are out of time. Thanks, Cecilia, we learned a lot today. I hope we hear more about her soon.

Conference: Two Months Later

Cecilia: Michelle has put me in her will! I have no idea what that's about yet!

Bonnie: Oh Lord!

Cecilia: I didn't want to rush in to deflect the connection. She has a number of pieces of real estate. Then she explained that she had fifty thousand dollars in cash but she gave it to her husband. He has bought a small franchise business. The first thing he did was lose his business checkbook in one of the home shopping clubs. Somebody walked by and got his attention, and somebody else came up beside him and took it. She was pretty upset because it's her money and that's all she has. She gave it to him and the first thing he does is to lose it.

Larry: Almost scripted. She opens up to him and her resources disappear, are amputated.

Cecilia: Exactly. He has never done anything in his life. She was filled with doubt about his business capabilities.

Bonnie: How old are they?

Cecilia: Michelle is 40 and he is about 38 or 39. The loss of the checkbook raised doubts and renewed fears of her becoming a homeless street person. Before all of this she was homebound. Joe (her husband) had to do everything for her, shop for groceries, run errands, and so forth. Now she's become more active. He has a supervisor from the franchise corporation

who checks in once in a while to see how things are going. Afterward, Joe and the supervisor come to the house to go over the books together. So in responding to that process she says, "Now I'm acting like a normal person. I don't want him (the supervisor) to see how I really am." She's cooking dinner and cleaning house. She had not done these things for years. Now she's going to the store by herself! The phobia that was so intense prior to this is quite diminished at this point. It looks like it's a very good business for Joe. He is very introverted and up until now he has been a "yes man" in order to live. Her response to that is, "He pisses me off." Because he never stands up to her.

Then there is her relation with Overeaters Anonymous. She's quitting. She's been there a year and a half. She says she doesn't need to be around those crazy people anymore. "Why do I need a sponsor that weighs three hundred pounds? Now that I understand why I'm fat, I'm okay with it." We talked about her fat and her pain about it. As we work on these things she deals with them in her own good time. She used to come in and have this flower-child appearance. Her identification is really with the sixties. She's still very much into social issues. She says she wants to quit OA because it's so self-oriented. Another thing that came up around OA is that she feels she never belongs anywhere even though she has many interactions with members of the group. One of the people had a party and apparently all the group was invited except Michelle. That precipitated her wanting to quit.

Larry: Does she have any understanding why she wasn't invited?

Cecilia: She doesn't. She couldn't understand it because she felt that she was close to the people in the group. But she had a conflict with a man in the group. The man was invited and she wasn't. She felt that she was actually closer to Laurie, the person giving the party, than the man was. She felt very slighted by that and could not understand why Laurie would have done that to her. But it reinforced the business of "I'm so different from everybody else."

Larry: She didn't talk to Laurie?

Cecilia: No, she didn't talk to Laurie. Her solution is to quit OA now and move on.

Larry: Whenever there's a possibility of breaking out of her underground isolation and relating she amputates it. The cutting off of her resources is a well-entrenched internalized pattern.

Cecilia: She wants to work to help the homeless, feed the hungry, or to do something worthwhile. I suggested maybe she join N.O.W. because it has more organization and maybe she could find some avenues there. I thought it could give her more choices and more structure.

The first part of last month she called and left a message on my machine. The message was, "I have been

having dreams. I had one this morning about my father that was so upsetting that even in my dream I called you. I wanted to call you, so remind me to tell you the dream on Tuesday in case I somehow block it out. I'm afraid of blocking because the dream was really upsetting. I think my memories are starting to come back. Bye, see you Tuesday and I do miss you." This was while she was gone on her trip to Pennsylvania with her daughter. I did remind her Tuesday. She said, "As I picked up the phone to call you, I realized that I was aroused. I have been molested and calling you to tell you about it aroused me."

[Cecilia stops reading her notes at this point, takes off her reading glasses and looks troubled. She addresses the group now.] What I'm having trouble with as I'm reading the notes today is that I feel I'm not there for her. I usually do write down what she tells me but I couldn't get myself into the notes. So as I'm reading this, I don't see myself in the notes. Michelle is not saying that. Instead, she's saying that I *am* present, that I'm important to her, that she's having urges to call me, to tell me important things. Funny I should be so blocked. When I go back and read the notes I think, "What did I say then or what could I have said." Those questions are really bothering me. I'm wondering how I can really be there. Maybe I'm not nurturing enough. I'm not there.

Larry: Are you concerned about that when you're with her?

Cecilia: No, afterward. When I'm in it, I seem okay.

Larry: It seems like you're there?

Cecilia: It seems like I'm there. But then when I sit back and read the notes and think about it, am I? Something is going on but I can't tell what it is.

Marilyn: That's very interesting because in fact you are very involved with her, very tuned in to her needs. I wonder if your cutting off your sense of involvement with her is a picture of how she cuts herself off from people, from memories, from her dreams. She now knows in her relationship with you that she is not going to be attacked and cut off. But she relates in a manner that nevertheless serves to cut herself off from you by getting you to not be there. So it sounds like what you're doing is exactly what she needs for transference development.

Larry: It may also signal the beginning of that fourth form of countertransference to organizing experience we talk about—diluting the potential connection out of unconscious empathy. She has been reaching out much more to you lately, letting you into her life. Your distraction may be your awareness of how dangerous connections are for her. She was even aroused when she called you.

Cecilia: I understand. That may be so. We've worked a little on the molest issue. One of the memories she was able to come up with is being in the house with her father. He had been playing with her and she liked it. She remembers thinking that she liked it and wanted more. But they had company at the time. She wanted them to leave so he could do it again.

Marilyn: Play with her sexually?

Cecilia: Yes. Then she somehow communicates this to her father. He humiliates her with, "You want me all to yourself." She thinks she may have been around 10 or 12 at the time.

From there we talked about her current sexuality. She has no sexual feeling at all for her husband. She's been aroused maybe twice in the seven years of marriage. She is very bright and she can express herself well, so that led her to talk about her first husband whom she had married in the sixties.

Mike: She feels aroused when she wanted to reach out to you by phone. But when she's actually in session seemingly engaged with you, you're not there for her emotionally. No one ever was there for her emotionally— except possibly when her father played with her. But she found out he wasn't with her either. When she leaves the session you're feeling like she felt when her dad, whom she enjoyed, left her, that the experience wasn't real, that it was just a fantasy. I think the contrast is interesting; that it seems like you're there with her in the session, but afterward you have doubts about how real the interaction was. I think somehow she has experienced that.

Howard: That's what she described with her OA group. She felt connected with Laurie but when Laurie doesn't invite her to the party she sees the closeness as false and cuts them all off.

Larry: So there's a sense of connection for the moment and then it's gone. The connection later seems unreal. And she is then humiliated for valuing the connection. She reports feeling aroused when she called you from Pennsylvania to tell you she had dreamed and to ask you to remind her about it. Is there something about whatever her connecting arousal is about that causes you to emotionally withdraw. If so, that would fit with what she tells you about wanting to be with her father sexually and his humiliating her for her desire. It also fits with only allowing herself to be sexually aroused with her husband twice in seven years. You are seducing her to reach toward you, to want to connect with you. And when she does it's arousing.

That's the treachery of the organizing transference—the minute there is a connection it is somehow ruptured. From this material we can surmise that the transference delusion is that when I connect others will reject my desire and then humiliate me for it. Does she also accomplish that rejection by being inappropriately aroused in her reaching out? Babies are aroused by mother's nurturing presence—was her arousal and desire not met with mutual enjoyment? It would seem so, based on the screen memory of her father humiliating her for her desire and in the countertransference your emotionally turning off to her after she reached out to you in a state of arousal,

Cecilia: She says, "I don't like to be touched. I'm phony, I'm real phony." Then she says, "I lost four pounds in Pennsylvania. I ate candy." She talks a little bit about her appetite. It's interesting how the appetite weaves into the molest. "My appetite is way down. It's so hard to believe. I never would have believed it. I never could have

thought my father would have done this to me."

Currently her daughter Sonia is leaving home; she's going to live with her father. Sonia is a gifted child and Michelle describes her own father as a genius. There doesn't seem to be concern about Sonia's relationship to her father.

Larry: During this same period that she's feeling closer to you she makes major shifts at home, cleaning and cooking, fixing herself up for meetings with the supervisor, and so forth. But in the same hour she tells you that even when she was feeling close with her OA group and with Laurie, they didn't feel so close to her so she cut them off. You worry that you aren't feeling all that close to her now either. Perhaps you, and perhaps also her group members, are ensnared in a "scenario," a symbiotic relatedness mode. That even as she wants you, you withdraw and so do they. And we could consider on the basis of past interaction the possibility of the scenario being reversed, that is, when you feel connected to her she distances.

The last time you presented her we felt the organizing listening perspective could bring her schizoid and autistic parts into focus. Today we see the potential benefits of using the symbiotic listening perspective, to think in terms of a partial internalized bonding dance being replicated in the transference and countertransference in which one yearns and the other withdraws.

This thread of symbiosis is undoubtedly important. But based on your earlier reports I would tend to listen to the issues she is working on as primarily organizing level rather than symbiotic. Viewed this way, we take her at face value when she says she's not like everybody else. It seems correct when she says that she wants contact with people but doesn't know quite how to achieve it. And what is the potential role of arousal in all of this? We don't yet have much direct mother material, so we have to listen to the father material with an ear to the possibility that it condenses and displaces, as on a screen, a memory of father with a much more important preverbal memory of a seductively traumatizing interaction with mother.

I am speculating that when she was an infant her mother was sufficiently tantalizing to produce arousal in the baby. But then when her yearning for contact with mother was aroused, somehow mother pulled away emotionally. So that in her infant thought system mother's presence was amputated by her own desire. The central delusion thus far is that it was she and her desire that killed mother. This organizing-level dynamic seems internalized in the transference delusion, which is producing a countertransference avoidance response. If the father molest memory is serving as a highly condensed screen or telescoped memory, then we might assume that some sort of rebuke was experienced from mother when the baby did orient in an aroused mode for contact. Perhaps your lateness served as such a rebuke.

When we are searching to understand early, especially maternal, themes, people's memory cannot picture, image, or otherwise remember the original infantile situation, so they have dreamlike "flashbacks" or construct "recovered memories" from later periods, perhaps with someone else, that captures the emotional quality of the earlier interaction. For example, was her mother the type who, just when dependency needs were being expressed in a strong and dynamic way, would pull away as though in lack of interest, like you report in yourself today? Or perhaps Mother, for whatever reason, believed that babies shouldn't be so dependent, so aroused, or so intense? Perhaps Mother found the baby's aroused sucking arousing and disturbing to herself and chose to withdraw the nipple just when the baby's desire was peaking. We have no idea yet but we certainly have to wonder about the actual nature of father's "molest," condensed as it is in memory with eating and Mother.

The transference and countertransference *are* the memories we have to have elaborated. Under these psychic circumstances we cannot assume the pictures or narrations she tells as memories are necessarily literally correct. But we can feel the power of the relatedness memories of arousal and withdrawal in the relationship. From this example we can see how easy it would be for someone to attempt to "validate" her experience and then to encourage her aiming her accusation at her father or even at you since it is the relationship with you that is stimulating the deep trauma.

You have many things to listen for as she feels closer to you. The arousal theme may become troubling to her or to you, but it needs to be dealt with frankly and openly explored. If you sense a problem you might quickly assure her that we have no idea what the arousal means now, but if arousal is part of what needs to be explored then we must find a way of looking at it. I say this so that the investigation process doesn't get defensively interrupted by fears of loss of boundaries in the relationship on issues of homosexuality—either in herself or projected onto you. The work is going great,

we'll look forward to hearing how it develops. Thanks.

Cecilia: Thank you. I really do have a lot to think about. Maybe it's best that she left her OA group. I could see them taking this molest memory and running with it. You're right, it needs to be elaborated, represented, and explored in our relationship. I'm glad I'm learning more about how to see and work with transference and countertransference.

THREATENED BY UNCONTROLLABLE FORCES: TWO MONTHS LATER

Cecilia: Ah, Michelle. She's gained a lot of weight recently. I think it came with her daughter leaving to go live with her father. Her daughter Sonia just graduated from high school. On Tuesday she was saying that she's down to zero functioning. She's just home. But she announced she's now over the amputee phobia.

Marilyn: She just announced it?

Cecilia: Yes. She said, "Well, I just don't have that anymore." Then she said, "And you don't even put yourself out as a phobia clinic." Before she came to me she had once gone to a phobia clinic and the therapist there didn't help her. Then she began wondering, "Why therapy? Why go on?" She was wondering why she was doing this. What's coming out now is that she has a phobia of dead bodies. And she's afraid of closets, chiffoniers. So that got us through Tuesday's session and she felt there was a reason to continue therapy. All she has in her life is coming to the sessions.

Now for last Thursday. "So how are you feeling?" "Hot, hot. I've been

sweating, it's so hot today! I always sweat a lot." "Tell me more about the sweating." "I just sweat a lot." "Do you?" "More in summer than in winter?" [Note: Session is on a hot July day.] She says, "Just a lot. This year I weigh a lot more than last year." "Have you gained weight since last year?" "Yeah 'cause I quit smoking." "Is the eating still like it was? Remember when you would leave the office and buy a dozen doughnuts?" She says, "And now I want them on the way here." So now she has anxiety before sessions rather than after. When I started the session on Tuesday, my sense was one of paralysis because I no longer know what to say. I'm very conscious of my responses. My sense of not being there for her has increased considerably. I felt like, "Good God, what am I going to say?"

Larry: Tell us more about the countertransference feeling. You used to know what to say but now you don't?

Cecilia: Well, I feel as I learn more, as I continue with the group, I'm more conscious of what I'm saying. And what *am* I saying? I feel like I don't know what to say anymore. It didn't used to be a problem. I just said what seemed right to say at the moment.

Larry: From our professional training we learn how to "do therapy." Then we move to another plateau, where we're trying to listen more to how the person relates to us. From the relatedness vantage point it's very difficult to understand what she's telling you. As we become more sensitized to how little we truly know about the people we work with and how difficult it is to figure out what's important, then we often really don't know quite what to say. Each minute we're struggling to see what relatedness experience can be defined and brought to light.

Cecilia: Right, because I've reviewed some of my older sessions and, you know, I'm in there way too much.

Larry: You knew what to say then?

Cecilia: Yes. I was really playing psychotherapist!

Mike: With the two organizing-level people I'm heavily involved with I notice too that the temperature seems to be a big deal with these people. She's hot and sweating. My organizing lady you all know about is always noticing, "It's hot," "It's cold," and I'm trying to find out what that's about for her. About the infantile state, the organizing state that she still lives in all day. I'm not sure how to understand it yet but I know temperature is a big deal.

Marilyn: Like the organizing woman I brought in. They're focused on everything but what's happening. Perhaps that's why the temperature

becomes important. It's the negative space.

Larry: As we've talked about before, the content per se is not so important. But Kohut in *The Analysis of the Self* (1971) alludes to temperature with preoedipal people relating to a concern about being without the warmth of mother's body, being on one's own to regulate body temperature and not being happy about it. He spoke of tension for merger with mother's body.

Marilyn: When a baby is born, its thermostat doesn't adjust for a number of weeks and the baby can't adjust it itself so the mother regulates it until the thermostat starts kicking in.

Cecilia: So she says, "Now I want doughnuts on the way here." "Now you want them on the way?" "Yep." "Did you get one today?" "No, I'm trying to diet. Yesterday when I went to the doctor. I decided I was going to try Opti-Fast again. But I got to six P.M. and couldn't do it. So I decided to try no meat and no sugar and see what happens. See if I can do that. The meat part is not that hard—I've done that a lot. But the sugar is going to be hard." "What did you eat today?" "I ate a vegetarian burrito." And then we got into a food thing. Do you want to hear that or should I . . .

Larry: Definitely. We're looking for contact points.

Cecilia: "I ate a vegetarian burrito." "Well, that's pretty good." "I was going to ask you if beans and rice are supposed to be a good protein substitute." I said, "Yes." "Okay, because I love them." I added, "The only problem is that if you buy burritos they have a very high salt content and often lard." "They do?" "Yes, it's best to fix your own." "Okay. I can do that." "And it's best to use brown rice," I said. "Okay. I've got brown rice." "And fix your own beans. Then you can spice them with condiments other than salt." "I use so much hot sauce anyway that it doesn't matter. I can't tell if I need salt or not so that makes it easier." I said, "You know, when you eat most fast food burritos you will gain water weight because of the salt." "Well, I go to Green Burrito. It's the new place that opened by my house. It's really good." "Is it?" "Yeah. A vegetarian burrito is what I had for dinner last night and I had one today, too. I can do that and then make hamburgers for Joe because he likes that. I can fix his dinner and that will work out."

Then she goes back to the sweating, "The doctor told me it's nothing," and she talked about bringing a fan to the office. "The doctor told me there is nothing they can do for head sweating," and she's wiping her brow. "I don't know why I do it. My mother didn't sweat at all and my father just poured his head off like I do. It's embarrassing." "Is that what's motivating you into trying to lose some weight right now?" "Part of it. It's just too uncomfortable. I don't like it at all. I've got to do something. I just don't like the way I've gained weight. I think if I lost weight I'd feel better."

Larry: It sounds like a nice connection around beans, rice, fat, and sweat.

Cecilia: It seems so. Then she says, "I had another dream about Sonia."

"Another one?" "Yes." "What was it?" "She came over to the house to drop off piles of junk. She was making messes all over the house but she wasn't living there. She was coming and going and dropping off piles of garbage and stuff and that was it." "Have you heard from her?" "No, I'm going to leave her alone and just . . ., I don't know. Her being gone doesn't bother me. It's easier actually, I mean if I don't have to see her anymore, I don't have to worry. I don't let myself worry as much because I can't check on her. It's not like she's expected to come home at a certain time. I just can't worry about her coming home late anymore." "I know last Tuesday you said you did worry about her a lot." "Yes, I always have. I know I'm afraid that something terrible will happen to her. I've always been afraid of that since I was pregnant."

Larry: I can't tell if the abrupt shift from contact around beans and brown rice is away from contact. Or if the dream about Sonia is an association that tells us something about what happened to her when she abruptly lost the maternal presence and with it the sense of her thinking self. The temperature associations may be dating her own difficulties back to infancy. The connection is going well. Is she overheated? Shortly before, she alluded to a genetic possibility regarding sweating, associating herself with Father, introducing the idea that her troubles may be rooted in a close relationship to Father.

Cecilia: "You think maybe the reason Sonia has left you is because of what happened to you in childhood?"

"Partly, I was afraid, I didn't want Sonia to have such a horrible childhood. It was hell. So every time anything went wrong with her I was just about in hysterics. I just panicked. I didn't want anything going wrong. Nothing. Absolutely nothing. And it pretty much didn't." "You felt you were there for her then." "Well it wasn't because of me, it's just circumstances that happened that I had no control over." "I don't follow you."

"Well, like kids who make fun of other kids. Or teachers doing something bad to a kid. I was afraid that something like that would happen to her. And something did happen with one teacher but I put her in another class immediately. It was a situation where I thought the teacher had spanked her. It was in preschool. And I went to find out why, because Sonia never did anything to get into trouble. She never got into any trouble at all. So I took her out of the class because I knew it couldn't have been Sonia. One time I got her some tennis shoes. I thought they were really cute but the kids made fun of her. They didn't like them and that just crushed me." "That crushed you?" "Yes. I didn't want to have to relive any of my childhood because if people make fun of your kids it's like they're making fun of you. I think it's because they didn't have to go through anything so that's why these kids can make fun." "So, you identified with what was happening to Sonia but more than that, it sounds like you were aware of your own pain as a child while you were protecting Sonia. Do you think you were an overprotective mother?" "I was overprotec-

tive. I still am. I wouldn't ever let her out of the house if I could help it. Just to go to school, I would drive her there, pick her up, and that would be it. I'm terrified that something is . . . I was terrified that something would happen to her."

Larry: Not only is she speaking of a frightening fusion of identity but she speaks in the present tense. Like something bad is happening to Sonia or to her in the present. She's getting along well with you these days. Is a merger sense threatening? Will something bad happen?

Cecilia: Possibly. Still in present tense she said, "I'm afraid that something might medically go wrong with her. Any time anything might happen. If she got just a little bit of a runny nose, I would take her to the doctor. But nothing much ever happened. It was so easy." "So where do you think it went wrong?" (In other sessions we had talked about how Sonia hadn't talked to her most of last year and she finally left her mother to go live with her father.) "I don't know. Maybe I was a bit overprotective with her. I guess I could have been a lot worse. I did drink and I did smoke there for awhile." Michelle had left Sonia with her father for two years when the child was around 2.

Bonnie: She left for two years and there wasn't any contact with her?

Cecilia: No, she was on an alcoholic binge.

Larry: There we have the dead body again. Right at the separating period, when the child needed to learn to be separate from mother, mother abruptly abandons the child. Tobacco and alcohol may represent an attempt to restore some of the bodily sense she had lost.

Cecilia: She's now gone to live with her father about half an hour away. About a month ago, she graduated from high school and left.

Bonnie: And her mother isn't having any contact with Sonia now?

Cecilia: Sonia came back once. She went to a party and met a fellow who lives near Mom. So she dropped by for a few minutes, brought the young man over to meet Mom and her stepfather and left.

Larry: Sonia really is declaring independence as forcefully as she can.

Bonnie: And you were saying that Michelle wasn't having contact with her?

Cecilia: She's cutting her off, yes.

Larry: That replicates when she needed to individuate before. "When she was 2, I sent her away for two years. Now that she's individuating as a young woman, I cut her off again." Is the reference to a dead body, the fear of the loss of Mother and how it's being replicated here with her daughter? And possibly how it may be going to be enacted with you?

Cecilia: She says, "I tried to keep Sonia from harm because I was so terrified." I said, "You have a sense of terror?" "Yes, I still do. I had it all the way through school. In high school it got a little easier. It's just amazing, the terror can come to me at any time and I have no idea what's going to happen. I may get up in the morning and everything seems like it's going to be all right, but by night time it's terror again." "Well, what happened to you?"

"Nothing, nothing happened to me. It's just I've never had any good feelings. I had such an awkward childhood. It was just the whole thing. It wasn't any good. It was the things that happened to me." "Something bad? I thought we had talked about some bad things in your childhood." "Well, to me it's not that bad." Two weeks ago she had talked about an incident when she was about 9 or 10 years old and she and her brother were left alone while her parents went to the grocery store. They were down in the basement playing. She heard her parents come back home. She heard them walking in the kitchen, putting the groceries away, and talking. So she went upstairs, opened the door to the kitchen, and there was nobody there. I said, "What did you feel?" "Terror." That was the first time she used the word *terror.* At that session she also told me that she hears voices. The voices call out her name. Especially when she's taking a shower and the water's running she hears her name. That was two weeks ago.

Larry: So she tells you about two "projection situations," a creaky house with a basement, and a noisy shower where she could project the voices that she wishes were calling her.

Mike: I would also consider the terror as arising now between you and her. I would go after it like, "Do you experience anything between you and me being terrifying?"

Cecilia: Well, it comes up but it just waxes and wanes. Sometimes she'll admit to it, she'll talk about it. And at other times she'll say, "Well it's not that bad."

Larry: It's bad, but "not that bad!"

Cecilia: I alluded to the terror in the basement and coming upstairs finding nobody was home and she says, "I can control the inside stuff but I can't control the outside stuff like an earthquake, or if the house fell on us. I couldn't control that kind of stuff but I controlled what I could."

Larry: Are the "outside" things like those she projected onto her daughter? The preschool teacher spanking her, the threat that disease might strike her?

Cecilia: That seems to be the case.

Bonnie: She can't control her sweating.

Larry: Recall our study of Searles's *The Nonhuman Environment* (1960). He emphasized that in early life infants experience the world acting on them rather than themselves as actors in the world. The subjective experience is that personal, mechanistic, forces of fate operate to determine life. She seems to feel that way about many things. They just happen to her. She has come to fear things happening to her, like hearing voices of her parents whom she wanted to come home, possibly to rescue her from whatever was happening in the basement with her brother. Or of someone calling her through the noise of the shower when she is naked and feeling stimulated in various ways. Think of the things she was afraid of happening to her daughter. Her daughter couldn't misbehave, it must have been the teacher. She has experienced all her life this way. "Outside" factors are uncontrollable and terrifying. From our vantage point the outside factors are projections from the organizing, or psychotic transference and her own terrorized state into the environment.

Those of you who have studied the Rorschach test know about the "little m" scoring category to indicate that the person responding to the inkblots has projected inanimate movement onto the card. In very young children we see inanimate movement responses, either because in fact their world acts on them a great deal or because they haven't yet fully learned to assume agency for their experiences. Even older hyperactive children often score a number of inanimate movement responses—presumably because as they whirl through the world many things reach out and grab them. In normal protocols of adolescents and adults we do not expect to see inanimate movement. Their world is animated with instincts projected as animal movement while human impulses and interactions are projected as human movement. They tend to experience control and agency over what happens to them. One interesting piece of research was done by a psychologist in the Canadian Navy. During a storm at sea in which the ship was threatened with capsizing, he tested sailors with Rorschach ink blots. He found a surprisingly large number of inanimate movement responses. The actual circumstances of feeling acted upon by impersonal forces influenced the way they were experiencing the world at the moment—as passive victims of circumstances, forces, and fates beyond their control. Searles (1960) makes us aware that the world is full of nonhuman, inanimate forces that people in primitive states of mind often feel threatened by.

We know with organizing-level issues to expect material that reflects the fundamental position of being acted upon rather than one of being an agent. Much of what people feel victim to in their own instincts is projected as forces over which they have no control. "I couldn't control part of my mind being lost (amputated) when my mother would disappear. I know my parents love me, I hear them calling my name. I can't help it. I can't control the temperature of my body or that I sweat like my father, or that I get aroused when I think of contact with a mother that can really feed me. All of these things just happen to me. If I begin to feel connected to you, I feel terror because I may become physically out of control, aroused and then you'll leave. I can't control your leaving me just like I couldn't control my mother or my daughter. Then I'll feel like part of me was amputated. Or worse, the very closeness I yearn for leads me to experience you like a corpse, another person I depended upon who has died on me."

Cecilia: She describes Mother as very passive and uninvolved. Life with Mother was very quiet.

Bonnie: Lifeless.

Cecilia: Lifeless, yes. I asked her, "What did you feel when you opened the kitchen door and there was nobody there?" She said, "I was terrified." I said, "Explain how it felt." But she

couldn't. They went back downstairs to the basement to wait for the parents to return. I don't know what happened to them. She couldn't tell me.

Larry: To a person who has developed more advanced object relations, "How did you feel?" is a relevant question. And they can generally give you some kind of a report. With her, I think all she can say to you is, "Things keep happening to me. I turn on the shower and voices appear. I heard my parents upstairs and I looked and they weren't there." In some sense at various times she doesn't experience herself as having a sense of personal agency, nor can she identify personal feelings. She doesn't have a sense of control, nor does she have a sense that, "I can rely on a human environment to be there for me." The human environment might as well be a dead body.

Marilyn: Yes. We're talking about a mother who's really lifeless, isn't in tune, and isn't involved with her child. We're talking serious deprivation that has been internalized as a state that is stored in memory by being compulsively repeated.

Larry: I'm enjoying this because there's a nice sense developing between you and her. The bean and burrito talk seemed like nice contact.

Mike: Yes, you tell her, "I know about brown rice. I'm going to give you brown rice, something nourishing."

Larry: "Too much salt and lard at those fast food places. Let's talk about how we can do better by ourselves."

Many people who have been

trained in traditional therapy find work with organizing states highly active and interactive. So conversation about beans, rice, and lard would seem, for many, to miss the opportunity to discover what the various meanings of food might be for Michelle. But the traditional search for symbolic meanings was never invented for or successful with organizing or psychotic states. I have written extensively (Hedges 1994a) on how idiosyncratic symbols and meanings are for people experiencing organizing states and how futile it is for the therapist to become preoccupied with the content of organizing states.

Because the person has never interpersonally bonded with anyone, our focus must remain on fostering connections that have the possibility of leading to a therapeutic symbiosis with the actual person of the therapist (Searles 1979). The point is not to teach the person to connect. A teacher or reparenting process could do that if simply learning how to connect was the point. The analytic focus is on the organizing or psychotic transference that functions to break or foreclose the possibility of a connection just when one is almost possible. That

is, what must be analyzed (broken down) is the primitive structure that destroys links between thought and feeling and between people. But we cannot frame for study the modes of contact rupture until we are beginning to have contact moments actually present to study.

The technical problem is that a person living an organizing state cannot connect. So the therapist is forced into an active stance. Look how Cecilia has repeatedly gone after Michelle and brought her back in. Then the therapist must find *anything* that the person is willing to connect about—rice, beans, lard, vacations, business ventures, movies, jokes—anything, any way the person will extend and allow interpersonal affective connection. Therapists often worry about being overactive or not engaging in deep, meaningful therapeutic conversations. This does not matter. What matters is that ways of connecting be found so that the modes of disconnecting can be analyzed in transference.

Bonnie: She didn't have anybody with any life in their bones at all. You and she are developing some liveliness.

Cecilia: I just can't imagine her mother.

CONTRASTING THE PSYCHOSES WITH ORGANIZING STATES

Larry: Let's try for a moment to distinguish what we see with Michelle from some of the more blatant forms of psychosis. With a person labeled "schizophrenic," we have a sense that

the mother's psyche constantly and damagingly intruded into the child's physical and mental states. That is, the child might be busy doing something and Mother would appear to disrupt the mental state or would fail to appear when needed, causing an explosion of the mental organization. The child's mental space is unpredictably destroyed or intruded upon. In order to fill in the void or to establish some sense of continuity, the child then draws conclusions or imagines how things are or might be and hallucinations and delusions evolve. That is, schizophrenic symptoms are formed when cognitions that might have entered into or might have been molded by human symbiotic contact were not met in a satisfactory way so that the infant develops idiosyncratic cognitions. But with people presenting organizing issues, such a disruptive experience wasn't there or it might have been there minimally or occasionally. With Michelle, you see, she wants these voices. She believes people want her. Her desire is for others to come and to take care of her. She knows you'll do a brown rice talk with her. So she tells you about poor eating habits and sure enough, your voice arrives and you caringly talk nutrition with her. She knows Cecilia is knowledgeable in nutrition. When we've talked about her before we've seen how terrified she can be of contact. Today we hear her reaching out for contact. But in the same breath she remembers previous yearning in which the hallucinated mother appeared and then she was left in terror.

I think a lot has happened in your connection since we heard about her last. We still see organizing features, but she wants a mother to be there. The suggestion is that even though her mother may have been passive and inactive, there were burritos—although they were loaded with salt and fat. We don't have the sense that Mother was overtly intrusive and destructive, so that she had to create hallucinations to fill in for missing object relations. She had to create hallucinations to find Mother. She had to listen very carefully for where Mother might be coming from. She seems hungry to come to session and finds brown rice nourishment from Cecilia.

Cecilia: I said, "So you think the phobia's pretty resolved?" She says, "Yes, I haven't been in a situation where I've been close to one, but I'm afraid of feeling the fear. But when I saw it on TV I was okay." I said, "The terror was gone at that time?" She says, "Yes, the terror was not there. I think now it's mainly getting over old habits and the anticipation. I anticipate that I'm going to be afraid. And that's what happens." Then she says, "I don't think I want to kill myself just because I had all these fears." (On Tuesday we had talked about her killing herself. There was no hope and nothing to live for because Sonia was gone, and what were the sessions for, and would she kill herself.) She says, "I don't think I really want to kill myself. Some things are better and I know that I can do some things, and I know that I must. I try to think of how it would feel if someone lost an arm. Nothing like that has happened to me. I haven't lost my leg or my foot like the kid on TV and so I think I can still manage."

She remembered when she had injured her shoulder and her arm was wrapped and she couldn't use her shoulder. She says, "Well, that was the first time when I broke my wrist." And then she shows me the wrist and says, "See it's still deformed a little bit. I couldn't use it then until they cut the cast off. The second time was when I dislocated my shoulder and then I really couldn't use my arm because my whole arm was bandaged." "So you see a reason for people living who have amputations?" "Well, I don't see that as a reason not to live." I said, "Okay." She continued, "If it's just that, you basically learn how to do things yourself. Therapists teach you how to do things, how to function, and how to do things for yourself."

Howard: That's transference.

Larry: And you started with brown rice and beans with no salt or lard.

Cecilia: She said, "If you were born like that, that's just the way you were born and you accept whatever it is that you have up until people start to talk about you. No matter what the differences are, you don't know it inside yourself. You don't think anything about it if you're born with a deformity. People say if you're born missing an arm you never know the difference."

Mike: That's heavy.

Larry: That really is. We're forming a picture of a mother who was not actively intrusive, but looking for her is active, arousing. Michelle knows that fast food burritos are good. She's had them. But she knows now they're not good enough because they've got salt and lard. Our speculation might be that early on in various ways there

was once a good-enough mother. "I was not deformed from birth. There was a part of me that was amputated." She addresses Cecilia, "Will you teach me how to live with my amputation?" And then later, after she's begun to find someone who's going to help her deal with the amputation, "I'm afraid of dead bodies. At some point my mother just died on me." We might imagine a fairly passive woman having a baby. During the first few months of life she was able to be there for that baby and to take care of the baby's every need. But at some point, as the baby begins to become more active and demanding, Mother can't stay with the baby so consistently anymore. "At first it seemed that a part of my body was amputated, the part that did the thinking about what I needed. Later it seemed Mother was dead."

One of Tustin's main ideas about functionally autistic children is that there was a mother and then somehow there wasn't. So that initially, whether *in utero* or in the earliest months of life, there was the physical maternal bond, maternal care that the child knew about. But then there was some gross physical or emotional deprivation that Tustin says might result from a severe depression in Mother so that the child loses the part of its being that was the nurturing part of Mother's body. The child closes off, retreats into a shell and holds on to hard objects in order to try to feel safe or real. But the main theory that might help us consider things here is that "there was once a mother who was part of my body and then that part was lost. And when that body died for me a part of my mind was cut off."

Cecilia: Okay.

Larry: She's afraid of relating to you because if she does get the help from you that she needs, you'll die on her like numerous other people have. Like Sonia is.

Mike: I'm concerned about her disengaging from you, like wanting to terminate. She's saying, "Well, you cured my phobia now I can leave. I don't want to come here." Perhaps you need to start giving her some words to help her know why she's seeing you. That it's not simply for a phobia.

Cecilia: I did that on Tuesday, so that in this session there's none of that talk about, "What am I doing here? What is this for?"

Larry: So quitting therapy and the suicidal content was about, "One of us has got to die." Then you said to her, "We could just keep relating after all, you know." But I think everyone here

sensed right away that we've got potential treachery in the organizing transference of "will you not disappoint me as well?" I'm impressed with how well the therapy is going.

I especially like your style of "not knowing"—just kind of floating along, staying with her. You know, whispering little sweet nothings, rice and bean recipes, and all. Because it's making it possible for her to connect. And she's telling you all sorts of wonderful things. So I think you should keep on not knowing anything. But pay attention to the countertransference feelings of not feeling like you're there. I think we'll learn from that. And go slow. We have now not only her fear of dead bodies, suggesting that the connection is threatening a transference loss. But we have your feeling that you're not there for her. The disappearing "psychotic mother" may show up at any moment, so be ready.

Cecilia: Okay. I will!

Four Months Later

Cecilia: I'd like to present Michelle again. After the last presentation I saw her twice. Things were going well but she stopped coming, ostensibly because of money. An insurance check had been delayed and she said she couldn't afford to keep coming. I wasn't sure what I had done wrong. So I kept calling her and calling her. Sometimes her answering machine was on and sometimes it was off and the phone would ring and ring, and then the machine would go on. Finally, I got hold of Joe and he said,

"Please stop calling because you make her feel really bad. You make her feel terrible when you call." But there was no explanation. I said, "Okay, I won't call anymore." Last Tuesday, I went to the office and thought, "Well, I guess I'll try and call her again." Because the insurance check still hadn't arrived. That was her excuse. She said she wasn't going to come back until the check had come in. I said, "Well, maybe I can hook her. Maybe I can get her back in and have her bring in another insurance form or give me some information." I really wasn't expecting her to answer the phone, but she did. I said, "Hi, how are you? The insurance money hasn't come in. I really would like to call the insurance company to see what's happening." And, you know, it had been such a big issue but she acted like it was no big deal. She said, "Oh well, you know it does take time." I asked her to come in because I was presenting to my study group tomorrow. I know the group had been important and I thought that might interest her. She answered, "You sound dependent on me."

Larry: Ah. There's the organizing mother. "Don't be so dependent on me."

Cecilia: Yes. I said, "I'm not dependent on you. I can stand on my own two feet." [Group laughs] She says, "You know, I've been talking to my neighbor about the possibility of moving to Philadelphia. But my neighbor thinks it's crazy to go and veg out somewhere like that." "She thinks the same way you do," I said. "But, what about our work. How will we get our work done if you move?" And she starts crying. "Michelle, you're crying." She says, "I've been having dreams. I dreamed I was talking to my father's secretary and she was telling me my father was having affairs. I know other people like him. The dream upset me so much, I woke up screaming." "Why don't you come in and we can talk this through. How about this Friday?" She says, "I have PMS right now. That's why I'm crying. Maybe Friday I won't have it anymore." She seems pressured and continues. "I had another dream. I was me but not me, and Joe was dif-

ferent too. We were married and we had five kids. We were in a big house and I was showing a volunteer worker the kids' rooms. It was me but it wasn't like me. It was me if I wasn't so fucked up." I said, "It was the you that might have been." And then I went ahead and set up the appointment and she came in on Friday.

Larry: Sometimes it's so much work keeping these people coming.

Cecilia: She comes in Friday. I go back to the insurance money. The check in the meantime had come in. I showed her the check, I showed her the letter. Again, she was very unconcerned about them. She sits rather quietly for a minute and says, "Well, why don't you ask what you need to know for your group?" "How are things?"

Larry: "I'm only here for your group, you know." (Laughter.)

Cecilia: Yes. Then she said, "I don't feel I need to come in. Everything is the same and I'm not going to change." "Well, maybe we can see each other so we can talk." "I have a good relationship with Sonia now and we talk." "What happened?" "I've been calling her. I've stopped being so critical and asking so many questions. I know when my father used to talk to me it really used to upset me." So I asked her if I upset her like that.

Marilyn: And what did she say?

Cecilia: She said I didn't upset her. I said, "Remember how we talked about how it wasn't over just because Sonia moved out?" "Well I know. I was acting perfectly normal. I missed my kid." It was really a very traumatic separation for her. She said, "In certain ways things seem better." "Sounds like she talks to you now." "Oh, yeah. She talks. She wants me to look at things when we go shopping now. She tells me all about her job and how the stupid boss treats her. She's smarter than I was. She knows how to handle him. I told her about the kind of problems I used to have at work. My self-esteem was so low I couldn't take it. But she does. She manages work well. She likes making money but she won't take any shit." "It's to your credit, Michelle. You've given her that strength." "No, I wasn't even there. It's from her father. He was like that."

"Michelle, things have really changed. Remember when we talked about you and Sonia and what might be the problem when she wouldn't talk to you?" She said: "Well, I asked her and she told me that I was too controlling. I was that way because I wanted her to be safe but I guess you can't keep people safe. I had a dream. I was afraid to tell you because you might think I really did it." "What was your dream?" "I was married to my ex-husband. I was giving Sonia a bath and then I had her lying spread eagle and I was humping her. She was 4 years old. She said, 'I'm gonna tell Daddy what you did.' I realized in the dream I had gone over the line. Why did I do this? I got nothing out of it. In the dream she's laughing. I told her that if she told I would go away and she would never see me again. She used to tell everything. If I did it to her I would kill myself. It was so gross. She was very verbal from the age of 1. She was talking. She knew she was not to be spanked and she would threaten to

tell or call the police for help. That's why I put her in preschool. I knew she was safe because she would tell everything. She used to get me in so much trouble because she would repeat my phone conversations to Joe."

"So in the dream you threatened to leave." "My father used to tell me if I didn't talk to him, he would leave. It was a creepy dream. So gross." And she laughs. "The sexual thing, I don't get it. Even in the dream I didn't get anything out of it. I almost called Sonia and asked her if I had done anything." "You've had dreams like this before. We seem to be getting pieces of the puzzle. Remember the dream with the schoolteacher, her bare abdomen, the cadaver, Dad, and you were about age 3 or 4?" "Yes." Silence. "On the phone you told me another dream."

Larry: Would you refresh our memory?

Cecilia: She had a dream previously where she was in a room and she knows that the teacher was naked. There was this woman, teacher, Father, and a cadaver. But she couldn't quite bring it all together except she could see the schoolteacher's bare abdomen. But when we would get to that kind of situation, usually we would have some kind of veering off where she would miss some sessions like what just happened. Maybe I should tell you I also had a fantasy one night when I was going to sleep. I don't exactly remember when it was in her therapy but maybe around some of this material with the cadavers, where I went to sleep thinking about her, kind of in that hypnogogic state. I could see this little girl's face in a very despondent, miserable state. It was so bad I felt I couldn't find words for it. These must be my feelings about Michelle. And I think my fantasy also registers my feelings about trying to reach her—she's so despondent I can't find words to relate.

"On the phone you told me about another dream. I wanted to go over that one again because I didn't finish my notes on it. It's the secretary dream." She says, "Well, his secretary typed up a list of all the affairs he had had. I was screaming in my dream I was so upset. Why would I be so upset?" "Somebody else was getting the love you so desperately needed?" "She was saying bad things about him. I was concerned she was besmirching his character." "It sounds like you were the little parent. You had to look after him." "Once his secretary did call me and asked why I didn't take him to the doctor because he was so skinny." "When did he last work?" "He worked up to September of 1988. He was almost 67 when we finally convinced him he couldn't work anymore. I found that out when his doctor called and told me to have him come in. I couldn't make him do anything. I couldn't tell the doctor anything either. We were never allowed to tell anyone anything. I finally did tell the doctor how he was. And when he finally did go to see the doctor, the doctor told him what I had said. He didn't get mad. But then I was mad. If he wants to die, go ahead. He really needed help, sometimes even to turn the ignition on in the car. I finally told

the secretary too. I said he was always skinny. The way I was raised, you don't tell anybody anything. And you left his mail alone. Once my mother accidentally opened one of his letters and she was terrified."

"What things were such a secret you couldn't tell?" "Certain things you don't tell, like your address, your phone number, and when you move, and where you're going. Even now I don't tell, I don't want anyone to know where I live." "You grew up in so much fear." Then she said, "So what about us?" "It's good to see you." "I want to continue our work. But I don't want to be what you want me to be." "Okay. I don't want you to be what I want you to be either. I only want you to be what you want to be." She continued, "I can't get volunteer work with people so I was thinking of working with animals. Sonia invited me to an animal convention in L.A." "Are you going?" "Yes, if she asks me again. I want to pay back. Do you think it counts?" "Yes it counts. Of course it counts. There's a tremendous movement to save the animals of our world." I asked about her cat and she tells me about Bronco. I said, "I would love to see Bronco." She tells me about Puff and how Puff is doing. Then I tell her about my cats and my dog. We connected around our animals. We ended the session and she's coming today at three o'clock with Bronco.

Marilyn: Has she brought her animals in before?

Cecilia: Yes. I think where I get caught up with organizing complexities is that I get into dream interpretation. I noticed that you didn't, Larry. You didn't interpret any of the dreams. Probably it would be a waste of time to do that, wouldn't it?

Larry: Well, yes and no. I think the traditional kind of interpretation is not helpful. Yet in some of the dreams you've made a few salient comments here. The connection is where the pay dirt is. She was connected. Too many questions or comments spoil things for her.

Cecilia: Well what I've found is that when we get into it too much then I lose her.

Marilyn: Yes.

Larry: That's it. But as we heard the dream in the sequence of the session we could see right away what it was about. She had just finished telling us about how she was trying to get Sonia to move back in. She's just gotten her clutches into this child again who has recently attempted to individuate, to declare independence. Then she has that incest dream that says she had gone over the limit, that she was humping her. That might be the one thing you might choose to pick up on. But not at the risk of losing her. Simply suggest that her need for Sonia is in danger of crossing a line that she might feel is not right. That's all. It's not that her dreams don't contain good primary process material that is subject to interpretation because they usually do. But with our high-level people, their psyche is embedded in those symbols. With our lower-level people it's generally not. So even though they may be generating dream pictures, we're not necessarily going to

have therapeutic movement as a result of dealing with them. It's helpful to know where she's at with Sonia. She's so happy she's got her back, but she fears she's gone too far in her mother love, either past or present. Perhaps the dream pictures her feelings that you crossed some sort of limit in coming after her with such determination. When did she have the dream in relation to seeing you on Friday?

Cecilia: It was between the phone conversation and the visit.

Mike: I'm wondering if this is about transference, you (mother) forcing, violating her.

Larry: "Is your dependency need in danger of crossing a limit?" It certainly would be a new twist on amputees, on missing parts. "If you, as my psychotic mother, feel that you're missing something and you relate to me, the child, as the missing part, then I become part of your craziness. I fear your dependency on me."

Mike: I've got to be honest with you about this case. I'm very impressed. I guess if you called me up and said what you said to her I'd say, "Hey bitch, you know, you're being intrusive. I don't want to see you." But she's responding to your intrusions. I mean, you intuitively went right after her and said, "You need to come here. I've got group next week and I need you." I think that was the only way to get her in and I'm marveling at it. I'm trying to think about that today. I mean, I'm really impressed that you went right after her and straight up said . . .

Cecilia: That's what you've all been teaching me.

Mike: And she's buying it. She feels the connection; then she has a transference dream to express the sense of a limit having been violated. She's doing great!

Cecilia: Yes she is. It's clicking.

Howard: Yes. It's amazing what it takes to get therapy going with organizing people.

Cecilia: What struck me is that she's going out of the house now. Because when she started therapy, she was so phobic she couldn't leave the house. She was so phobic about amputees that Joe used to run interference. If he saw an amputee over there he'd steer her away and they'd go someplace else.

Howard: I'm thinking she feels it's important for you to need her whether you need her or not. I mean, I think that's the issue and my sense about it is she did come when you mentioned that you needed her for the group because she felt like there's somewhere on this planet where . . .

Cecilia: "I'm needed."

Howard: That people . . .

Cecilia: "Care about me."

Howard: I think I would interpret that at an appropriate time, that she needs to feel needed and how that is for her. She likes it, is responsive to it, but also feels it crosses a line.

Cecilia: In my needing her, she needs me.

Larry: You said, "I can need you and yet stand on my own two feet." I think you've got to stay with that theme.

Cecilia: Okay.

Larry: "You feel that if people need each other then they're endangered, that it's frightening, or that someone may disappear or die." It seems we have here a piece of her history. Was this done to her? Was she used for others' dependency needs? She wonders if she is using, abusing her daughter. To need is to use or abuse the other. In the dream she's humping her daughter. So there's dominance, a taking advantage of, and an injuring. So if you're needing her, where's the danger line?

Cecilia: That was an interesting phrase wasn't it? "I've gone over the line."

Mike: Yes. Fairbairn talks about infantile dependency verses mature dependency. I think that's what she's got confused. She's operating with a very infantile dependency paradigm. If I need to depend on you then I need to merge with you or I need to dominate, abuse, or kill you.

Larry: That's "over the line."

Mike: Yes.

Larry: I think what Michelle needs to hear is, "Just because people need each other and value each other does not have to mean they've crossed that line into being exploitative of each other. You've known damage from that line being crossed. The question is, did someone cross the line with her in a literally incestuous way, because it could well have happened, or are we talking about crossing the dependency line? That is, at some point when she was an infant did her mother keep intruding so that she couldn't form her own mind?

When we think about the earliest organizing state, in principle, we're thinking about the child who wants to have experiences and reaches out in some way or another to an optimally responsive environment. But if the environment responds too early or too late, or faultily, or too intensely or intrusively, then the child's mental space is violated and the child's mind doesn't develop well. Khan (1963) speaks of cumulative strain trauma to designate the damaging long-terms effects of many seemingly not-so-abusive intrusions or negligences that leave the infant in a state of chronic strain. This seems like a transference representation of the way she was damaged. She had a mother that too much wanted to go after her like you were going after her. And while that may have been stimulating, it was done in such a way that made her afraid. "You need me too much." Her mother had a missing psychological part and needed her so much that Mother intruded. In the course of intruding Mother went over that line, which was experienced as baby's space, and damaged her.

So is it a representation of her organizing process or is it a representation of something that in fact happened to her later? The picture is forming that there's been a destructive intrusion somewhere in her life, but what is the nature of it? Often the incest fantasy set at a later age is a way of representing the primary intrusion of the psychotic mother across that line into damage.

How can a person picture strain trauma that happened so early? We sit here trying to imagine what the first months of life might have been like and to construct interesting little fantasies that might apply. We can barely make sense of what it might be like and what these intrusions of the overstimulating or psychotic mother might have been like. But we do have that dream of hers stuck in that basement apartment with the curtains closed from the inside, completely encapsulated. The average person doesn't have any way of representing that. But incest is a cultural motif of crossing a line that shouldn't be crossed, going into an area that is strictly taboo. The "promise not to tell" can have been an instruction from, say the brother or the father, but may represent the child's being timelessly lost in the exclusive primal relationship with Mother. It's the third-party view of my relationship with Mother that structures it, that permits my psyche to enter into relationship with cultural rules. The incest theme provides a culturally transmitted image that can represent what happened to me when I had a mother who intruded and damaged me by her intrusions whether they be positive or negative intrusions. The intrusive damage is known only to us (Mother and me) and I am prohibited from telling anybody anything, even my address or phone number.

I'm always prepared with people who are searching their psyches and their pasts for overt genital incest to say to them, "Perhaps you were, and if so we'll keep trying to explore it. But, since you have some doubts about it, what other possibilities are there?" And to try to go into some of these other ways in which parents cross lines to the point of creating for the child a sense of molest, domination, or exploitation. But whatever it is that happened to her, she fears she is doing it to her daughter. And the circumstances and timing suggest that this theme applies to her relationship with you who have come after her in need.

I'm eager to hear where it goes from here.

Cecilia: Thanks, Larry, and everybody. This has been helpful.

Larry: Thanks, Cecilia.

THE SEARCH: FOUR MONTHS LATER

Cecilia: A lot of changes have occurred with Michelle. She is going to divorce Joe now. He had an accident with their business truck. He rear-ended someone. She had been thinking about it anyway. This was the final blow. He seems to her like just a blob that lives with her. She has realized that he doesn't think for himself. Joe just wasn't getting the work done. The financial adviser told her to sell the business she bought for Joe because she has to use her inheritance money to meet the monthly bills, because he is just not making it.

Sonia is back now; things didn't work out with the stepmother. We've talked about how the relationship with Sonia needs to be different and she feels that it is. She realizes that before she was too close and overprotective.

Larry: You told us she had been concerned about being alone if she asked Joe to leave while her daughter was gone. But with Sonia back can she afford to throw Joe out?

Cecilia: Now she can afford to throw Joe out. But there are new rules in the household. She is going to treat Sonia like an adult. She will have her own quarters like an apartment so that she can come and go and Michelle is not going to be interrogating her about every little thing she does.

And Sonia has a boyfriend. So that's where we are. Overall she's looking a lot better. She seems a lot brighter. The weight is still a problem and she's still on Prozac. I can see that there are a lot of traumatized areas that we're not going to get to any time soon. I think it's going to be hit and miss for awhile. We touch on things, but we just can't stay with them. She talks to me as if she's cured. I'll say, "We still have a lot of work to do," or "There is still a lot of pain," and she says, "Oh really? I thought we did all that."

Let me read the process notes I brought and we can go on from there. I am trying to be more attentive to her cuing. She begins the session by telling me about Sonia and Joe. Then she tells me a dream. "My parents are with me and my father has just died. As he is lying in his coffin he rolls over on his side. I went to my room and then I went to find my mother and I saw that she was crying hysterically." I said something about the recurrent theme of corpses. She said, "You know I have always believed that dead people can grab you. I learned that they can sit up from gas." And she starts laughing, just laughing, and so I laughed with her because the image of a corpse with gas sitting up was so funny. I said, "The corpse phobia is with us still." "I guess."

Larry: We have never related her phobia to the corpse of Father. We have talked about her "dead" mother.

Cecilia: Well, we have talked about the dead bodies father worked on. [Father was associated with work involving corpses and as a child Michelle was from time to time exposed to a dead body when she spent time with her father at work.]

Howard: But in the dream this father rolled over. He's a corpse but he rolled over.

Larry: In his grave.

Cecilia: Yes. Then there is silence and I begin to notice movements with her head. She does these funny movements. I said, "Dad died first?" She said, "No. That's the way it should have been. We all wanted Dad to go first but Mom went first." "So you arranged it the way you wanted it in your dream?" There is a silence again and she changes the subject. She says, "The business went up for sale last Tuesday. I told Joe to sell or I'm getting a divorce."

Larry: Let's stop a little bit. Why did we lose her?

Cecilia: Well, I'm noticing that this is recently happening more. And actually when I was reviewing these notes, I'm loose with her. But at the time, I didn't see the looseness.

Howard: What do you think the theme was?

Cecilia: I think the theme is grieving.

Howard: Grieving?

Cecilia: I thought that the dream was about grieving. She is longing for her parents still and I don't think she has had anyone to grieve with. I don't

feel the same connectedness we used to have there for awhile. I'm trying to reach out to her, but she's not giving me much to go on.

Mike: [To Larry] Could I ask a technical question? I haven't heard a lot of dreams from organizing people. Is there transference in dreams with these people?

Larry: Yes. But transference appears at the level of the "organizing breach," which would be the nature of transference at this level. In the relatedness Cecilia is dead or in danger of dying and haunting her from her coffin. That's the potential transference meaning.

Cecilia: She says, "I miss Dad, someone to call and ask about things." I say, "You used to do that?" "Yes I did, but when I had my gallbladder trouble, he said I had lung cancer." "How did you feel?" She said, "That's how he used to talk to us all the time. Dad would make fun of my illnesses and try to humiliate me. Mother died of cancer but Dad didn't know about it ahead of time because if she told Dad, he would ridicule her. He was quite merciless."

Larry: He would ridicule her for having cancer?

Cecilia: Whatever their weak spot was he would ridicule. "So when I was sick with the gallbladder problem he said, 'You are going to die of lung cancer.' He would say such things, then he would laugh. He thought that was funny. I have always been afraid to go to the doctor. I rarely go to the doctor." "So doctors scare you?" "Well, I have a high tolerance for pain." "So doctors hurt you?" "Yes." I said, "Why don't you call me when you're in pain and we can talk about it. Perhaps I can be there for you." She gives me a vacant look, just stares at me and says, "I can't depend on Joe." I ask if she is wondering if she can depend on me. I feel she has put me to the test also, you know, with the previous problems we've had. "Sonia said, 'I'm glad you let me move back in.'" Then she starts laughing again. She said, "Of course I would let her move back in. You need a backup. I have no cushion. I have no parents anymore." And she gets very emphatic at this point and says, "Joe can't do anything."

I said, "You are without parents. You feel you don't have anyone. Maybe you're still grieving for your parents. Were you close to your mother? You hardly ever talk about your mother." She laughs again and says, "Sonia asked me the same thing. I told Sonia that you often ask me that. I tried to be close to her but she wasn't interested. She didn't even go to my wedding. She went out to lunch with my sister-in-law instead that day." That was when she married Joe. "Mother was really attached to my brother. She did whatever he wanted." I said, "So was your mother pretty active in your life and with your brother? Was she working? What was your mother like?" "Mother worked teaching up until one year before she died." "It sounds like she was pretty close to your sister-in-law." "Yes, and my sister-in-law has Münchhausen syndrome. She likes surgical procedures. She goes from hospital to hospital getting operations."

The sister-in-law, the brother, and the mother were very close. Michelle was never a part of that closeness. So she says, "Sonia realizes my brother is a dick. I heard her saying so to her boyfriend. I am glad she sees it so I don't have to say it." Then she told me how they had fought over the inheritance. They had to go to the bank one day, jointly, and the brother, in the middle of the bank, was yelling at her saying, "But Dad always loved you better." She says, "He didn't really love me." It sounds like they were both blaming each other for not having parental love. "Your father turns on his side. He turned away from you or toward you, and what was it like?" "Toward me to scare me. I see men who look like him and I'm terrified. They both didn't pay any attention to me. I used to do anything I wanted. When I was 16 or 17 I came home at seven o'clock in the morning and my mother was sitting right there in the living room. She saw me come in and she never said a word." "She didn't ask you where you had been?" "No. I was pregnant but they didn't know it." "How was your pregnancy?" "I loved it but I was terrified to have a girl. I was afraid that the same thing would happen to her that happened to me. I said, "You mean the molest?" She looked puzzled. I said, "Remember when you told me about having been molested by all those people?" She said, "No, I really wasn't. It wasn't a sexual molest. I was just exaggerating. It's that we moved so much and I never made any friends."

I go back to the dream. "Maybe inside you're crying hysterically, like your mother is crying in your dream."

"Mother was just not interested in me. She didn't like me. I wasn't a cute little girl. I was a mess. I got fat at 8. And I only took baths once in awhile. The kids used to make fun of me. She just didn't like me. I don't like my brother. He's not a nice person." Then she pauses and does the funny movements with her head again. I say, "So you turned to your father?" "No, I didn't. I didn't like him. I didn't even like sitting next to him." "Why is that?" "He used to play with my hair. In the car I used to sit in the back seat so that he couldn't." "What did he do that upset you so much?" Then she shows me what he did. With her long hair she took it and flipped it like this [gestures]. But the way she did it, there was a sensual quality that she apparently had experienced. I said, "Well your hair looks nice, Michelle." She said, "For years I didn't go to the beauty shop because it hurt to have my hair touched. I said, "Well, maybe that's why you don't go to the beauty shop very often now." She said, "Why?" "Because your father touched your hair in that way. It hurt you." "Oh gee. I never thought of that. Wait until I tell Susan at the beauty shop." That was the end of the session.

Cecilia: But I feel like we're kind of wallowing. I feel I'm not anchoring.

Larry: It's hard to take hold of her, to find a place to connect.

Cecilia: It really is and part of it is I feel like I want to go after the molest a little bit, but you know, in one session she'll talk about it. But I can repeat it in the next session and she'll deny it. My impression is that she remembers much more than I thought she remem-

bered but she can't tell me about it. And I don't want to encourage her toward producing a false memory.

Larry: Why do you say she knows a lot more about it than she's able to tell you?

Cecilia: Because she will sometimes float into a kind of disassociated, fugue-looking state and she'll dreamily tell me, "You know I was molested by my father, by the doctor, by my teacher, by my neighbor." And then she will flit off someplace, but I'm stuck because of the dreamy state. You know it kind of catches me in ways and at times when I'm not quite up to responding to her in maybe the way I need to. If I ask something leading, like "Follow the dream," I hit a wall. I'm thinking to myself, she is just not going to let me in. I can't do this right. I've tried to pursue, like say, the father rolled over. Then I'll come up against a wall. Even in this session I had thoughts of "I'm not doing this right. I've just got to get into this." But she gets loose or she changes the subject or something. I think it's disorienting me. And I'm not pursuing things that should be pursued. I'm not picking up the cues well.

Larry: It's not that you didn't think of them at the time, but more like you were aware you might have followed them but it wasn't going to work?

Cecilia: Well, I do ask questions and then it doesn't work and I think I didn't ask the right question or I begin to reproach myself in the session as we're moving along.

Howard: Do you feel her criticism of you?

Cecilia: Well, I feel the wall. It's like

she's going to be in control. She's going to say what she wants to say. That's basically what I feel is happening. Part of it may not be that it's loose, but that if she doesn't want to talk about the subject any longer she will change the subject. My feeling is that she's much bigger and more powerful somehow than I am.

Howard: That comes through when you talk.

Cecilia: My sense of it is that somehow I need to break through that. But I don't know how. And yet she wants to come. I think something new is happening too. She's calling me and leaving messages on my machine, like the time when Sonia was coming back, she called and said, "I am so glad that Sonia is moving back home" so I called her and responded. She said, "Oh you didn't have to call me. I just wanted to let you know."

Larry: She didn't need the interaction, she just needed to inform you.

Mike: She didn't need anything from you really. But maybe she felt *you* did.

Cecilia: I think you're right.

Mike: There is a punishing quality to that. You return her call, "I don't need you today. Fuck you." I think she continually does that. I think there's a part of her that wants to connect and then when you show up she vanishes.

Larry: There is a wish, a yearning, but no follow-through connection. We've been tracking this woman's organizing issues for a long time as she tries to find you. Our literary prototype of organizing issues is Franz Kafka. In all of his books it's like this. There is the search, the reaching out, but somehow the sense of connection is never quite made. He searches and even when the world attempts to respond, something bizarre goes on at the border of the interaction. The interaction never succeeds in producing useful contact.

ORGANIZING COUNTERTRANSFERENCE CONTRASTED WITH SYMBIOTIC COUNTERTRANSFERENCE

Larry: I want to pick up from the standpoint of countertransference. If you had reported that kind of countertransference, with a person working on symbiotic issues—that she's bigger than I am—we might turn it around and say you are now responding in proxy for her infantile self. That what you're feeling from her is Mother, big as life, and "I am just a little girl. No matter how I try to reach Mother, Mother is not there for me." That would be the way we would try to formulate, try to massage, to work that reversal form of countertransfer-

ence. That is, there is style, consistency, method in the madness when symbiotic issues are involved. If you are being cut out, unresponded to, punished, or whatever the quality of it is, we assume that in the interaction she is somehow showing you what was done to her emotionally. Here we don't quite have that sense. She shows the inclination to always be searching for the nipple, searching for the object, but no inclination to be able to hang on, to nurse, to interact, to benefit from the contact. Instead she changes the subject, is evasive, looks dissociative, contradicts stories she has told you; in short, she flees or freezes in the face of potential connection.

Howard: It doesn't seem so much like an active aggressiveness but more that she can't quite make the connection.

Larry: Yes, I'm thinking that the countertransference is to your own overstimulating and failing psychotic mother. You know how I use that term *psychotic mother.* A transference structure remains in all of us to mark our blocking reaction to when our mothers failed to meet our extensions. When we work with a person like this where we reach out and reach out, our most primitive frustrations are roused. I think the countertransference to organizing issues often registers our most primitive responses to when our early mothers failed us. So, there you are, trying to connect, but you can't. She is not there. So it leaves you feeling frustrated, lost, loose, disorganized. She is bigger than life. She's in control. You have no opportunity for profitable exchange with her so this kind of countertransference isn't necessarily telling you anything about her or her interaction with her mother like it might be if we were studying a symbiotic structure. Rather it shows you what happens to you when you feel the persistent disconnections. Her disconnections leave you with your own organizing core—your own helpless inability to connect to your early mother. I feel like this is one of the reasons that the countertransference at this level has been studied so very little, because our own most primitive kinds of responses get activated when we cannot achieve in the relationship the kind of connection we need to sustain us.

Cecilia: You know, that suddenly explains why I've been having all these strong thoughts lately. I have a friend who has a little baby and I look at that baby and I think, "My God! How did I survive that age!" That's where it's coming from. And I couldn't make sense . . .

Larry: Can you say more about that?

Cecilia: Well, the baby is about 9 months old and we see a lot of each other right now. I look at the baby and I think, who was there for me? How did I ever live through this age?" We were sitting outside the other day and my friend said to me, "What are you thinking? You're so lost in thought." I said, "Oh, I was just thinking about my psychotic core." Looking at this baby I keep wondering how I made it because my mother was very, very ill. She "had" to get married and in those days that was a terrible thing. So I don't think that she ever quite got used to the idea of having me. I keep thinking about her mental state, her illnesses, and wondering how did I survive? Who was there? Who would come and pick me up when I cried?

Larry: I'm asserting that your primitive feelings of not being responded to are now coming alive in your relationship with Michelle.

Cecilia: Okay. It's suddenly very clear. Now tell me what to do with it? [Group laughs.]

Larry: Keep sucking your thumb! [All laugh!]

Cecilia: Sucking my bottle!

Mike: And hope something comes out of it!

Larry: Yes! We end up using the countertransference here differently. If we saw her issues as more symbiotic and you were having these feelings, then we would assume that she was using your personality and your relationship with your mother to stir up reactions through projective identification. You would then be trying to verbalize with her how helpless and disorganized you feel in the relationship, how much you want to relate to her but that it seems as though she's not there. You would try to show her that the countertransference is a projected representation of her own infantile frustrations, that in the relationship she is mothering you the way she was once mothered. With symbiotic or borderline issues we would be encouraging you to speak your feelings. We would be urging you to find ways of speaking your reactions so that in doing so, you would be interpreting her infantile position vis-à-vis her mother in the symbiotic dance.

With organizing issues we don't think that the countertransference necessarily works in that way or that speaking the countertransference is necessarily interpretive. In this case the countertransference is simply that burden you're stuck with as a part of your professional work. Her constant turning away makes you feel crazy! No one has yet been able to show us any systematic ways across different cases of using our own organizing experiences trying to relate to our own absent and failing mothers or to our own organizing cores, for interpretive purposes. But the interpretive technique I've been teaching for organizing issues

uses our disrupted functioning to notice the ebb and the flow of the connection. That is, there have been times in the past in which you have felt Michelle could address you, could reach out, could get her mouth around the nipple, and could hold on and take a little bit from you. But right now, during this time period, you are not feeling that. You tried several times in that hour to offer her something but she was not able to make use of it.

Cecilia: We're not going anywhere.

Larry: Instead you're left with your own organizing fantasies from your own "psychotic mother."

Cecilia: She is evoking them. They're really coming up a lot.

Larry: About all you can do with them is to realize this experience brings forth aspects of your own nature and of your own history. By turning away, refusing, or breaking contact she is reviving your memories of when your earliest mother couldn't provide for you, didn't give you nurturance, couldn't let you be responsive to her. But I don't believe we're going to be able to make rich use of that deep and personal material by finding ways to speak those feelings like we might with symbiotic issues. With better-structured issues the person would, by now, know exactly how to work you to make you feel punished, lost, lonely, hurt, and would, through projective identification, work the relationship in such a way that your feelings would be extremely relevant to the relationship. I don't believe that's the case with Michelle. I think your feelings are more or less irrelevant to her material except that they register the approach and flight, the search for a connection and the compulsive destruction of the connection. If the issues were more symbiotic you would feel more consistency. There would be more style, more "method to the madness." You would know the interaction was tapping your own early object relations, but you would also know that you were being moved, cajoled, manipulated in some way in the particular feeling. Then we would try to feed back into the interaction your feelings in terms of a projective identification. You would be feeling that there was something peculiar or something alien about the way this woman was doing something to you. The way it is you are not even able to say that. You are only able to say, "Well, here I'm lost. I am sitting with my friend and I am thinking about my psychotic core, and I think about how my mother was ill and wonder how she could have been there for me."

So Michelle is stirring it all up, but she's not working it with you, not purposefully engaging you in order to show you the details of how her early experience went. I think this is a very important distinction between the countertransference to organizing and symbiotic issues. Now the time may come in Michelle's work where your being regressed and feeling lost and bizarre will have a place and must be spoken but we don't know that yet.

You see, when you address Michelle with the general question, "Tell me all about yourself" you are implicitly asking her to establish a transference, which would be to reexperience a total breakdown in her relationship with you. No one wants to experience a breakdown. And we cannot expect our clients to do something we have not done ourselves. In our own therapy is the place to regress to our own helplessness in our psychotic core. If you have done so, you will be clear on what you are asking her to do and, in time, she will hear the request and also know that you know what you're asking of her. If a therapist has not experienced his or her own surrender to primal helplessness, then the therapist will not be able to help the client do so. But occasionally we are required to regress ourselves in relation to our client and we need a consultant on board to stay close by if that needs to happen because we can't be confident of our ego boundaries and reality testing under such circumstances without outside support for ourselves. But Michelle's wall is very strong now so about all you can do is to feel the shutout and the frustration in whatever ways you can.

Bonnie: You suggested last time, Larry, that the marital relationship that was threatened be somehow fostered in order to keep her life at least for the time being more organized and stable. What happened with that? I guess you [to Cecilia] probably encouraged her to stay with him and she rejected that. How did that go?

Cecilia: Well, there was a lot of effort in that direction. Her husband even had a few sessions with a therapist but he didn't follow through with ongoing sessions.

Larry: When we're dealing with people who live full time with organizing issues, it's so hard for them to find a nice warm cave and living companions to go home to at night. Regardless of how bad the relationship is, viewed from our perspective, when it's a live-in relationship and it's working in some way or another, it seems to provide some sustenance for so many of these people. I felt if there were any way to preserve the living arrangement, that might be best in terms of sustaining the therapy, at least for now. But two things happened. One, her daughter decides to move back in so she's not going to be alone if she asks Joe to leave. And then immediately following that Joe wrecks their business truck, further threatening her resources with a lawsuit.

The relationship dynamic is perhaps tied up with all the "molests" you keep picking up on. She goes to Father, she feels his warmth but then comes the physical intrusion and she feels guilty if she doesn't let him hold her hair seductively, but it hurts. I don't know how quickly you can begin to work that one, but I think the whole dynamic of guilt with Joe may relate to molest guilt. "Someone is interested in me. I have to respond." But

then she feels intruded upon and injured by the interaction, something to be alert to as potential transference. Then she says, "It was my uncle, the doctor, the schoolteacher, and the others." Then she backs off and says, "Well, no, not really." I'm thinking that she has a wisdom that it's hard for us to possess. She says, "Yes it is true. In some special way all those men molested me. But there is something more operating. My guilt. My need for a man. My need for a connection. There is my feeling that I have to open myself up, I have to go to work with my father and sit beside him while he deals with corpses because he needs me or because it's the only thing I can get. I have to let him play with my hair even though it hurts me." Then she hurts for years because if she hadn't let him play with her hair she would have felt guilty, or perhaps worse, lonely. But if she does, then she feels intruded upon and injured. I think she's saying, "This is the dynamic of my life and it has come into play in every relationship with a man." And, of course, we are watching for the molest to be experienced in the transference.

PRIMAL MOTHER AS MOLESTER

Cecilia: Okay. So now what do I do with my personal countertransference? Just understand it?

Larry: Tell it to someone who cares! [Group laughs.] Seriously, understand it as best as you can. I don't think there's much to do with it right now except just be aware. As you begin to study the countertransference with her and notice the kind of thoughts

and fantasies that come up, you'll begin to identify what happens in you when there's an organizing-level disconnection.

I find that until therapists have learned how to identify the loss of contact with a particular person, they fail to realize the person has silently left the interaction. Our narcissistic and symbiotic needs tend to blind us to the moment of disconnection. But then you learn to notice, "She's gone. I just thought about my psychotic mother." Meaning that right now she just did to me what my mother did. She skipped out on me. At that moment just say to yourself, Aha! We had a moment's connection or a close connection here and there she goes off again. I feel the uselessness of my interventions. When we can pull it off, our technique is to quickly go back and track it, to call Michelle's attention to it. "Something earlier was going on, we were having a conversation about so and so. You seemed interested and stimulated. It seemed like we were feeling connected and then you changed the subject. What can you tell me about that?" Time and again, just when you almost make a connection with her she shifts the subject. It's like a multiple personality who "shifts" personalities the minute the therapist makes a connection. We saw that this hour. She was not going to tolerate a connection.

I advocate tracking connections and disconnections, the approach to and flight from an experience that might lead to a bonding kind of interaction. I advocate studying the way the person accomplishes both procedures and then engaging that person in a study together. In the process of collaboration we can together generate pictures and stories about mothers and babies, things from movies, fairy tales, and anything else that can possibly bear on the problem of representing how the person persists on relating and interrupting the relating. I have come to believe that the critical therapeutic event or thera-

peutic action with organizing states is that *de facto* during that discussion, the connection is being sustained. That is, after all, what a mother tries to do with an infant, to seduce her into symbiotic relating. Baby is there and isn't there. Mother waits and when the baby orients and is momentarily present, suddenly Mother does anything and everything to reinforce that connection. She smiles, she gurgles, she coos, she makes faces, sings, she plays with the baby's lips or toes, anything, because a mother knows "I am going to bond with this baby by bringing her into connection this moment and holding her here a bit until she drifts off again." Baby will stay connected in this way so long as the baby can stand it, then the baby looks away again. A good mother lets that happen. Baby seems to look away to "digest" the contact and then comes back for more.

But the erratic mother, the intrusive mother, the inadequate or overstimulating "psychotic" mother won't sense those moments when to be there for the child and when to let the child drift away to digest the stimulation. She will be going into the child's space when the child isn't ready and leaving the child when the child is available for connection. The net result is a child with pockets of organizing experience that show up later in therapy as organizing transference. The symbiosis doesn't form, bonding doesn't occur—at least in the areas affected by mother's erratic and frightening responses. The therapeutic tactic is to learn how, with each person, to track that connection and disconnection, to learn how to hold onto it, and to find ways of encouraging him or her to study it with you. The almost inadvertent but critical result of the study is that you are at that moment in fact giving that tickle, that coo, that thrill. To hold the person there seems to move him or her toward a dance that we two learn to do together. The holding leads to things that we two can talk about and enjoy together.

When I first started advocating this way of working I was often surprised at how readily the person caught on to connection as a concept and displayed an instant and intuitive understanding that the therapist had at last found the difficulty that had been eluding the person for a lifetime. People become excited about the invitation to explore the contact dimension. You had her

talking with you, connecting with you for a while before this last interruption. You and she were actually having conversations and enjoying them. It took a long time to get there but you two got there. Now we've had this disruption probably because of the connection and its treacherous transference meanings and the former ability to sustain contact is, for the time being, lost. I have confidence it will return. You're having to wait quietly now and talk to your own psychotic mother until Michelle gets back in a place where you can draw her into emotionally connected, interactive relating again. Thanks, Cecilia.

Cecilia: Thanks to all of you. This has been disturbing but clarifying and helpful.

Six Months Later

Cecilia: Things have been going so well that Michelle was about ready to come in twice a week. We had agreed to start and then she called and said she couldn't come in at all because the annuity check people had made a mistake.

Larry: There you go again. The connection gets good and she has to flee.

Cecilia: They had sent her too much money so now she was going to get less money. So until that evened out she couldn't come back. I talked to her several times about consulting with a financial planner, but I don't think she's going to do that. But in the last session she said she was going to buy a van for her daughter to travel in.

Larry: She can't afford therapy though?

Cecilia: Can't afford therapy, no. I talked to her about the reality of buying the van. Then she changed her mind because Sonia is in no shape to handle extensive travel now anyway. Sonia was fired from her job, because they accused her of stealing money at work. Sonia denies it, but she got fired anyway. So then the trip was on again. She's leaving on her trip today, with this ne'er-do-well boyfriend that she's been supporting. They're going on a cross-country trip in the van Michelle bought. Part of Michelle's inheritance was a time-share condo in Hawaii for a week at the end of the month. She was taking Joe with her. She was going to go on the plane blindfolded. She wanted to have her eyes all cottoned in case there were any amputees. Joe was going with her. That was the plan. Her anchor with Joe is increasing, though he won't, or can't, get another job. But then she's again going through the same scenario, "I'm going to leave him." So we talked about how she needed him to accompany her on the trip. And about who was going if Joe wasn't. The upshot is that she canceled the trip. She said I could go with her or she could let me have the condo for her time-share. I explained to her why I really couldn't do that, that I'd love to, but that I couldn't accept it. She said that she had never met anyone like me.

Larry: What did that seem to mean?

Cecilia: I think in terms of the previous five therapists, that no one has ever kept calling and asking her back in. One lady she saw frightened her so much she literally ran out of the office screaming. The lady never called to see if she made it home all right or anything.

Marilyn: To me it means that no one has ever cared for her like you have.

Cecilia: I'm the only person currently in her life who is not taking her money. Because you know Sonia was ready to take quite a chunk for the van. Joe took $40,000. Her brother, whom she won't talk to now, tried to take her half of her inheritance.

Larry: You wouldn't take the free week in Hawaii.

Cecilia: Yes. Maybe I'm making some inroads into some trust.

Larry: Something's shifted.

Cecilia: Something has shifted. I think in my not accepting any of her deals she trusts me more. I'm still charging her the same fee that the original medical plan was charging. I kept it at that level so she could come in twice a week. So I haven't raised my fee in the last couple of years. I think she's beginning to register some of that now in terms of trust.

Larry: Feeling safe takes a long time, doesn't it?

Cecilia: Yes it does. It really takes a long time. So she called to cancel her appointments since she has no money. I called her back this morning. I told her that it was just to check in on her. She answered the phone, and that's new. I said, "Well, I'll call you back soon so you can come in for a special session so we can stay in touch until the annuity gets straightened out." She said, "Okay." Before, when I wanted to do that it was a struggle to get her in.

Larry: To keep up the continuity during the break?

Cecilia: Yes.

Bonnie: Do you think she'll come back?

Cecilia: I think she'll come back. This thing with the money is similar to the fantasy of moving back East and is similar to her imagining leaving Joe. None of these are very real. But she's told me something new. This is how she explains to me about the breaks in therapy she needs. When she was a child her father frequently abandoned them. One time they were starving when they lived in Tennessee. He just left for a year and then came back. Then they'd move someplace else. Or just when she'd adjusted, as she did in

Nevada, he would come and move them again. So we think that maybe it's that pattern, that she had to leave me. At least that's a start toward thinking about the frequent breaks.

Mike: She hasn't been able to get rid of you. But she regulates the contact with breaks.

Larry: She tries to reach out to you with the offer of the condo, because other people relate by taking money from her. Your refusal to take advantage of her leads to a period of closer working together but, predictably, in fairly short order she finds a reason to stop it.

Cecilia: It's too much contact.

Larry: I take it when you do get her back, you know the general way I've been advocating studying her, which is to try to study the manner of approach, the form of contact, and how she manages the break *during* the sessions. You've done some of that already. But I think that's going to be very important in the next round, because she continues to live it out in big ways. She'll be there until she makes the connection, and then she'll disappear. It would be so much better if that would happen *during* the sessions where you can study it together, rather than over a month or two break where it really can't be studied. You may not be able to bring the sequence under closer scrutiny in actual sessions for a while but I would certainly try.

Cecilia: You know there have been points where contact has occurred and I was able to address it.

Larry: Yes, I know. That's the direction to move things.

Cecilia: But then it gets ticklish when she feels too close and then she arranges for the money to run out so she can take a break.

Larry: I will be interested to see if Father's abandonments play a part in this pattern or if that's a telescoped memory of Mother's inability to stay in contact.

Cecilia: Well, that's where we are. I'll be doing a session with her soon and then maybe I'll know.

Larry: Okay, thanks. Always glad to hear about Michelle.

HOLDING ON TO CONTACT:
SIX MONTHS LATER

Cecilia: Lately I've been taping some of my sessions with Michelle and listening to them. I find in the moment I often miss breaks in contact that I catch when listening. I've typed some notes from the tape of the session I want to review today. During the first part of the session I was tracking her pretty well. But later in the session it seemed like I dropped out. Perhaps I was tired, and I just let her talk more or maybe something else was happening. Overall I felt it was a remarkable session because she brought some things she had never done before.

Michelle had baked cookies, dreamed, and brought pictures from her vacation. I say, "Oh, how wonderful! Cookies, dreams, and pictures. You've brought so many things tonight! The cookies look wonderful!" "I made them last night." "Well, thank you so much. These pictures are great! Now, who is this?" "This is a kid at the pet shop. I took the picture to show Sonia that kids over there look like the kids here. That's when we were still going to move over there. Don't you think so?" "Yes, absolutely, psychedelic shirt, baseball cap, and long hair. Yes, long hair and jeans." Michelle is laughing. "Of course out here he wouldn't have posed. He finally told me to get lost. His friend was laughing in the background. But they enjoyed it." "That's nice." "Of course they don't have the attitude that . . ." "Some kids do here." And why I stepped in and finished the sentence, I don't know.

Larry: That was your thought?

Cecilia: Yes. What I heard on the tape that I never heard before is that we do lots of talking together. I fill in for her. It's just happening for me subconsciously. I wasn't aware of it until I heard it. I couldn't capture that in the transcription, but maybe this is an example of some of that. "Well, these are great pictures, and where is this?" "Oh, that's out at some dam, I forgot the name." "Oh, what beautiful country. And this looks like a church and a graveyard. Oh, look at those trees. And this, Michelle?" "Oh, those are two deer. They're small aren't they?" "Yeah, they look so small." "Yes, they're overpopulated. They're all over the highway." "How dangerous." "Oh, they want you to kill them." "They do?" "Yes." "And these two little guys were close to the road. It's really sad."

And I go onto the next picture. "This is beautiful." And I show her the picture and she says, "That's at the arboretum." "How are you feeling? How did you enjoy all of this?" "It was pretty, yeah, but after a while it's not

that big of a deal." "Yes." "Joe liked it more than I did." "It's beautiful." (Animated discussion of pictures continues.) I hand her back the pictures.

"And these are the cookies." "How come you thought of bringing me cookies?" "Because I made them last night. Normally when I make them we eat them before I get a chance to bring any." We both laugh. "For once I lucked out! So what about this?" "These are four different dreams." I was pointing to the sheet. "I just wrote down what I remember," she says. "And at the bottom there's an actual something that I remember. A lot of death dreams. I just divided them up into different dreams." And this is the memory: "I am in preschool. I am preschool age. Some people take me to a little circus like in a shopping center. I sit in the front row, and I'm afraid that the elephant will step on my feet. Also the clowns run at me, and I'm afraid." I had this dream again, this morning. Here's the dream: "My parents come alive again. They have no money because my brother and I got it all when they died. We're all living together. My brother no longer has any money, and he's still working. I ask him what he did with his money. I think that we should reimburse my parents. Nobody really connects with me. People just come and go. I keep going into bathrooms to pee, which finally wakes me up. When I get to the part of going to the bathroom . . ."

And we start laughing, or I laugh, I don't know why I laughed. Then she laughs. "I have those dreams about peeing that wake me up all the time." "Every night?" "Yes. I keep dreaming I'm looking for a bathroom, or I find it, and there's somebody already there. I suppose that when I get old . . ." "You'll wet the bed?" "Yeah, unless I'm wearing Depends or something." And we start laughing again. "I have a lot of dreams like that, that's really common. Every week I have those." "What?" "Having-to-pee dreams." "But that's just a need dream, or something. Like Freud called it." "What? A need?" "Yes, a need, you know like if you're cold you dream you're cold. Or if you're hot, hot." "Mine are that I have to pee." And I respond, "So then you wake up. Well, we'll study what comes up around that." "What? Having to pee? I thought everybody had these dreams." "Well, no." And she interrupts me. "When I was a kid I had them and I actually wet the bed. I can't remember what was going on." She pauses, and I say, "Well it could be reminiscent, you know, of the stress you suffered at that time. But what's interesting to me is that your parents come alive again." And she says, "I have that dream a lot." "That's been a recurring dream for years or months, Michelle?" "I think just months. And in the dream I know they died, and they know it too." "What does that mean for you?" She pauses for a long time. "Well, just think about it, what comes to mind?" She's silent. I say, "You and I are together now. Think, as you and I work, about what comes to mind?" "About them dying?" "Yes, about your parents dying. The dreams are recurring, and we've been working pretty consistently. We've got some good work ahead of us, but we have some good work behind us. We've been together for three and a half

years. Of course we've had some breaks, but otherwise we've been fairly consistent. I'm wondering, is there something about the dreams that occurs to you now?"

Marilyn: Could I interrupt for a second? What are you thinking and feeling at that point when you said "We've been together for three and a half years?"

Cecilia: Well, I was trying to hold her, to reach out to her. In the previous session, I had said to her, "Michelle, are you ready to touch on some of your childhood stuff?" She said "I would rather die than do that." So these are kind of holding statements. Sometimes I'll say things like, "Well you and I are a little family." Or, "What happens in your life is important to me."

Larry: In the six months since you've reported on her I'm impressed with the increase in the spontaneity and interconnectedness of the interaction. It's been like pulling teeth for the last three years to have any kind of a conversation, and then it would be sort of fragmentary. I thought that you do these little "pulling together" things to foster the interaction and here to get a fix on that dream—possibly in the context of transference.

Cecilia: Yes. I find if I don't hold on to her firmly that she's off and away to something else.

Larry: In this dream, her parents have returned. Now what does that have to do with the transference? I thought that's what you were going after.

Cecilia: Yes, I do here shortly where it's "We're a little family." These dreams are coming out for us, so that we can work on family issues through them. Right? Then she says, "Joe told me to tell you that everywhere I go I see my brother. I said, "When did that start?" She said, "When I first started to see you." Her father had died in January, and she came in April of that year. And that's when that started. And she thinks she sees her brother, even though it might be a black man, or somebody who is totally opposite race-wise, or anything, and she thinks it's her brother. And we just touched on it that one time.

Larry: Is he following her?

Cecilia: No, it's just that she's afraid of him, and she thinks that she sees him. And it's apparently quite prevalent in her life. But this was the first she'd dared tell me. "In the dream my brother is there, our families are there, and nobody is getting along, but everybody is there. I can tell on my brother." And I let that one go. Only later I realized that I was a part of the family there—"our families are there"—but at the time I missed it. It's a biggie, and I don't know, my head was elsewhere. I missed completely. That "she could tell on him."

Larry: Tell on him?

Cecilia: Tell on him so that she could have some power.

Larry: Some power. Her parents always protected him at her expense.

Cecilia: Yes. She laughs, and I laugh. "Michelle, we're both laughing. Are we laughing because it's sad?" "Well, I'm kind of ashamed because I kept trying with my family. That's why I'm not pushing Sonia." And here she gets off again onto Sonia.

Larry: How subtly she leaves the contact. You're worked so hard trying to stay with her over the years. How quickly she leaves contact. Here you have her talking about family and talking about "us." She's just come back from Hawaii, she's brought you things. She's feeling connected to you, she's not going to go away. She dreams of the family coming back together. You are included. She dreams of at last having control over her brother. And just when the two of you are enjoying the moment she leaves by changing the conversation to her daughter Sonia.

Cecilia: So we go into that a little bit. "I'm not going to try with Sonia."

Larry: What is your fantasy about had she stayed there with you? Would she have cried? Would she have gotten angry?

Cecilia: At times in the past when she was in more pain and these points came up she would start to cry. She cries from such depth and so profusely that I see where she would want to avoid it. And yet we need to go there. But it's just such an incredible depth, the tears and the deep heaving. When she gets that uncontrollably sad I want to reach out to her, and one time I did. I asked to sit next to her. Later on in another session she told me not to do that.

Larry: Too frightening.

Cecilia: Too frightening. And part of it is also because all this time, you know, all the struggle I've had in getting to know her, she's been checking me out. She's been testing me. In case we don't get to it, I want to mention that she said during one session, and later in this session that she was talking to Joe about me, and wondering where on earth I was coming from. Because by now they had figured out that I wasn't in it for the money, and that I wasn't a lesbian. I wasn't going to make a play for her. They couldn't figure out why I was staying with her through all of this.

Larry: Why you were interested in connecting to her. This is the organizing family problem. Why does someone want to relate to us?

Cecilia: She said she doesn't believe in altruism. So she compared me to cops who will stick to a case for twenty-five years.

Larry: No matter what.

Cecilia: No matter what and finally solve it. That made sense to her. So I think maybe tears might have come. But she switched to talking about Sonia and I missed it completely until I heard the tape. "I'm not going to try with Sonia like I did with them, because I know it doesn't work." "Tell me about the trying." "Well, it's just that you're trying to convince somebody to like you and to care about you and that you're worth something." And I say, "Yes." "It doesn't work. You can't convince them. It doesn't work. They feel that way or they don't." "But this was your parents, Michelle." "Yeah." "I've tried with friends and it doesn't work with them either. I've tried with Sonia. I am just going to be there and she knows it. And if she doesn't want to use it, she doesn't have to." "Right. But with us, and the work you and I are doing, we need to look at what that was about for you when you were home, and nobody paid attention to

you. You touch on it, but you run away from that. Tell me, what was that like?"

She's quiet, and I go on. "You tried to get your mother's attention, and it didn't work." "You mean how I felt when it didn't work?" "Yes." "Just empty," she says, "I guess." "Do you remember any particular incident?" "Well, this was about twenty-five years ago, I brought them Christmas presents and my brother cried because he said he couldn't afford to buy them presents. And that they would like me better because I bought them something and he didn't. And so from then on they hid everything I ever bought them." "They did?" "Yeah. They would hide it so he wouldn't see it and get upset and cry. And he never bought them anything that I know of, and he used me as his excuse. And they never saw through him. They would hide my stuff, and it would make me feel like dirt." "It made you feel like dirt?" "To think that they were concerned about him, and weren't considerate of my feelings." "They never considered your feelings?" "They always hid what I got them, and I would get upset. I don't see what it would have to do with him at all. I didn't buy the stuff to make him feel bad. I bought it to make them feel good." And I say, "So, did they open the presents after he left?" "Well, we were hardly ever there at the same time." "How old were you?" "I was in my twenties." "And your brother?" "Nineteen." "So he could have bought them presents, too?" "Yes, but he didn't want to." "Well, that is painful. What strikes me most is your feeling like dirt."

"Well, you know, it doesn't matter. Nobody cares how you feel. So at the end I was giving them things like . . ." and she pauses. "One time Joe and I gave them a 5"×7" picture of the three of us." She laughs. I said, "This will be good." She's smiling broadly, now. Sonia, she, and Joe. A family picture. "'Watch,' I said to Joe. 'They will act like they like it, and we'll never see it again.' And they did." And she's kind of laughing at the end of each one of these sentences. "And when my mother died, my father gave it back to me," and she kind of laughs. "He said, 'Here, I don't need this.'" She laughs again. "No, they never cared, so I was just supposed to shut up . . ." And I interrupt her, and I say, "Why do you think they reacted like that to you?" "I don't know. The only thing I can think of now, is that I was always trying to prove that I was better than my brother. But that's really stupid." "No, that's not stupid. You did it out of a tremendous need to be loved, to be found as their child."

"When we had relatives over, I was told to stay away from the house." "What were you doing, did you embarrass them?" "Well, the only thing I thought was I was heavy. But I did ask my father and he said it was because they were so mean. I had to wait until I got mean enough to stand up for myself. And it's true, they were extremely mean. The whole family was really mean. But then I was thinking, why couldn't he stand up for me?" And I say, "That's a good question. But that doesn't mean you couldn't belong to the family." "It was really funny. My father had a cousin who

moved out here, and Dad knew him. He had met him and his wife, and he went out to their house. Joe had to show me where they lived." "Joe knew better than you did, huh? I almost get the impression that your mother and father were hiding something, or that they wanted to hide you."

"They hid things all the time. My grandmother didn't know I was married, and didn't know my brother was married and had a kid. They thought the kid was mine when they saw him. They thought the kid was mine because I was the oldest. My whole life was hide and don't tell. Don't tell we're moving or how old we are." "Such a sense of suspiciousness. I'm not sure where it's all coming from. But your dream is telling me that you want to work this through because your parents keep coming back. You need to bring them here to share the problem with me, because you and I don't need to hide it any longer." "Well, I don't care. I'm not hiding anything anymore." [Cecilia's voice tone indicates an end to the close emotional sharing.]

Larry: Oooh, off like a gust of wind, huh? After that beautiful contact that she just made.

Mike: I would have melted if you had said that to me. [Group laughter.]

Larry: I'm really glad you brought these notes because I think what we're looking for with organizing clients is always this detail. When the person is there, and then they go. And it's taken so long for you to be able to have her emotionally present. I'm amazed at how much of the hour she's there.

Cecilia: Definitely. I can feel it.

Larry: But each time there's a possibility of affective contact, she's off and running. You pulled her into the here and now, and you made good use of the dream with its transference potential and the problem that she wants to solve. The problem of her parents constantly dying. Just when she offers them a gift, they go off into some sort of secret.

Cecilia: Okay, she says, "Well, I don't care." And so I say, "Last session I said, 'Are you ready to talk about some of these childhood pangs?' And you said you would rather die than to talk about your childhood." "No," she corrects me. "I said, 'than relive it.'" "Than relive it?" "I don't remember a whole lot." "Do you think you were depressed?" "Oh, I'm sure I was. I know I was now. I didn't know I was depressed when I was 7." "You know you were depressed when you were 7? What incident comes up?" "When I was 6, my father dumped us in Florida. I was with my mother. My mother was pregnant, we were starving, and the baby was born in February. He died, and they kept him somewhere." We had discussed this some time ago, and so I say, "You mean in the closet?" "Yes, they buried him in the summer. He died in February, and they buried him in June. Dad said, 'Did you want to see him?' And I said, 'No.' 'Cause I asked him. I don't know if I found the box or whether he showed me but I asked, 'Where are you keeping him?' My dad said, 'Oh, he's right here in the closet.'" [Recall Father's business involved corpses and embalming.] And she laughs. "There was no door to the closet. It was right next to the toilet, and the light in the bathroom didn't

work." We both laugh. "It had like a sheet or a curtain." "And the light didn't work so you couldn't go there in the dark?" "And Dad said, 'Do you want to see him? I'll get him out so that you can look at him.' 'I don't want to see him.'" Then she stops. "I can imagine what he must have looked like by then."

And I say, "So there was no light in the bathroom. The closet was dark, and the baby's body was in the closet." "Yes, in the pine box." "So you were scared going to the bathroom. And did you have to go often?" "I don't remember." "I wonder if there is some connection between the dream, going to bathroom, the baby's body, the coffin? It's something that you felt . . ." She interrupts me, 'Doesn't everybody dream about going to the bathroom if they need to go?' [Group laughter.]

Cecilia: I say, "No!" [Group laughter.]

Larry: That good old neutral attitude, "No!" [Group laughter.] She can't identify the fear about the embalmed baby next to the toilet. She calls it depression. But she knows she doesn't want to relive it!

Cecilia: She says, "Oh, I thought it was common. Just because I . . ." And I interrupt her and say, "You dream this every night?" "No, just sometimes. When I dream and I have to pee at the same time. It happens about every week at least." "So at least once a week . . ." And she interrupts me, "I dream that I can't go, and then I go. And then I have to go again, so I have to go find another one." "In the dream?" "Yeah, in the dream." "So you're searching?" "Yes, for relief."

"You're searching. Like your parents were hiding everything, you're searching for everything. Your parents hid real basic family functions, and you're searching for basic family functions." "I used to not be able to pee anywhere." "When you went out?" "Yeah," she laughs. "What was that all about?" "I don't know. I just didn't want anyone to hear. Now I can pee anywhere." "Well, that's good!" We both laugh. "You don't care if anybody hears it? So, were you very shy?" "Yes, I was kind of ashamed of things everybody does. I didn't used to eat in front of people. I used to practically starve." "You wouldn't eat in front of anybody?" "Yes, because I can't close my mouth because of well, because they didn't get braces." "Because of your teeth? Well, you don't have buck teeth, I see." "No, I thought I did." "You thought you had buck teeth?" "My lower jaw is back. I should have had braces to correct it. And the only way to fix it now is to break my jaw, which I wouldn't do. I thought I had buck teeth, and then I thought my top lip was too short. I even told my parents, and they didn't say anything. They never said that it wasn't." "So you believed it," I say. "Why did you think your top lip was too short?" "Because I couldn't close my mouth. See?" And she shows me, and for the first time I notice that she can't close her mouth, and her jaw is receded, it's not a clear jaw line. "When I was sick I couldn't hold a thermometer in my mouth." "Oh, I see. But can you close your mouth now?" "I can't hold it that way, see? It's . . ." "I see, it's a misalignment of your jaw that could have

been fixed easily when you were a child." "No, they didn't fix anything unless they had to. You have to suffer. If something broke, you had to suffer a few days first." "So here you go, you're searching, searching for a place to pee." "I still think it's normal. If Freud talked of need dreams then they must be normal." "But we still need to know what the unconscious message is."

Larry: You're not going to let her get away this time! [Group laughter.] Are you all appreciating how hard Cecilia has to work?

Bonnie: Good job. [Other affirmations.]

Larry: There's a very nice conversation you two have going. What a contrast to how it used to be.

Cecilia: Yes.

Larry: You finish each other's sentences.

Cecilia: Yes, you do get that, okay, good. "We still need to know what the unconscious message is." "I had some other ones, too. Where you can't pull your pants up? Like you peed somewhere, and you don't want anyone to know? So, I'm trying to get my pants up, my jeans, and they won't come up." "So you can't get covered up again." "I have a lot of those dreams where I'm walking around naked and I'm wondering why didn't I wear clothes, but no one ever notices." "But isn't that the way it was with your parents? You were there, but nobody noticed." "It's just as well, I'm glad they don't." Notice how the tense changes for her. At this moment she is in the present with her parents and no one else noticing her. She then starts almost imperceptibly slipping away here as she moves from the (very much present) pain of not feeling noticed as a person to how hard she had to work so that people would notice her or so her parents wouldn't yell at her. "I have a longing to be noticed, to stand out in a crowd." "To be special? You're special to me." (I am trying to hold the personal contact.) She laughs. "I'm the craziest person you have?" I interrupt her, "No, not because you're the craziest." She interrupts me, "Well, I could stand out if I let things," she pauses, "If I hadn't hid so much I would have stood out a lot more than I do." "If you hadn't hid so much? Hid what?" "Everything that went wrong. I always tried to appear normal and right, so that my parents would like me."

Larry: I'm glad she got to that line, "I always try to appear normal." Because I was relating that to the early part of the hour, when she's showing you the pictures, and she's showing you the boys, and then right after that she talks about people taking pictures. I was aware of how she was focused in on the mimical aspect of the boys first, and then more specifically. "That's what you do there, people go, and then they take pictures." She is so preoccupied with "what people do," the mimical self, and I think here she relates it to, "I've never had anyone come after me and help me find a way to be me. All I could do was to imitate what I saw."

Cecilia: Right. "Yeah, they tried to make me normal." I'm sorry, but I stopped typing at this point.

Howard: Were you still having your energy at that particular moment?

Cecilia: My energy drops shortly after that. She goes on to tell me how she tries to be normal. And also how she wants to stand out in a crowd. Though I tell her that she's special to me, and that she and I are our own little family, as she slips away my energy and animation drop. It's very dramatic on the tape the way we seem to simply lose interest in each other. Our voices drop to a bored, energyless drone. I was surprised at how responsive I was to her pulling away. I don't know if it's always been so pronounced but it certainly was this time!

Larry: It seems like she's caught in a contradiction. The only thing she knows how to do is to try to be normal. To mimic. But what she longs for is somehow to be noticeable. She's tested you, and she feels that you have noticed her. She is relieved that she doesn't have to try to get you to like her like with family and friends.

Mike: I think it's the longing. She wasn't picked out of the crowd in her family, she wasn't special to anybody in her home.

Cecilia: Her mother never related to her at all. What strikes me most is that the whole time she's been analyzing me in terms of why I'm so intent on sticking with her. No one else ever has and she can't understand it. It's inconceivable that I would simply be interested in her, would like being with her, would find it enjoyable and challenging getting to know her. The rest of the session she kind of just took off into her own monologues, and I pulled back.

Bonnie: So you serve somewhat as

an anchor, in keeping her here? And when you aren't interacting that same way, then she just begins to float off?

Cecilia: She seemed to float off, and at that point in the tape, I can't quite understand what she's saying anymore, because her voice drops down.

Larry: She goes somewhere else.

Cecilia: At the end of the session we roamed around exploring what she would like to become someday. What she would like to do. She says, "I don't believe in altruism." But then she tells me about doctors who were in the war, and how I'm like a dedicated doctor. Maybe it was a quality that doctors, nurses, and police had, because they can really move in to care about someone. She wants to do something to help people too.

Larry: So she's attempting to identify with you?

Cecilia: I said, "Well, someday you will too." And she said that no, she didn't have that quality. I said, "Well,

whoever you are, whatever you are to become—someday it will come, it will come from you. That's the exciting part about our work. That it will be a wonderful surprise."

Larry: And to hear about this hour is a wonderful surprise as well. The overall interaction is more animated and full than ever before. And we see how hard you work to hold her in the present. We also see how when you lose energy she fades away. Ideally, if you had been able at the time after the energy fades you would have tried to call her back, focused a discussion on what was happening, how you both were fading and why. So there's much work to do but she's clearly in the best place ever to be doing it. In the next phase it will be important for the two of you to notice how this mutual flow of energy, of interaction works between you.

Cecilia: Thanks. I'll keep working. The group support makes it possible.

7

A Similar Degree of Helplessness

Our group earmarked a day to discuss some general issues of concern rather than do a case or go over readings. Ian had recently joined the group. He had been practicing therapy for a number of years and hoped now to enrich his work with object relations concepts and peer review of some of his cases. We began discussing the transference and countertransference implications of personal disclosures on the part of the therapist. Ian began talking about a woman he had been seeing in therapy for some time. It was actually painful for her to talk or to interact with him. This was the first we heard of their work together but we were able to follow it up in subsequent meetings.

ON DISCLOSURES AND LEARNING ABOUT FEELINGS

Ian: She is persistent and insistent in telling me, "I can't tell you things about me unless you tell me things about you." I've tried a number of ways of responding to her but she keeps coming back to the same thing. Finally, a few months ago I began telling her a few things about myself. She brightened and seemed to come to life in a way I had not seen before. I've told her about my kids and certain things I've been doing. Last week when she again asked me to talk about myself I said, "You know, I do tell you things about me and I don't mind doing that. As a matter of fact, I've told you some things about me tonight. This is how I'm feeling, this is my experience of you, these are my emotions, this is all about me. This is who I am." She said I was mean, cold, distant, and not gentle enough or something. I said, "I'm sorry it feels that way, but I have to tell you that I do have angry feelings at times. I have anger in me and sometimes when I work with you I get angry, and that is part of me."

Larry: I think she's giving you a very important part of herself when she says that you're mean, that you're angry. I think that's going to be the clue to your eventual understanding in transference of the internalized, overwhelming, overstimulating mother. You're a person and your capacity for love, anger, impatience, and other feelings is fine, but how will she use you as a person to re-create what she once experienced as a disruption of her personal sense of continuity and contact with the nurturing environment?

Ian: She's made comments about how I stare at her, stare through her. She doesn't like the way I look at her.

Larry: I would think it interesting to encourage her to relate all of these feelings as soon as they occur. That you're being mean, you're being cold, you're being distant, you're staring through her. Until you get a moment-to-moment report of what's happening with her, you won't have a sense of where the thin thread of connectedness is developing and what experiences intervene to prevent contact that she might otherwise be able to use for growth.

Ian: Yes, I've urged her to do that. Only a few months ago she'd have feelings, and then she'd write me a letter three days later and say, "I was having these feelings." I said, "You know, it would really be helpful for me

to know when those sort of things happen. Let's bring your feelings into the room." She's been working on that a lot. A couple of weeks ago she actually said, "You're doing it now."

Larry: All right! Those are the moments you may be inclined to consider what you're doing to elicit those feelings. She will experience you doing something. There may or may not be much reality in what she says you're doing. But what to watch for is the way she is *using* her experience of you to prevent or to break off a feeling of connection to you. Studying the approach for contact and the way contact is foreclosed is our central technical tool for studying the organizing transference.

Of course there may also appear a bonding pattern, a mode in which meanness will be experienced as a way of connecting to the sadistic mother. But I think with her most of the time you will be studying the formation of ways of achieving disconnection rather than connection. With a person presenting symbiotic structure for analysis, we're aware that what they're terrified of is the abandonment, the loss of the connection, the connection that means safety, comfort, love. With the organizing experience, the central terror is around the danger of connecting. That is, there has been something frightening, intrusive, traumatic, neglectful, or disorganizing about connections with others in the primordial past, so human contact is regularly warded off. In Bion's (1962) idiom, thought links between self and other are not formed, the links between sensations and thought potentials of the human milieu are broken rather than joined. The etymology of "consciousness" is two people coming together, knowing something together. That's how babies learn to know. They circulate their sensations through mother's thought system in order to know, in the human sense of knowing, about themselves and others in the world.

Ian: There's something else I forgot to mention. She tapes every session.

Jeanna: Does she really?

Ian: Yes, she catalogs every session we've ever had. Between sessions she listens to the tape five or six times. We've talked about her need to do that. She says she doesn't know why she has to do it but it helps her to listen to them. She says she doesn't remember what she does in the sessions. The only way she has to remember it is to play the tapes back.

Karen: The early memory can only hold the image of Mom for certain lengths of time, whether it's five minutes or a day or two. With that tape she's allowing the image of you to be there again without your actual presence.

Larry: Has she asked for a picture of you yet?

Ian: She had asked me to bring pictures of my jazz band and things like that.

Larry: I think she may want a picture of you, because I doubt she can remember what you look like when she leaves the room.

Ian: Out of sight out of mind. She's coming to my public lecture tonight. That's been one of her ways to know more about me. She said, "I'm going to

come to the lecture because when you do lectures, you talk more about you. This is a way for me to get in there."

Larry: Perfect. The whole notion of the neutral therapist who maintains anonymity and who avoids personal disclosures was evolved for work with neurotic personality organization. And to a certain extent it's still the best backdrop for most work with preoedipal personality organization. But often when we work with lower-level issues, people want to know something about us. To blindly maintain some kind of *a priori* rigid personal boundary system that the person is not capable of understanding is to my way of thinking unempathic and rude. She really wants to know some things about you and she may not be able to form a connection with you until she discovers the reality of you as a living, breathing, acting human being.

Sometimes we hear, "I've been telling you this and this about me, but I don't know anything about you." When it comes in that form, it can be dealt with very readily, "That's not true, you probably know me better than the people I live with. You don't have to know the facts about my personal life in order to know very deeply and accurately who I am. From our interactions you know me quite well."

In general we avoid disclosure. But when it seems indicated the question often comes up, "How much shall I disclose and where should I place the limits?" I say that most things these people want to know probably can be spoken first and questions asked later. If you ask questions first you often create problems for yourself. I suggest simply that you use your judgment in not disclosing any areas that may be upsetting. But the ultimate criteria I suggest for not disclosing when working with lower-level personality issues is simply when you don't want to. We all have a private life that in one setting we may share, while in another setting we may not care to. We all have many private matters we don't want to talk to various other people about. We all have issues that are simply private. So any time there's private material that we simply don't wish to talk about, that's a good enough criterion for saying, "Well, this is not the kind of thing I generally talk about to other people. You want to know it. Your curiosity is good. You feel hurt and deprived that I find it private. Let me think about it. I'll get back to you but right now, I don't feel comfortable talking about that." Usually it doesn't get to that. But if you have that in the back of your mind, then you know where disclosure would stop.

The other danger with lower-level people and disclosures is the problem of envy. If you have a rich, full life, and you're doing this and that, you make lectures, and you've got a family, while this woman goes back home to an empty apartment, and she has no friends, no family, and no one that she can talk to, how long before the hatred is going to begin to emerge? It will eventually be unavoidable but why fuel the fire, why force the envy prematurely by disclosures you can tactfully avoid?

With more differentiated people, we become less inclined to disclose. If

we felt that facts about ourselves would cure anybody, we would make copies of our autobiography and in the first session hand them out. We don't believe that facts about us ever made anybody better. But we do know that many people, with limited areas of development and for a variety of reasons, feel a certain urgency or desperation to know things about us. We try to judge what that's about and try to interpret all the way along, of course. But I don't think that there's any purpose, in principle, in withholding nonprivate factual information about ourselves from people with lower-level issues when people seem to be truly needing information. I'm not even certain that when dealing with well-developed neurotics that the standard ritualistic rule, to hide behind a blank screen, is always the best way to go. Because even with well-developed people, there are a great many areas of their personalities that are related to preneurotic issues that have not been retrospectively reorganized into the neurotic structures. Some disclosures at certain junctures may be important for maintaining empathy or for establishing connection with split-off aspects of personality.

The general principle involved is that disclosures will affect and may interfere with the development of certain transference features. But our profession talks out of both sides of its mouth on this issue. We have all heard that the transference is delicate, and very easily tampered with by anything we say or do. I am inclined to think that most of the time it's our narcissism that believes we are so significant in every detail of our presentation to clients, though it is true that any particular detail may be singled out to project a transference reaction onto.

The more recent thinking that is certainly reflected in the new laws and ethical principles about relations with clients, holds that transference continues in its tremendous inexorable power for years after analysis or forever. This line of thought suggests that transference is very robust. That there's hardly anything we can do to stop transference development and that transference is never fully "resolved." My view is that the whole question about disclosures and client relations in general has to be evaluated in terms of the individual in analysis and what transferences are likely to develop for what purposes. *A priori* policies simply serve to close our ears and stop our thinking. Why disrupt an otherwise workable relationship by withholding information there's absolutely no reason to withhold? Too often the failure to disclose when there is an authentic need for information or empathy creates more problems than it solves. I promise you that not every request for disclosure can be used as a projective device so why be stupid about it all? The urgency and need of course, must ultimately be subjects for analysis, but at the time, analytic restraint may risk upsetting the relationship.

Ian: At times, in her quest to ask me about me, I've thought what she wants to know is what it's like to have a life.

Larry: Exactly. She simply wants to know. Her experiences have not adequately informed her and she's ashamed to be so naïve and she's too frightened to ask anybody.

Ian: She's got nobody else to talk to about that.

Larry: She wants to know, "What is life like out there in the real world?" You see, we think she knows. She gets in her car, she goes to the shopping mall, she goes to the grocery store, she goes to work. But she doesn't know what human emotional life and human relatedness are really like.

Jeanna: Particularly behind the scenes. I mean, what happens inside people's heads, feelings, fantasies, relationships.

Larry: She doesn't even know what goes on at the office. If we had a videotape of her at work we would likely see a whole group of people relating to one another. She might be able to "pass" but she can't truly relate to any of them as real, living, breathing human beings. And she knows it, all too painfully.

Ian: Right.

Larry: She doesn't understand what human life is all about. So for you to tell her stories about your family, or a little incident with one of your kids, or something like that and how things affect you, I think it's like a mother reading fairy tales or talking about this or that little incident. It provides a basis for safety, for basic trust in simply being with you, for developing human understanding, and eventually for nourishing symbiotic connections.

One of the things we're aware of with people presenting early-level issues is that they don't experience feelings in the ordinary meaning of the word. Our old model for treating neurosis says these feelings were repressed, stuffed "down there" somewhere. So by hook or crook with correct interpretation the feelings have a chance to come "up" into the light of day. This model does not serve well when working with preneurotic, prerepressive relatedness forms. We know babies have biologically based affects from the moment they're born. Research has now identified that within the first hours and days of life mothers can identify some twenty-six affects in their babies. So affect potential in newborns is tremendous. But it is the mother's ability to identify and relate to different affects that is crucial. Affects are not feelings. Affective potentials are biological givens. To have feelings is to be able to understand at an interactive level human conventions regarding the categorization of somatic experience. "I'm feeling angry at you." An infant doesn't have the slightest idea what that would be about. Some stimulus simply evokes physiological potentials. Feelings are learned phenomena that categorize or represent various affective forms of self and other experiencing that many people with limited relatedness experience simply have no understanding of.

I don't have to tell you that part of our job as therapists is frequently to tutor people about what they're feeling. This is what mothers do in the symbiotic period. They actively regulate affects with actions and activities while simultaneously teaching activities and words that go with somatic states and interpersonal situations. I have written extensively about how emotionality in human relatedness

has been considered in psychoanalysis and how affective exchange is the first and most basic form of human communication (*Hedges* in press).

Ian: That's interesting because about a year ago we did exactly that. I was talking to her about feelings. She says, "I don't know what feelings are." So we spent about six months talking about anger, talking about sadness, talking about loneliness, and so on.

Larry: Right.

Ian: She'd tell me a little story about her life and what happened to her. I would say, "Well, it sounds like that would be anger." Then she would write down notes about that and take them home. This is anger. This is sadness.

Larry: We forget that this is a natural process that ordinarily happens in the mother–child emotional bonding relationship. The child will be experiencing something and the mother early on will respond according to the affects she perceives. Later she will put words on the nature of the experience, and on the nature of the feelings. Later more complex metaphors, images, and stories will be added to fill in the complex spectrum of human emotionality.

Sabrina: Even in storybooks, too. "Why does this little boy look sad? Why does this one look mad?" We teach our children about feelings through pictures and looks, and things that are descriptive.

Ian: The thing that strikes me the funniest about what we're talking about is that I've done all this stuff without having the slightest idea what I was doing—simply flying by the seat of my pants.

Sabrina: Yes.

Larry: A good human being who is sincere and trying to connect to such a person is intuitively going to go in the direction you have. A great many people are not going to have the patience to do it or they're not going to be willing to do it. They may even be so doctrinaire about what therapy is supposed to be as not to believe such things are part and parcel of analytic therapy. But I think this would be the natural direction that an empathic person would go in. However, from this point on, having some ideas about organizing transferences and countertransferences will be of a great value to you in terms of expanding and elaborating what you've begun with her. An intuitive and well-meaning therapist can get a person to the point where there's a relationship that supports the person in her life. But such work remains essentially supportive. A lot of old guard therapists would call such a woman a "lifer," meaning that she will require relationship support until one of us dies. Analytic work from here, however, entails a study of transference, resistance, and countertransference. So we want to hear about her again, in the not too distant future. We'll want to hear some actual sessions in which you're able to make notes of exactly what happens in sequence. It's initially difficult to remember interaction sequences with someone whose personality is essentially unorganized but we have to follow the process to look for movement toward connection and events that serve to foreclose connection.

Ian: Except she tapes every session so . . .

Larry: Great! So bring us some notes next time. Choose a session that has a little life between the two of you. And let us take a look at that life.

Ian: Okay.

Larry: Thanks a lot, Ian.

Ian: Sure.

HOW LONG PROCESSING REACTIONS TAKES (A FIVE-MONTH FOLLOW-UP)

Ian: This is a woman I've been seeing for about four years. She is 48 years old. She had come to several of my public lectures. But it took almost six weeks to set up the initial appointment because she wouldn't leave her name or number so I could return her phone call. For the first year of therapy every session she would disassemble my couch and put the cushions up in front of her so that I couldn't see her. I ended up talking to these cushions. And several times she walked out of the room holding a cushion in her hand in front of her so I couldn't see her leave. She would leave the cushion in the waiting room. There are variations on that theme. At times she would have me turn around and not watch her when she left, so that she could put the cushions down.

Sabrina: What did it mean to her to do that?

Ian: She wanted to be invisible. There was something excruciatingly uncomfortable for her about being seen. I have always had a difficult time being with this woman. I've wanted to terminate my work with her on many occasions. We went through a period of time when she was able not to put the cushions up. We did a lot of general exploration about life, humanity, and emotions. We did a stint where I more or less educated her about emotions because she didn't know what they were, didn't understand them. So we'd pick anxiety, depression, joy, or whatever, and we would work that through until she felt she had some grasp on what the emotion was. We spent time connecting somatic symptoms and sensations with emotions and feelings. We talked about situations and what would be a normal emotion to experience in the circumstance. This woman just did not know what it was to be a person. She would tell me she needed me to talk, for me to point her in the right direction, and for me to guide her. I was very reluctant to do that. That's what I want to talk about today, about my reluctance. I finally did begin to guide her and teach her basic things that I realized she simply didn't know about. In retrospect, I think that it was very helpful. This woman has no friends. She was married once when she was 20 for a year. Her husband beat her repeatedly. She finally ran away from him. Disappeared.

She was born in Wyoming in a one-room cabin with a dirt floor and never had any friends there. Her father was extremely abusive and her mother was a very strange and critical woman. It was in discussing her history that we studied the material about hiding. The only place she could go in her house that was safe was under her bed because there were no rooms. She feared her father and felt that the only way to survive in the family was to be invisible. So she spent a great deal of her time hiding under the bed.

Instead of talking to me she writes and brings me letters. I wish I had the last one she wrote, but she wouldn't give it to me, which is very strange because she always gives me her letters. The letters are really incredible. There are two different things of importance in them. One is that she will write a letter just heaping me with praise for my patience and my ability to be there, and the amount of time and effort I've put into working with her. Then I'll get a letter that is just scathing, that rips me to shreds. For example, in the last letter she wouldn't give me, she called me, among other things, a sexist pig. She sent me a card once that had a cat on the front of it and it said something about wanting to scratch my eyes out. So she can write about intense emotions but she never shows them. They are never directly expressed.

She tape records every session and has this catalog of tapes for the last four years of the sessions we have had. She will tape the session and then for the next week listen to the tape every day. She says this is the only way for her to process what we have talked about because in the session she is totally oblivious to what's going on. She can't compute what's happening. So she says it's not until two or three days down the line that she is able to listen to the tape and actually hear what we talked about. I once suggested they served as a transitional object to keep me with her. She really didn't like that idea. And in response didn't tape the sessions a couple of times to prove to me that she didn't have to. At that time I told her, "You know it's okay if you want to do that." And she started again.

She wrote me a letter several weeks ago in which she talked about how difficult things have been for her. The only woman she has any connection with at all, who is 80 years old, has been put in a distant rest home and she's been distraught about that. She's not going to be able to see this woman any more so she is essentially totally isolated at this point. She told me that in the last year she has put on 75 pounds by eating compulsively. She's got to weigh about 350 now.

Things are just not going well for her. In the last several weeks she's gone back to pillow hiding again. She's back behind the cushions so I've become very concerned with that. She goes home at night after work and scarfs. She eats everything she can get her hands on and has not been able to stop doing that. She had been in the Weight Watchers program for a year or so and had been doing very well. So she's really taken a turn for the worse in that regard. The last session she spent most of the time behind the pillows again and brought that letter that really ripped me to shreds. She has this tremendous ability to take anything I say and transform it into an attack. If I say, "Hello," it may somehow get transformed into an attack. So I find myself afraid to say anything.

Jeanna: Do you tell her this?

Ian: Yes. We talk about that a lot. We talk about how difficult it is for me. She wrote in the last letter about removing some things from the tape that I had said. One of them was how it seems important for her to please me in the session. I was trying to understand what it must be like to be her. She translated that into I thought I was superior to her and that all men are sexist pigs. She does that quite regularly.

Sabrina: And that leaves you . . .?

Ian: Dumbfounded sometimes. I'm astounded at what I can say in the name of empathy, which gets transformed into a blatant attack.

Larry: In response to your empathy, your attempt to connect, we see the rageful disconnect or refusal to connect. The overwhelming (and to the infant, psychotic) mother appears in transference to thwart the contact. In your remark about how important it is for her to please you, you were reaching out to show her that you wanted to be with her, to join her in her space. I believe your comment was empathically successful because of the break-off transference reaction that followed. The woman is terrified of contact for reasons suggested in the small history you gave us. Contact can only be abusive.

Ian: I've found myself feeling very sadistic toward this woman. I'm not sure why that is, because I don't generally feel that way with people. One of the things I'll do, for example, is when she comes into the office she'll maybe say "Hello" or something and I'll say "Hello" and she'll sit down.

Then I'll sit and wait for her to begin speaking. She's told me time and again that my waiting for her to start is really painful for her. She needs some kind of communication from me. But even armed with that knowledge, I'll still sit and wait. It's almost a sadistic, angry feeling that I get toward her. I haven't been able to figure for myself why I feel that way, other than I must be incredibly angry with her. I feel myself being almost punitive by just sitting there and waiting. I'm even consciously aware of a belief that I must be punitive, and that I will continue to be. So that's been worrying me about how I'm feeling about her.

Sean: In what you're describing about not saying anything to her for fear that she's going to turn what is intended to be a statement of empathy around as an attack, she's putting you in a position where you're becoming more and more invisible. In some way is she bringing the experience to you of how it is that she's needed to hide all these years? While we see few signs of symbiotic structure in what you tell us about her, it's possible that invisibility is for her a way she experiences a certain self and other connection.

Karen: I like that.

Sean: There is a hatred, a despising of anything that you attempt to bring to her. She destroys it; she pisses on it; she turns it to shit, and attacks you in the process.

Karen: And you're even uncomfortable with having feelings toward her.

Ian: Yes. I am.

Sean: It seems like you're needing to hide your thoughts and your feelings from her because she is somehow

going to turn them around and use them against you.

Ian: Yes, that's very true. I remember not long ago listening to one of your cases when you were talking about how you hated this patient so much, and weren't able to speak that. My fantasy is that I could never speak my sadism to this woman because I would never see her again. I've talked to her on occasion about my anger. I've talked to her about feeling helpless. I've talked to her about no matter what I say it's not the right thing, and how I become scared to say anything. That all seemed to go okay. But when I talked about my struggle being in the relationship and how I get really afraid I will say or do the wrong thing, she says, "What a horrible person I am for inflicting that upon you. I shouldn't come here anymore because it's so difficult for you."

Karen: Her attacking self-pity is a way of deflecting the insight you have to give her about her own behavior and what it provokes in you. What she does with that possibility for connection is get into a wounded-victim position, deflecting again your attempts at contact. I am struck by how much of her private world she is sharing with you. I see those letters as a window into her private world, as if she's doing this inner dialogue with you at all times but you only get these quick glimpses.

Ian: Oh yes. I'm sure she is. We've talked about that, too. I'll say something to her and I can see the gears turning. Nothing comes out, but you can see it being processed. I've said to her on several occasions, "You know, I would really be fascinated about what's going on in there because I can see it going on but I'm not ever hearing it come out." So it will come out in a letter. But as she says in one of the letters I have here, it takes her a week to process her experience and to be able to put it into words. In this one-page letter she says, "It has taken me eight hours of concentrated effort to write this letter." There are four short paragraphs in the letter, so it is laborious for her to express herself but she does. I've found myself in the last months feeling increasingly ineffective, helpless, lost, frustrated, and angry.

Sabrina: Which are all her feelings.

Ian: I know that's true.

Sabrina: Including that your situation is impossible, that you can't get out of it.

Ian: Right. Two weeks ago we had a conversation in which I vocalized how difficult it was becoming for me and how frustrated and helpless I felt at times. But that even though I felt that way, I wouldn't be throwing her out like her last therapist had. I explained that I saw my reactions more as something to be interested in and concerned with. That the way we affect one another is a problem that she and I are going to work on together and work it through. I think she understood that she was not going to be thrown out. But I feel like I'm working myself into a pit I don't know how to get out of. I think I'm aware of where these feelings are coming from but I don't know what to do with them.

COUNTERTRANSFERENCE: CONTRASTING SYMBIOTIC AND ORGANIZING

Larry: Your dilemma offers us an opportunity to get a sharp contrast between the way we might think about countertransference to symbiotic material versus countertransference to organizing material, which I think this is. The role reversal formulation you are speaking of, Sabrina, often gives us a lever when we are dealing with symbiotic material. We can do a lot of things with it. We hear ourselves representing Mother with the person in analysis as child. Then we are able to reverse it so that our reactions represent the child and the person in analysis is the mother. Then we are able to say, "I'm now feeling what you must have been feeling for years."

But when we're dealing with experiences that are less organized, less related, the countertransference is more often to the overwhelming or psychotic mother who was internalized in infancy. That is, the countertransference reaction reflects a primitive emotional response on our part. I think of an infant's primary attempt to organize channels to Mother, first *in utero* and later in the postnatal nurturing environment. The success of the reaching out, the organizing attempt, is dependent on the receptivity and responsiveness of Mother's body and mind. The image I have is of an infant sending forth a thousand invisible tendrils of some sort. It's easy to think of a hand reaching toward a mother's breast, face, eye, or other body part. What will be the mother's response to the reaching? Will the tendrils find a place on Mother's body and in Mother's mind to attach themselves?

The current thinking on touch, whether literal and concrete or metaphorical and abstract, emphasizes the motivation, the intent of the one touching (Brazelton and Barnard 1990). Mother must *desire* to make contact. I think of Michelangelo's Sistine Chapel version of God and Adam reaching toward the touch that gives human life its meaning. The spark of human life comes from two beings actively reaching out toward each other, wanting to be in contact. If we think of a child either *in utero* or in the extrauterine environment sending out mental or physical tendrils toward the environment, then what we hope for is some kind of response that will provide the sense of being empathically met, contacted, so that the child is encouraged to sustain the extension of those primordial tendrils.

Whenever we're dealing with organizing issues, whether in a limited or a well-developed personality organization, we are going to be studying situations in which the person is in active, motivated extension toward the therapist, with the hope of a sustaining response. When studying organizing material it is not so much the *way*, or *style*, or *mode* in which Mother responded that is decisive. Instead, the organizing transference is a record of faulty responsiveness, of early maternal failure, the failure to be there in the needed way at the needed time though the fault may have nothing to

do with the real mother. An activity issue that might look similar from a behavioral standpoint, when studied through the lens of the symbiotic (or replicated) transference would be embedded in a stylized way of relating. But when viewed through the lens of organizing transference, the memory will be of early contact attempts coupled with the person's internalized reactions to the failure or rupture of contact.

With your woman, Ian, your reaching out and successfully connecting revives the frightening abusive-parent transference. She turns that right into "You're a sexist pig," an attack that seems based on primary identification, almost a "monkey see, monkey do." If we are looking at that interaction only with a symbiotic lens, we are going to try to understand the mutual attacking, the internalization of the vicious objects, the turning of passive trauma into active victory, and so forth, all of which might be other ways to understand her. But the crucial thing to understand about the organizing level is that there are moments in which you are oriented and extended toward her waiting for contact. But as soon as you are oriented, "I am here," and she believes you, then the organizing transference becomes activated and the vicious mother or father of the organizing period appears to her. You are not responded to in terms of your empathy, but rather you are seen as a threatening monster and she reacts ragefully to fend off the danger.

The predefense patterns we expect to see are those mammals use to react to danger: flight, fight, or freeze. At that moment in time what we've got to learn from the individual client is exactly how this person learned in infancy to break off, to destroy, to turn away from, to rupture contact – contact that might have the power to engage her in a symbiosis. At this moment of potential contact we get into the specifics of each person's developmental history, prenatally and postnatally, in terms of organizing channels that were attempted and what the nature of the traumatic breech was that caused the person never to reach out again.

Winnicott (1965), in his paper on birth memories, says that the basic pattern of the mind forms according to the ways in which there was early traumatic impingement. Using birth trauma as a prototype for considering early impingement on the child's sense of "going on being," Winnicott says that ordinarily we have no reason to feel that the birth process is traumatic. The child has already had many frustrations living in the intrauterine environment, being constantly squeezed, subjected to numerous chemical changes, the mother's movement, and so forth, so that a normal birth need not be traumatic and may be very relieving. But if the birth process is prolonged or overly intense, there is an impingement into the child's mind, the child's sense of "going on being." The child reacts to that impingement. The longer I study these early prenatal and postnatal impingements, the more convinced I am that human infants are equipped with genetic knowledge of the fear of death. If

the umbilicus is twisted or the placenta disturbed, or if the warm body of Mother cannot be found, I believe infants react with a strong terror of death and go into frantic somatic reactions and constrictions designed to ensure survival. But the death fear trauma forms a primary persecutory template in the mind that influences all subsequent development.

When a child is forced to react, to respond with an assertion of the life force or instinct before the child is ready to respond, the *pattern* of having to respond prematurely to the impingement becomes the basis for subsequent thought and is necessarily persecutory in nature, leaving a traumatic imprint on the infant mind. It leaves a pattern imprinted in which interpersonal contact is paired with the fear of a monstrous intrusion. The mode of fending off the intrusion – fight, flight, or freeze – likewise becomes a fending-off pattern that is influential in the person's subsequent personality development. The persecutory pattern remains a a foundational template to all later experiences. We might think about all the varieties of possible reaction to intrusion. But the bottom line is that what somehow gets registered in memory is, "Never go there again." Connecting in that way is too painful.

So, Ian, as you begin to invite her to go there again to the connecting place with you, to the remembered pain of overstimulation and abuse, the only thing she can hear is the traumatizing parental response. Then you wonder why she so misinterpreted you. If we're thinking and behaving the way we ordinarily do with other clients, working on projections and projective identifications, then we miss completely where the organizing experience leaves people. It does not serve us to study the ebb and flow of transference and countertransference as scenarios. What has happened here is not an interaction or interpersonal flow, but rather the compulsive cessation of the interactive flow based upon the organizing transference, the "Never go there again."

Ian: So in transference I become the terrifying organizing mother to her when I make an empathetic contact?

Larry: Exactly. When you reach her and she feels touched by your intention, yes. Then she must stop the flow of relatedness. An archaic fending-off mode emerges and in the countertransference you are left high and dry wondering what just happened. This feeling unresponded to no doubt stimulates deep feelings in you of when your mother of infancy failed to respond to you or when you felt pushed away by her.

Ian: Her mind works it a particular way each time, and she experiences my approach as a persecution, an attack, or a disruption?

Larry: Yes. And to her it is *absolutely real*. In such moments when the person allows the organizing transference to govern his experience with you he is in a presymbolic thought mode that is concrete, sensory, immediate, and lacks the usual reality testing. You are not merely behaving like the mother, but at the moment in her awareness you *are* the persecuting mother/other. The usual split in the ego between experiencing and ob-

serving (Sterba, 1934), which we rely on for transference interpretations does not operate when organizing experience is in focus. It is for this reason I advocate that some third party be involved as a case monitor or manager, perhaps from the outset of therapy when significant organizing transference is anticipated. I strongly recommend having a colleague meet with the client occasionally to see how things are going, to see her when you're not available, to make notes of the state of the therapy, and to serve as the observing ego when the transference psychosis is firmly in place. I am convinced that the majority of accusations being made against therapists today are derived in one way or another from the activation of psychotic features associated with the organizing transference. To your woman the things you do to her are real.

Ian: I've attacked her, intruded.

Larry: Yes. But pay close attention to the fact that you are *really* there, actually wishing to reach out to her. The place of potential contact is very real. When she feels that reality, that's where the break-off occurs and that's when the psychotic mother makes her appearance and you become the real intruder, the real molester, the real abuser. She is absolutely convinced of the reality of your intrusion and its damaging or hurtful effect. In fact, you are there. In fact you are reaching out. In fact your intent is to reach her, to touch her with yourself. This contact moment that permits interpretation contrasts sharply with interpretation of, say, a neurotic transference where we both understand we are engaged in a chess-like game of symbol manipulation, a game of illusions, an "as if" experience.

It's my belief that most, if not all, negative therapeutic reactions, malpractice suits, and ethical complaints are rooted in the problem of the organizing transference being at the moment completely indistinguishable from reality. When we engage a person at this deep level we are playing with fire—and we may get burned. If we are not successful in getting the person to distinguish current reality from organizing transference, we will either lose the case or risk a lawsuit aimed at our "inappropriate" conduct, which for the patient is real, being based as it is on our really reaching out, and of our really taking hold and engaging him or her at a level and in ways that have not happened since infancy.

Ian: I really have a sense of that. It could be dangerous.

Larry: Yes. And when you do get that psychotic response I think it's such an important thing for us to pick up on the confusion of transference reality with our interactive reality. It is real. They will say, "You really did this to me."

Ian: Yes. I really understand that.

Sean: In thinking about the organizing-level patient I've presented here, I find myself often reluctant to make contact on that level with her. Because if I do I have to be willing at the moment to face the psychotic mother in her, with a psychotic reaction to me. It's the psychotic experience in her that she's bringing. Something in me wants to hold her in such a way so that a psychotic reaction doesn't come up.

But that's no good because it's inevitable that psychotic reactions come up if you're going to make contact. It's a real tightrope to walk.

Larry: Absolutely. Melanie Klein is quoted in Strachey (1934) as observing that analysts are frequently reluctant to give "mutative interpretations" because in so doing they are inviting the full force of id energies to be directed toward themselves. This danger certainly applies here.

I've talked with you before about the organizing countertransference in terms of what happens to parents in the first four months of a newborn's life. By the fourth month they have bags under their eyes, they are overwhelmed, the marriage is falling apart, sex is in trouble, everyone in the family in one way or another is about to kill each other. Countertransference to organizing states is often similar. Harold Searles (1979) has written that countertransference to psychotic states is chaotic, it is disruptive, it is somatic, and it feels perfectly terrible. Winnicott (1949a) feels that hate is an inevitable and appropriate response to psychotic elements in transference. But we are now in a position to go further. What we can now add is that if we are tuned into the organizing layer of our client, then it activates the organizing layer in ourselves. We work to get a satisfactory response from our client. When the client is unable or refuses to connect or connects and disconnects by going psychotic on us, it reminds us of the primordial time we reached out to our mothers and got an inadequate or painful response.

Ian: Which would be to address

what I was saying before about the sadistic rage I'm feeling.

Larry: That's right. Now we have to look at that as your transference reaction to your organizing or psychotic mother that is being stimulated by her nonresponsiveness. At the symbiotic level we are more likely to think in terms of projective identification, that is, that she is projecting sadism into you. At this level I am more inclined to say that even as you reach out and she feels your contact intent, her primordial transference response is to break contact with a vicious response.

Her predefense is to fight. She attacks you, bites you, and now what is your response? I'm thinking at that point it is not a sadistic projective identification you are responding to. But rather, this recalls for you when your own mother in her own way refused you, got angry, or bit back.

Ian: I didn't want to hear that! [Group laughs.]

Larry: Our time is up. Let's return next week to your woman, Ian, because it seems we all have much to gain by looking at your work very closely.

Ian: Sure thing.

WORKING THE CONTACT MOMENT (ONE WEEK LATER)

Ian: My picture of her is a woman from a Marx brothers movie. The Marx brothers always have these women in their fifties or sixties, overweight, hysterical, with high-pitched laughter who are all over the place. That's the kind of a presentation she gives. Very frenzied at times. She told me last week that her mother always accused her of being too loud. Her mother said she was ashamed to take her anywhere because she was too loud.

Two other things really interest me about her. She never answers a question. No matter what question I put to her, she will not answer it. She will only give an answer to it circumspectly. At times I've become interested in that process and asked her the same question maybe seven or eight times in the same session and never gotten an answer. Something like, "How did you feel when your husband did that?" "Well you know how men

are," and she'll go into this thing. I'll say, "But about your husband, how did you feel when he did that?" "Well, you know in 1963 . . ." and there's this story but never an answer to the question. I don't think this woman has ever answered a question in the four years I've seen her in therapy.

The other thing that she does is talk about me in the third person. She's very disturbed by my looking at her, which seems connected to her wanting to be invisible. She'll say things like, "Now he is staring a hole through me," or "Now he is thinking such and such." She talks about me in the third person, as if I'm some sort of object in the room. My question to her is, "Who are you talking to? Who is that person in the room that you're speaking to about me?"

Karen: So she relates to you as a thing?

Ian: Right.

Larry: Kafka's story, "Metamorphosis," has been talked about by many as what it feels like to be psychotic. It's a story of a young man who was very responsible. Every day he put on his coat and tie and got on the train to go to work. But as he began to decompensate, the family, which had been dysfunctional while he was functional, slowly had to move into a functional position. He wakes up one morning a cockroach. The family sits outside his room and even pokes into the room but they are always talking about "him." "What is he doing now?" The whole family talks about the psychotic in the third person. Kohut (1979), in referring to this story said, "This is how so many of our patients felt as children. They were talked about in the third person." They were never addressed. They were not seen as real, live human beings to interact with. But rather, "What is he doing now?" And so your woman was always an it, a she, the baby, the child. And that attitude on the part of the parents makes it very difficult for a child to grow up feeling like a person.

So much material relating to organizing issues has to do with features in the nonhuman environment as we read last year in Searles's book (1960). So often it's, "I'm not human either." In another paper we're going to read soon by Victor Tausk (1919), a woman speaks repeatedly of an "influencing machine." He did a diagnostic study on a woman in a mental hospital. No one could do much with her. She kept talking about this influencing machine. He suddenly had the idea of asking her to draw a picture of the machine. It was a crude picture of her

body. She experienced her body as a thing that influenced her, but it wasn't her. When we are dealing with very early levels of psychic development, we want to be tuned into the experience of not being a person who could be addressed or related to.

Ian: I can certainly feel that with her.

Karen: I'm relating to what he's saying. In working with my organizing-level person and trying to use Kernberg's principles with respect to object relations, I'm really moving into what's happening here. I, too, experience my attempts to relate either as falling flat, or as the person rejecting a transference interpretation I'm making. So I, too, as I'm hearing you, Ian, I'm feeling, "Where do I go now?"

Ian: I've been feeling that for the last three years.

Larry: I think as we go around the room we all are dealing with people who are functioning predominantly in this mode or who from time to time drop into this level of experiencing. How helpless we feel because all of the standard therapeutic interventions do fall flat. And even if routine or standard interpretations are accepted, you end up having the sense that they didn't touch anything. Even if the person is more or less cooperative, or says, "Yes, yes, I'm sure you're right." Or even if a person can repeat our interpretations, they don't hit the mark or they're not usable.

Ian: Speaking of hitting the mark reminds me of one of the things she said last week. We were talking about her compulsive eating. I was asking her about the feelings she has when she comes home and starts to stuff herself. I asked what she felt about herself at those moments. Her answer to me was that I didn't understand. That she has no self. There is no self. That I kept missing that. That she has no self, that she's not like other people.

Larry: She can say that to you because it's true.

Ian: And she always says that there are no thoughts. That there are no feelings. She complained that I'm constantly trying to find them and that they are simply not there. Which I thought was very insightful.

Larry: Yes. People are seldom able to admit that, because they know

others will think them crazy. They know people are supposed to have thoughts and feelings. They know people are supposed to have a self. If you don't have any of those things you must be bonkers!

Ian: I thought that was an accomplishment when I heard it.

Larry: Absolutely. To be able to say, "Everyone else has a self. I don't. Other people have thoughts and feelings. I don't. I have no idea what you're talking about. You ask me questions. I don't know how to answer them." I find it remarkable that she trusts you enough to tell you those things.

THE MIMICAL SELF AND THE FALSE SELF

Larry: I think that her words ring true for many people organized or unorganized at this level. But they're seldom able to acknowledge it. As you know, I've formulated at this level the idea of the "mimical self" to contrast with Winnicott's (1952) notion of the "false self." Winnicott's idea is that the false self arises during mother–child relating in consequence of the child's conforming to the maternal demand so as to have access to the mother. If, in trying to form a symbiosis, the child sees that Mother is available in this way, and not available in that way, then he or she will mold him- or herself to fit the mother's nature. The false self is an ego structure based on conforming to the demands of the world in deference to one's own wishes and inclinations. The false self that is universal can be said to be essentially masochistic in nature in that one en-

dures pain and/or deprivation to get some form of love or connection. I have written about Bergman's film, *The Passion of Anna*, as a brilliant study of how our deepest passion, based on our earliest bond to Mother, is essentially false, masochistic, perverse, and self destructive (Hedges 1992).

In personality organizations we call symbiotic or borderline, we are aware that there is a certain personality warping. Learning to fit our needs in with Mother's personality is a project we all had to accomplish. I am of the belief that with every one of us, there were a great many areas of early potential that did not fit within the personality requirements and limits of our mothers. That is, if we imagine a baby to be born with a thousand possible ways to connect, the good-enough mother might be available for 300. In order to find her I must organize my response system in certain ways. But what happens to the other 700 potentials? Or, consider the possibility that in order to find her I have to warp some of those potentials, which might have better possibilities or might have more creatively gone in different directions. I had to position myself in certain ways in order to form and guarantee a safe bonding connection with her.

So I believe that at the bottom of every one of our personalities, there is a whole series of unmet possibilities. The more I'm able to tune into this level in myself, and the more that the people I'm working with are also able to tune into these primary or foundational aspects, the more I'm becoming aware of how many ways we each were unable to find a mother's love when we needed it. I think that even if a good strong symbiosis was formed, and even perhaps where later separation-individuation partially occurred, it is still important for us to be able to talk about the unmet potentials of the organizing period.

I think at the bottom of all of our personalities are spontaneous and creative parts of ourselves that never got fully responded to and that remain undeveloped, simply because our mothers didn't know how to or didn't want to respond in a way that tuned into various aspects of our natures. Each one of us had a mother who had a certain personality that was finite. Though the baby's potentials may have been met adequately, what about those essential potentials that remained unmet (Jorgenson 1993)?

So with your woman we have a lot of unmet potential. To the extent that the child conforms to the maternal demand, we can talk about a false self, which is also ego structure. Or we could talk about a true or an integrated self, which is the extent to which the baby's own true needs and the mother's personality meet and work things out to begin a spontaneous and creative line of development. Integration of essential potentials results when the child is not merely conforming, but when two are working together to develop an emotional mutual cuing dance based upon an appreciation of mutual need, demand, desire, and request. We might talk about a true self forming out of negotiation with the object relations world (Bollas 1989), and a false self forming on the basis of a demand from the environment that the child adapts him- or herself to.

I have added to these considerations the concept of a yet developmentally earlier mimical self, an imitative self (Hedges 1994a). This concept describes simply, "monkey see, monkey do." Homo sapiens has far more potential for mimicry than any of the other primates. We have a remarkable capacity to ape, to imitate, to copy others. The example par excellence, is Jerzy Kosinski's *Being There*, which was filmed with Peter Sellers and Shirley MacLaine. In *Being There*, there is always a television set that Peter Sellers is mimicking. Kosinski himself arranged the screenplay so that what is on the background television—the commercial, the speech, the political rally, whatever—is aping the main action on the screen and vice versa—the live action apes the TV. Then there was that wonderful sex scene with Shirley MacLaine, the greatest love scene ever filmed! [Laughter.] She is passionately in love with Chance (the mimical character) but can't seem to rouse his interest. Finally she asks, "How do you like it?" He is watching the television over her shoulder. He has no idea what she is asking and all he knows to say is, "I like to watch (meaning TV)." We watch her mind turning, "Oh, he likes to watch." So next we see her wildly and passionately masturbating for him to watch on this giant bearskin rug with the jaws open to the camera. Meanwhile Chance is up on the bed watching TV, standing on his head aping the video calisthenics, occasionally glancing at but not being quite sure exactly what she's doing over there on the bearskin rug. In this film and novel we have a brilliant picture of how the whole world responds to people who live in the organizing level, continuing to think that they know things that they don't because they can imitate. There is an appearance of being a person, an appearance of living normally in the world, a semblance of being human. But the appearance is totally misleading. The person, like your woman, has no self, no true thoughts, no knowledge of what human feelings or interactions are about.

Ian: As you're speaking, I'm thinking of things about her that really fit what you're saying. For example, she has had this job at an office for fourteen years where she writes procedures. And she can do that well. Many years ago she got a promotion and it was a big step for her. But in that promotion she had to interact with other human beings . . .

Larry: And she couldn't do it.

Ian: She couldn't do it. For two weeks she tried and failed dismally. She went back to writing procedures and is still there now.

Larry: That's a very good example. She can perform skills requiring cognitive intelligence and imitation. She knows how people, things, and procedures are supposed to be. But when emotional or relatedness intelligence is required she is completely lost. She was so traumatized in infancy that she withdrew totally from human interaction that would lead toward becoming human through symbiotic relating.

Ian: Right.

Larry: Many of these people have spouses and families. Yet, as you examine the family life, you can see it's a strange kind of family life. Again, achieved by imitation. But if you ask the person to tell you about his teenage daughter he can't tell you anything. He can give facts but not anything characterological or what it's like to interact with her.

Ian: Which explains her not being able to answer any questions because that involves some internal relatedness process. Instead she gives me a story that she has stored in some file somewhere.

Sean: We left off last week with Karen bringing up projective identification and its relation to countertransference. You suggested that Ian's emotional response was an outcropping of his own internalized "psychotic mother." I am interested in your weaving that into your thoughts here.

Larry: Projective identification is most useful as a listening concept when we're talking about the way the symbiosis forms and functions. When we think this way, of course, we are considering two different relatedness levels that are not necessarily distinctly separated in any given individual's life experience—the organizing level and the symbiotic level. "Levels" are, of course, metaphors to describe two different listening stances or perspectives, which we define somewhat arbitrarily for our own thought and-communication convenience. The perspectives are defined by reference to what we believe are different kinds or levels or stages of human relatedness. We see many instances with analytic speakers where we may find it helpful to listen alternating from an organizing to a symbiotic perspective. As a concept, projective identification forms the interface between these two defined modes of interaction, of relatedness intelligence. We might imagine that the child organizing his or her environment forms primordial impressions of the good mother and the bad mother depending upon what happens during the early organizing reaching attempts. We might formulate that in the transference the woman relates to Ian as though Ian were that original good breast or bad breast. Since that mode would be a primary way of experiencing the world for her, we might formulate using the notion of projective identification that she then makes him become her fantasy by her engineering of or perception of the interaction.

But this is a very sophisticated formulation, much more toward what we ordinarily consider from a listening standpoint symbiotic. When the analytic speaker comes in and forces us into a certain stylized position, we infer that the pattern is based upon the way he or she once lived emotional interactions with the (m)other. That replicated transference is what we listen for when considering the internalized symbiosis and all of the so-called borderline and characterological conditions. Either I as the analytic speaker am experiencing the analytic listener as a good breast or a bad breast (so-called affective splitting), or I may experience myself as a good self or a bad self (also affective splitting). The crucial twist for countertransference interpretation becomes possible when I (as analytic speaker) reverse the experience with my listener. I will then mother my listener in the way I was once mothered.

In Alice Balint's (1943) paper we read on primary identification, we learned that the earliest mimicry or identification thought mode is mobilized by the infant to deal with traumatic experiences. I identify in a total or gross body way with the trauma my mother provides me. In all subsequent relationships I relive bodily what was done to me by doing it to others. I have often said that the psychoanalytic "golden rule" is that "we do unto others what was done unto us." These are features of the symbiosis revived in the replicating transference or at least these are helpful ideas about how we might listen to the replicated character dimensions. No one knows the best way to observe or formulate what's "really" happening in analysis, but listening schema concepts like projective identification and primary identification seem to do a fairly good job of keeping us in our chairs attending to the relating processes.

Returning to your question, if we are listening to earliest organizing strivings we can't count on stylized forms of interaction with identification and projective identification operating smoothly and predictably. Because if somehow arrested at the organizing level, the child has not been able to form reliable relatedness channels with which to continue development. Presumably, what has happened is that this mother was somehow not ready to receive this child. Sometimes it seems to us that the mother's womb was not optimally responsive. Perhaps there was some toxic substance passing through the placenta. Perhaps the arteries in the umbilicus were hardened or constricted. In one man I saw some years ago it happened that in the last phases of pregnancy the mother was forming Rh antibodies in an attempt to kill the child. As a fetus he knew his mother was trying to kill him. So sometimes early organizing structures are formed in utero. But for convenience in discussion it is easier to consider a real baby interacting with a real mother.

Let's suppose that along with the mothers of Tustin's autistic children, this mother is depressed due to life circumstances not her fault or of her making. Say something horrible has happened in her life. Perhaps her husband was just killed in an automobile accident. She is left bereft with a baby. When that baby needs mother to be thinking and responding in the way that Bion (1962) suggests is critical, the mother simply can't do it effectively, efficiently, or sensitively. She is preoccupied. So instead of the baby forming primary thought modes within the context of ordinary sensual and consensual reality, the baby must precociously begin inventing his or her own private ways of dealing with the world like any other animal would. And so various psychotic constructions arise.

Many autistic children indeed look and behave like animals. They are often seen as wild. They may identify with animals and crawl around on all fours baring their teeth, somehow understanding well the animal in them. Tustin (1981) talks about the child's withdrawing into an encapsulated state. She maintains that these autistic children regularly draw and talk about a black hole. When she unraveled the riddle of the black hole, she found that the black hole is used by the child to express a place where Mother once was, where love once was! These children had a mother in utero. They might have even known Mother in the extrauterine environment. But in some way or another their contacts with that mother were experienced as under- or overstimulating enough for them to blot out object relations potentials and to construct a private encapsulated world.

Tustin also talks about the entangled children who are autistically withdrawn but psychically remain somehow connected, merged and confused with the mother. The bottom line of what we are considering is that, if for whatever reason, the baby and the mother do not match up in a way in which the human thought and relatedness system can be satisfactorily assimilated, the living tendrils that ordinarily link the mother and child in a symbiotic dance, simply do not adequately form. With some autistic children and other psychotics we have reason to believe that there was a genetic, biological, or constitutional defect or problem so that no matter how creative or attentive the mothering, a symbiotic dance could never have formed. The baby couldn't make use of the available mothering because of some preexisting factor or concern. But the vast majority of people we see in our consulting rooms tend to be functionally organizing or psychotic because the subtleties of the infant's needs did not match the available caregiving processes. When thinking about the mismatch there has been an unfortunate tendency among researchers and therapists to blame Mother. There certainly must be inadequate mothers. But most of the time I find the trick is to discover the fault with the mothering process without faulting the mother. Many times I am convinced that no matter how good the caregiving may have been, the

child was simply not able to make the transition from somatic sensual life in the womb to psychic life in the symbiosis.

Sean: Could you comment on how to see the moment of psychotic transference and how to make use of it?

Larry: Yes. After the client has attained some sense of comfort and safety in the presence of the analyst (which may take several years), it becomes possible to begin tracking the approach for interpersonal emotional contact. After we learn to identify the mode of approach we then begin to learn exactly how this person manages to foreclose contact completely or rupture contact that is about to be made or has just been made. Then, in a daring move, immediately after the break or breech, we may feel confident enough to interrupt the client and ask if we can retrace a few steps and see what just happened. Like, "Wait a minute. Can we go back a bit? Something just happened. We were talking about such and such and you were telling me thus and so I thought you were a little nervous about it, or you were excited about it, but that we had a moment of sharing together, of feeling each other's presence. And then I felt like you left the room, or that you weren't here anymore." We might use any words that convey the sense of leaving, disappearing, or being invisible, based on whatever language he or she may have given us about the withdrawn state. "You and I were connecting and then something happened. Can you tell me about that?"

We must actively seize those moments in which we feel a potential presence and then a loss of presence. It takes awhile before a listener gets to where he or she can do that, because each speaker has his or her own special way of obscuring moments of potential contact. And they almost have to forcefully and immediately bring them back and try to capitalize on the fleeting moment of presence. If you wait three minutes, they are so far away you will never bring them back. When you first stop the action and ask for a replay, you will get a vacant, unknowing stare. What you are asking will not be understood. But I promise it won't take many times before they catch on.

Sean: Now, when you say, "bring them back," are you talking about sustaining the connection?

Larry: Exactly. That's the goal, that's where it seems that the therapeutic action actually exists for organizing states, in analyzing the momentary appearance of the internalized "psychotic mother" and then finding a way of sustaining the connectedness that could never before be held onto. What's being confronted in this maneuver is the fundamental psychotic or organizing-level delusion that has governed this person's ways of relating. By calling the person to return to being emotionally alive with us in the here-and-now interaction, we hope to show that we are not the psychotic mother of their delusion, that safe, satisfying, comforting, and/or stimulating interactions can be managed with us as "exhibit A" of people in the world. By deliberately fostering, seducing, creating in any way possible these moments of contact and then capitalizing on the fleeting

contact and trying quickly to grab it before the person gets too far away, what you are in fact doing is sustaining for a moment that contact.

I don't know how many different ways different therapists might be able to sustain contact, but I've observed that by attempting to hold the person to discussing exactly what has just happened between us, exactly what the person just experienced that accompanied the flight from contact, people soon become willing and able to sustain the conversation, even if their rupture mode is a fighting one. At first they may be startled. No one has ever said to them, "Wait, come back. You were here and then you ran away—I *want you* here with me. What happened just now?" People seem rather quickly to grasp intuitively that you have correctly seen and fixed on something of crucial importance for their lives. Now mind you, this taking hold of the contact moment cannot safely be attempted until well into the process of feeling comfortable together. People sense the importance of your insistence on "our being here right now" and studying the process of our coming together and going apart as a new adventure. I find it consistently uncanny how people almost immediately feel the rightness of it once they trust the positive motive of the therapist.

Anything you can do to create and to sustain the contact is important. The therapeutic action here seems to follow the principles of classical (Pavlovian) conditioning. *With organizing experience stopping the withdrawal is the interpretive act.* The interpretation is, therefore, not really verbal but implicit in the activity of the therapist, however the blocking of the withdrawal is accomplished. What happens in the long run is that by catching and sustaining the contact moment through interpretively holding the person in an engagement, people learn that they can tolerate contact stimulation of various kinds and intensities. They learn through discussion of contact moments that they do have an option to relate to people emotionally and realistically. Often when therapists begin this technique they may be able to catch the speaker only once an hour. I have often said that the 50-minute hour was never invented for these people. Half-hours held more frequently and/or brief phone contact in between is probably more effective much of the time because the contact can just as easily occur in a short time. And 50-minute sessions with organizing states are often very difficult for the therapist as well as for the client.

Ian: I agree with that. It's grueling to be with her for an hour.

Larry: It can be terrible for the therapist. Struggling to be present with and relate to someone who doesn't know how to relate is simply taxing. I've watched therapists work well with two or three twenty- to thirty-minute sessions a week and two- or five-minute phone contacts. The point to

all of this is creating contact, so that withdrawal can be studied. Long, laborious, useless sessions with repetitions and reflexive content are unnecessary and hard on both participants.

Ian: That makes a lot of sense to me.

Larry: I believe what we've doing over time *de facto* is that we're conditioning what Searles (1979) calls a *therapeutic symbiosis*. We are teaching and learning mutual cuing and beginning a dyadic dance. It's not what we talk about, not the content of the dialogue that's important. Rather, the critical thing is finding ways to sustain contact in the face of myriad impulses and maneuvers cleverly designed, through a lifetime's experience, to avoid contact, usually through fight, freeze, or flight types of activities. We know a symbiotic borderline person is terrified of abandonment. Organizing people are terrified of contact because the initial contacts that might have led them toward symbiosis, but did not, were traumatizing for some reason.

We're out of time. Next time you present, Ian, please bring some detailed notes of a session or two and we will look for moments of potential contact that can be worked during the hours. Thanks for your case.

Ian: Thanks. I got some helpful ideas today. This lady is truly difficult to understand and be with.

Eight Months Later

Ian: In our last conference, Larry, you suggested that the sadism I'm feeling in the countertransference

might be my own stuff, that is, not something projected into me by her. I still haven't sorted that out for myself.

She got mad at me and took seven months off but we're meeting now again and I worry about the sadism.

Larry: My tentative formulation is that she is calling the sadism out in you. She is provoking it through her unresponsiveness. And yet because I feel her object relations are so limited I'm not sure that what you're feeling can be considered projective identification, that is, an inner sadism of hers that she is managing to rid herself of by putting it into you. She doesn't appear to have well-defined scenarios. You mentioned as we were getting started a minute ago that your own father died of illness when you were 11 months old. So very early on, your mother must have been quite unavailable.

Ian: That's very true.

Larry: I think of a child who knows the breast, who knows comfort and who has it. And then at 11 months, or sometime before, because his mother goes into a preoccupation or a depression, he loses much of the goodness of what he believed was his. How insistent that child must become, insistent almost to the point of sadism, because that's the point in development one would be in the oral sadistic phase (at 11 months). The child says, "I know that nipple's there, I know you've got milk, I know you can give me what I need, damn it, come back!" And almost biting to get what he knows he needs and is there. Or alternately, the child who loses a good experience but still has Mother around may experience her preoccupations or depressions as sadistic and, in the symbiosis, identify with them.

Ian: Both fit very well. Because I almost said that to her last night. I said, "I know you're in there, I know there's something in there, and I really want it."

Larry: Right.

Ian: She said, "I'm not giving it to you." [Group laughs.]

Larry: She felt you were being mean to her. If we felt for sure that this was a structured symbiotic scenario, it would be worthwhile to start talking about it right away. It still may be worthwhile to talk a bit about it. Or since she's feeling you're being mean, you might simply say, "I know it may be that I'm being mean, and it may very well be that there's something about me that when I know there's a possibility of connection I go after it very firmly. So I really appreciate your telling me when it seems like I'm being mean, or telling me to back off. Because on the one hand I think our work has to go forward, with your finding a way to relate to me as an example of all other people. But on the other hand, there's no point in your suffering or being uncomfortable with me because I'm being so pushy. I feel like this last seven months you stopped because I was being too pushy, because I was wanting too much from you. I was wanting to connect with you, when you didn't want such an intense connection. I really hope that doesn't happen again. I hope that whenever you're having trouble with me, you tell me to be quiet so we don't lose time again."

I think you might make use of your reaction in a variety of ways, but probably not quite in the scenario way.

Sometimes we talk about people who show mostly organizing features but who also display some symbiotic threads. But in my experience, the symbiotic threads that they have made are almost always built qualitatively upon the foundation of organizing patterns. It may be as you and she learn to work this, that a symbiotic scenario with both active and passive sadistic replications will develop and you will then talk about it and work it as we would with borderline or characterological features, but it's too soon to tell. This is the advantage of having several different listening perspectives at your disposal. You can listen differently when her relatedness mode shifts. So we have here an interesting example of how an important part of the countertransference may relate both to your own persistent symbiotic need to hold on, and the sadistic flavor which may be a part of a projected replication of hers.

Ian: [Relieved] I hope so! [Group laughs.] Another thing that has happened in the process of therapy, is that last year she reconnected with her father. She went back to visit him and spent a couple of weeks with him, bought him some clothes . . .

Larry: Still in his isolated one-room cabin?

Ian: No, he's living in town now, in a little house. He's very old, and he's not well. She got him Meals on Wheels, and she got a housekeeper to come in and take care of him. This is the first time in years that this woman has spoken to her dad. She has really made a reconnection. Now she calls him periodically and talks to him.

She's come to see him as not all bad, as well as seeing her mother (who died a few years ago) as not all good. She's come a distance as far as that goes. Before, she wasn't having any of that. There was no doubt that Mother was perfect, and Dad was all evil and she didn't even want to hear about him.

Karen: So do you experience a split transference in terms of your being the idealized object as well as being the devalued object?

Ian: Yes. I feel both. She tells me both. She tells me how brilliant I am, how verbal I am, and how talented I am. Then she tells me how punitive, mean, and aggressive I am. I hear both.

Karen: Kernberg might say that's an entrée for you to interpret the split-off defense, by simply making an observation. Like, "I'm struck by earlier in the session, you seem to have experienced me in a way that was very brilliant, aware, and alert, and able to give things to you verbally. But now your experience of me is one of being quite punitive, and not having much to give you that's worthwhile."

Ian: Whenever I say anything like that, it gets transformed into an attack. If I were to say what you just said, she would say, "Why are you ripping me apart? Why are you so critical right now? Why are you telling me that I did this wrong?"

Karen: [in a role-play mode] "So it sounds like you're experiencing me right now as the punitive, assaulting dad with you being the helpless, victimized child."

Ian: [picking up on the role-play mode with Karen] "There you go again. See I'm wrong. I shouldn't be that way. I should be able to see you better. I'm all wrong."

Karen: "Then how are we going to find a way out of this?"

Ian: "There is no way out. I'm stuck, I'm going to be here forever. I'm going to die this way."

Karen: "So part of our connectedness right now is in feeling a similar degree of helplessness."

Ian: That was good, Karen. I really like that. Especially that, our connectedness is "in feeling a similar degree of helplessness."

Karen: I mean, I would just follow it.

Larry: Tell us more about what you're thinking.

Karen: I was illustrating, the way I understand Kernberg does when working with these more primitive, preoedipal people. Part of the definition of borderline organization is primitive defenses with a lot of split-off parts. So part of the therapeutic task is integrating these split-off parts, is being able to identify them as they are operating in the transference, and to be able to label them in the moment. And to make interpretive remarks that are based on hunches, where a split-off part might be the castrating mother with the helpless child, or the prison guard with the angry, rageful inmate. You're really trying to capture the flavor of these split-off emotional parts in the context of what's going on in the transference and countertransference, with the goal being toward integration, the aim of seeing all of the myriad ways that these split-off parts

get repeatedly and self-destructively enacted.

Sean: I like that because the split-off parts are funneled through or are displaced into the transference and countertransference. That's part of the interception that Larry speaks of (Hedges 1983b), to pick up and to intercept those part selves and objects as they are transferred to you, right?

Karen: I think Kernberg is on the same track as you, Larry. I like what he's doing.

Larry: He's very thorough and systematic in his object relations approach.

Karen: Yes, he's very systematic. What he teaches is looking for dyads. Look for the dyads in terms of split-off parts that are getting acted out in the transference. I heard him speak at APA recently. His attitude seems to be, "Don't worry about making mistakes, because what you're doing is you're using your countertransference to feel what might be going on for the patient." Ask, "Who am I? What actor am I? Who are you? What's going on here?" Label it and look for the patient's reaction. See if you're on the trail or not. If you are, go with it. If you're not, then sit back and wait for what emerges next. It's an interesting way of bringing the borderline transference into view.

Ian: The dilemma I've had with her is that I can't find the damn trail. Because every time I say something like that, she says "I don't understand. I don't understand what you're saying."

Larry: My response to Kernberg,

okay? [Group laughs at the coming challenge.] You know I have always considered his thinking to be brilliant and pioneering. I really appreciate your articulation of his style, because it's clear, concise, and workable. However, you've gotten twice from Ian, "Fine, but my lady won't let me do that. And part of this is, of course, how primitive and non-trusting she still is. Now I have several things to say. I feel like in the long run Kernberg's ideas clearly mark the way to go. But, if you think for one minute that a woman like this is going to pick up on such things early on in the therapy, while she's still in the organizing state, it won't happen. Because when you're looking for those dyads you're fundamentally looking for projective identifications, for split-off borderline part-objects, and for symbiosis. You're attempting to define what I call a symbiotic or borderline scenario, a stylized interaction pattern. A set of such scenarios is likely to emerge with variations in them like those you describe Kernberg working with. When you work this way you listen for a scenario, an internalized dyad in interaction that has a certain character, a certain style, a certain mode of relatedness. But when you two did this role play, I heard the woman in therapy breaking off the possibility of a dyadic interaction, not creating one. You Karen, went emphatically right for something that was correct. And just at the moment that the connection was about possible, just when you were able to speak an understanding of this dyad, the person living in the organizing

state has to break the empathy, is compelled to somehow break the contact.

I also like what you said about the spirit of Kernberg working with borderline transferences. "Don't worry so much about whether you're right or not; you're trying to identify these things to label and to sort out split-off images." But the therapist working with organizing rather than borderline issues is in the position of, "No matter what I try, no matter how I attempt to show object relations as split-off part objects, just at the point when I'm there, when we're at last connecting, she blows me out of the water." But that's no reason for us to be discouraged or not to continue to try to identify these images and themes. We just can't expect it to work as clearly and consistently as Kernberg would like it to go.

It's like the mother who speaks to the baby long before the baby can understand. The mother must keep speaking. You can't stop speaking just because the baby doesn't respond the way you want. The baby will only learn speech by watching your activity and hearing you talk. So your woman, Ian, will only ultimately get in a position to deal with these split-off dyads, and with the replicated scenario aspects that have developed with part objects, as a result of your being able to talk with her about them as you go along. But at present the dominant motif is not defining symbiotic dyads or split-off parts. The dominant motif she presents is the blockage of all potential connections every time you're in danger of emotionally touching her, because that's the way the organizing transference, the psychotic mode operates.

Ian: That's certainly what it feels like.

Larry: I liked where the role play finally got to, because your last words were, what?

Karen: "We have a similar degree of helplessness."

Larry: "Helplessness together," which is wonderful. Because on the one hand, the split-off parts are spoken. Perhaps accurately, perhaps not, but there's certainly a movement toward coordinated speech. Here's my translation. "I felt you emotionally touching me, you're crazy. Don't touch me, get away." And the response from the therapist was, "Well, then, not only do you feel helpless, but I feel helpless, and that's where we are." Which is a really nice way of defining and summarizing where things are.

I would add to the Kernberg-styled role play to adapt it to the organizing experience. "Let's consider for a moment what has just transpired between us. It seems as though you have given me many ideas with which to speak to you. You seemed to be following me. But at the point I actually spoke and tried to relate to you, that's when our interaction somehow broke down." (Note the impersonal "something just happened." This mode of impersonal expression seems to best empathize with the organizing level sense of lack of agency.) "Do you know why at that moment it was not possible for us to pursue our connection? Do you know why you were not able to say, 'Well, gee, Ian, that's an interesting idea. What other ideas do you have? I don't understand what happened to our conversation. Can you help me see what happened?" Why couldn't you have said, 'Oh, that makes me think of the day my father beat me, or the day my mother took the nipple out of my mouth.' Is there any way you can tell me how and why you are not able to collaborate with me in terms of developing stories and pictures together? As opposed to simply saying, 'No, that doesn't go anywhere.' " Because at that point, Ian, you're trying to engage her in talking about the actual interaction that happened right then, which would not be the replicated scenario transference, but rather would relate to sudden appearance of the organizing, "psychotic mother" transference. You see the split-off objects or the scenario, you talk about them, and then she says, "This has no meaning, you're worthless." At that moment, you're dealing with the organizing, rupturing transference. Whereas in the work up to that moment, you're trying to define the scenario or borderline aspect. Is there more to tell us about the session last night?

Ian: Yes, just a few more things I want to tell you about the session. She was saying something about having wasted three days of the weekend she had off. She had done nothing. I said something to her to the effect that we've talked about this before, how she takes days at a time and does nothing. I'm always struck by the fact that she doesn't seem to be connected to anything, to have a passion for anything, or to have an interest in anything. She said she doesn't read, she doesn't go anywhere, she has no interests. I asked her about TV. I said, "Do you ever watch TV?" She said, "Yes, I do a lot of that." I said, "Well, maybe there's some interest for you in television. Why don't you tell me a little bit about your experience with TV." She said, "No." [Group laughs.]

Larry: So you found a place of potential contact. It sounds as though she may to be able to tell you that she really gets turned on to certain characters, or certain shows.

Ian: Well, that's what I was hoping.

Larry: But she's not going to let you connect. No contact for you.

Ian: There's a better part coming, though. She says, "No, I'm not going to tell you." I asked her a little bit about why she felt she couldn't tell me, and she just shut down. She wouldn't talk, she put the pillow back up to cover herself. She wasn't going to tell me anything about TV. I started to go after her a little bit, "You know I'm really feeling cut off. I want to go after you. I know you're in there. I want to know more about this. You must be having some thoughts about why you don't want to tell me about your TV interests." She sat and sat. It probably took ten or fifteen minutes before she finally said something to the effect of, "If I tell you what I watch on TV, you're just going to be critical of me again, and tell me it's bullshit, and it's crap, and I shouldn't watch it." I said, "Gee, that's interesting. I wonder

where you got the idea that I would do that?" She said, "Well everything I say you think is rotten and horrible." We talked about that. About my being so punitive and critical. I told her I was sorry the things I say hurt her because that certainly wasn't my intent. I was really concerned about that. She said, "You know, just like now, you're always yelling at me." I said, "It's interesting that that's how you perceive it, because it seems to me that I'm speaking very calmly and quietly. I'm not feeling angry or critical. I invite you to listen to your tape of the session later on tonight, when you're in a different space. Go back and hear this part. It's conceivable that I'm talking very quietly."

Larry: When the transference psychosis is in place the split between the observing and experiencing ego (Sterba 1934) does not function and the person's reality testing is temporarily blocked so in transference you were angry and yelling. Here you *are* the parent who criticizes her as rotten and horrible and who yells at her. Our knee-jerk response to this kind of transference accusation is to be defensive, to correct the person's views. We do better if we accept the attacks as being set off by something we did or said. But we know that contact or the threat of contact rouses the internalized traumatizing transference.

Ian: Some more time went by. She finally said she watched Sally Jesse Raphael. I said, "Oh, really. What did you see on Sally Jesse Raphael." She said, "It was a program about men who hate women." [Group laughs.]

Sabrina: You set yourself up for that one! That's great, though.

Ian: I said, "Oh, really. Tell me more about that." She said, "No." [Group laughs.]

Larry: Once again, as you're ready to make an empathic step, she senses it and is bound and determined to prevent it, to shut it off. The close-out is an automatic, overconditioned response to empathic contact or the threat of it.

Ian: She wouldn't tell me any more about it. She said, "I don't want to talk about it. I don't want to say anything about that show. That's what it was about, that's enough. I don't want to tell you anything else." I said, "Okay, anything else you watch on TV? Is there anything else?" She says, "I like to watch movies. There's a movie that comes on every night at 9 P.M. on one of the channels, and I'll watch the movie for the evening." I said, "Is there a kind of movie that you like, is there anything that you really enjoy? Tell me about a movie you saw, something that really caught your attention." She said, "Well, there was a movie about a therapist whose patient tried to kill her." [Group laughs.] I said, "Could you tell me about that movie?" "Well, in the movie the therapist is this woman, and there's this crazy patient. The woman came to her as a woman, but she was really a man. And he set out to kill her, and he was following her around, and the end scene was the patient and the therapist struggling in front of this log shredder, a branch shredder that tree trimmers run the branches through. They're

struggling, and the patient is trying to throw the therapist into the log shredder and kill her and shred her up. But at the last minute, the therapist wrestles the patient around, and manages to get the patient's coat caught in the log shredder, and it shreds the patient to bits, and that's the end of the movie." She said, "I really liked that part." [Group laughs.]

Larry: What does she like about it?

Ian: She wouldn't tell me. I said, "What is it about the movie that you like? Does it relate in any way to you and me?" I said, "You know it's really interesting to me that the two shows that you were able to tell me about had to do with men who hate women, and a patient and therapist who are trying to destroy each other. And she said, "What's interesting about that?"

Larry: The automatic cut-off again.

Sabrina: Did you tell her?

Ian: Yes. But she said, "I don't understand."

Larry: She can't permit any empathy, can't tolerate connecting to you. Not understanding is for her a common way to fend off contact. The reason she loves these is of course, because they mirror her in some way. But she can't or won't relate to you on that basis. In transference she (the male or aggressive part of her?) wants to destroy you, but it's she who always feels destroyed. So, even though in fact she regularly cuts you off, thereby destroying you, what happens is that in the process, she always accidentally gets caught in the shredder, and it's she who is shredded at every one of these points of contact. She finds something satisfying in that. It's like the movie represents the story of her soul. It pictures the self-destruction she must compulsively repeat in the relationship.

Karen: I think that's a beautiful interpretation. Would you speak that to her?

Larry: Yes, I would try.

Sabrina: It's so graphic.

Larry: But the problem Ian faces, which is no reason not to speak, is that she's going to say, "See, I told you it would happen. You're being mean and critical again." So even if he tries to connect through such an interpretation, she will ensure that it is she who gets shredded by him, not directly necessarily, but as he tries to connect, her coat will accidentally get caught.

Karen: I wouldn't look for her agreeing.

Larry: No, and that's why there's no reason not to speak it. Except that what Ian has to be careful of right here is not so much agreement, or disagreement, but he just lost her for seven months because of pushing her for contact. He has to be very careful at this point not to lose her again. So he might choose not to push her by interpreting. We have to let Ian use his own intuition here. Ultimately it must be spoken because these images represent so well the state of the organizing transference. The other television theme of men who hate women likewise reflects her inner world. She has more to say about this topic but refuses, again making contact impossible.

Ian: Very well spoken. You all certainly see the mess I'm always in. [Group laughs.]

Larry: Tell us what happened next.

Ian: That was right at the end of the session, I don't think we said much more. I said, "I found those TV shows really fascinating, and I think they have a lot to do with you and me." We said a couple of words. Then she was out of there.

Larry: I bet! Knowing that you had just lost her for seven months, and not wanting to lose her again it was probably best to just receive her TV talk.

Three Months Later

Ian: I read the transcripts of the earlier case conferences, and I found them very useful. It's really different going back and reading the verbatim conference. The replies, the feedback, and the input were all very useful to hear again. I find myself feeling a lot better about this lady now, since I've presented her several times. I'm not nearly so angry with her. After reading the transcripts, listening to the input, and processing our interactions for myself, the sense I got in my session with her last night is that she's much better. But I realize that it's probably me who's better, not her! [Group laughs.] Little has realistically changed for this woman in her life, though she and I have come a long way in our process together.

Larry: And you're getting so much better!

Ian: Yes! [Group laughs.] An event occurred that brought me back to what you were saying last week about how with organizing people we have this tendency to see relatedness even when it isn't there. But I noticed that my feeling better about our interaction certainly does have an ameliorating effect on our relationship. Because as I'm feeling different about her our interaction is affected positively. She does seem to be a little more responsive, which is what the session last night was about.

Larry: She's aware that you're improving?

Ian: Yes, I think she is. [Group laughs.] She has slowly been getting more comfortable, a little more conversant, and a little more connected. The week before last when she came into the office, the first thing she did was to turn off all the lamps, which I'd never seen her do before. She turned off all the lights, sat down on the couch and proceeded to pile all the pillows on top of herself, so that I couldn't see her.

Marilyn: Like neck high? Could you see her face? Was she going back to the womb?

Ian: She completely covers herself up. There must be a certain sense of safety for her to be able to come in and turn all my lights off and climb onto the couch and cover herself like that. I hadn't seen her like that for quite some time. When I talked to her about what was going on, she didn't know. She said, "I don't know why I'm feeling like this. I don't know why I want to do this, just for some reason I feel that I have to hide tonight." We talked

about why she might be feeling that way, or what's going on with her.

Larry: I'm thinking she may be regressing to a former plane. Or now that you're improving in the way you approach her, she may be returning to earlier material that was not well understood with the hope it will be better understood now.

Ian: Yes. I think it may be she's returning for better understanding because, as you'll see, I managed things quite differently with a very different outcome. She stayed hidden until during the last part of the session I said, "Listen, I want to try something different. I'm thinking that hiding in darkness and under the pillows has to do with some kind of fear you're experiencing right now. I'm thinking that it has to do with fear about me, because I'm the only other person in the room." I said, "I wonder if you would be doing this if I left the room, if you'd still hide, or if you would come out, and turn the lights on. So let's just experiment and see what happens."

So I turned the lights on and moved my chair over right in front of her. I said, "Now, let's talk about this. Let's talk about the fear, and let's talk about what's going on." She said, "I don't have any sense that I'm afraid of you." I said, "I can't help feeling that since I'm the only other person in the room here that whatever's happening has got to have something to do with me. There's some kind of uncomfortableness. I'm wondering what your thoughts, feelings, or ideas might be about that." She said that she didn't have any, like she always does. By that time the session was over, so she left. I had taken a brave leap and called it an experiment. And it seemed she completely sidestepped my moving in for contact.

But she came back in last night. She brought a piece of paper with her on which she had written a bunch of stuff, which she tends to do when she processes something. She told me that after last session she went straight home, and tried to gather her thoughts about what she was experiencing. She said, "I have to do that right away, because if I don't do it right away the memory disappears and I don't remember the session at all." There are a couple of interesting things in what she wrote. First, from my talking about the feeling of the relationship we were having in the room, she translated what I said into, "I want to know what you think of me." She said, "I got out of it that you wanted to know how I felt about you. So I wrote down a bunch of things."

Larry: Which really is exactly correct. That's what you wanted to know. Maybe not so concretely, but nevertheless . . .

Ian: Right. That's not what I was asking, but that was what I wanted to know. The first part of the paper was about how wonderful she thought I was. She talked about the other therapist who had thrown her out. She talked about the group therapist that she had been to, and the other therapist that she had gone to briefly. In all this I stacked up very well. She thought I was dedicated, attentive, and empathic. She added, "And sometimes I feel like you're a drill master."

Larry: A drill master?

Ian: Yes, then she said something about, "You keep on me if you don't get the answer that you want from me." As if I'm trying to make her do something. Oh, I forgot to say that the very first thing she said about my turning on the lights, and moving my chair closer was, "I was trying to process how I was feeling about that when you came over and got on top of me."

Larry: A drill master on top of her.

Ian: Really interesting statement.

Karen: What would you do with that? I can't wait to hear.

Larry: I'm not going to touch that. [Group laughs.]

Ian: I didn't touch it, but I thought a lot about it later.

Marilyn: What was her affect when she said that? Was she aroused? Was she alarmed? Was she flat?

Ian: When she said those words? I think she was pretty flat. She was remarkably comfortable last night. The lights were on, she didn't have any pillows in front of her, she was sitting there talking to me. As a matter of fact she said, "I'm being brave tonight," when she came into the room. Also on the paper was something like, "I think about the session, and I think about what's going to transpire, what you think, what you feel, and how I'm going to respond." Then she said, "As I was writing that, this emotion came up, I could see myself running out of the room, screaming in terror."

Larry: That's remarkable. Because given her nonverbal behavior in that last session, you attempted to put into words her feelings. She couldn't recognize your words at the time, but when she gets away where she's not in immediate fear of the situation, and writes down her thoughts, she's quite able to say she's afraid. It's as though you've given her permission to have those feelings. To be frightened of you, to imagine running out of the room screaming, because, being a drill master on top of her, your demands for increased contact are terrifying. She express the aggressive (drill master) and the dominant erotic (on top of me) aspects of your relating to her and feels like running away screaming.

Ian: Her image helped make me aware that sometimes I do demand too much from her, that she doesn't have the capacity to give what I ask of her sometimes. We talked about that, she made that really clear to me—that I expect too much.

Karen: I'm not so sure I agree that your demands are excessive. When you're working with a schizoid patient like this, if you're not somewhat active in your work, then it's dead space. I see nothing therapeutic coming out of it. I don't see silence or passivity with these folks as empathy. I see it as resonating with a bottomless pit. So in my experience, I think it requires being somewhat active. I can understand from her point of view that some activity could be perceived as a drill master. In a subtle way you are pushing her. But is that so bad?

Larry: I agree with your thinking. Obviously, it would be very easy to expect too much from this woman. But I think you've gotten tuned in to how to resonate with her. So you dared to turn the lights on, go over and sit next to her, and say, "I'd like to talk about what's going on between us.

I think you're afraid of me." Well, she can't respond emotionally, at least not right away. But I don't think you expected too much by doing that. Now, if you had been disappointed that she couldn't verbalize right away, that would have been expecting too much. I think had you not expected this of her, you would not have gotten what you did get later. I think it was very important to do what you did. Because it did stimulate her need to represent. The complication, of course, is that people don't become extremely withdrawn for no reason. So when you take active steps toward her there's not only the transference reaction, but also the danger that you're actually replicating an intrusive trauma. But your intuition seems great here. It worked to good advantage.

Ian: It was a wonderful thing. It was very nice. I was surprised by what she had written down, and how articulate she was about it. Remember when we started we had whole sessions with hardly a word.

Karen: I think one of the hooks, at least in my countertransference with this sort of patient, is feeling responsible, personalizing the response you're getting, when in fact part of the scenario that's being represented is the patient as the antagonized child, and you as the intrusive, abusing parent. And those roles reverse themselves periodically where you feel antagonized by her being sharp with you. So it's a whole engagement.

Larry: So to the extent we're working with a replicated symbiotic transference, if you're not in there actively, the scenario cannot be replicated. But another angle is that we're looking for the way in which the organizing-level contact gets broken. Many times you move in and she disintegrates. It's easy to say maybe you've overwhelmed her, and her ego disintegrates. My theoretical position is that at that moment in transference her internalized psychotic mother appears and her mind flies into a thousand pieces out of terror. That's what you've got to focus on in time. So, yes when you move in and she fragments or disintegrates, we see it happening. We believe her. But rather than formulating what you see as mere fragmentation, I prefer to view it as an organizing or psychotic transference reaction.

The working material is *how* you move in and *how* she fragments so as not to be in contact with you. She expressed it so beautifully. She can imagine running from the room, screaming, which is not a disintegration, but flight. The disintegration, the loss of function in the moment, however, may be basically the same thing, an emotional flight. She runs from the room screaming. In multiple personalities we see flight from the therapist in terms of personality switching. But when we're locked into the descriptive psychiatric view we don't have any way to think about what's happening in the relatedness or any way to work with her.

The moment of disintegration or psychic flight is an expression of when her transferential mother (or father, because she had that harsh abusive father), moves toward her to make contact with her. What remains in memory as transference is that disintegration, which happened repeatedly with both her mother and her father when they moved toward her. Either there was this horrible abuse, and her ego did disintegrate or she hid under the bed—dark with pillows might be a way of remembering that. When you look at her disintegration as a memory instead of a psychiatric symptom two things happen. One, you realize that this is what we're here to work with, not something to simply be avoided or cured. But also you're very respectful of the disintegration as memory and go very slowly because you realize unraveling these moments is the essence of her therapy.

Ian: I see that. I certainly feel better now. My tolerance has increased a lot as I work with and process my feelings of uneasiness. That's what I was saying in the beginning. I feel more acceptance of something in myself. I'm really okay with who she is now. I've let go of my need to get her out of herself and make her into who I want her to be.

Marilyn: That's major.

Larry: She said that. And she said you stack up well. "The other therapist threw me out."

Ian: Yes.

Larry: She's realized that you're dedicated, that you're loyal, and that you're present. She is performing tasks, showing she is willing to learn from you. We always learn from and for someone. I learned that in Education 101. The professor said, "Simply review in your mind everything you feel is important that you have ever learned, and you will immediately remember *who* you learned it from. It was somebody you knew, teaching you, and you were learning it from and for that person. All ego skills are learned in connection with another person. It's why we're gathered here to learn from each other the subtleties of therapy. And to the extent you accept me or others in this group as your teachers, you know who you learn from and for. Now that you have "settled down," Ian, she can learn better from you—you as a special person she wants to do things for.

Ian: Later on in the session she acknowledged that I accepted her, but that she sure as hell doesn't accept herself. She was mad at herself. All of that came out of last week. Then Thursday and Friday she went to a two-day workshop on how to build effective relationships. She brought me the flier describing the workshop. We had talked about it in her previous session—about her feelings about going to it. She was really scared and anxious. The day she went to the workshop, that night I got a telephone page. She said, "The workshop was great, I had a great time." Which was not what she expected, and not what I expected.

Marilyn: She actually reached out and called you. Wow!

Ian: I'm thinking back to last night. We were talking about her response to me in the task master/drill master role. I was asking her why she was experiencing such terror and how she felt I was being overly critical. She said to me, "One of the things I learned in the workshop is that communication is 65 percent nonverbal, and 35 percent verbal. I think one of the difficul-

ties I have with you is that," and she laughed, "you don't do anything." She said, "I don't get any interpretable nonverbal feedback from you because you just sit and look at me. I talk and you always look the same." Which isn't how I experience me at all. "And only last week you did a lot."

Sabrina: It isn't how I experience you either. You're a very pleasant and animated person.

Ian: She says, "You're very stern, and you're always looking at me as if you're displeased." But the times when I don't look stern, if I look excited or interested, or if I get enthusiastic at all she goes into that third-person mode. She did that a couple of times last night, which I thought was interesting. She said, "The only time I get any real interpretive feedback from you is when you get interested and relaxed. Every once in a while you take your shoes off." I said, "What do you make of that?" She said, "He wants to go home." She flips into the third person. Whenever I come out of character for her, or come alive she goes into the third-person mode, and she'll say something like, "My, isn't he excited all of a sudden."

Larry: The human interest or excitement when you take off your shoes says, "I'm here." It's not "I'm going home." I think that the third person is her way of breaking the contact, of distancing when the situation threatens more intimacy. Perhaps it was her parents' way of squelching any signs of spontaneous life in her.

Ian: Yes, I get a sense of that.

Larry: I'm thinking with her that before calling attention directly to the third-person mode, you and she need to reach some understanding that however she experiences you and speaks to you is okay and full of possible meanings. So it's important that she lets herself say what comes to mind. Then you can move into, "It's really interesting when you slip into speaking of 'he.' " I would not want to make her self-conscious and let this speech mode go into hiding, because it seems crucial when she slips into it. Later in the process you'll be able to say to her, "I think you're aware not that I want to leave, but that I'm here and I'm very comfortable with you. I think that when you felt I was comfortable with you, 'he' appeared, so as not to deal with my being very much present and comfortable with you." That's the interpretation, but you can't just drop it in from out of the blue.

Karen: The moment I find I can do something like that is immediately after that connection moment has occurred. Like immediately *after* it switches into "he."

Larry: I say to let the contact go forward, then once you realize it's broken and the focus has shifted somewhere else, stop the action and go back to the break.

Karen: Like immediately, before the defense goes up.

Larry: Before she gets too far away, but not while it's happening. We want to leave the connecting alone; it needs to be fostered. Just after it's passed, call it back for study.

Ian: I think I've made that error before in trying to grab it in the moment, and it goes away. As a matter of fact, I think I did that last night a couple of times, and then we're both

lost because it goes away and we can't go anywhere. As a matter of fact, in listening to the tape I realize that the entire session was me pursuing this lady and her evading me. You can hear the whole process. I'm going after her this way and I'm going after her that way and she's slipping this way and I'm chasing her around the room. The whole hour is like that.

Larry: What we're always trying to figure out with people whose relatedness is so limited is how are we going to get their cooperation in studying and expanding the awareness of the contact moment. How are we going to set up a dialogue about the contact moment? But now finally she's giving you ways to focus it. She's giving you pictures and words. She's giving you things that you can capitalize on. Just like giving you those words and pictures on paper, but giving them to you after the session. She's playing into your hands now. She knows somehow where you need to go with her, which is to study the relationship. You've been saying relationship all along, but she is now giving you ways to say, "Aha! I think you're absolutely right."

Marilyn: There's a toy I think is called a "water-willie." It's shaped like a weenie and very slippery. If you hold it too tight, it pops out of your hand. If you don't hold it tight enough it slips out. You to have connect with it in just the perfect way or it pops up or slips out of your hand and contact is lost. That's what it feels like you're saying it's like to try to stay in contact with her.

Ian: Very much so. I can't hold her too tightly or too loosely or she gets away! [Laughter.]

Marilyn: So the task is to figure out what the optimal way of contacting her is.

Ian: This lady really challenges my therapeutic skills.

Larry: Working with her is like holding a slippery water-willie.

Ian: Yes.

Marilyn: And you also realize that anybody in your role would be having that experience with her.

Ian: I think that's what the case conferences have helped me see. It's been useful getting feedback about my work and seeing that it's a tough case, a tough job, and that despite my frustrations our work is inching forward.

Larry: I found when going over the case conference transcripts, that your work is the kind that every therapist identifies with in horror. This may be a more extreme situation than most therapists have faced, but none of us knows if the next person walking through our door won't pose this same problem for us. We all experience this contact problem in various, perhaps less extreme ways. How do we begin to find ways of focusing on the contact moment? How can we begin to get the person to focus and study contact with us? What forms does contact take and how many ways do our people develop for blocking or stopping it? How hard it is for any of us to be regularly and fully present when we are with another person. I think of E.T. and the Reese's Pieces you're putting out for her, slowly reeling her in, drawing her toward you. And she's starting to eat out of your hand. A therapeutic symbiosis is forming.

If you were not sensitive to and intent on working the transference and countertransference her therapy could be easily derailed as it has been a half dozen times before with other therapists. On a behavioral level she's incredibly shy, untalkative, quick to take offense, eager to criticize, and slippery as hell! It would be easy for a therapist to dismiss her. Or we could imagine the folly of a simplified recovery approach that would seek to define her feelings about the abuse (which would have to be fabricated because she has no feelings in the usual sense). It would be easy for her to be influenced toward recovering memories of violence and molest and for the therapist to be active in "validating" all of this and to promote recovery by confronting her perpetrators. That entire approach would be a collusion with her resistance to establishing a transference psychosis. But it would be simpler and easier on the therapist! Thanks for keeping us tuned in to your work, Ian.

Ian: Thank you.

ACKNOWLEDGING STRANGENESS: A YEAR LATER

Ian gives an extended report of the many areas in her life that now bear the marks of relating. He reports her more realistic progress with weight control after he relates the compulsive eating to a wish to have her mother back. Her mother had died several years ago. For years the two of them ate meals together. When she was needing mother she would eat. Then the discussion took an interesting twist.

Larry: As you've listened to these various encounters with people in her life, because she's definitely attempting to relate, can you tell how much of the poor reception she gets is that she's a very strange lady and people mistreat or neglect or are rude to her out of lack of consideration, or disgust, or whatever? Or how much may be that there is average expectable relating going on, but her psychotic transference messes thing up? Do you have any feeling for that?

Ian: She's a very strange lady. She relates to me in a very strange way. And I think she does that with everyone else. I think they pick up on that.

Larry: But there are many times when decent people can sense that there's a good but strange person who's in some kind of confusion and they go to extra effort to be kind. Then you have an average, expectable lunch going, with a strange edge to it. What I'm asking is as you've listened to all these new interactions she's trying out, are people in her life actually mistreating her, or is it when a connection starts, the psychotic mother appears, and she feels mistreated, or can you really tell?

Ian: I don't think I know the answer to that. My first response is that I think it's probably both of those things working at present. She is strange. And she does interact in a strange way. But I think she distorts to a great degree the interactions that do take place and her distortions feed back into the relatedness to make it go sour.

Larry: Are you able to talk with her about that?

Ian: Some. Let me tell you about a

videotape of her I got to see. She's worked for this large hotel for a very long time. They gave her an awards dinner for being an outstanding employee. She's been there reliably for twenty years, never missed a day, and she's very dedicated. The party was videotaped, and she brought me a copy of the videotape.

Marilyn: She wanted you at her party.

Ian: She wanted me to see it. It was a fascinating tape. I took it home and watched it, but I don't know if I can describe it. Here's this party, and here's all these people, and there are banners, and there's a cake for her, and the guy is giving a speech.

Larry: People trying to treat her like a human being.

Ian: She said to me, "This really doesn't have anything to do with me, they do this with everybody. And it was just that my turn came up. They had to do this because it was my turn to be recognized, and they threw this party." I said, "I think they did this because they really appreciate all you've done." But she wasn't going to buy that. It was fascinating to watch this tape, because all these people were in this restaurant—sixty or seventy people. And she comes in, and from the time she walks in the door until the end of the celebration, she is just excruciatingly uncomfortable. It was very apparent.

Marilyn: She needed your pillows, and they weren't there!

Ian: That's right. It was apparent that this was not the kind of environment that she looks for. She's just on guard, and her eyes are darting the whole time.

Larry: Frightened. But people know this about her, so do they just move on around her without seeming to notice . . .?

Ian: Yes, they just went right on with the party.

Larry: It's interesting to see how accepted she is. They understand that she's somewhat strange, and yet she's devoted, loyal, and reliable in a variety of ways, and so they're kind to her.

Ian: Yes. I think they've learned how to work with her. With where she is in life.

Larry: What did she want you to see in it?

Ian: I think she wanted me to see that.

Larry: The strangeness?

Ian: The uncomfortableness. She didn't request that, but that's certainly what I saw. I'm not certain what her motivation was.

Larry: I'm fishing now. One of the things that these lower-level people sometimes want us to know about is that they're weird, that they're strange, that they're awkward, that they're crazy, that they're sick, or whatever the feeling is. I think well-intentioned therapists too often try to "normalize" people and avoid a frank discussion of their truth. "You know, these people must see you as an unusual or strange woman. You're quiet, you stay in your corner, you take breaks by yourself, you don't go out to lunch with them, you don't relate to them. You and I can understand why all of this is so. You and I can understand that you are the way you are because of your history. And

we also know that's not where you'd like to be, and that you've wanted to reach out to those people many times. On this tape it's very clear that people care for you, that in their own ways they like, value, and respect you. But I think you want me to see that there's something very very different from you and other people." We try to bring out whatever words are likely to fit for them.

You've all read Margaret Little's (1990) account of her analysis with Winnicott. What tremendous relief she reports when Winnicott says, "You're really quite ill, you know." Then she knew that he saw her, that he understood what she was up against and the struggle she has had her entire life. So for a woman who doesn't want you to look at her, to bring you a videotape and to show you that, it's like she really wants you to see something.

I guess the reason I'm thinking about it is that every time her father or mother saw something strange, weird, or "idiotic" about her, they would cruelly point it out or talk in the third person about her. It would be humiliating and abusive. She knows she was considered an idiot child by her parents. That's her self-concept. And she also knows she moves around in the world in strange ways. She watches television, she knows what people are supposed to behave like and she knows she's not that way.

Inside she's an idiot child, and she knows it—let's not kid anybody. I think some frank recognition of that as she experiences it, and your seeing whatever distress there is about that, fits well into the context of what you're trying to do in terms of forming an honest relationship with her. It can be used as a springboard for the future, of how she doesn't want to be in that place forever. But because of her history that's where she is now. It gives an opportunity to ask, "How are we ever going to find a way out of this?" It sounds like you're doing some of that. But I always wonder if it's frank enough for the client.

Ian: I think I've been pretty frank about it. I said she's done a lot of ancillary things, like groups and so forth, and she's gotten a lot of feedback from people when she's gone to groups that she's very bizarre, that she's very strange, and that they can't connect with her. And so we have talked about that.

Larry: So she knows that you know.

Ian: Yes, because we've talked about it. And we've talked about the strangeness in the relationship between her and me and how uncomfortable and awkward it is for both of us. We've grappled with that in many different ways.

One of the things I mentioned before is that this lady never answers a question. No matter what you ask her, you're not going to get an answer to the question. And this is one of the things that drives me up the wall. So if I say to her something like, "How did you feel about that experience?" she'll say something like, "Well, you know I was watching a television show the other night . . ." and she'll go off on a tangent and she's totally gone. Her answer may turn out to be tangential

but it leaves me hanging. "Well, how did . . ." and I'll ask her this question five or six times, and I'll never get an answer. Actually, two weeks ago, we were talking about it, and I said "You know, it's so frustrating for me to try to get an answer out of you, to just get you to say 'yes' or 'no' or 'black' or 'white' or anything." I don't remember what the question was, but we were going around and around about it. Then about the fifth time I asked her, she looked at me and she said, "No." with great volume. And I said, "All right!" And we both celebrated that. I think that was the first time she had ever answered a question.

Larry: Freud says that "no" is where the human mind begins! Was she able to feel the strength and directness of that?

Ian: Yes, and we both got a real kick out of it.

Larry: So there was a connection at that moment.

Ian: But boy, it was a chore to get that to happen, let me tell you. It's incredible the way she gets around it.

Larry: You've really gotten the relationship where you can demand a connection, Early on, you never could have done that with her. But now she's shown you that there's enough connection, enough basic trust, so you can pursue her like that until the two of you are connected in some way. This seems to me the way it's got to go. The lack of interpersonal connectedness is what makes her different, what makes her seem and feel weird. She's so terrified, because the minute she connected with either one of her parents, it was going to be abusive. So when she finally comes out and says "No," it's like she's fighting through a lot to get there, to say that.

Ian: Very much so.

Larry: It's nice that you're both able to celebrate that, the strength of that connection.

Ian: Yes, I think you're right. I don't think we could have done that a couple of years ago; she was nowhere near that.

Larry: No.

Ian: She was nowhere near where she is now. I've really seen her grow a lot.

Larry: I'm impressed with how you've been willing and able to stay with her—basically to wait it out gently seducing her until the moment you can risk pushing her a little in a way so she can respond directly and emotionally to you. I think it began that time when she was hiding in the dark under pillows, and you turned on the lights, moved your chair up, and asked her to tell you what was happening right now. That was such a strong moment because you felt you had enough of a bridge to her to be able to cross that bridge and almost command her to stay put, to "connect with me." And she did.

Ian: There've been a lot of changes. But they sure seem to take forever!

ISSUES IN CASE MANAGEMENT: THIRTEEN MONTHS LATER

Ian reports the laborious progress and his perennial discouragement because the work goes at a snail's pace. But she now carries on conversations with him regularly, probably the only ones in her life, and it seems the first ones ever in her life. She's making more active steps toward weight loss but that means to her letting go of mother and the possibility of making new connections, so that's slow. Ian has encouraged her toward community involvement, which she's been doggedly pursuing. He reports the following discussion.

Ian: Here's what I did a couple of months ago. I got the adult education catalogs from the community colleges around her. And I said, "Listen, I want to go through this with you. I want you to look at some things that you could do to enhance your career. Because, number 1: You need to do that to feel good about yourself. And number 2: You've been at this job for twenty years now. You haven't moved, you haven't gotten a raise, you haven't gotten a promotion." She's living paycheck to paycheck. "We're in an economic recession now and people are losing their jobs. If you get laid off, in two months you'll be on the street. You have no savings, you have no retirement, you have no anything." So I said, "I want to look at these with you and see what you can do." She picked out a bunch of computer classes, word processing, Lotus, and others like that. And she took them. She took them all.

Larry: She could be really good in that area.

Ian: Yes, because she works with

computers. She has gone to all these weekend workshops, and she took those classes, and it was good for her. I mean she felt good. She mastered many things. I said, "Gee, that's marvelous. Now, put that on your resume, because you could get the ax any day." There are people being laid off all around her, jobs being chopped.

Larry: Right. Isn't that amazing, that she's not touched?

Ian: Well, I think it's because she's been there for twenty years, and that she does what she does very well. I think it would take two or three people to replace her. So the hotel hangs on to her. She's said a lot of her co-workers have been fired. I told her, "Listen, you need to stay in therapy. But if you lose your job, you can't stay in therapy. So you need some new job skills just in case." So she took some computer classes, and she did well, and enjoyed them. She even talked to a few people. . . .

I got her to go to the gym at the hotel. I got her to enroll in an aerobics class on her lunch hour. But then they laid off a bunch of people, they restructured, and now she doesn't get a lunch hour, so that was the end of that. But she was doing it. She won't walk in her neighborhood, because by the time she gets home it's dark and she's afraid, and I can't get her out of the house. . . .

She will do damn near anything I tell her to do. If I say, "Look, this would be good for you to do," she'll do it. She went to a singles party a while back. I said, "I found this in the local paper. This might be good for you to go to. Why don't you go?" "I've never-

been to one of those in my life." I said, "Why don't you go?" And she went. [Group laughter.]

Marilyn: That's more than most people would do.

Ian: She came back, and I said, "How was it?" She said, "It was horrible. Nobody talked to me and I felt terrible." I said, "Well, I'm so proud of you for going. We'll try some different things and hope they work out better."

Sabrina: Her background had no stimulation. I mean living under the bed and all. She needs someone to provide her with some interest and stimulation. You're really going out of your way to find these things and bring them into the session. That must mean so much to her. Who has ever shown such interest in her?

Ian: I'm sure she "loves me to death" for it. [Group laughs.]

Larry: I'm thinking of all the places people go to get together. Classes are fairly innocuous, and people aren't going to attack her, but there's also limited interaction. If she were going to activities in churches or social clubs there would be more conscious awareness of socialization, of people. I'm thinking that she's less likely to be persecuted in these settings than in other places. As we know, the slightest connection sets off fear and internal persecution trauma.

Ian: I think you're right.

Larry: Is it time to tell her she's got to have more experiences with people so we can pay more attention to what happens to her? "Even if the experiences are painful and difficult at first, it's the only way we're going to get some sense of how it is that you're not putting yourself forward so that people can relate to you and give you things that could be good for you."

Ian: I think you're right. I think I'll do that.

Larry: On the heels of feeling some-

what successful about the classes, now might be good timing. We need a place where she's getting experience being around people, not in a work or class-room setting. Perhaps interest groups where there are discussions and lec-tures.

TRANSFERENCE ANALYSIS AND SKILLS

Larry: But let's be clear on what this is all about. As therapists our focus isn't educational or social, or supportive. There are plenty of other people who can perform such tasks better than we can. Our business is studying transfer-ences and resistances to transferences. You and she have broken out of the worst part of her crippled and abusive past in your relationship and you will continue to do transference analysis between you. But one thing that we know helps along therapy at these early developmental levels is use of parallel transferences to broaden the experi-ence potential. People used to be wor-ried about "splitting the transference," but that's a concept we now under-stand as useful when undoing neurotic repressions is the task at hand.

All of our preoedipal, preneurotic people take to groups, classes, milieu therapy, and develop parallel transfer-ences that can be most useful in fostering their personal development. For some people we find that they can first experience and speak difficult transference developments outside of the consulting room with others. The most difficult experiences come with the therapist. But the early phase of working through occurs with many others in other places. Yes, this woman could use some socialization.

I have written extensively on the relationship between object relations deficits and the failure to develop many ego skills (Hedges 1983b). As object relations gaps are filled in or bridged by therapy the areas of faulty or missing skills and learned problems need opportunities to develop. I be-lieve it is not out of place for an ana-lytic therapist to be empathetically attuned and supportive of the person's efforts to develop skills. And transfer-ence is frequently attached to various talents, skills, and learning deficits (Hedges 1983a). And I certainly reso-nated with your practical concern for skill development in case she got laid off and the therapy was threatened. I have also written extensively (Hedges 1994a) on the importance of giving priority to the practical concern of protecting the ongoing therapy with organizing people. They often get into messes in the world and if we don't give immediate and practical help, the therapy will end by sheer carelessness or lack of knowing how to stay afloat in a complex world. With a woman who is and always has been so isolat-ed, having people in her life also lets her begin to breathe and stirs up transference experiencing that can be put to use in sessions as well. The hardest kernel of psychotic transference has been cracked as you have been able in a beginning way to show her how she avoids connectedness with you. But with over 40 years of complete social isolation she needs as much expansion of her relatedness possibilities as possible to work through the organizing transference. She clearly knows this and trusts you in this regard because she is certainly expanding her purview—even if it seems slow to you! Remember, only a few years ago this woman would have been considered totally untreatable. A few therapists might have seen her as a candidate for lifelong supportive therapy. But no one has heretofore believed that the kinds of transformations she has made with you were even possible. In some sense, your analytic work with her is just getting started as the two of you feel a therapeutic alliance. In another sense, the "impossible" task has been accomplished in that she now sees the key to her growth as connectedness to you and eventually to others. She's mustered enormous courage to go into the world for the first time and dare to relate. She's willing to follow your suggestions and trusts you enough to march straight into the face of pain and humiliation because she now knows she must, and she trusts you to stick it out with her. I feel very optimistic now about what you two will accomplish, though we know it will still be slow. But Ian, no matter how long or difficult the road for her to find satisfaction in life may be, she has broken out of her lifelong prison of terror. Nothing can stop her now! I hope you continue to enjoy her.

Ian: Thanks. I will.

8

Lost in Time and Space

Laura's description of her work with Karen illustrates graphically how people living organizing experience have difficulty keeping their thoughts and feelings effectively oriented in time and space. Fortunately, we have just enough early history to point to the way Karen's difficulties originated. Also we have here a therapist who is able to be sensitive to, and who is willing to puzzle about, the exact nature of very unpleasant sensations in the countertransference. In a prior case conference Laura had brought for group discussion her feeling that Karen was driving her mad by leaving her feeling woozy, disoriented, frightened, and out of control with her client. Processing her bewilderment with the group, coming to see her countertransference sensations as difficulties in orienting in time and space to her client, gave Laura a better footing. What follows is a three-month follow-up that shows how the two are managing with Laura's fresh perspective. Also illustrated through the imaging of the case, and some dreams in particular, is the impossibility of decoding symbolism employed to express the approach and avoidance of interpersonal contact at the organizing level.

Laura: I have been seeing Karen for fourteen months twice a week until six weeks ago, when we moved to once a week. She is 30 years old, single, never married, and attending business school and getting excellent grades in a very difficult program. She is very accomplished academically.

She first came to my office to interview me. She had the names of several therapists and she was interviewing them. She has a very snobbish, elitist quality in her voice. I thought, "Whew, she's not going to like me, I'm miles dumber than this one. She's going to go find somebody really intelligent that she can talk to." She asked me a lot of very probing questions about my theoretical orientation. I found myself utterly unable to speak like an intelligent human being. I thought, "Whew, good riddance" when she left. I was sure she would find someone else. A couple of weeks later she called me back to say she wanted to work with me. I was terrified. I thought I would be found out!

Larry: So the countertransference was you didn't think you knew what you were doing? It seemed unlikely you could connect to her.

Laura: Absolutely. I felt like a fool. This all started to make sense eventually. She dresses in very expensive clothing, but she manages to look like a bag lady. Her clothes are not ironed. They're not clean. They don't match. Her hair is somewhat mussed. If she has makeup on at all, it's sort of on sloppily. She looks like she's just been through a wind storm and had to dig things out of the bottom of her closet to wear. Which I think she does.

The first time she came for an appointment she got lost on her way to my office even though she had already been there once. She got lost and didn't make it to her appointment at all. She called in a frenzy, very apologetic that she had gotten lost. We rescheduled and the next time she made it. Karen is usually late. She usually has had a terrible day leading up to coming into my office. Her first presenting problem was men. She always chooses inappropriate men. They're either married or unavailable. They're always much too low class for her to even consider a permanent relation-

ship with, but nevertheless she gets obsessed with these guys. At the time she started seeing me she was obsessed with this guy who was a construction worker, went from job to job, often unemployed, divorced but still in love with his wife, and very unavailable for her. When she meets men who are what she would consider appropriate, she's just not interested in them, she has no feelings for them.

Her second problem she initially described as anxiety. Small tasks would become huge mountains instead of little molehills for her. She would become completely paralyzed and incapable of dealing with them. One example was that she was supposed to write to a speaker who had been invited to come and talk to one of the school's programs. She knew the man, having worked with him. So she was supposed to write to him to confirm that he was coming. She could not do it. She just couldn't do it because she had to write even this simple note absolutely perfectly. She simply couldn't write it until it was too late. It had gone beyond the point of being polite and she was just in a complete frenzy about it and horribly ashamed. That was the beginning of what I came to understand as a terrible confusion in time and space. I came to understand it as more than merely an overperfectionistic way in which she would get tangled up in tasks she had to do. She continued to get lost on the way to my office. Or she would lose her car keys and spend hours looking for them. She would have someone with her going through her whole apartment looking for her car keys. She looked in her purse at least thirty times, but the thirty-first time there they were. That terrified her because she knows she must have seen them on one of the thirty times she looked. She thought she had not seen them because she needed them to be lost.

My countertransference when I'm with her is horrible. It's just really intolerable. I feel like I have a hangover when I'm with her. Or like my head is stuffed with ground pepper. I can't think. I'm almost physically dizzy. I can't conceptualize anything. It's an awful feeling, terrible. At first I thought, "Well, I don't know what this is. Maybe I shouldn't see her in the mornings, maybe I should schedule her in the afternoons." It didn't work. Now I'm again seeing her mornings and I'm experiencing this disorientation and it's a terrible feeling. My underlying fear is that I really am stupid and this is just the first time I've ever noticed it. [Group laughs.] I've been denying it all these years.

Cindy: I guess we know how she feels! [Laughter.]

Laura: Karen told me she thought she had been adopted at birth. I asked her to check out the facts with her mother. She said, "Oh, I couldn't do that. I've never talked to Mother about my being adopted. Mother won't talk about it." I continued to encourage her to do so because I felt there were some primitive disturbances, and some early history would help us piece things together. She finally did talk to Mother and came in to tell me with great excitement that no, it wasn't at birth. "I was 3 months old when they finally brought me

home." Her parents had been in the process of arranging the adoption when she was born and placed in institutional care. She would turn blue and there was concern that she might have a congenital heart condition so she was hospitalized during the first two months several times for extensive testing but nothing turned up. She was with foster parents another month before the adoption process could be completed and the foster parents concluded that the blueness was because she was a "breath holder" when she didn't get her way. So from the beginning she was seen as a willful, stubborn baby. But her parents were willing to take this bad baby on anyway. So Karen began her life in her adopted family as a bad baby. Her sister, the natural child of the parents, was four years older.

Larry: So we have here not only the institution and the hospitalizations with intrusive testing, but foster parents who drew the conclusion that she was stubborn, willful, and a bad baby as the way Karen was greeted the first three months of her life. So each time the child attempted to put out organizing tendrils to orient herself to the world, to find a maternal body, something happened to interrupt the possible organizing attempts — at least four and possibly more times. And then she was given to a mother who received her as bad and who had questionable empathy herself so that she provided no apparent bonding experience at all. Something isn't going right for the infant and she's experiencing or expressing her distress in breath holding. So before three months she's already experiencing difficulties relating to the world around her.

Cindy: I'm imagining this screaming baby crying and crying and when she can cry no more there is silence and tenseness with tight lung and heart muscles leading to blueness.

Larry: Was she left to cry too long?

Laura: My interpretation was, "I don't think you wanted to live. I think you were trying not to be alive." That felt right at the time. It didn't feel like rage. It felt more like terror and frenzy fighting off a depression. She continued being the problem in her family. She remembers people saying all her life, "What's the matter with Karen?" Her parents would be in the study with the door shut. She would listen and they would be discussing, "What's the matter with Karen?" There was always something bad, something wrong about her. The older sister, Linda, was perfect. Linda was a genius. Linda was Dad's child. They were both adopted but she was the one that Dad took places. Linda and Dad would go to museums and do intellectual things when they went on family trips. Mom and Karen would go shopping. Linda was always in gifted classes with special tutors. When she came home from school she was locked in her room. She never watched television; she did homework and studied every night. Karen would sit on the couch and watch television with Mother, but she always knew that was because she wasn't bright. There was something wrong with her. She didn't read well. She didn't get along well with the children at school. She said, "I really was just a terrible problem child."

When I would ask her what exactly was wrong, the examples she could give me would be very minor, ordinary childhood things. "I got into an argument with a girl at school about lunch pails." That was horrible. That was an indication to her parents that there was something dreadfully wrong with her. They had her in therapy when she was between 8 and 9 for about six months. Mother said the therapist said she was schizophrenic. I have not been able to verify that. We haven't been able to locate the therapist.

Larry: Mother told her that in this recent talk?

Laura: Yes, Mother told her that recently. As they were growing up she continued to be the bad girl and Linda was the good girl. Linda went off to college and was getting a Ph.D. in a very specialized technical field when she had a nervous breakdown and was hospitalized. She has never been able to work since. That was seven years ago. Linda has since married. She remains in therapy and on medication for depression. Karen went to a college in the Midwest where Mother had gone. It seems the family shipped her away where they wouldn't have to deal with her. She joined the right sorority like she was supposed to, and presumably started off doing all the right things. Then she decided she wanted to be a ballet dancer and that was the wrong thing. She started spending all of her time dancing, running, and vomiting. She was bulimic. She also started taking speed, partly to lose weight and partly to be able to keep up the dancing.

Larry: All this frantic activity seems a manic defense. She is away from home—dancing, running, vomiting, taking speed . . .

Laura: Frantic. I was surprised when she told me those things. It took her about three months to get them all out. I was surprised because she seems so staid, so very conservative. She's also very religious. She has a born-again Christian kind of tightness about her. She does not have a sex life, only a male friend. I was very surprised when she told me about this period of her life when she dressed all in black and took drugs and was bulimic.

Arlene: Was this around the same time her sister was having her breakdown?

Laura: It was just before, yes. She was still the family screw-up then. While her sister was succeeding, she was shipped off to the Midwest. She experiences her mother as simply not seeing her at all and making up things about her. Mother would tell people that she was at a different school than she was and would tell them that she was doing this, that, and the other thing that she was not. Though she later became accomplished academically, at the time Mother presented her as much more successful than she was. This embarrassed her. Father was this utterly driven, horrible man. One of her memories of him is that he would get up at four or five in the morning in order to rush off to work. He would take a cup of steaming hot coffee and practically pour it down his throat. She remembers once saying to him, "You couldn't possibly have enjoyed that." His response was, "The human body needs a certain amount of fluid." She also thinks she should be able to exist on four to five hours of

sleep and be a tremendous success in everything she does because that's what Father would have expected. Father, in the meantime, has come down with what she sees as his just deserts. He now spends his time getting drunk, dying from a rare form of dementia. He is pretty much noncommunicative. He's out of it. He stays at home with Mother taking care of him. She presents it as this horrible sounding scene. He screams at his wife constantly to do things for him, to fix this or that, to do all sorts of things. Mother just takes care of him and takes care of him. Once a year Mother hires someone to take care of him and goes away on vacation. They never are able to hire the same person again.

Arlene: Karen doesn't live there though?

Laura: No, she has her own apartment. It's such an impoverished emotional life this family has. On birthdays the tradition is that Mom has a cake for you and you sit and Mom takes your picture with the dog. Mom's dog is a schnauzer. In college she was caught by her sorority sisters vomiting. She was thrown out of the sorority.

Larry: For vomiting?

Laura: For vomiting, yes.

Cindy: Because she was bulimic?

Laura: That's what she says.

Larry: So they must have been ready to get rid of her.

Laura: They tossed her out on her ear.

Bill: Just looking for something.

Laura: I'm sure she didn't fit into the Midwest social scene. She came back here (California) and that's when her sister had her nervous breakdown.

That's when the pressure was on Karen to do something to succeed; she also had the opportunity. Finally there was a possibility that she might actually make something of her life. So she started graduate school and has done phenomenally well. However, she is utterly compulsive. I mean she works constantly. She works a night job to make a living. She is way over her head and always horribly anxious. They have papers due that are supposed to be about a page or a page and a half long. She will turn in twenty pages. She does this week after week after week. She very much overdoes everything.

Larry: We know it's more difficult to write a short paper than a longer paper. What it requires is that you orient to your material accurately.

Laura: Right. I think that is exactly the key. She has no way of orienting to what's important, to what's enough, to what's normal. But she's doing fantastically well in the program. She has taken on a part-time job with her department. Of course, she needed more work to do! She was already taking a full load, working nights, and auditing yet other classes. She's going on job interviews with prestigious firms. She's already been offered a position when she graduates, which will be nice because I would like to be paid. [Group laughs.]

Arlene: You mean you don't get paid?

Laura: Well, this becomes the crux of how we finally began to confront the countertransference. When she first started with me she said, "I've been to the college health center and I've purchased the insurance, but it's not good until January." She started with me in September. So in January they will pay fifty percent of the fees. So I charged her simply the co-payment until January. Then we would be set to go with the insurance at full fee. Well, usually when I see someone and they expect to subsequently have insurance coverage I'm immediately alerted and say, "Wait, there is a potential problem of the insurance company not paying for a preexisting condition and you need to know about that." I didn't discuss the issue with her as I always do. I just figured, "Well maybe she knows what she's doing because she seems a lot smarter than me."

Larry: I wonder if that's the nature of the mother–child relationship?

Laura: It might be.

Larry: We see how confused Mother is and how Mother dissembles to her friends. I wonder if in infancy Karen assumed that Mother was correct because Mother was bigger and smarter. Yet her mother was inconsistent, confused, and maybe even bizarre. So in the countertransference you failed to orient yourself to her so that your needs in the relationship could be appropriately insured.

Laura: And her mother wasn't her mother anyway. It was somebody who showed up when she was 3 months old and who doesn't seem, from what I know of her now, to have had the empathy required to deal with an infant. So I just let this insurance question go. I let her handle it. By March I sent the forms in to the insurance company and they want another code number. I gave her all the codes and we redid the forms. It got to be late summer. She was paying me her share all along, but so far I haven't seen anything from the insurance. By now we have a large insurance bill. I was gone the month of August on vacation. I think time away from her helped me to sort out, "Wait a minute, I don't always feel this way on Monday morning, only Monday mornings with her." So the time seemed right but I can't remember exactly what allowed me to take the matter up with her. She was talking about how people don't know her, how people have problems understanding what's going on with her, and just how lost she always feels. I told her, "I have this strange experience when I'm with you that I think may be really important for us to understand. I feel disorganized and confused and it's a really odd experience. I'm almost physically disoriented and dizzy." She looked kind of shocked. At first she was worried about what she was doing to me and I said, "That's not what's important. What's important is that I think I'm on to something with this feeling. I think I'm experiencing something of what you feel and of why people leave you, because anyone who gets close enough to feel this is also likely to feel confused and perhaps frightened." She started to cry. She said yes, she thought that was true and she does feel that way. We clarified various aspects of mutual confusion and fear in a very useful and personal way. We felt very close to each other. It was a very good session. The next session she missed. [Laughter.]

Cindy: Surprise!

Laura: Surprise. She called later that afternoon in the usual frantic, apologetic frenzy and put this long story on my answering machine about how she had been ready to come to session but she was running a little bit late. Then she had a flat tire and the Auto Club took too long to get there. After this long and labored explanation she assured me she would see me next time. Next time she arrived pale. She looked really, really upset and told me that she had finally contacted her insurance company. They made a ruling and they were not going to pay a cent. She was horrified. She handed me two checks. Her own check co-payment and her mother's check for the very large amount of money that was owed by the insurance. She said that after our last session she had felt completely stuck, convinced that she does have an unconscious and that it's trying to sabotage her. She called it her evil friend Skippy. Skippy did this, not checking into the insurance, and not paying attention so that she could continue the therapeutic relationship. She had gone through that whole week talking to her friends, really struggling, thinking she had to quit therapy. Friends offered to pay for her therapy. She finally decided that, no, she would pay for it herself and she went to her mother and asked her to pay the back amount due. She had never asked her mother for money before.

Larry: Has Skippy appeared before?

Laura: We had talked about Skippy off and on. Skippy who loses the keys, the person who can't get the job done.

Larry: How did that come up?

Laura: In the Doonesbury cartoon some years ago they were doing George Bush and his evil twin Skippy who was invisible—so that's where that came from. Her evil friend Skippy just screws everything up for her. It was a very powerful experience for her to see how she had managed to jeopardize her therapy. She said, "I have to go down to once a week because I can't afford twice a week." I let her. I'm now seeing her once a week. Often she misses even once a week by forgetting, showing up late, or getting tangled up somehow. So that's where I am with it. My sense is to just let things go as they are for now. But I don't know if I should be pursuing that.

Larry: She didn't check with her mother if her mother could help her with the second session on an ongoing basis?

Laura: She doesn't want help from Mother or anyone. She has a male friend now who actually is almost suitable and who could afford to help her and offered to, but she said, "No." She did not want that. She graduates in June and she had been offered a job which, if she takes it, will allow her to pay my full fee and come more often.

Larry: I find it's altogether too easy for therapists to be understanding when someone says, "I don't want to go to my parents to ask for help with therapy," or "I don't want my friend to help me out with it." As though that were an issue simple to understand, when someone obviously needs therapy as badly as she does. I think the issues are often more complex. At this point she clearly realizes that the

therapy is important and she realizes that you are on to her.

Laura: Absolutely.

Larry: She's afraid she is trying to sabotage therapy but she's content with cutting it to half and then missing much of that. How do you understand it?

Laura: With Mother, she would say it's because Mother holds money over her head and manipulates her with it. Last summer Mother wanted to go to Germany on vacation and wanted Karen to go along because she didn't want to go alone. Mother proposed that they go to Germany and that Karen take a course in Berlin, which she needed to satisfy some requirement. So she went. But Mother at the last minute expected her to pay for her own ticket. She said, "Mother doesn't understand. I work a low-paying night job, for crying out loud. I don't have that kind of money." She was crushed having to tell Mother, and Mother absolutely not understanding—telling her once again about what a failure she is. How come she can't pay her own way, and so forth. When she goes shopping with Mother, Mother wants her to buy these expensive things. I told you about this the last time I presented her. She's terrified to go into Mervyn's because she's only shopped at Robinson's with Mother. The idea of going into Mervyn's where she could actually afford something just terrifies her. She wouldn't know what to do. On the other hand she cannot afford to shop where her mother wants her to shop, so she doesn't shop at all. She just has all these expensive clothes her mother coerced her into buying that are wrinkled and badly cared for.

I think it's more my getting so close to understanding her that's the problem. I don't think it's the money. I could have offered to adjust the fee more but I didn't. I think she needs to back off, to have some room to not have me there. But I'm not sure about that. I don't know if I should be running head over heels after her and not letting her withdraw like that.

Larry: I appreciate your being cautious about it because you're not clear about what it means. But you could say, "If you wanted to arrange to come in twice a week, we could probably negotiate something or figure out some way of pulling it off. But it sounds like for right now you're more comfortable leaving things the way they are. Perhaps later we can talk about it." This leaves open the possibility that there might be ways. If and when she wants to think about it there are no doubt some possibilities that could be explored. But you may be right in just keeping quiet for now.

Laura: In that session where she didn't ask me if she should go to once a week, but told me that she had to, I said, "I don't like that. I think you need the twice a week but we'll try it and see how it feels for you." Now I haven't seen her for two weeks, she said because she's had interviews and things.

Larry: Your comment raises a minor phraseology issue for me, particularly with "organizing" people. To me, the "you need it" still rings of the medical model, prescriptions, and things like that. I prefer introducing

the symbiotic "we." "We are working on things and it will be difficult for us to continue at the same pace or with the same intensity once a week. For us to feel together in our work and to enjoy the same continuity that we have seems important." This highlights the idea of a mutual need being mobilized here, which is the way symbiotic states develop—two personalities learning how to interact spontaneously and intimately in a way that works for both. "We both need each other in order for us to do this work together and we will no doubt be able to hold things together with once a week, but we'll feel the difference. It won't be quite the same and at some point we may need to talk about increasing our time again." Keeping it in the symbiotic "we" with an open-ended future gives linguistic aid to the project of establishing what Searles (1979) has called the *therapeutic symbiosis* from which two can later individuate.

Laura: That's much stronger. I definitely have a fear here. She is about to graduate. She does have an excellent job offer. This man has now asked her to marry him. This has all happened in the last month. But she's just not thinking about any of it. She's straining just to get through the week. This is a heck of a time for therapy to fall apart, particularly given the sister's breakdown when she was at the peak of her success.

Larry: On the surface it appears that things are just coming together so wonderfully for her. But from her manic frenzy we can infer that she feels quite differently. So often with organizing people when the therapeutic interactions finally begin to take hold, that's the point at which they want to cut down, withdraw, or take a break. To them it feels like things are getting worse or things are getting more threatening. If one chooses to intervene it may be important to be definite and firm. "This is a critical time in your life, our understanding of your family, your friends, and our relationship is just really getting going. I know all of this may feel uncomfortable or even at times frightening, but I certainly feel we should try to keep up our continuity and intensity—even if it's tough to do so." What I'm saying is this: we know that what terrifies people when they're living in an organizing state is interpersonal contact. The psychotic transference becomes mobilized when contact, connecting threatens. Depending on how we assess the situation and the strengths operating at present, we may decide to (1) support the person in backing off or de-intensify the relationship for now with the idea that later we will need to get things going more fully; (2) interpret the resistance to the growing interpersonal connectedness, showing an awareness that the person can indeed back off but that such a move probably isn't necessary and will definitely slow down our work; or (3) do as I have just suggested and come on like gangbusters, making clear that you are in this one hundred percent and you intend to do everything in your power to see that she stays and does the work of relating that you both know is important for her to learn to do—no

matter how much she really doesn't want to.

This last almost coercive approach should be reserved for situations where you judge the challenge as something the person is currently ready and able to respond to but needs a firm nudge and solidly committed help to dare to open up the Pandora's box of miseries that are bound to be released when the psychotic transference opens for analysis. And with her and this feature of disorientation, a strong road map might be facilitating. Clearly the therapist at the time also has to be willing and able to take on the challenge as well. There is no room here for the passive attitude of the classical analyst who treats neurosis. Framing the psychotic transference for analysis requires a mutual commitment of two as well as considerable potential background support (finances, transportation, medication, hospitalization, the use of a case manager, and so forth).

With Karen, if you chose to be firm, you might say, "All of your life this or that awful thing has happened to you. You have agonized endlessly. Now you have somebody on board studying with you what's going on. We have a lot of preliminary ideas. We have a certain sense of continuity. And we have enough intensity in our relationship where even after my vacation I was able to say to you what I said about my feelings of confusion and disorientation. It seemed to hit some important place. I feel like we're moving forward in a way that's bound to be disturbing and at times even terrifying. I feel like our cutting down right now slows our momentum in a critical way. Yet I can understand how uncomfortable it might be for you and how going easy for a while might seem the best thing to do."

Cindy: My experience is that you seem so much closer to her now. I think she may feel very ill. As you were talking I thought, "I'm going to pay attention to how I feel," because I started to feel really sick to my stomach and I'm wondering if she has difficulties taking in and holding on to your care, especially now that you seem so much closer.

Laura: Yes, she does. Once after she had missed a session, in fact, it was the session with the flat tire, I said, "I know that you didn't get a flat tire on purpose, but I want you to know that when you're not here I think about you and I miss you and I look forward to our time together." That was almost too much for her to take. The idea that I could think about her when she wasn't there was very frightening.

Larry: So your hunch, Cindy, is that the bulimic symptom may have something to do with Laura's caring?

Cindy: I felt sick to my stomach and then after you stopped talking I felt okay, so I thought maybe it was part of your moving in close with your interpretations of her disorientation.

Larry: So you think the bulimic symptom may have something to do with the threat that some type of personal contact may be on the verge of being taken in.

Bill: She missed a session after you interpreted the transference by using

the countertransference. Maybe she perceived herself as a bad object for you like she always was for her mother and that had an adverse effect on the bond with you.

Laura: She did, and we've been talking about it ever since. But luckily there is this split-off way of talking about the evil friend Skippy who is the bad object. She's frightened of how she makes people believe her bad self and how she does damage to people, distances herself, and then loses her relationships. But it's all slightly disowned. It's this unconscious part, this evil friend Skippy.

Larry: I recall we had our last case conference on her just a few weeks before your vacation. You were just beside yourself in terms of feeling crazy with her, not knowing what to do, and worrying about how you were going to keep your sanity during the hours with her. So you presented her at the case conference in which you began to pull together some of your thoughts about her. When you came back from vacation you were ready for her. You moved right in in a way that she feels. And then of course we have the missed session, the flat tire, and then she presents the insurance news. On the one hand it seems, "Well, that was what had to happen." But on the other hand, the insurance problem had been hanging over her head since February and she could have checked on it and made it happen much earlier.

Laura: Exactly, it was when she felt my presence that she . . .

Larry: Called and made them reject the claim. So right at the point when there is meaningful contact the break occurs. When we track the organizing experience that's what we're always looking for, the way in which what I like to call the "psychotic mother" appears to destroy any possibility of sustained relatedness.

Laura: I even wonder if she actually had a flat tire. She very well might not have.

Larry: She simply may not have been able to reach you.

Arlene: Mother changes facts to make them look better. She is so compulsive about other things. You know, one-page papers are twenty-page papers and everything is worked toward achieving perfection. But nevertheless she doesn't quite make it to her therapy. The way we talked about it before was that when it comes to dealing with the facts of the world, there is this enormous amount of energy designed to get things operating in a cause-and-effect chain. But when it has to do with relationships she becomes much more confused. She doesn't know how to orient to people, to object relations, to people's bodies or to her own. So all that compulsive behavior wins her marks of excellence in certain places in the world, but she is a frantic mess trying to produce it. But in terms of the world she can often make it work. In object relations she doesn't have the same power to make things finally work. If anything, she begins to connect in such a way that it drives people crazy. It's driving you crazy, the result being, of course, that she can't connect. And what's driving people crazy, her way of reliving the psychotic transference with Mother? Does she mimic

somehow all the things Mother did that drove her crazy, all the inconsistencies, the lies, the misrepresentations of facts, the manipulations, the last-minute surprises, the attacks, the miscalculations? She was a bad girl from the beginning, and always seen as a problem. To what extent was it Mother's responsiveness to her that drove her crazy?

Laura: I neglected to mention that the way she stopped her bulimia was a 12-step program. But the way she relates to the program makes it a substitute for the addictive process. She got through most of the 12 steps, but she got to some point where she could not own everything and be responsible for everything.

Bill: How do you deal with people like that? I've always had difficulties with that. They go to a 12-step program and switch addictions. You don't want to be rude, intrusive, or inappropriate and say, "Well, you're doing that with this, too." Because the program means a lot to them. They're really invested in what they're doing.

Laura: But when she came to me she was disillusioned with that program. She said, "It worked to help me stop throwing up, but something is still very wrong. I don't know why I can't completely work the program, but it's not enough." That's when we started talking about the unconscious. She has also been in previous therapy before and this guy would challenge her irrational beliefs about, "Why can't you get a 'B?'" She said, "I tried real hard to do that but I couldn't do that either." It was one more way she was a failure. You reminded me of trying to please the male authority figures, the professors that she's trying so hard to please. They're father figures and she knows that and she can never please them because sooner or later they'll find out she's a complete flake.

Bill: Has she had any significant male relationships in her life?

Laura: No, just with these inappropriate males until this last one proposed marriage but I have no idea where that's going. She isn't at all related to him.

Bill: The "unavailable" you said?

Laura: Yes.

Bill: Do you think that might be an unconscious seeking of abuse, like with Father?

Laura: That's what I thought at first, but as I got to know her better I realized it's much less organized than that. She's supposed to be grown up, so she's supposed to be interested in men, so she will choose some that are kind of, you know, you really don't have to talk to them or anything, you just have crushes on them—a very adolescent-seeming and very disorganizing kind of relating. With the male authority figure there is a much more fearful relationship. There is not, at least consciously, a romantic fantasy there at all. She has simply got to please them and get their approval and she knows that she never will.

She has a very odd kind of lack of information about her father's family. With her mother's family there are cousins and other relatives she can talk about a bit, but there is very little she knows about her father's family. She just doesn't know. Apparently they never interacted much. My first thought was that because she's adopted, she didn't consider them her family. The dressing and the inappropriate men was like an identification with her fantasy about her real mother, who must have been this lower-class woman who she really feels like.

Cindy: But she has no idea of who she is in this family. She doesn't have any idea of who they really are.

Laura: No. There is no real sense of them as people. She says that she always felt like she didn't belong with them, even though she didn't know that she was adopted. She always felt like she didn't belong there, they weren't really her family.

Arlene: So was Karen surprised when she found out that she was adopted?

Laura: It just fit because she always knew that she didn't really belong. And because she was able to say that, I also thought she would have some fantasies about her birth mother or curiosity. But she has none that I can see.

Larry: She doesn't speak about her family as though they're humans nor does she have curiosity about humans. It's the organizing quality that's not connected to human beings.

Laura: Your mentioning the non-human reminds me that she had two dreams very early in therapy. In one dream she was in this house with her mother, who was half robot. Her mother and another complete robot were coming after her. She flew out the window, set the house on fire with them all in it, then flew away.

Larry: That's an interesting version

of the old fairy tales! "I don't belong here. I am of royal blood and these peasants who raised me are just robots."

Cindy: "I have magical powers but I am alive. They are mechanical and destructive. I hate them and I want to kill them."

Laura: The second dream was about a little girl, "But I knew it was me," she says. "She had on this very elaborate mask with rhinestones, feathers, and jewels. And people were trying to get her to take off the mask. But I knew the girl didn't want to take off the mask because underneath her face was horribly burned and scarred." I interpret that the fire she set burned her as well.

Larry: She didn't completely escape the family fate. But she hides behind something that's nonhuman. She's real, alive, scarred, pained, and self-protective. What does she feel like to you now?

Laura: She knew that dream was about her and she knew it was about coming alive, shedding the mask in therapy. She feels her ideas about herself all fall apart. It would make sense to think that she identifies with her fantasized birth mother and that's why she looks like a bag lady. But no neat ideas about her finally make sense. They are all confused. I worry that all of this is my attempt to come up with something to hold on to, some kind of structure so that I don't feel her awful unformed chaos and that I don't feel so crazy when I'm with her.

Larry: You're trying to become oriented to her, but every attempt collapses.

Laura: I feel like I'm being sucked into a black hole.

Cindy: Laura, when she talked about the dreams, I would be interested in how she felt about those dreams, or if there was any emotion. I mean with the scarred face, "Aren't I lucky I had the mask to cover it up," or, "Oh my God, what if anyone ever saw it?" What were those dreams like for her?

Laura: It was more, "I can't let anyone see this. It's just too awful." In the first dream there was very little feeling. She was frightened and that was about it.

Arlene: She wasn't in touch with the anger at all?

Laura: Not really. She's very bright. So she knows that dream has to mean anger as well. But she doesn't have the feeling; it's not there. There isn't even sadness. She was just frightened. Her intelligence simply doesn't connect to her body, her feelings, or to relationships at all.

Larry: It is not clear to me that it's anger. I think about the agitated chaos that's possible in infancy when Mother cannot be formed.

Arlene: Because anger is a posture? Something somehow organized with a communication purpose, isn't it?

Larry: Right.

Laura: If I could put the structure of anger on it maybe I would feel better. She can't hold any of the structure I keep trying to contain her with. These don't fit.

Larry: Which, once again, is one of the characteristics of working with organizing material, that we try to put a structure on it as we try to understand it. We try to decode a symbol. We try to get into the psychotic material and understand the nature of the psychotic world. I've worked with therapists caught up with "getting into the psychotic material." One seeks desperately to create a sense of "understanding" it. Yet what has been understood? Nothing. It's nonsensical. Psychotic content is not anything we can hold on to or truly make any sense of. Which may be the experience of the prebonded infant. Bonding begins with a psychological orientation to Mother's body. Without that, a bond cannot evolve and one cannot hold a steady orientation to the world except by obsessive rituals or frantic activity. The first ground to feel oriented by is Mother's body. She never had such grounding and has been disoriented in time (Mother's rhythms) and space ever since.

Laura: I am always so busy trying to look for the feelings in between the reporting of this and that. But there just aren't any—only intense work and frenzy. No sadness, anger, attraction, hope—maybe deep despair and agitation. An orphaned baby for sure.

Larry: With well-developed people the symbols and language are chosen because they represent one's self, even if imperfectly. We embed our personal experience within the symbolic language structure as we grow up. People who have never had a constant experience of mother and then of substitute mothers, never learn quite how to substitute things. The basis for organized language is metaphor, comparison to original constants, knowns, givens—she had none and so her en-

tire metaphoric system is flawed. We find organizing symbols don't carry the expressive power we might expect. Or their symbols are not metaphors but work differently somehow. Several years from now, when you have a better sense of what her comings and goings and trying to reach for you and backing away from the contact mean to her, you may return to these dreams and suddenly have some sense about how those symbols served her purposes of trying to express idiosyncratically something about the connecting and the disconnecting moment. But although the images are compelling, vivid, and interesting to us now, how to understand them at this point in time is an enigma.

I'm feeling that the way you're reporting today is drastically different than the last time you spoke about her. You are more oriented and patient.

Laura: I'm prepared. I think that my sense of her is somewhat different. It really made a difference to speak the countertransference. I still feel it with her. I still feel disoriented when talking with her, but I don't feel so tormented by it. I am now interested in what it's all about.

Larry: Before you seemed totally enmeshed in the disorientation and hangover confusion experience. It seems now you're standing somewhat outside of it, experiencing it, but also noticing it, watching it, feeling her through it.

Laura: I haven't seen her for two weeks.

Cindy: So if you had seen her this morning?

Laura: If I had seen her this morning I would not be able to talk about her so clearly as I am right now.

Arlene: You need distance for that.

Laura: To organize it.

Cindy: I think she may well need some distance from you too. I'm struck by the formlessness of it all. You're saying you get very much touched by the sense of formlessness and uncertainty. You carry it, you speak it, you feel the chaos.

Laura: I find myself doing the same thing she does. I keep trying to organize it. She keeps thinking if she can make a better schedule, you know . . . I feel that too. Let's organize this thing into some kind of a framework. But it won't go. It doesn't happen. There is no organization. Only frenzy and chaos.

Arlene: "Let's not see her in the morning, let's see her in the afternoon."

Cindy: But Laura, despite these wonderful insights, this good work, and these developing understandings, isn't there somewhere this little question, "Can I really go anywhere with this person?"

Laura: That question comes up. But I know there's a person inside there somewhere looking for me. She never has had a mother to organize around and I know she needs one and I'm it.

Cindy: Yes. In therapy we have to start there. We acknowledge that there is humanity there that can somehow be reached, that can organize, given the right opportunity.

Laura: The human in Karen is mostly held together by the intellect. There is enough intellect that she knows something is very wrong. She cares about that, and wants to do something with it. Something. I don't know if she's prepared to take the big plunge now. She backs away. But there's no point in delaying.

Larry: After we heard your case last time people had a number of questions focusing on basic body orientation in time and space. We talked about maps and about trying to find one's way safely through time and space. By thinking of basic orientation as an ego function we see that something fundamental is learned through the infant's basic physical relation to Mother's body. If you can't learn to be grounded in Mother's body you can't learn to be grounded elsewhere and you are always somehow lost or groping for directions. We are well aware of great differences in how people orient in time and space, of how each of us relates to maps and directions.

Cindy: Laura, when you talk about her it seems like there is a lot of sadness.

Laura: It seems really sad to me. In spite of how confusing and how frightening it is to be with her, I feel a lot of caring for her. I really want us to be able to do something, for me as well as for her. When she was born she lost everything and has never recovered her orientation to life. I know I have to be an orienting beacon for her and I know I can be.

Larry: Thanks, Laura, you're helped us focus on something basic in all of us, something somehow always present in organizing experience—how lost we can be in time and space and how crucial orientation is to the organizing experience.

9

The Secret Escape Hatch

When working with preoedipal issues, fears of breakdown, internal emptiness, and death are almost always present in one form or another. Winnicott (1974) has discussed these fears that something catastrophic will happen in the future, as memories of what has already happened in the infantile past. Winnicott formulates that the sense of omnipotence that an infant is born with ideally undergoes a series of gradual and bearable disillusionments in the earliest months of life as the infant comes to understand that the environment is not subject to his or her whim and does not always react quickly or appropriately with the needed responsiveness. If Paradise exists *in utero*, it is lost in fairly short order in extrauterine life—but, it is hoped, in ways that are manageable for the infant and supported by the environment.

To Winnicott's discussion I would add that these fears, which are memories of breakdown, of terrible inner and environmental void, and of psychic death in infancy, emerge in the psychoanalytic situation when the analytic speaker begins to sense that these memories of primordial terrors need to be reexperienced in full emotional and somatic force within the analytic transference. That is, the analytic speaker is starting to realize that the internalized experience of the "psychotic mother" of infancy is about to make a terrifying reappearance that cannot be avoided if the speaker is finally to be able to understand the nature of his or her organizing-level structures and how they operate in daily life.

When the organizing experience begins to emerge in psychoanalysis and dynamically oriented psychotherapies, the internalized mother who kills (by being unavailable in the needed way) and the internalized infant who suicides (by withdrawing from an anticipated cataclysmic relatedness experience) become the focus for transference and resistance study. The acting out of the organizing transference may take the form of a series of alternating attacks on and withdrawals from the therapist. The resistance to the terror of reexperiencing the organizing transference in full-blown emotional and body forms may become manifest in a negative therapeutic reaction in which, by precipitously ending the treatment, the speaker simultaneously represents by acting out the withdrawal from and the angry attack on the psychotic mother and the withdrawal from and the suicidal attack on the infant self.

But there is not only the danger of an uncontrolled ending of treatment; there is also the extreme danger that as the person successfully revives the infantile delusion in a transference psychosis, he or she will be functioning very concretely, nonsymbolically, and without benefit of ordinary reality testing. We then see the murderous and vengeful attack on the internalized psychotic mother acted out in the arena of accusations of abuse by the therapist that reach ethics committees, licensing boards, and courts of law. Or alternatively, the identification with the aggressor (that is, the internalized psychotic mother) is acted out in moves toward self-mutilation, self-destruction, and suicide. Under the conditions of a successfully revived organizing or psychotic transference both the analytic speaker and the analytic listener are in realistic danger.

In case consultation when I raise this concern therapists frequently respond, "Oh, this person wouldn't ever really sue me," or "She talks of suicide often but she would never really do it." My response: "Who gives you to know the exact nature of the psychotic delusion you are working so hard to revive? You say you 'trust' your client. I say that attitude constitutes a potentially very destructive dual relationship! Psychosis, even in subtle almost invisible forms, is never to be trusted. Too many people have been badly damaged in gross and subtle forms in the first months of life in ways we cannot know about until they emerge in transference memory. Analytic speakers need to be able to express the murderous rage and suicidal despair of a traumatic or strained infancy within the context of the therapeutic relationship. "So," I ask therapists, "what are you doing to get ready? What precautions do you have in place to protect both yourself and your client from the powerful forces of hidden or not so hidden psychosis that you are inviting into your relationship in order to transform?" I have written at length on these realistic dangers and made suggestions regarding what steps therapists can take well in advance to be ready for the unleashing of powerful psychotic energies in the transference (Hedges 1994a, 1994b).

We are about to witness a suicide. As the reader will see, everything that could be done to prevent it was done. It seemed that everything was going as well as could be expected under the circumstances until the shot was fired that ended Anthony's life. The story demonstrates the power of psychosis. It shows that life's circumstances are not under our control and that accidents do happen. It illustrates the tragedy of not having treatment funds available for people who desperately need treatment—an issue exacerbated with the advent of health maintenance organizations and managed health plans offering limited benefits.

Anthony's suicide tells of the widespread circumstance of people who are the sickest being sent to clinics staffed by overworked therapists who have limited training and limited supervision in the treatment of psychotic constellations. Often, these very ill people are seen primarily by student interns because of financial considerations. Anthony's tragedy tells of the inability of such clients to cope with changing therapists, a widespread circumstance that happens annually as large numbers of psychotherapy students rotate training settings. And finally, his story tells of the extreme danger of the unregulated emergence of recovered memories. Therapists tend to welcome revealing stories and recovered memories, often without understanding their condensed dreamlike nature or how to contextualize them within the developing transference situation. Here there wasn't time.

The first case conference to be reported was held several months prior to Glenda's having to terminate her work with Anthony. You will see how carefully thought through and carried out the transfer to another therapist was achieved. The second transcription is a three-way conference with both therapists and me, held a few days after Anthony's shocking suicide. So far as I can tell everything was considered that could have been. So far as I can tell everyone did the best he could. And yet—the fatal shot was fired. Anthony had lived his entire life in confusion and pain. Finally he used his secret escape hatch.

GLENDA MUST TRANSFER ANTHONY
TO ANOTHER THERAPIST

Glenda: I've come to a crossroads of not knowing what I'm going to do yet in my personal and professional life in September [three months away]. This passage in my life finds me feeling freed from a lot of the commitments I've been involved in for many years. Now that I've completed my training and obtained my license, I'm left trying to decide whether to start private practice or to go into mental health administration. I've given notice at the clinic where I've been seeing people whom I'm leaving in September. I said, "Well of course I'll take Anthony with me." But as my personal possibilities began unfolding, Anthony showed a level of pathology that began affecting me deeply. The problem for me has been how to stay detached just enough to be able to help him, and how not to have so much maternal preoccupation, which at times has been just as strong as I've ever had with any of my children when they were little. The background, but ever-present suicidal risk, has made an incredible mutual attunement necessary. My part was possible because I was in supervision with Larry, and was able to move us forward really slowly. Anthony and I have been meeting two times a week, which is really not enough for this kind of therapy with a person who has so many deep needs, but it was all that could be arranged practically, even in a low-fee clinic. But twice weekly was enough to get the process of attachment going.

With the suicidal risk emergency again this summer I really pressed to get additional consultation here and elsewhere. There had to be more safeguards, like a psychiatrist active on the case and a hospital available. But he had no health insurance, so he had to be seen as a county client. With our work going intensely but my not being sure if I was doing everything I could, I often felt alone and out on a limb. I know in the heat of it all I felt resentment. You know, "There's Larry sitting coolly in his supervisory chair. I love the theory but when I'm walking through the thick of it I feel so frightened and alone." All the while Anthony's writing me this stuff that's just grabbing my guts, confusing me, tearing me apart. I mentioned Anthony again to Eleanor, the head of the clinic where I'm working. When it came again to the threat of suicide and how clearly dangerous this was, she said, "You are seeing this client at great risk. You've got to give him an ultimatum that, whether he wants to or not, he has to go back to the county for psychiatric evaluation and follow-up. I had sent him to the county when I first took him on. We all agreed that he probably needed medication, but he refused to take it. And the psychiatrist he saw at the county had no rapport with him at all and did no follow-up. As we all know, public services are severely limited because of funding. So my position became one

of strongly recommending but not forcing him to take medication at that time. But since he refused to take it I worked with him without medication.

But this time I had to come down with the ultimatum of "If you want to keep working with me, you've got to go to the county. You've got to go today. I've already called your boss and set up an appointment." The boss is the one who had brought him to see me in the first place because she was afraid he was going to kill himself. So his boss went with him. He agreed to go because he was scared of my dropping him, which is what has happened in the past with therapists. Many therapists have dropped him when he's gotten into regressed places like this. This maneuver was my way of taking over control and saying, "You have to do this. You have no choice. And if the psychiatrist says you have to be on medication, you have be on medication. I am going to risk you being mad at me, that's just the way it is."

Larry: His boss actually took him to the county psychiatrist?

Glenda: Yes. I called her and I told her what I was going to do. I had a release to talk with her and I knew how supportive she had been with him in the past. I didn't ask her to take him. But I wanted her to be aware so I talked to her first. When I talked to him, I said "Your boss is willing to talk with you." She did. She was very supportive and she went with him to see the doctor.

Fred: Good for her!

Glenda: Then I got further involved, in that I talked to the psychologist he was seeing at the county clinic for intake. These visits have been worthless in the past so after much soul-searching I decided to become involved to be sure he got what he needed. He doesn't tell her anything, that's the whole problem. When he goes to the clinic he doesn't tell her what's really going on. So she didn't see him as very suicidal. But I talked to her and told her about some of what was coming out, the suicide danger, and the possibility of the emergence of multiple personality material. She said, "Okay, we'll get him to a psychiatrist right away." Because she was going to set up a medication appointment for three weeks away.

I decided to go with him to see the psychiatrist, again to be sure everything got communicated. Since his last visit had been such a dismal failure I went and saw the psychiatrist first. It really helped a lot, because this time, this psychiatrist was really concerned. We finally found a guy who was concerned. I gave him the case material, and told him I felt like I was in over my head with the possibility of multiple personality coming out. I said "I've heard about Anafranil. It's supposed to help with compulsive symptoms." Anthony was ridden with rituals and punishments by this time. He had great anxiety about his boss being transferred to another job site, and over my announcing that I would be making some changes in September. Also, he is typically depressed in the summer and now his father is coming down on him harder. Although Anthony is in his early thirties he still lives in the family home and takes considerable abuse from his father.

Everything was so bad that he didn't have a moment's peace, a moment he could be free of his rituals and self-punishments. The psychiatrist agreed that Anthony might be a good candidate for Anafranil. I said "Great!" The Anafranil has helped greatly.

Andy: Anafranil helped?

Glenda: Anafranil helped. I stayed in the interview with the psychiatrist and Anthony and it went great. Anthony said he would tell everything, that this time he would be honest. And he was. He was comfortable and the psychiatrist liked him.

Andy: Great!

Glenda: I had come to believe it was necessary to intervene directly and forcefully, to really take him and help the county workers relate to him because otherwise it's impossible. People discount him because he doesn't engage right off. The psychiatrist liked him and said he would let him take control of the medication because of his control issues. He would let him go on and off as he saw fit, but then would see him again in two weeks. He told him all the possible side effects. He was very thorough and careful working with Anthony's fears.

Larry: Every time I've followed a therapist going through this kind of active process with the county or an HMO I find it helps greatly.

Glenda: Really?

Larry: Yes. Professionals working for the county, for public clinics and for managed health companies are greatly overloaded. They see so many people coming through, that all they can provide is what is demanded. Unfortunately, patient care isn't the concern, rather the squeaky wheel gets the oil. If an overloaded worker sees a therapist who is shepherding someone through the system, he will stop and pay attention, exactly like you're reporting. I have come to advocate the therapist taking such an active role. It would be better if we had a parallel case worker or case monitor to intervene instead of yourself, but that's not always possible.

Glenda: Well, in any event I saw him decompensating and felt something had to be done. You all remember from when I presented him before that his family is completely useless. They don't see any problem at all with him, which no doubt is how he got this way in the first place—a complete insensitivity to human need. The next day his punishments were gone, which to me is amazing that these marked symptoms would simply dissolve like that overnight. He said his punishing side said that he would cooperate. But he doesn't know if it's the medicine, or what.

Larry: Well, he certainly got a lot of holding in one week. You, the boss, the psychologist, and the psychiatrist all attended to him skillfully, so it's hard to know how much is the medication and how much the holding.

Glenda: Two days later I arranged to meet his boss. He had wanted me to meet her a long time ago but I had held back. He had wanted the internal mother here to meet this external person. So I did. I went to his job. It was like bringing a friend to meet the family. That's what it felt like. I met his immediate supervisor that he's worked

with for several years, and saw where he worked. He said it helped ground him more. Somehow when I gave him our special double handshake in the parking lot there, in the external, real world instead of in the little womb, cocoon of my consulting room, it gave more connection of our work to out there. So those things had been going on in addition to the medication. The massive thing that blows me away is that all of this deep psychological stuff, talking about organizing issues and multiple selves, and how to handle all the material coming out is great, but when it comes to alleviating a severe symptom, sometimes a chemical is really crucial.

Larry: Absolutely.

Glenda: The medication eliminated the rituals and punishment that were driving us crazy. He was diagnosed at the county as an obsessive compulsive disorder. He went back to see the psychiatrist yesterday. I called the doctor afterward to see how it went. He says, "Oh, it's really nice that you called." I said, "What was your perception of Anthony and the medication?" He says, "I'm just delighted. It makes me feel like I'm useful to see the reaction so quickly to some of the symptoms. You know he's a bright guy." I was glad he had this positive feeling.

Larry: He sounds like a good man.

Glenda: His demeanor was really good with him. He was not the authoritarian, macho medical person that Anthony had feared at all. So that brings me back again to my feeling less anxiety, but still feeling guilt that I can't do more.

Anthony gives me a journal every month. At first the journals had been a very concrete account of what had transpired in the sessions. Then they moved to the "Dear Glenda" format, which was what I had suggested to get to more of a feeling level, which made the journal much more intimate. This month there's the letter at the beginning of May that has Myrna speaking. Myrna, he explained, is the 7-year-old playful female child in him. Myrna says, "Miss Glenda, please don't think Anthony would molest a child." This relates to his father's fear that if you're a summer camp counselor like Anthony was a couple of summers ago that you will be suspected of molesting. Myrna says, "He would never do such a thing. I see everything he does, and he doesn't hurt other people. A lot of times he hurts himself." Then she says, "He does very bad things to himself. I'm getting very scared and I want to cry. Please help him stop, Teensy gets scared." Teensy is a little stuffed rabbit I gave him. "Teensy gets scared too, and Buster, and Ozzie and Harriet. Melissa says to tell you about the bad things he does to himself. Will you help him if I tell you? I'm only a kid and I don't know what to do. Please tell me what to do." This came earlier when the pressure was developing.

Larry: Yes.

Glenda: Things were getting so bad, that he didn't know if he would be able to call me if he had a suicide feeling. Then he got into the part where "I'll do anything, just don't leave me. I'm doing everything you tell me now. I'm

going to the county. And I'm taking the medication. I'm calling other people now when I get frightened." I've informed him that after September I am leaving the clinic and I'm not sure exactly what I'll be doing or where. That I don't know for sure if I will be able to continue seeing him. I told him that wherever I went or whatever I chose to do, that if at all possible I would find a way to continue seeing him, but that as of now my plans had not firmed up and I could be without employment, without an office, and taking some months off. Myrna's letter to me continues, "You know, you're the best therapist I've ever had. This is the closest I've ever been able to get to anyone." I had been sharing some of my feeling about feeling trapped with his telling me he was going to kill himself, that he had a secret escape hatch but wasn't going to tell me his plan. So anyway I forced him at that time to tell me his plan. And then I insisted that he bring me the knife he had planned to use. So then he said he had no secret escape hatch anymore.

Larry: I worry here that Anthony fears that whether or not you leave him in September is somehow dependent on his cooperating, being a "good patient." He gives you his knife and says he has no secret escape hatch but is he just conforming to what he thinks you want from him?

Glenda: Yes. I considered that possibility myself but gradually ruled it out because his anxiety was increasing dramatically, he said, because he no longer could kill himself if things got really bad. He writes, "I see where I made you feel trapped, and I feel sorry. You may be right that I was testing you to see if you would drop me. It's kind of funny that you were trying to be the perfect therapist."

I was telling him that sometimes I can handle things comfortably and sometimes I can't. "It's funny you were trying to be the perfect therapist, and I was trying to be the perfect patient. And that we were both driving each other crazy." [Group laughs.] You know, true, so true. He continues, "There is something to say against perfection. I cried all the way home and all night. The thought of not working with you is the most upsetting thing that has ever happened to me. I listened as carefully as I could to everything you said. And deep down I know you're right. It's just that I think you have done the best job that anyone has ever done, and I have faith that you can still do the best job. I'll also honor your wish to do what's best for you." This refers to earlier when I had felt it necessary to bring in my needs, that I wasn't sure at this time where I was going to be in September or whether I'd even have an office and that kind of thing. I have pledged to continue seeing him if at all possible and I've said that if I can't or we have to take a break for a while that I would be sure he had a good therapist and that he could keep contact by mail if he wished. So he keeps talking about my taking care of myself, and how he's trying again to put it that my going over things so carefully is trying to take care of him too. He says, "I know that I can't be with you forever, but I don't want it to be over this soon."

This next journal entry is about the medication starting to work. "I wanted to call today, but I'm trying to give you all the space you need to continue working with me. Thank you for telling me what I would need to do that." He used to place emergency calls frequently, which posed practical problems for me. I've been limiting, as best I could, the drain he can be on me. Trying to explain, like if you're with a kid all day, and you say, "Look, I can't stand it anymore. I have to go and cool off for a while, so I don't get mad at you." You know, that kind of thing. You have to take care of yourself so that you don't throw stuff on the kid who is just doing his thing. That was how I was feeling. He was just doing his thing, the despair and suicide rumination—he was just doing his thing. And yet, you know, there was the part of me that was getting ticked off, weary of his 24-hour-a-day needs. He said that no one has ever told him they might need a break from his intensity. They have simply dumped him. As a result he's always believed that he's too much to handle and sooner or later he will be abandoned. He said when he first came, "As we go, I'm going to be too much to handle, and you're going to drop me like everyone else."

Larry: Let's review. He had gotten to a connected place with you where he's never been before about six weeks ago. Then came the gut-wrenching letters, full of psychotic, sadomasochistic sexual fantasies and confused thoughts including his secret escape hatch. This fits what we usually expect with organizing people when they finally feel the contact. They somehow withdraw—here he fragments and becomes suicidal. Then you arranged the county evaluation and meds. Shortly thereafter you had to begin telling him that you may be leaving. And now he's begging you not to leave him, promising that he's not a child molester and showing you how good he can be. Quite a sequence to follow what may have been the best connecting experiences of his life. It's hard to tell if he's suddenly improved because of the meds, the containment, or the fear that you're going to drop him for talking about sexual feelings. I have the sense that the function of the letters that you found so gut wrenching was to rupture the closeness that had been building. But then seemingly, in his mind, in response to his fragmented sexual fantasies you tell him you may be leaving and then he promises to be good. It is terribly complex and tragic that just as he starts to trust you you have to consider the possibility that you may have to stop seeing him.

Glenda: I know. He says, "I'm terrified at the thought of facing life without your help. My elimination of physical punishments." I mean, you know that's just unbelievable. "The reduction in number and frequency of rituals, and improved sleep are all helpful." He was not sleeping at all at one point. "I had extended feelings of well-being after your phone call the other night. I've noticed that my vision and hearing seem to have improved." Remember, I told you earlier how he used to feel like things were flat, two-dimensional. "I've been no-

ticing more details in everyday things." He said when he came into the office as his punishing self that he could see things much more vividly. Now he is saying that even when not in his punishing self he's seeing things much more vividly. "I've also noticed more conversations around me. In general, I think all of my senses have been broadened. I definitely have less tunnel vision."

Larry: Interesting he can *see* better, more vividly. He's attributing this to the medication, but we're also aware that the way the medication came was through all of the other relations that surrounded and contained him. The way I'm interpreting that letter, is, "For some reason I had great investment in the psychotic activities, the rituals, the punishments, and so forth. When I was told by you that I could not do those things anymore and I was given a pill to stop me, that energy has now gone into being able to maintain good feelings and to see things more clearly." I don't mean to downplay the importance of the medication at all—but it does have a context that's important for him as well. The investment in the psychotic mechanisms has shifted, but we don't know exactly how to interpret it. Like what exactly is more clear and vivid to him now? That life is better when he cooperates? Or that if he allows a psychic regression he will be thrown away?

Glenda: The part of him that people can respond to is becoming more available, he says. He says people at work are noticing he's laughing. And it was Myrna who could finally laugh, the depressed child inside. He said he is more aware of people talking, so he can get more involved in conversations. He's afraid of becoming dependent on the pill. But his boss said, "Well, it may not be much different than being dependent on Glenda."

Andy: In other words, if he wants to remain in therapy with you, his punishing part has to be on the side of healing.

Glenda: There wasn't a way I could directly influence the punishing part. We tried many things and talked a lot about it. You know, "Tell the punishing part, you've got to go along with me now." But nothing gave us control over it until I was at my wit's end and told him what he had to do. Then the punishing side volunteered to help out. I see that his acceptance of the chemical is the fact that it happened in this trusting, or at least demanding, environment.

Larry: Yes. This firm approach seems warranted at the moment but I do worry about hidden resentments. It's always best if the psychotherapeutic material can unfold unhampered and unpressured, so nothing has to go underground. But realistic dangers have to be considered and responded to.

Glenda: He has enough deep paranoia that he could, I'm sure, counteract whatever the chemical could do. But he's expressing that whether he loses me or not, he is concerned about my well-being, which seems to be a developmental move for him.

Larry: It seems more out of fear he will lose you. I think he's in a terrible bind. He began connecting with you and senses somehow that you can help

him be more human, alive, and real. But no sooner does he start connecting to you then the psychotic/erotic letters appear to rupture contact. Then you say you may not be able to continue working with him. Well, he can't tolerate interpersonal contact, but he hates to be dropped for being bad, for needing a connection and then having his regressive experiences perceived as bad and then, once again, being abandoned.

Glenda: I made a commitment to myself during that soul-searching walk on the beach I told you all about, of saying to myself, "Don't lose track, you really need to see yourself as a transitional object here. You have gotten as much as you possibly could have out of this year for him. And you can walk him through a transition to another therapist, just as you did at the county." If I were staying at the clinic I would continue to see him. Because now the pressure of finding somebody better, who has more experience, and can work with him "better" than I could has lessened. Because I now know that the connection is the important thing, and I've been able to mobilize other resources to help me maintain that connection.

Larry: You're now seeing that there is nobody who knows more about Anthony and what he needs in order to be able to grow than you do.

Glenda: Well . . . [Group laughs.] I went to a friend who has been in this field for years. She said, "You just walk into these situations and then suddenly you're it! Farm out whatever you can't do yourself." [Group laughs.] And that's really what I've been doing.

After all I've been through I now have much more of a sense that I could continue to work with him successfully, if everything was staying the same. But the down side of it is my own life passage I'm in. Evaluating whether I want to be a front-line therapist and take on the phone calls, the hospital, the beepers, and all the commitment the way I get involved. Being a therapist is especially taxing to me because I get deeply attached. I really have to work on detachment. However, I also see that part of my ability as a therapist is in the capacity for connection I have and for being able to be very absorbed in the clients I work with.

Larry: I agree.

Glenda: So my question for myself now is do I want to go back and learn some short-term treatment models for just hitting superficial stuff, with the way the mental health field is generally going now? You know, "This is all I can provide for the moment, come back later and we'll see what else we can do." But part of my struggle is that in this depth work the possibility of helping a person transform his or her life is very appealing to me. It's so human, so very real, and so very needed. And I see there are so few people who have trained themselves in it. And resources for training and depth therapy are dwindling. Even though there are so many desperate people who need it. Studying psychoanalytic work is very appealing. It gives the most satisfaction, there's no question about it. How else can the client ever be given much that is useful and sustaining? Managed care as it's

going is ridiculous—nobody's needs are met by it but the business people who are running it. My psychiatrist friend says psychoanalysis is the crème de la crème, really the only way to transformation that lasts. I always felt like that, but I didn't know that much about it, and rejected it in some way. And then, of course, it's been mostly limited to medical trainees until relatively recently. I've also experienced the satisfaction that comes with the beauty of what often happens in learning the psychoanalytic way. It's about practicing it that makes the difference. It's so human, so real and so worthwhile. It justifies the heavy investment of resources it takes.

Larry: Yes.

Glenda: What it comes down to again is here's this client I have to find a place for. I called the clinic where I picked him up originally before I transferred to where I am now. Is there any possibility of his coming back there? Because that was an agency he knew. He had been there several times over the years and worked with several different therapists. The director knew he was high risk and was reluctant to re-admit him. I protested, "But he was there before, he's cooperative, he comes regularly and pays his fees." I'm wanting to more or less take his hand and lead him to a new therapist while he still is seeing me. I really want to do a careful and lengthy transition process. I've come to terms with my not being personally able to carry him when I don't even know where the hell I'm going! If things turn out in September that there's any way I can continue, I will. But I have no current prospects and no way to foretell what my situation will be. I have to make preparations now for him since I know the adjustment will be very difficult for him and will take considerable time. I have not yet been able to concretely say, "You know there's a therapist so-and-so at such and such a place who wants to work with you. I don't know where I'm going to be working so I can't count on being able to continue with you."

Larry: Is he going to be able to understand that it's not that he's bad, or has overwhelmed you with his regression, but that there's a transition in your life, and you don't think you'll be able to take him into the new phase?

Glenda: That's what I'm trying to convey.

Larry: I know there's not much time and there are so many pressing issues, but in the time you have left I would certainly watch for primitive transference reactions. Whether you have an opportunity to work with them yourself or whether you pass the information on to his next therapist, now may be an important time for observing organizing level resistances and transferences. Like what is his reaction when Mother is preoccupied with herself to the point that his needs, from his point of view, mean nothing? Or can he even get that far? Is he feeling that you're dumping him because he upset you with his psychotic/erotic talk? Since I read that loosening as an effort to flee from the danger of the developing connection, we might surmise that it happens every time he tries to feel close to anyone. So he then

believes they dump him because he talked dirty—after all, the dirty talk does function for him as a repetitive predefense pattern to flee from, to rupture relating. And now that his fear of losing you is mobilized, we see a freezing pattern. So there's a self-destructive, or other destructive quality to sharing sexual preoccupations, as though he knows well that sadomasochistic erotic talk will wreck any relating. Also sure to disrupt relating is frank suicidal preoccupations—the secret escape hatch with the knife. He knows this from past experiences of being "too much to handle." If this nightmare is what results from attempts to feel close to a person, from attempts to feel more like a valued person himself . . . what utter futility Anthony must feel.

Fred: Do you feel your relationship with Anthony has contributed to your thoughts about wanting to get out of doing direct therapy?

Glenda: Yes, it definitely has. Definitely. There is no question. I don't know if being so deeply involved is good for me personally. I'm sure Anthony senses this. And in ways I try to tell him that in my discussions of my dilemmas for future career plans.

Larry: Few therapists attempt to deal with this very difficult kind of client in the deep connecting way you have done. Certainly not so early in their careers. By now you have discovered, through all your consultations with people, that Anthony is the kind of person who has always been considered untreatable. And that this view still remains widespread. Advice, suggestion, medication, hospitalization, and support are how these people are ordinarily responded to. They are the unwanted, the mistreated, and the abused, and neglected of our world. You have seen for yourself. Over all these years with a half-dozen therapists, no one has ever been willing or able to reach out to Anthony in the way that you have. The clinic director doesn't even want him in her clinic because he is "high risk." His response to threatened closeness is a bizarre, sexualized grasping, and threatening ruminations of suicide which are all bound to send people running. Yes, there are many kind-hearted people in the world who can see that he is suffering and want to lend a helping hand, like his boss. But to take on the project of relating to him, given the bizarre sequences he is compelled to repeat, is demanding, frightening, risky, and burdensome, to say the least, no matter how important the work or no matter what the rewards. Our society simply has no humane place for these people and no motivation to care for their needs.

Glenda: He wouldn't have gone to the county even once if I hadn't made him. He was afraid of humiliation and abuse like he has experienced there before. He wouldn't tell people what he was dealing with because he was afraid and he refused all medications, so if I hadn't run interference, Anthony wouldn't have gotten anything.

Larry: He wouldn't have gotten treatment at all until there was some major crisis, and even then only a quick, cheap patch-up job. You have tackled the kind of patient other

people have been afraid or have not wanted to take on.

Glenda: You encouraged me in my work with him. And yet how much, I guess that's my question, how much can you give? When you don't know any better you just get involved and then you're stuck. And how many thousands or even millions of people need what Anthony got—even if I could only give it for a year? I didn't know when I started what it would take to make a connection with him. And I didn't know I would be needing to break it off this soon either. I hope he doesn't see my leaving as due to him. I've explained it carefully to him again and again.

Larry: With experience you can learn in the first interview to see the depth of this kind of problem. I can often pick it up even over the telephone. And then it's a question of given your available commitments and resources, are you currently able to or do you want to work with this person at this time in your life? At the point where you started with Anthony you just took whoever was assigned to you at your clinic. You had already begun working with Anthony when we started talking about him here. I was supportive of you because I felt you could do the work, and you have. It's been a spectacular piece of connecting work. And we have had a vivid dose of his predefensive resistances to experiencing his psychotic transferences in therapy with you. If it had been possible for you to continue seeing him, we could have studied over time his moves toward connection and the emergence of the psychotic mother transference and how it prevents or ruptures connections. Anthony was up for the work. He has suffered his entire life and your devotion has offered him hope. You, too, have been up for the work and have really hung in there with him. Tragically for both of you, the work is now being interrupted. It was promising to be a truly powerful growth experience for both of you. Anthony has had a glimpse of what it means to be treated like a human being, to be valued and cared about for the first time in his life.

But I've also supported you in terms of deciding whether or not continuing to see Anthony is right for you. If I had been supervising you when you started with him I would have alerted you to what it would take to work with him. We would have considered the time and personal investment factors and decided if it was right for you to take on such a major commitment at this moment in your life. I often discourage therapists from taking on people like this who, given the current circumstances of their lives, they have no business taking on. The alternatives at a beginning juncture are to choose time-limited modest goals or, if the person seems motivated for more, to try to locate a place where they can continue therapy for an indefinite time to do the work they want and need to do. Often in managed health plans the best thing a therapist can do is to help validate and define the magnitude of the need and then help the person aim toward some depth work outside the plan or to think about future therapy possibilities in terms of employment, insurance options, and so forth.

I believe Anthony is treatable. I feel like the work you've done is the best possible kind of work. I don't believe anyone else knows better how to make a connection with him by now than you do. But, of course, we never quite got him going long enough so we could begin studying how, in resistance and transference, he is compelled to disconnect. We have before us a lot of potentially illuminating material but its meaning is now incomplete and clouded because you are likely to be leaving him. Finally, someone who wasn't upset or repulsed by him or his needs at last had a chance to see what it is he does to alienate people, to make sustained and rewarding relating impossible, and then you announce you're leaving, right after he starts letting it all hang out. What would be required for his treatment is a practical living circumstance that can support frequent contact, motivation on your part to connect for a long period of time, and good psychological health on your part, including the ability to regress, to feel utterly helpless, and to be able to make use of consultation. Because as he shows you his internalized psychotic mother you will inevitably feel shut out, alienated, and helpless at the deepest and most agonizing layers of your personality.

The prevalent view, as you know, is that this man cannot be treated psychologically. I think that's entirely wrong. The problem is that resources are scarce and therapists aren't generally prepared to experience themselves so deeply. I've had occasion to watch a number of Anthonys treated quite well—to watch their lives and their relationships undergo major humanizing and life-giving transformations. The demands are always intense, but I must say not always so chaotic as they have been with Anthony. We have many other examples of this kind of treatment being done successfully today. (See Giovacchini 1979, Hedges 1994a, Little 1990, and Searles 1979.) In our field we have lots of choices, and we need to find the kind of work that suits our personalities, our capacities, and our tastes. But you didn't know any of that when you were assigned Anthony.

Glenda: Right. I hadn't had the experience of it. These things are not taught in graduate school.

Larry: I think early in practice one feels less choice than later. But now, based on your experience, you will know right at the first interview whether you want to work with a person or not. Many people do not find this work so demanding or taxing but love the intensity, the intimacy, the involvement of it. I personally do not. I can do it and I can enjoy it but it taxes me greatly. You now know what it takes to connect with a person at this level and the personal demand this work makes on a therapist. It's been an immensely valuable learning experience for you.

Glenda: Oh yes, no question.

Larry: I think I told you the first time I followed a woman through a case like this some years ago. In fact she was working for the county in a

setting with some treatment options. One schizophrenic woman attached herself to this therapist. The therapist came to me and said, "I would like to find something out about myself. I've been working with psychotics superficially in day treatment for a long time. I may continue, I may not. But I would like to have some sense of what depth treatment is like. Will you supervise me on this case?" We worked together weekly for several years with some very good gains before the patient's husband was transferred out of state. In our last supervisory session the therapist told me, "I can't thank you enough for being with me, for supporting my work with this woman. But I now know that I will never do this again. It takes more from me than I care to give. I now know that and I'm glad I do." At the beginning she didn't know that, and you didn't know either. Some therapists choose the work, many do not. Most are unable to connect deeply enough to even understand what the person's expressive needs are and so remain in ignorance and misunderstanding of what this type of work is even about.

Glenda: On my beach walk I also thanked God for sending me Anthony because there's been an enormous transformation in me. My friend said, "You're never going to forget him."

Larry: You'll never be the same.

Glenda: No, I'll never be same, because there's been something especially illuminating in his being able to articulate what's happening with him. It's a highly magnified version of the basic human struggle. I'm going to miss him a lot. He has given me a vision of ourselves I never had before.

Larry: The thing that this particular man brings that many other people functioning at this level don't is the unusually clear and beautiful articulation of his experience.

Glenda: Yes. And his way of using metaphor. He even said, "My strong point is my imagery." Like when things have gotten tense between us, I have been able quickly to metaphorically flip over into, "Well, Watson, my boy, this is really something isn't it?" In our play to discover difficult things, he's been Watson, and I've been Sherlock Holmes. His punishing side is called "Slippery." He said, "When you talk quietly to me about Watson and Sherlock it makes such a difference. I feel we're safe together."

I think his writing has been very important too. When I do transition him to someone, there's got to be some way of our maintaining some form of at least token contact, because I do care about him and he needs to know that. Even the psychiatrist mentioned it would be good if he could have some way of continuing to write to me and maybe occasionally of our getting together—like visiting a distant relative. But before I make any promise I need time to regroup, to reorient, to reestablish myself. It does feel like a leave of absence, and it may be that I'll come back full force as a therapist. I don't expect to give it up completely or forever, but I do feel a need for some space, and I'm not so sure how exactly to get that.

Larry: That may be one of the things you can mention to Anthony. I think it's important to make it clear to him how much he has contributed to you and your personal growth, so that he'll have a sense of worth as a result of that. Try to tell him in every personal way you possibly can what he's meant to you and the ways in which you've grown, how valuable it's been, how much he's given you, and how you'll never forget him. I think that would be very important for him to hear.

Glenda: I will.

Larry: Some of these cases, as you know, go on for years. I would encourage you to talk with him, and make it clear that you're taking this time and this space for yourself, and that right now you cannot continue with him. Make it very clear that it doesn't have anything to do with him. Yes, he's been difficult. He knows that. Yes, you've made each other crazy at times. And yes, he's given you a hard time, no question about that. But you and he have been working on those things and he's given you all he's got, and you've given the work all you've got. Things between you are now going very well. So that's not the reason you're taking a leave. If you wish, explain some of the details of your personal life that make this time a transition for you. There's no reason why you can't disclose your reasons for leaving him. To him this relationship is the first breath of life he has known. The more real you can make it for him—even though it has the limitations of a professional relationship— the better he will be able to hold on to it, to have some hope about overcoming the abuse he has endured. I only worry, of course, that he won't be able to make use of any of it because the delusional transference is so strong at present. But you might write a termination letter for him to have and read in the future when he's in a different frame of mind.

Glenda: Maybe I will.

Larry: You're shedding a whole part of your life right now and preparing to begin something fresh. If Anthony can be a part of that, so be it. If not, we know that with you he felt a stronger sense of connectedness than he has perhaps ever felt in his life. Let's hope he can transfer that possibility of connecting to someone new rather than using it as ever more proof that he is truly bad and that there's no point in going on. Thanks for sharing your work with us, Glenda. And good luck with this transition.

Glenda: Thanks to all of you.

Six Months Later, Shortly Following Anthony's Suicide

Larry: I'm really glad you two could meet with me today. I was concerned about you both. Glenda was so deeply connected to Anthony for so long that his suicide last week not only was a shock but it was bound to be deeply disturbing. It shakes one's soul.

Glenda: I gained some detachment in the transferring process. I grieved a lot about not being totally what Anthony needed. In finding it necessary to take care of my own self I hated having to transition him to someone else. I went through a lot then.

Larry: I know you did. We reviewed it every week. You were a wreck for a long time.

Glenda: Right. So now I have somewhat of a removed view. I'm really glad Charlene and I are in this together. Because we've continued to talk regularly about Anthony ever since she started working with him. We've been processing things right along. He sent me two letters and I wrote back. So I wasn't cut off from what was going on for him but I was more detached because I had let him go to Charlene.

Let me read a few parts from his first letter. He is saying he has his regular ups and downs. "Charlene is doing a super job in keeping me afloat. Okay, now some unfinished business." This was the end of September. I had stopped seeing him in the beginning of September. "I am still convinced that the letter and limericks Carol (another of his internal personalities) wrote you upset you enough to change jobs. So I'm repeating my apologies. I know you said they weren't a factor, but this is one time I don't believe you. I made a mistake and I am very sorry."

Larry: The power of psychotic delusions always astounds me. We talked about the danger of his not believing you. He knows that when he regresses he alienates people. And he also knows at some level that the regressive psychotic/erotic talk is pre-defensive, that is, by upsetting or unsettling the other it serves as a flight from intense relating—the other falters and/or withdraws. So at some level he knew it was his intention to protect himself from the anticipated traumas of transference relating and that he could do so by alienating you with erotic talk, could upset you so you would pull away. So when you tell him that isn't true he can't believe you because that's the way he's constructed the world. If I recall correctly, that was the place in the sequence when he revealed his suicide plan to you. A psychotic expression of what he has to do (kill off the self), and was in fact doing by alienating you in order to escape intense connections, which for him have been orally intrusive. Wasn't drinking your urine and blood part of the sadomasochistic representation?

Glenda: Yes. So I had a lot of anxiety about what to write back. I told Charlene I wanted to do something that's therapeutic for him but it also needed to be genuine. So the letter I wrote said something to the effect that, "Yes, your revealing some of your innermost thoughts did scare me at times. It made me feel like I needed to get more help. Remember that was the time we got you to the county psychiatrist for medication." So I acknowledged that it had scared me but it had led to our using auxiliary resources to feel safe together. And that it was not anything he did that made me leave the clinic. I reaffirmed that many things in my personal life came together that resulted in my leaving. So I validated his thought and fear that he

had indeed upset me and didn't just say, "Nonsense." Because I felt like I had always been genuine with him. He would have known if I had ever been dishonest.

Larry: Absolutely.

Glenda: I said, "Remember, you were always afraid of me dropping you as others had. I didn't drop you. I carefully handed you over to one of my best friends who is a wonderful therapist." I tried to interfere with the thought that again he'd been dropped.

Larry: We know with him we were dealing with a primary process fantasy that operates outside of ordinary reality, more like a dream or a delusion. And we know that delusions, inner reality, usually supersede the facts of external reality. In the course of your time with him you were able to get him out of the delusion at times and to get him to receive some things from you. But we know that primary process delusion has a life of its own that preempts objective reality. So even if you are genuine and even if you try to give him information to modify the delusion, it doesn't mean that the delusion gets modified. He let forbidden parts of himself, sensual desires and (perverse) oral need-derivatives be expressed and he believes that disaster always strikes when these hidden aspects (needs) are revealed. And when we consider that the fragmentation and erotic delusions seemed to be the direct result of good connection and the threat of the psychotic mother having to be reexperienced in transference, then we can say that the expressive intent of the perverse talk and the suicide ideation was to break the connection, to flee the relating by frightening and alienating you. So he believes his intent succeeded. And sure enough, you left. Since his internal structure scripts abandonment for his despairing, demanding, oral sadomasochistic self, he can only believe that you dropped him because of his regressive expressions. It suggests to me something of his earliest relation with Mother. That somehow he came to believe that it was his fault that she kept dropping him. Since we infer that she was somehow sadomasochistically orally intrusive, it may be he learned that the only way to gain relief from her traumatizing intrusions was to be regressive and get her to drop him.

Glenda: I'm sure you're right. This is what he says in the next letter. "Thank you for your letter and for confirming what I have always sensed was true."

Larry: Did he say what it was that was true?

Glenda: "Your honesty has helped me decide what I have to do in the future. Again I'm really sorry for scaring and upsetting you. I didn't mean to."

Larry: So he didn't believe you. His delusion that you were scared away by his regressive ploys continues. You cannot convince him that you had your own reasons. He now is convinced that he has to kill himself because there is no place where his true self can ever have a chance to exist. Did you have other ideas about what he might have meant?

Glenda: I didn't know what he meant, of course. Then he goes into

things that are happening. He's having lots of ups and downs with Charlene, "But it's not all her fault. It's really a rough time for me. I miss you and Susan."

Larry: Susan was his boss?

Glenda: Yes. The boss who was transferred to Santa Barbara.

Larry: I wondered if work was going badly without her to protect him.

Glenda: I talked with his current supervisor after he killed himself. She said he was excited about Christmas because he was going to Santa Barbara for Christmas dinner. He didn't talk to her about who he was planning to visit, only that's what he was going to do. He had gotten a new car, he said, and he was going there. "Oh wonderful," she said. Then at the last minute he tells her it was canceled and that he wasn't going. She talks with Susan after this has all happened and Susan says she never invited him for Christmas dinner. And there is no new car.

Now we come to Charlene. He is revealing more and more to Charlene. He is saying, "I'll take whatever punishments I have to. I promise I'm going to reveal all to you."

Larry: I don't like it already. The punisher, Slippery, is back and he does not approve of Anthony's total revealing intimacy with Charlene.

Glenda: He wants to tell Charlene things and he is telling her. For the first time he has revealed two memories of his father sexually abusing him at age 5. He never, in all the time we were together, mentioned any such memories.

Charlene: The transition he made to me I felt was a very good one. It really went very smoothly. It seemed like he had connected.

Larry: I had the impression from Glenda's last report that he was doing well with you. But the apparently rapid connection bothered me, since this man isn't given to connections. And now I hear that sexual talk has started again, oral no doubt.

Charlene: We had dealt with the sadness of losing Glenda. I had encouraged him to write her a letter if he felt unfinished. That's when he wrote her. I feel like I was at an advantage working with him because I had enough history on what had happened to be able to encourage him to be open with me. He had been afraid that he had scared Glenda off by talking about having sexual feelings for her. I gave him reassurance that he wasn't going to scare me off.

Larry: A wonderful reassurance, but given that he believed he has always succeeded in breaking connections with sexual talk, your reassurance surely fell on deaf ears.

Glenda: He thought I was very strong, but somehow he wasn't going to spare you as much. Charlene does a lot of work with the sexually abused. So she was probably coming from a place of, "lay it on me."

Larry: Right. The perfect person to tell a molest memory to. She makes clear she is ready to hear them and she's not going to be pushed away by them. Of course he doesn't believe any of it. He isn't going to really connect again because it's too scary, so he hopes to once again push the (intrud-ing) other away with talk. Now we have a recovered or constructed memory of being molested by his father who has worried about Anthony being considered a sexual molester at summer camp.

Charlene: Right. So we talked about him being able to talk about sex or the sexual things that he felt had scared Glenda. I told him he could go ahead and share them with me. I told him he could give it to me a little bit at a time if he chose.

Larry: So your usual therapeutic approach of helping people recover memories of abuse falls into his delusional intent to alienate you with sex talk. Refresh my memory, what exactly were the sexual things he believes he shouldn't have said?

Glenda: It was a poem in one of Carol's letters. I read the poem at case conference. I was emotionally distraught with the intrusive feeling that it had. You [Larry] commented at the time that it seemed the real world was not as attractive or compelling as the sadomasochistic world of his fantasy. It was also the letter he wrote to me in which he said that he loved me. It was from Carol. He wanted to drink my urine and drink my blood and that kind of thing.

Larry: That was the point at which he got into material that he knew was perverse, crazy, and alienating in nature. And this all immediately followed the time when his connection with you was better than ever? And by then you also know your plans would likely take you away from him but you had not yet told him that?

Glenda: Right.

Charlene: He told me about his father sexually abusing him, prior to sharing the old Carol limericks. He said he had a memory of his father abusing him and I encouraged him to tell me about it. It was when he was 5 years old. His father took him down to the basement and fondled him genitally. His father had told him that this is what men do to boys and not to tell anyone. I listened to that and told him it wasn't his fault. I asked how he had felt about it. He said he felt like something was wrong. He shared another memory with me the following week. He remembered his father orally copulating him. He shared the oral sadomasochistic limericks with me after that. I was continuing to reassure him I wasn't going to leave him. That I didn't have any place to go and he didn't have to worry about that.

Larry: It seems clear from all of the material that there was oral level intrusive abuse, no doubt from the early mothering process. While father may-have molested him, the recovered memory seems likely to be a screen memory condensing (1) oral intrusive trauma from infancy, (2) father's later humiliating abuse, (3) father's accusations that he was a child molester, and (4) that he was being asked to "swallow a lot" in relation to all of this Glenda and Susan transfer affair. His dream representation is to have a shiny new car (self) and be invited to eat (with a safe mother figure). Whereas what he is being asked to deal with in reality is a taxing connection, delusion, and loss. And now a therapist who states her intention to connect with him no matter what. He said he had to test

Glenda. Of course he doesn't believe Charlene either. This all feels like another intrusive molest with him at the receiving end (passive, feminine, oral).

Charlene: He was also having some difficulties at work as far as feeling rejection because he was real sensitive to that. The other workers would have lunches and not invite him or invite him at the very last minute. He knew they really didn't want him there. I suggested, "Let them know it hurts your feelings when they ask you at the last minute." So we were working on very basic things like that.

Larry: But again, your best possible approach, which is to support and encourage him in connections with others does totally bypass his lifelong knowledge of how terrifying connections are and how he has learned to do everything in his power to make sure that he does not connect. He is being a "good patient" and talking about his social problems like he knows he's supposed to do. And you're giving the expected "good therapist" response of encouragement and support. But we know that the basic delusion and the disconnection of the psychotic transference is silently active in his attempts to alienate you through sexual talk.

Charlene: Then he shared those two memories of the sexual abuse and then the Carol limericks. I was able to be objective and not overreact. But I did ask him who this Marie in the limerick was. Because it was Miss Marie getting screwed over by all these other bunnies. He said Miss Marie represented himself and him getting screwed over by everyone. I've wondered if in his revealing the oral sexual abuse and my reinforcing that he didn't deserve that, if that increased the rage at his father?

Glenda: I just located that disturbing letter from last April, one that shot my anxiety up so that we had to get him evaluated and medicated. The letter said, "I am taking the plan off the shelf. My escape hatch." He talks about his desire for revenge toward his father. But there had never been any intimation about sexual abuse. Only the severe verbal abuse and perhaps physical abuse when he was younger. He says, "I have been alternating between periods of being upset and panicking and sort of calming myself down. I remembered my escape hatch plan and I got it down from the shelf, figuratively speaking. It is all set and ready to go so I am sitting here deciding what to do. I know it is really up to me whether I commit suicide or not. But I am using my promise to you as an excuse to keep living. I am just thinking of his [father's] verbal abuse. I often relish the thought of what the suicide would do to him. It would be the ultimate revenge for all the suffering he has caused me. I would get in the last licks and there would be nothing he could do. It would be the best way to shame him before the world, which would probably destroy him emotionally. That thought is very satisfying." That is when my anxiety shot up because it seemed like revenge was such a potent motivator for him.

Larry: Yes, it seems strong. He certainly must have had a great deal of vengeful anger at his father. But I'm not sure exactly how father fits in, except that he feels weak, feminine, passive, and helpless in relation to fa-

ther, authority figures, doctors, and men in general—Miss Maria getting screwed over by all those bunnies.

Glenda: The next week I got him to the county. His next letter says, "I don't like it. I am going to take the medication, as you said, but I am angry about it."

Charlene: As we look back at this, the question is, was he getting stronger? As the memories of his father and vengeful feelings towards his father were coming up, was he getting stronger in his rage against his father so he could actually do what he always wanted to do—to humiliate him in front of the world and emotionally destroy him—because he felt he was in a stalemate with life?

Larry: You're suggesting that the only way he felt he could get even with his father was to get revenge by humiliating him in this way. And that he was experiencing Glenda's abandoning him as a replication of the abuse he suffered from his father. [Then to Glenda] Would suicide be a way of getting revenge for your leaving? And a way of proving his strength to you, of humiliating you for not being able to receive his true self?

Glenda: Possibly. He felt like he was a coward. I said it was courageous to live. He said, "I don't believe that."

Larry: No, because for him . . .

Glenda: It was cowardice to live because life was just a stalemate, nothing would ever change. No one could ever be trusted with his true feelings. We went to the memorial service. His parents didn't come.

Larry: They didn't come?

Glenda: No.

Charlene: No.

Glenda: Only three siblings.

Charlene: There looked like several other relatives.

Glenda: They kept saying, "If our parents could have been here they would have thanked you." Our feeling was that they didn't come out of shame. It was a shock. He did it with a gun to his head.

Larry: In his mouth, I would suppose. Where was he?

Charlene: He was at home, the day after Christmas.

Glenda: He had written some letters to Charlene that the family found, which is why they called her. But they don't want to give her the letters.

Larry: You might try again to get copies of them.

Charlene: They don't even want to show us the letters.

Glenda: Charlene said she wanted to understand more about what had happened, that she had been working with him. What we want to know that might be in the letters is, at that end point, was this a continuation of the feeling of hopelessness and despair? In the last letters we know about to me he says, "I don't feel normal yet, I don't feel a part of your world yet." Was it that deep despair that motivated him or was it more out of strength and determination, I am going to do what I've always wanted to do, to get revenge? Do you know what I mean?

Larry: I'm hearing you. I don't know whether you will ever find out the answer. I know when something like this happens we feel helpless and somewhat guilty as though we might have prevented it if we had just under-stood it better, or done something differently. To me it makes almost too much sense for us to merely think that he'd been despairing all these years and finally just threw in the towel. Anthony didn't just quietly take some pills and drift away. It was a violent destructive intrusion into his head. It would be consoling to think that he has been a pained, passive person all these years and that as a result of telling someone his molest memories or fantasies, he mobilized his rage at his father, gained inner strength, and then sought to humiliate him, to become active rather than passive, and to get revenge by killing himself. But this isn't the way psychotic delusions usually operate. When the molest is "remembered" and told in a "validating" setting, the violence usually gets aimed directly at Dad, not at the self. He could have made public accusations or begun a lawsuit like so many people today who believe they are recovering true abuse memories in therapy. I fear that the shot in the head delivered by a secret weapon is an expression of a psychotic delusion that we simply cannot totally fathom. If I had to speculate, I might think that it was Charlene's solid intent to connect and stay with him that once again terrified him that his psychotic, infantile abuse was going to have to be relived. In desperation, he whips out "abuse memories," which Charlene invites, and the Carol limericks to prevent the possibility of Charlene holding onto him. Then he was stuck with the intense longing for Glenda and Susan and a great fear of connecting to Charlene. From this past sequence with Glenda we know that it is better for self and other to be killed than to connect. I think he was hopelessly stuck and delusionally did the only thing he could think of—end the self.

In studying organizing experience we always encounter enigmatic expressions and we perennially try to make sense of them. We call them symbols or representations of something, completely forgetting that organizing or psychotic experience is presymbolic, prerepresentational. Organizing expressions cannot be symbolically decoded. Rather, as we study the main and really the only relational motive in the organizing resistance and transference, it is to prevent or to rupture any possibility of interpersonal exchanges that might threaten, given every mammal's incessant search for contact with other warm bodies. If we had been given the chance to unravel this with Anthony my speculation is that the knife and gunshot—the secret escape hatch—express somehow a psychic death that happened somehow in infancy through an oral sadistic intrusive trauma that he lived out, replicated.

From the limited information I have, it appears that the ideal longing is for a shiny new car/self to be connecting with a nurturing/Christmas dinner/other. But for fear of having to relive some violent, traumatic, and infantile penetration (in the head) that comes with interpersonal connection, Anthony either becomes false in the relationship or fends it off by repulsing the other with oral sadomasochism

and the threat of suicide. Revenge doesn't really seem mobilized emotionally in Anthony at the point where he ends the threat of self and other connection. The revenge talk seems to come from mimical self formation. The motive is to fend off the other by doing or saying something he thinks may make sense to the other—"My father molested me and now I want revenge." I don't believe a word of it because this kind of thinking doesn't stem from his central delusional terror of relating. There is a national epidemic now of people saying, "My father abused me and I want revenge." I think he is mimicking. This suicide arises from a lifelong delusion of believing that by perverse regressions he could fend off traumatic intrusions and end the sense of self and other—to obtain relief from threatened relatedness.

This sketch would take a lot of time to fill in through psychoanalytic resistance and transference study. Thinking this way, the gunshot is an expression of some element in a delusional sequence—that it actually happened is a tragic accident, a trigger pulled when the distinction between the objective fact of death and a delusion of ending the self was not being effectively made. It's why I say we can't "trust" the organizing experience—it is, after all, dreamlike, the product of condensation and displacement. The delusion is always unpredictable and always surprising in how it is represented.

My formulation, which must remain unvalidated through therapeutic study is that his contact with Glenda, and to a lesser extent with Susan and Charlene, stimulated the ideal Kafka-esque fantasy of mother love. But because of infantile trauma, actually enjoying that love had to be blocked by somehow repulsing the other. Glenda is visibly shaken by his perverse sex and suicide talk. Charlene's defense against this penetration is that she isn't going to be bothered or be sent away by either one. Everyone was expecting that he could cope but he felt that he was being asked to swallow a lot of confusion, of connections, of destructive intrusions into his idealized dream that his delusion prevents him from realizing. Why he flees by means of repulsing the other with sexualized talk, and why he further fends off connection with secret weapon self-destruction talk are questions that can only be answered by understanding his earliest developmental history. Extended transference and resistance study usually allows sufficient approximations to be able to define the organizing delusion and through its definition to allow the person's relatedness patterns to be transformed. But before we were allowed to get into a systematic study of transference and resistance the secret escape hatch was opened with a shot and Slippery got away.

Charlene: There was an October letter saying, "I am falling into a very deep depression." He was going into his annual holiday depression. "I often wish I was dead." Prior to the last session I had with him, there was an increase in this intrusive thinking, the mental activity that he had going on.

We had talked about it and he said that he couldn't make out what was going on. It was just a lot of voices, male, female, and so forth. He couldn't sleep at night. He would be awakened with them arguing and that was really bothering him. The psychiatrist had just increased his medication at the county. He did say, "I am having more thoughts about dying."

Suicidal ideation was not firm enough that either I or the psychiatrist could force hospitalization. Anthony had no medical insurance, but we did speak of the possibility of hospitalization at a county facility to help keep him comfortable and safe. He would have none of it.

Glenda: We had made the transition of the knife that he had given me, which was supposedly the secret escape hatch. We gave it to Charlene. Though I asked, there wasn't any mention of anything else, any other possible weapon or plan. And it was a gun he had that he did it with. We have no idea where the gun came from, though a newspaper article suggested it was his father's.

Charlene: He said in the last session that he had decided he was going to be open with me. He was going to tell me everything and take whatever punishments he had to take. So, I wondered what was the punishing part that got expressed? If the shot was the punishment.

Larry: How are you doing?

Charlene: How am I doing? It was real shocking to me. I just couldn't believe it. Of course, I went through feeling guilty. Did I have him revealing too much too soon? Should I have picked up on something sooner? But, there is that part of me too that realizes that this was his decision. He kept his last escape hatch so secret that no one could stop him.

Larry: Of course.

Charlene: I believe that somehow this is what he wanted to do.

Glenda: We've talked a lot together. What we came to is that he was in a lot of suffering. And he saw no end to it.

Charlene: He was intelligent enough to realize that he had a rough row to hoe. He was a very peculiar person. He was very intelligent and had a very sweet, gentle quality about him, but he wasn't accepted really by anyone, any place.

Glenda: That last letter to me says, "I am not a human yet." When he first came to me he felt like he was a germ. "Although I am not part of your world yet, I am closer than I used to be. I am not a somebody yet, but I am closer than I used to be. And I am not normal yet, but I am closer than I used to be. I hope someday my world, or at least part of it, will coincide with yours." That is so poignant. That isolation of "no matter how much I connect, I am different and I am left out here by myself under this crazy dome that separates me from everyone else, left with these crazy voices inside."

Larry: I am not human. According to the way you're thinking, possibly in his mind the most human thing he ever did was to take up that gun.

Glenda: Some act.

Larry: To make him human?

Glenda: Right.

Larry: To get revenge? To stand up

to his father? To refuse to be manipulated like a thing?

Glenda: My feeling was that he was finally somehow getting out of this unbearable stalemate with his family. I got out of my unbearable stalemate with him by announcing my ultimatum. With the gun he announced his.

Larry: Yes.

Glenda: I thought, "We are in a stalemate here and I am going to have to push it." He didn't like it, but we then were no longer in stalemate. It feels like that's what he did with his father. Somehow he got out of the stalemate. He could either have felt like he lost or won. We don't know.

Larry: But you feel he got out of the stalemate.

Glenda: He lost his life, but he did act decisively, humanly.

Larry: I see what you're saying. The last time he was in this stalemate it was you who took the action. But at this point in time you believe the stalemate wasn't with you in transference, it was rather with his real father who was continuing to put abusive pressure on him. We have no control over that. At least you [Glenda] had some measure of connection, some measure of control over the stalemate process because it was with you in the transference. This time it did not come up in the transference, so you [Charlene] did not have the same opportunity to respond, to give an ultimatum. All he said was the domes are going up again, I'm depressed, I'm not quite human. Your question is, "Did he feel in a realistic stalemate with his father and did he feel it could only be broken by the shot?"

Glenda: Yes. That's what I wondered.

Larry: How are you doing with it yourself, Glenda?

Glenda: I've been using all of this information. I processed so much of my losing him in supervision and case conferences. I talked to the county psychologist. She says, "If the patient has not changed his commitment to death, the therapist can only get in his way for awhile." Well, that somehow rang true. It seemed I was interrupting this path he was on to kill himself, trying to give him my hope. Trying to give him my human connection, but how much can you literally do it for someone else? You can be available, but how much can the client use? I felt somewhat helped by looking at it that way. The psychiatrist was appalled. That's the word he used. My feeling is that I got him as much help as I could. At the end I didn't feel out on a limb. I did all I could.

Now I walk along the beach and I say, "Oh Anthony, we worked so hard together and it wasn't enough. I wasn't able to give you the feeling that life was something you could cope with." That's more the feeling I have. A deep sadness that all the help that could be offered wasn't enough.

Charlene: Although he had connected at some level with me, he was only seeing me on a weekly basis for his hour session and writing in his journal. He wasn't calling me in between. We didn't establish that. That wasn't part of how we were working together. He called me once to help him with the county, but that was it. So the dependency, the dynamic connection with me, wasn't the same at all.

Glenda: What comes up for me about the whole process of treatment with him was that in my doing this type of work with him, of literally fostering connections, our process began getting much more fluid. But when I had to leave, all that was lost. Like he had tasted something good but couldn't count on being able to have it on an ongoing basis or ever again.

Larry: And he had become more articulate. He was finally able to state to you many things about himself.

Glenda: We come to supervision and we're wanting to use the new theories to help people like this. I'm angry to think that the current state of the art has real possibilities for these deeply disturbed people, but that the benefits of current psychoanalytic research cannot be provided to them given the resources our society is willing to allocate to these very damaged people.

Charlene: You're saying these people can be treated?

Larry: Absolutely I say they can be treated. But we have to have the necessary resource, which is considerable. If we don't see in advance the long-term resource available for transformational work, however, I say supportive psychotherapy is the way to go. It's more humane to provide limited support than to give people hope that because of available therapeutic and financial resource can't be fulfilled.

I've watched a number of therapists on a once or twice weekly basis augmented with phone calls manage to work well with many of these organizing or psychotic people. They work with them four, six, eight, or more years. But you see, no one can know at the beginning all of the psychotic dynamics. Who could have talked ahead of time about the revenge motive as a humanizing feature? Who could have known about the emergence of the memories or fantasies of molest by his father? Who could have imagined that in order to survive and break the stalemate he would feel it necessary to shoot himself? Who could have imagined in advance that at the level of infantile oral intrusive trauma he had developed a predefensive pattern of flight from the threat of relatedness through alienating or frightening the other with sadomasochistic perverse talk? Or that the infantile memory of psychic death provided relief from traumatic intrusion? Who would have thought Anthony would shoot himself to avoid the threat of relatedness? It's fine for us to sit here afterward and formulate dynamics, but there are so many active delusional factors involved that no one can know in advance how they might manifest themselves in the therapeutic process or be acted out in this way at this point in time. We could see dangers and a lot of high-risk pointers. But in every one of these organizing or psychotic cases there are continuous overt or background suicide threats and the ongoing dangers of a psychotic break and self-destructive acting out. There is very often abuse and molest. We have no way to say ahead of time how psychotic transference might constellate itself during the course of therapy or in

the transference psychosis so that a man would suddenly shoot himself. He was very slippery. He concealed the way out he had planned and surrendered the knife to cover his secret. Or perhaps the knife really was the plan and later, in desperation, he found his father's gun.

Another feature may be present that I've seen before in cases like this where somebody has suicided. There would occur an accidental fluke, a change of life circumstance that dovetails with the central delusion and becomes an important precipitant of the suicide. Here there are two factors I would call unpredictable flukes. One is his boss, who had been supporting him, being transferred. In denial he creates a reunion fantasy. "She didn't leave me. She's invited me to eat Christmas dinner at her home with her family. I'll go in my new car. I am now a human being." We can see a psychotic formation arise in relation to that unexpected change in circumstance. The second fluke was that you [Glenda] had to stop seeing him. Your life took an unpredictable turn and, like his delusion predicts, when he connects, he alienates the other and in the process both self and other undergo a psychic death. The very supports that might have sustained him through a series of stalemates and transference crises in such a way that they could be confronted one at a time failed him through fluke changes.

Glenda: Yes.

Larry: The treatment process that might have helped him work through his psychotic resistances and transference could not be completed.

Another possible dovetailing fluke is that his father began renewing abusive pressure and verbal abuse at this same time. And also possibly a fluke, we don't know when, where, or how the gun appeared. I recall one particular circumstance of a woman who was in treatment for many years and was doing extremely well. She had gone back to school for professional training and as part of state certification had gotten an apprentice position in a good firm. But by a fluke, a curious set of circumstances, the emotional situation of her psychotic childhood was actually and vividly replicated at her employment site by an abusive supervisor. After this woman killed herself, all of the other employees banded together to have the severely critical and abusive supervisor fired from the company after twenty years of tenure. The supervisor had been sadistic toward many people but had actually pushed this vulnerable woman over the brink. The fluke was that the way in which the supervisor was torturing her replicated the exact emotional dynamics from her infantile past. The woman was forced to apologize and apologize for things not her fault and was finally found dead in her bed holding a pillow her therapist had given her. This, after twelve years of excellent therapy. Can you imagine what that did to her therapist?

Charlene: Oh my!

Glenda: Wow!

Larry: The therapy had been going very well. But what nobody can control is the way reality can impinge on these people and cause them to suddenly disintegrate. Those of us who reviewed the case had the distinct sense that had this particular fluke not occurred, this woman had integrated amazing things and she would have become a very competent professional in her field. Her vulnerabilities were all but healed but this replication did her in.

Glenda: So external reality continues to unfold and you don't know what kind of impact it may have on a person's deep vulnerabilities?

Larry: Exactly. And that is true in some sense for all of us. But because one of the developmental deficits of these people is the occasional or frequent inability to tell the difference between internal and external reality, if something hits in just the wrong way before they are completely stabilized, disaster suddenly strikes and we can't control it. In reviewing your case, we can easily go back and say, "What if I had done this, and done that. What if?" But as you review it, I think I hear both of you saying you behaved in . . .

Glenda: We did what we could do.

Larry: You did what was possible to do for a man who had a great many deficits. It was unfortunate that the two people whom he was hoping to work through stalemates with could not stay with him any longer and he had to end his self.

I was interested to hear you say earlier that you felt perhaps he found the peace he had been longing for. I had a very moving experience early in my career. It was in a social and not a professional setting. After a sumptuous dinner sitting by a blazing winter fire, this particular man, an artist, chose to start talking to me, a young psychologist fresh out of school. He talked very movingly. He said, "You know I am schizophrenic." Well, I didn't know. It didn't occur to me because we had all been having a perfectly sensible dinner conversation about art and literature. He said, "I have gone crazy three times." And he proceeded to describe how absolutely horrible it was to lose control of his thoughts and have to be hospitalized, medicated, restrained, and given electroshock. He said, "I have made up my mind I am not going to go through that confusion and pain again. Each of those times was so unutterably agonizing, so absolutely awful. Now I know what craziness feels like and if it starts to happen again I am not going to start on the medication. I am going to kill myself. I have gone over it with all my friends and family. They all understand. Nobody likes it, but they all understand." I don't know if he ever became ill again or if he ever killed himself. But I knew the man meant it. We now so often hear of people wanting the right and the means to kill themselves if they have a terminal illness and don't want to suffer an undignified and painful death.

Anthony had a secret plan and an intention to use it someday. From the standpoint of treatment, the gunshot seems a tragic accident. But in another sense I hear you both saying that he may have meant it. He was prepared to use his secret escape hatch if he ever needed to. He wanted to feel human. He wanted to have a car and a family that loved him to be with for Christmas dinner. Some people live in pain so unbearable that we have no way to even imagine it.

Charlene: Right.

Larry: You two have been close enough to him to feel how unutterable such agony is.

Glenda: Right. I really have felt that. The worst was not feeling human and believing there was no hope.

Larry: I believe there are a great many people in this world who are needing psychotherapy for similar conditions and who can be treated. Simply because we have a few tragedies, because the dynamics click wrong, or because we have a fluke of reality that ends tragically, I am not prepared to back off from the treatment of organizing-level people. Each therapist has to evaluate what is the resource that will be required for each piece of treatment and can it realistically be mustered? I'm sorry to say that too often it cannot be. I've coached a number of therapists in working with organizing people in wonderfully successful transformative long-term intensive therapy. I have also encouraged therapists to refer the patient out—perhaps to a public or nonprofit clinic—because they don't want to or cannot do the work. Or for them to come to grips with the fact that supportive therapy and not long-term transformational therapy is in order. Without tremendous ongoing resource we simply can't treat these people. And of course, these days we're becoming alarmingly sensitized to the very great risk that as the transference psychosis falls successfully into place the person cannot at that moment test reality and the therapist delusionally becomes fused with the original perpetrator of infantile abuse. The result is that the therapist becomes falsely accused in ethics committees, before licensing boards, and in courts of law.

Glenda: It is risky, but I worked with every bit I had.

Larry: Absolutely.

Charlene: For myself, in retrospect, I feel like I wasn't prepared really to handle this great a challenge. He had come to our agency and seen many therapists. I really should have considered additional supervision so that I knew exactly what I was dealing with. I knew I was dealing with a high-risk person who had major psychiatric problems. I might have gotten more involved. I might have been more attentive.

Larry: So that's the part you can hold as your guilt. "Perhaps if I had done more . . ." But realistically, how much more can any of us do?

Charlene: I wasn't willing to give any more. I know for next time I won't take on clients that may need more than I'm prepared to give.

Larry: Or you take them on in a limited or supportive format. Almost every therapist in private or clinic practice sooner or later has someone like Anthony in his or her case load. Someone deeply disturbed with limited resources who is motivated to relate. The therapist hopefully finds some inner or outer resource, some financial, or some time resource to try to meet the need. We need to know more about the Anthonys of the world and what it takes to give them adequate treatment response. You can see he was accessible. Time, resource, and his peculiar dynamic unfortunately caught up with him.

I would like to see a case like this presented publicly, in terms of what his struggle was and what the outcome was, so that therapists can be warned, can be aware. This is a personal as well as a social tragedy for all of us. If you would like more time to think together I will be happy to review Anthony and your reactions further.

Charlene: Great, thanks.

Glenda: Thanks. We both agree that Anthony's tragedy should be made known so other therapists can benefit from our experience. [Session ends]

Anthony's tragedy is presented here for readers' consideration. Some may feel more could have been done to prevent his suicide. I learned long ago that supervisional hindsight, like Monday morning quarterbacking, fails to take into consideration just what being caught in the situation was really like. It's easy to call the shots better when viewing retrospectively. I wanted to present this tragedy for everyone to think about and for the opportunity to consider how the psychotic or organizing transference silently and dangerously operates. I hope we all have had a sobering learning experience from Anthony's tragedy. I especially appreciate Glenda's and Charlene's courage in sharing this experience.

IV

WORKING THE ORGANIZING EXPERIENCE

10

The Organizing Transference

MIMICRY AS A BASIS FOR THOUGHT

The organizing transference arises from experiences the neonate or intrauterine infant undergoes in trying to organize reliable channels to the environment that ensure the safety and continuity of physical and psychological life. When the child is reaching out or extending in some way to form a channel or path to the maternal body, either inside or outside the uterus, the interpersonal channeling or connection is facilitated when that extension is met (reinforced) in a timely and satisfying manner. Winnicott's (1949b) formulation is that the infant needs to maintain a sense of "going on being." Any impingement on that sense prematurely activates the psychic system and forces the child to begin thinking precociously.

During the age period of about four months before birth to four months after, the infant's neurological system alternates from rest to activity. The child actively arranges numerous sensorimotor experiences. The child may be looking, listening, or experimenting with movement, sounds, or touch. Under optimal circumstances the infant is not required to problem-solve in response to impingement, intrusion, or trauma. But when there is impingement into the sense of comfortably going on being, the child is forced to react, no matter what the nature of that impingement is. Such things as an Rh factor, the presence of some undesirable chemical, or a shortage of food or oxygen in the placental blood could each provide a considerable impingement for a fetus.

Psychological studies suggest many ways that the mother's psychic life and her relation to her environment before the child's birth may impinge on the child's comfort and sense of safety, thus activating alerting mechanisms and thought processes. Any intense or prolonged environmental stimulus or deficit could impinge on the psychic world of an infant. Winnicott holds that impingement forces the infant to begin thinking, to begin problem solving before that infant might otherwise have done so, before that infant may be fully ready. Under such circumstances, a child's basic thought patterns are responses to (persecutory) impingement. Winnicott had witnessed many childbirths and saw no reason to assume that birth, per se, need be traumatic. The baby has been in cramped quarters with limited possibilities for some time. The baby is ready to leave. There is an exit. The exit is large enough and the baby's musculature is adequate to traverse the birth canal. The process can occur and so the baby transitions from one sort of environmental circumstances to another. The baby is prepared for birth, already having experienced many tolerable frustrations with the intrauterine environment. Traveling down the birth canal may even be satisfying and positively stimulating in various ways. Midwives maintain that putting the infant immediately onto the mother's belly and letting the infant's own instinct to move to the breast occur, is also activating. In other mammals the licking of the baby's body seems to stimulate deep tissues and to enliven the newborn. So there may be many aspects of the birthing experience that are stimulating to the child, or soothing and comforting.

However, says Winnicott, unusually long or unusually intense birth experience may provide a trauma that can serve as a prototype in thinking about early impingements. If baby's first thought (*in utero* or postnatal) occurs in response to an actual traumatic intrusion, then the first thought mode upon which all later thought modes are based is persecutory. Winnicott addresses the Kleinians who speak of observing persecutory anxieties in clinical situations. He believes that these anxieties exist because persecution (impingement) *has already occurred*. There is a fear that persecution will happen again. The child experienced primordial impingement or persecutory intrusion with the result that the basic pattern of the child's mind became interrupted and organized around anticipating or guarding against intrusion. The child scans the environment for more persecution because that is the foundational experience. Such a child was deprived of a secure "going on being" experience until the perception and motor equipment naturally evolved to tolerate gradually increasing frustrations, delays, and other maternal shortcomings. In an optimal situation by the third, fourth, and fifth months, a mother and a baby are interacting in many ways. But a baby who has experienced traumatic intrusions perennially maintains a guard against further intrusion and in doing so has already lost much of its potential flexibility.

Even in optimal situations, Alice Balint (1943) still holds that the infant's first thought processes arise in relation to trauma, even if minor. The subtext of her paper is that primates have an innate capacity to mimic. Human babies mimic their mothers in order to gain understanding and mastery over what is happening to them. Before cause-and-effect thinking can occur, thought originates based upon primary identification at a gross body level (mimicry). An infant sees the mother smile and the baby smiles back. Mothers imitate the baby and the baby reciprocally imitates the mother in an endless circle leading to the mutual cuing process of the later symbiotic period of development.

Hedges (1983b) speaks of the "mimical self" as an expectable aspect of psychic and somatic experience at the organizing level. People who retain organizing modes of interacting as a significant feature of their personalities live with mimicry as an important way of being in the world. One client spoke of having a series of cassette tapes, one to tell her what to say and do in each situation of her life. To the extent that any part of the personality retains early modes of organizational striving, mimicry of human life and activity—in contrast to resonating emotional interactions—may predominate.

Anna Freud (1951, 1952, 1958) and Winnicott (1952) emphasize the role of maternal care in augmenting the protective shield during the period of early infantile dependency. Khan (1963) has introduced the concept of *cumulative trauma* to take into consideration early psychophysical events that happen between the infant and its mothering partners. The concept of cumulative trauma correlates the effects of early infant caregiving with disturbing personality features that only appear much later in life. Cumulative trauma is the result of the effects of numerous kinds of small breaches in the early stimulus barrier or protective shield that are not experienced as traumatic at the time but create a certain strain that over time, produces an effect on the personality that can only be appreciated retrospectively when it is experienced as traumatic.

Research on infantile trauma and memory (Greenacre 1958, 1960, Kris 1951, 1956a,b, Milner 1952, and others) demonstrates the specific effects on somatic and psychic structure of cumulative strain trauma. Khan (1974) holds that " 'the strain trauma' and the screen memories or precocious early memories that the patients recount are derivatives of the partial breakdown of the protective shield function of the mother and an attempt to symbolize its effects (cf. Anna Freud, 1958)" (p. 52). Khan further comments:

> Cumulative trauma has its beginnings in the period of development when the infant needs and uses the mother as his protective shield. The inevitable temporary failures of the mother as protective shield are corrected and recovered from the evolving complexity and rhythm of the maturational processes. Where these failures of the mother in her role as protective shield are significantly frequent and lead to impingement on the infant's psyche-soma, impingements which he has no means of eliminating, they set up a nucleus of pathogenic reaction. *These in turn start a process of interplay with the mother which is distinct from her adaptation to the infant's needs.* [1974, p. 53, emphasis added]

According to Khan, the faulty interplay between infant and caregivers that arises in consequence of strain reactions may lead to (1) premature and selective ego distortion and development, (2) special responsiveness to certain features of the mother's personality such as her moods, (3) dissociation of archaic dependency from precocious and fiercely acted-out independency, (4) an attitude of excessive concern for the mother and excessive craving for concern from the mother (co-dependency), (5) a precocious adaptation to internal and external realities, and (6) specific body-ego organizations that heavily influence later personality organization.

Khan points out that the developing child can and does recover from breaches in the protective shield and can make creative use of them so as to arrive at a fairly healthy and effective normal functioning personality. But the person with vulnerabilities left over from infantile cumulative strain trauma "nevertheless can in later life break down as a result of acute stress and crisis" (p. 56). When there is a later breakdown and earlier cumulative strain trauma can be inferred, Khan is clear that the earlier disturbances of maternal care were neither gross nor acute at the time they occurred. He cites infant research in which careful and detailed notes, recorded by well-trained researchers, failed to observe traumas that only retrospectively could be seen as producing this type of cumulative strain trauma. Anna Freud (1958) has similarly described instances in which, "subtle harm is being inflicted on this child, and . . . the consequences of it will become manifest at some future date." (p. 122)

Psychological theory and infant research (Stern 1985) are rapidly adding ideas to help us think about what the experience of the infant may be like during the organizing period. These concepts help us grasp the kinds of early mental structuring that can be listened for in the analytic situation: (1) basic primate mimicry and primary identification, which give rise to the "mimical self" (Hedges 1983); (2) later adaptation to the maternal environment giving rise to the "false self" (Winnicott 1960), seen most clearly in the later symbiotic bonding period; and (3) stimulation experienced by the infant as intrusive strain trauma (Khan 1963), causing an adverse reaction of the infant that sets off an adaptation in caregivers resulting in what can be thought of as "an internalized vicious circle of mutual misadaptations."

In listening to a person living a pervasive organizing experience or to a person living out a pocket of organizing experience, how might we begin to identify aspects of their experience that might be considered transference from the organizing period?

CONSIDERING WHY SYMBIOTIC BONDING DOES NOT OCCUR

One way to begin is to consider that babies come into this world ready to attach themselves to a (m)other. Bowlby's (1969) work on attachment has shown that human babies naturally seek attachments that make the human emotional exchange possible. If the child does not move toward bonding, if the child fails to bond in an overall way, or if parts of the personality are left out of the bonding dance, there must be a significant reason why this otherwise natural, expectable process did not occur. It is helpful to picture an infant extending through vocalization, perception, or movement—striving for a connection, seeking warmth, stimulation, nurturance, or a sense of comfort and safety. If the mothering person, for whatever reason, is not able to meet these extensions in a timely manner or does not know how to, or is unwilling to, or meets extensions with negative response, the extensions withdraw and/or atrophy. The baby simply does not reach in that way any more because there is no gain, no percentage, or perhaps even pain associated with that kind of extension.

In Freud's (1895a) earliest paper considering issues of primary repression at a quasi-neurological level, he suggests that an attempted pathway that goes unrewarded by pleasurable experience or that meets with painful experience is intentionally blocked against future extension. Bioenergetic analysts (Lowen 1975) think in terms of various systems of involuntary muscular constrictions that become chronically fixated, creating body rigidities and blocks in the flow of natural energies so that future extensions are blocked because they are experienced as painful.

The reason all people, in various ways, can be said to retain psychic and somatic modes of organizing experience is that there is no such thing as perfect mothering. Current infant research suggests that mother and baby may only satisfactorily connect 30 percent of the time (Tronick and Cohn 1988). In these earliest months every baby has reached out needing, wanting, and questing in various ways. Her quest may not have been met because no environment can possibly meet all of these quests with perfect timing and empathic attunement. So various experiences occur that teach every baby to avoid or to withdraw from certain forms of contact where appropriate environment response is absent, missing, or negative.

It is helpful to picture a rooting baby who gets so far as to have her mouth almost around the nipple when "something happens" (internally) so that rhythmical sucking never starts. The receipt of nourishment, comfort, and safety from contact with mother is foreclosed. The mouth stiffens and the baby loses the nipple, or perhaps pushes it out or turns away, arching her back and screaming. This image comes to mind when we hear of a person approaching a therapist searching for human connection. The person extends, reaches out, yearning for human contact. Then "something happens." They're suddenly just not there. Their questing personal presence in the room has somehow vanished, though their mimical conversation and activity may continue.

Many, if not most, practicing therapists, presumably due to their own history of bonding experiences, fail to notice for long periods of time that the client has figuratively left the room, vanished from the interaction. Mimicry prevails, so the person "passes" as interacting, when he or she is not at all involved emotionally. It becomes helpful to distinguish behavior that serves as grasping, clinging, or *attaching* from patterns or modes of interpersonal interacting that constitute reciprocal emotional *engagement*.

Franz Kafka's literary work portrays organizing themes throughout. He himself must have lived significant organizing experiences to be so exquisitely sensitive to them. In *The Castle* (1926) the hero searches endlessly for a way to reach that nipple up on the hill, the castle. He doesn't even have an identity beyond the initial "K." He believes that he has been sent for and that he is needed as a surveyor, one who defines boundaries. But the castle is elusive, endlessly denying him human recognition. K. extends himself in one way after another attempting to reach the castle, to prove that "I was sent for, I am wanted, and I have a job here which involves living in the castle village and drawing boundaries."

Kafka could not bring himself to finish the book, perhaps because this story was about his own life traumas. But in soirees he read it to friends and told them how the book was to end. All his life K. searches for a connection to the castle without finding it, always frustrated, always almost making it, just about having the castle within grasp. But each time suddenly and inexplicably "something happens."

The phrase "something happens" is of great importance because when people living organizing experiences extend themselves for contact it often lacks an explicit sense of agency, of "you" or "me." The experience is more one of, "I'm reaching, wanting, grasping, almost connecting, or attaining and then something dissolves, something happens." The subjective experience is more one of an impersonal force operating to attract and then, when the possibility of connection is felt or is within grasp, the attraction dissolves, vanishes almost imperceptibly. One client talked about a wind coming up and all is lost.

In Kafka's proposed ending to *The Castle*, K., on his deathbed, has all of his friends gather around him. He still has never been able to directly contact the castle. Suddenly an unexpected messenger arrives from the castle with a cryptic note. The note, in effect, says, "You may stay and work in the village, but not because you were sent for, and not through any merit of your own, but for extraneous reasons." This is the essence of the organizing or psychotic experience: not feeling quite human, not having an identity, not feeling received by the human world. People living organizing experiences often say, "I'm weird. I'm different. I'm not quite human. I'm like a robot. I don't belong. I live in a glass bubble. I exist behind a glass wall that separates me forever from others." They somehow know that the experience they are living has never entered into an interpersonal bonding dance that lets people experience themselves as fully human. People living organizing pockets know that this part of their personality is strange, crazy, psychotic, or weird, and that it cannot find human resonance.

In Kafka's *The Trial* (1937) he poses the question, "What is my guilt?" In the end the protagonist bares his chest to the knife. His guilt is for being alive, for wanting more than his mother had to give him.

IDENTIFYING ORGANIZING TRANSFERENCE

Identifying transference experience from this level of development begins with the assumption that if psychological attachment, the bonding dance, has not occurred or has only partially occurred, there is a reason. And whatever the reason, it occurred historically in the earliest months of life. Evidence of closed-off psychic channels for human connection and somatic constrictions that make extensions painful are retained in the personality and in the body structure in ways that can be observed in later life as the organizing or psychotic transference. This earliest of transferences represents learning experiences of the infant that occurred whenever he or she emotionally extended or reached out and was somehow turned away, not met, or negatively greeted. The questing activity was met with environment response that taught the infant not to strive in that way again. The "never go there again" experience effectively marks organizing experiences that later can be identified as transference.

11

Working Through
the Organizing Transference

THE CONCEPT OF TRANSFERENCE PSYCHOSIS

The specter of madness has haunted humankind for centuries. But the systematic study of insanity arose only in the nineteenth century, coinciding with the industrial revolution and rise of urbanization. Whether the increased awareness of insanity arose because more craziness was being produced by the changing conditions of human life, or whether the increased social demand for more coordinated cooperation in working and living situations brought insanity more into public view, is a question that remains unanswered. Relabeling the problem *mental illness* has been credited with leading to more humane treatment for people suffering with various pronounced forms of mental disturbance. But now after more than a century of intense scientific and clinical study of various symptom clusters or syndromes, a radical paradigm shift is emerging in the way that psychological organization is conceptualized (Hedges 1992).

The word that best describes the new conceptual approach is *relatedness*. Jacobson (1954, 1964) described her psychoanalytic work with more deeply disturbed individuals as a study in the way people represent themselves in relation to others. Numerous self and other representation studies followed until it became evident that human mental life itself could be considered as systematically organized in layerings of representations of the way people experience and represent themselves in relation to the various ways that they represent others through different phases of human development. According to this metaphor each layering arises out of or is built upon the ways that previous experiences of self and other representation have been laid down in psychic memory.

Memory itself has come to be considered a function of the way a person's experiences of self and others have come to operate. According to this view the most important features in the human environment are other humans with whom the developing child has significant intimate daily contact. Mental structure itself is thought to arise from and to be dependent upon early relatedness experiences. Mental efficiency, cognitive and affective styles, memory organization, social skills, intelligence, and creativity itself are the product of early relatedness experience and bear the indelible mark of those whom we were first attached to and first learned to love and hate. Relatedness intelligence is thought to develop in early childhood and to provide the foundation for many possibilities and restrictions in our capacities for satisfying and fulfilling lives.

The relatedness thought paradigm conceives of early relatedness experiences as having established psychic representations that serve as memories associated with physical constrictions and psychological restrictions that limit, distort, and under-mine our capacities for joyful, loving, and creative living. Our understanding of madness thus has a new face. Human madness is universal and it relates to unfortunate experiences we each had as infants and toddlers that have left us with a series of greater or lesser limiting relatedness assumptions that have systematically exercised a devious and destructive influence upon all subsequent layerings or levels of our psychological organization.

While poets and philosophers have long been fond of pointing to universal forms of insanity, the first psychological writer to suggest that a *forme fruste* (morsel) of intense delusional belief can be seen in almost every case of psychoanalysis was Hammett (1961). The term *transference psychosis* was suggested by Gitelson to Reider (1957), who uses the term more descriptively and etiologically because it is less dynamically precise than its Freudian analogue *transference neurosis*. Rosénfeld (1954) describes how psychotic manifestations are linked to the psychoanalytic transference so that the patient includes the analyst in the delusion. Little (1958, 1960) uses the term *delusional transference* saying, "In practice one finds certain patients who cannot use transference interpretations; the difference between these and other patients is qualitative not quantitative" (1958, p. 81). By 1981 she collects her papers on the subject in a book entitled *Transference Neurosis and Transference Psychosis: Toward a Basic Unity*. Transference psychosis then becomes a develop-mentally earlier transference manifestation that contrasts sharply with transference neurosis.

Wallerstein (1967) summarizes the Freudian concept of transference neurosis as follows:

> On both clinical and theoretical grounds the transference neurosis has long been established as the central technical and conceptual vehicle of psychoanalysis as a therapy. The usual course of psychoanalysis and of the development of this regressive

transference reaction is characterized by the familiar reactivation within the analysis of earlier (i.e., infantile) experiences and also of earlier (i.e., infantile) modes of reacting to and mastering those experiences. At times this reactivation within the analytic transference can (temporarily anyway) sufficiently lose its "as if" quality to become near delusional. Classical analysis is, however, usually protected against such extensive reality disorientation by the split, described by Sterba (1934) into an observing (introspecting) ego alongside the experiencing ego. It is this observing part of the ego which in its guardian function enables one constantly to maintain distance from, and exert reality mastery over, the transference illusion. [p. 551]

Little (1958) points out that in the delusional transference or transference psychosis the saving "as if" quality is gone. At the moment of experiencing, the analyst *is*, with a strong sense of authenticity, the idealized and deified as well as the diabolized parent. Ferenczi (1912, 1919) first describes how actual hallucinations can be evoked in and by the analytic hour and shows how some patients are overwhelmed by impulses and act out their psychic content in the analytic hour. Wallerstein (1967) presents two analytic cases in which, in the unfolding of the transference, the expectable split in the ego did not occur and the ego was "overwhelmed by the intensity of the liberated affects" (p. 577). Reider (1957) points out that psychotic episodes in psychoanalysis occur under two circumstances: either a previous psychotic state is reenacted, or an identification with a psychotic person is reenacted. Wallerstein's cases illustrate both kinds of circumstances. He calls for "setting forth more explicitly the range of specific circumstances under which these ego vulnerabilities occur and the intrapsychic functions they serve" (p. 583).

Since that time various writers have addressed these issues in terms of the traditional concerns of psychoanalysis, but only now are we in a position to let our attention turn to the issues as they emerge within the new relatedness paradigm, within the context of the earliest self and other representations. Hedges and Hulgus (1991) have put forth a series of dimensions along which the ego's earliest experiences can be listened to in psychotherapy. But the central therapeutic approach, as with the establishment of the transference neurosis, relates to that moment when the delusional transference or the transference psychosis is activated within the analytic relationship. There is much to be said about the nature of this organizing level transference structure and how it can be framed for analysis. Here the focus will be on the working-through phase and how the therapist may position him-or herself to empathically interpret psychic extensions of the client. How empathy can be expressed regarding the wall or block to interpersonal experiencing is the central technical problem and requires precise thinking and precise timing.

EGO VULNERABILITIES AND HUMAN TOUCH

Hedges (1992), in an extended discussion of psychoanalytic empathy, raises the central questions of, "Empathy with what, and what forms will it take?" Kohut's last

talk at Berkeley (1981) is cited wherein he calls for the elaboration of a developmental line of empathy that extends from complex verbal-symbolic activity with
advanced issues of the Oedipus complex downward developmentally toward
increasingly concrete forms of postural, facial, and gestural empathy. In a symposium, *Touch: The Foundation of Experience*, Brazelton and Barnard (1990) trace
the philosophical, epistemological, interpersonal, and curative aspects of touch
throughout the ages, concluding that human experience originates in empathic
forms of actual physical touch.

As depicted by Michelangelo on the ceiling of the Sistine Chapel, touch is
critically involved in conveying the divine spirit of the Logos to the human soul.
Symposium participants agreed that the critical feature of human touch that
conveys the human spirit from one person to another is the motivation of the one
touching. Hedges and Hulgus (1991) discuss at length a specialized form of
interpretive touch which is appropriate—and at times necessary—for extending
human empathy to the earliest organizing levels of self and other representation, to
reach the earliest ego vulnerabilities. They take the position that the earliest task of
the infant is to organize channels of contact to the maternal body and later to the
maternal mind.

People pervasively living organizing-level experiences in later life or people
attempting to revive for analysis a pocket of organizing-level ego vulnerability have
experienced an arrest in psychic development during a time in their lives when
physical contact with the maternal body was the only way that the infant mind
could be effectively contacted. As a result, the organizing or psychotic block is a
somatic one—an internalized fear of emotionally reaching out and touching others
or allowing touch by others in ways that were experienced in earliest infancy as
traumatic. At certain well-defined critical junctures with such people, the analytic
regression takes them to a level where any attempt at distinguishing the psyche
from soma fails—where psyche and soma are truly the same experience.

Successfully framing for analysis the organizing-level somatopsychic internalization entails meeting the person at the level of the arrest—which means at the level
of physical contact. Such interpretive touching is not for the purposes of making
either the person in analysis or the analyst feel soothed, comforted, or safe per se.
Rather, the invitation to make interpersonal contact on a physical level—when
offered at the exact moment that the internalized rupture in contact is activated—
serves as a physically concrete, empathically timed, interpretive response on the
analyst's part. The offer of physical connection in effect says, "I understand that in
your primordial past when emotional contact with others was a present possibility
you somehow experienced what was offered as traumatic. We are here to study
what went wrong during that period so that you have been cut off from various
kinds of human interaction and personal fulfillment. Throughout your life whenever the possibility of intimate interpersonal contact has been offered it has been
necessary for you to move into a 'fight, flee, or freeze' pattern (Fraiberg 1982)
because your learning experiences had taught you that human contact is fright-

ening and dangerous. I am here with you now. You experience our being together and feeling close as a primordial threat that you must avoid at all cost. This is not true. We have been together for a long time. Certain kinds of trust and continuity have developed between us. We can stay together and enjoy human closeness. You do not have to fight me. You do not have to flee contact. You do not have to freeze in fear. We can make contact with each other that is wholesome and fulfilling for both of us. Can you hold my hand now? Can you work to overcome your overwhelming urge to split away? Can you stay with me a few minutes so that we can both know that we are human, that we care for one another, that feeling close is a good feeling, that contact with each other can be safe?" For many people this will be the first time since infancy that an invitation to be together has been offered in such a way that it can be accepted—albeit not without fear and trembling and not without a difficult follow-up working-through process.

What follows is a vignette that gives a picture of what working through the organizing transference can look like. Needless to say, the forms of infantile trauma are infinite, so that the working through always looks different as the person's own history has to be revived in transference and resistance memory.

BEYOND THE UNTHOUGHT KNOWN

At the organizing level the discoveries are not unthought known, they are puzzling, traumatic, and unknown. That is, the internalized compulsion to break contact, in whatever form that rupture takes, forecloses knowledge of how one withdraws because it is predefensive in Fraiberg's (1982) sense of fight, flight, or freeze, and exists at the somatic level of neurological conditioning rather than the psychic level. The known is at best that the connecting other is somehow dangerous and that connections are to be avoided—much as any prey "knows" danger situations that are to be avoided, though it may not have explicit knowledge of what it feels like to be in the hawk's talons or to fight for its life. The subject can only struggle to somehow control the danger emanating from intersubjective contact with the other—through imitation and various manipulations involving moods, guilt, and demand, because the impetus is basically a defense or a fending off of threatening stimuli associated with survival.

Whatever desperate maneuvers the person uses or however he or she experiences the other impinging, the function of the activity is self protective. The neurons function on a quasi-instinctual avoidance of threat basis, thereby making it impossible to observe and to analyze whatever personal reactive potentials might emerge in the absence of defense. The activity presented to us does not tell us the withdrawal story, only the predefense used to fend off reexperiencing the original sequence of primary neuronal activity involved in the first terrified flight from (dependency) circumstances that are judged or misjudged as similar to the potential interpersonal connection of the present. The activity that can be observed is inevitably an outward directed response to what the other is doing or not doing rather than to potential internal dangers or potential overstimulation. That is, the predefensive activity is directed toward the persecutory object's activities, real and/or projected.

Freud (1920) set the stage for understanding this externalization process when he envisioned an organism with outward-turned sensory receptors developing an energized protective shield. The defense activity against external impinging stimuli is effective enough so that soon the organism begins to project the cause of impinging internal stimuli onto the outside in an attempt to control them with the protective shield as well.

The persecutory pattern and the modes of breaking contact are not where we find the action to be understood, to be analyzed. Their function is predefensive avoidance. The technical problem is how to stop the predefensive action and let the terrifying organizing transference sequence unfold. The original impingement, according to Winnicott (1949b), is into the continuity of being, into the infantile sense of "going on being," into the sense of being alive and safe. Because the early impingement intrudes into life's continuity, the infant is obliged on the basis of a survival instinct to react. And the pattern of this primordial reaction constitutes the first thought pattern. Since it is in response to impingement, this primary governing template that influences all subsequent thought is necessarily experienced as persecutory in nature. The persecutory template then exists as a fundamental foreclosure mechanism that operates with many faults until later in life when it can be analyzed. One fault is that one is always on the lookout for certain classes of impingements, projecting them onto situations that may have similar cues to the original one but are not the same. Another thought fault occurs when the person is monitoring the environment for certain classes of cues that spell danger and tends to miss whole other classes of danger situations, thus setting up a vicious circle of maladaptation and leaving one a sitting duck for real exploitation coming when one is not tuned into danger situations that common sense would otherwise warn one about. A third problem is the wholesale importation of some form of fear response (learned in connection with infantile sensorimotor capabilities and under conditions of total dependency) into situations of later life that might be characterized by more diverse and reliable sensorimotor modes and the capacity for psychic independence.

Behavioral conditioning studies have manipulated in endless research experiments an array of proximal and distal cues to positive and negative reinforcement situations, showing without a doubt that mammals are readily conditioned to all types of peripheral cues. The classic example is Pavlov's dog, but instrumental conditioning studies have demonstrated a series of kinds of learning and extinction curves involving incredibly complex sequences and combinations of cues to which subjects "neurotically" and "psychotically" become conditioned. Harlow's cloth monkeys and rubber spiders are the best known. But Pavlov's dogs and Harlow's monkeys are only the simplest kinds of experiments from a massive body of elegant conditioning research. They stand out in the public imagination because their lessons are clear and graphically portrayed. One trial conditioning is commonly observed when strong aversive stimulation is provided – and this singular fact is of great interest to the present discussion.

In understanding conditioned fear of interpersonal contact, we have yet to appreciate and specify the wide variety of dimensions involved. Bion (1962, 1963, 1977) and Grotstein (1981) speak of predator–prey anxiety, and the critical dimension of binocular vision. Lacan (1977) speaks of human evolution according to complex ocular environmental cues. Tomatis (1991), the French audiologist, envisions human evolution as an ear that has grown a body – highlighting the importance of the auditory. Suskind's (1986) imaginative novel *Perfume*, as well as infant research into smell suggests the power of olfactory stimulation in organizing early mind. All these basic conditioning examples point to the critical and central place of infantile sensory perception in conditioning the organizing level transference structure. Kafka's work (1926, 1937, 1979) abounds in sensory imagery.

Fraiberg's predefenses point to the biological means of managing impinging stimuli that become experienced as threatening. These modes likewise become incorporated into the early transference structure. We have reason to believe that considerable conditioning occurs before birth and we are able to observe it directly in the hours, days, and months after birth. Stern (1985) cites infant research to demonstrate that in the earliest months perception and response is not even mode specific. For example, a sharp auditory stimulus may cause the baby to close its eyes in an attempt to flee the sound. Infant research demonstrates that sensory input of all types is responded to globally and amodally at first. The distinctions in the sensorimotor modalities we commonly think of only slowly evolve out of a much more general and interrelated stimulus–response system operating at birth. Such fusions and global sensorimotor responsiveness also appear when the organizing transference structure is being experienced.

This is all to say that what cues are being conditioned to what traumatic impingements in infancy is a complex matter and is anybody's guess what is happening at the time of early experience. Khan's (1963) concept of "cumulative trauma" makes clear that even the best-trained infant observers do not know how to interpret cumulative strain trauma at the time it is occurring because such stimulus–response sequences operate invisibly and silently in infancy. Only *retrospectively* when childhood disturbances or adult breakdown under stress occur can it be inferred that damage was being done to the child that could not be seen at the time (A. Freud 1958).

What was learned, what was conditioned in infancy was a predefensive reaction, a behavioral means of blocking out classes of environmental cues that were present proximally and distally in the original infantile trauma situation. Faulty responses to cues may have been further mislearned because of fused, global, or amodal perception and motor response operating in early infancy. What lies beyond the defense is a set of sequences of terrifying responses that Winnicott has sketched out

in broadest terms in his "Fear of Breakdown" paper (1974). Green's (1986) formulations regarding the dead mother must be governed by similar considerations.
Because the impingements of commission or omission are persecutory in their effect
in infancy, the only way to manage the stimuli is to withdraw and to defend in
whatever way the organism can manage. "I have learned to be in relationships by
learning mechanisms of disconnection from the other in order to feel safe and to
comfort myself." To understand the contemporary relational attempts of the adult
subject or the relational activities of the interacting other do not tell the story. The
intersubjective field is foreclosed by predefense. Knowledge of the prerelational
past is required but in its details forever unknowable in principle. Its effects can,
however, be charted and defined in a systematic exploration of the transference
psychosis.

FRAMING THE ORGANIZING TRANSFERENCE

In framing the transference psychosis for analytic study, there is much room for a
Kleinian understanding of splitting and projective identification (1937, 1952, 1957)
as well as Tustin's (1972) formulation of confusional or entangled autism, which
resembles Mahler's (1968) symbiotic psychosis. But such considerations are developmentally later than the organizing transference that blocks the infant's movement toward projection and projective identification. That is, the infant reaches
out. To the extent the extension is received and experienced as pleasurable the
reaching in this manner is reinforced and a channel is found to the maternal body
and mind. Conversely, if the reaching is not actively rewarded, is ignored, or is
actively punished in some way, a block to ever reaching in that way again is
conditioned.

Between these two extremes there is a world of sometimes finding, sometimes
not finding—along with whatever result is conditioned to whatever proximal and
distal cues may be present in the moment. That is, Tustin's confusional or
entangled autistic child did connect enough with the externally perceived mother
to have its psychic mechanisms confused with hers through early splitting and
projective mechanisms, whereas her encapsulated autistic self was once connected
at the physical level, at the sensuous level, but the sensual connection was ruptured
prematurely and traumatically so that the child could only build a wall that served
to block out incoming stimuli that might have built a sensuous bridge to the
mother's psyche. One might further consider other oral-level compulsions involving food, addictive substances, and tactile (sexual) sensations. Here one might
imagine that there was once a reaching, and a certain finding. The overall fate of
the finding is recorded in the way the symptom operates on the one hand to find,
bring, and conserve needed and comforting aspects of the object, and on the other
hand to expel, repel, and destroy the aversive and unwanted aspects of the
connecting object.

In analytic listening framed in terms of confusional or entangled mechanisms, a part of the psyche was presumably once open to early interpersonal connecting and to the development of splitting and projective identification mechanisms. But another part of the psyche had an eye to biological safety and so maintained enough distance and disconnection to avoid anticipated dangers—even though there may have been a faulty or globally determined assessment of the central or peripheral cues in the persecutory situation. The action that is later displayed responds to these faultily interpreted cues and focuses on the external environment because there is no way the internal terror responses can be viewed. They may have occurred only once and then been foreclosed from reexperiencing by the blocking of the fear response. That is, the predefensive safety mechanisms function to keep things out of the psyche, to keep life at the somatic level, to prevent elaboration through reflection. This means not only that knowledge and experience in these areas cannot be elaborated through subsequent experience. It also means that allied experiences remain distorted because they are isolated. But most importantly it means that the foreclosed potential experience is not part of Bollas's (1987) "unthought known," to be recovered as memory, because it was never actually known—only fleetingly and instinctually apprehended in a gross and globally perceived manner and reacted to with helplessness, terror, withdrawal, and total blocking. Bollas refers to early preverbal, prerepresentational mother–infant experiences that make up the basic working knowledge of our personalities but have not become the subject of systematic thought until the psychoanalytic relationship brings the experiences into the realm of the experienced and thought.

The foreclosed area of the organizing-level experience remains essentially unknown but marked with dread. That is, the unthought known is comprised of living modes of interaction, affects, and moods that conserve early experience with others. The foreclosed area contains only dread and terror of vaguely experienced unknowns related to dependency connections—such as the fear of breakdown of functioning, the fear of an empty or persecutory environment, and the fear of starvation, abandonment, and death. When any cues similar to the proximal or distal cues present in the original learning situation present themselves in subsequent experience, an instinctive predefense of fight, flight, or freeze occurs, preventing contemporary assessment and response to what may be more objectively happening in the moment. The predefense is a struggle for survival and held onto tenaciously.

Primordial memories that conditioned the predefensive responses are from such an early developmental period they globally fuse and confuse (1) the sensorimotor modalities involved, (2) the nature and source of stimulus cues arising from inside and/or outside the body, (3) whether the attributed agency is self or other, and (4) whether the central sensorimotor focus possesses an attracting or an aversive quality as it is confounded with peripheral and nonrelevant cues. If we needed a working definition of psychosis this would certainly be it. Transference psychosis results when the analyst becomes a part of this confusional, delusional perceptual motor system — as is inevitable in the working-through process of intensive psycho-therapy and psychoanalysis. And when symptoms and memories are constructed to express the primordial, life-threatening trauma, they take on a realistic halluci-natory vividness of life-and-death proportions. This vividness of recovered memo-ries corresponds to the phenomenon of dreams that have hallucinatory vividness — the fact of importance upon which Freud built his first theory of mind and the unconscious (1900).

ORGANIZING TRANSFERENCE:
CUTTING OFF THE PASSIONATE LINK[1]

One patient had the following experience during a phase of the working-through process of the organizing transference. She had been away with her family for the weekend with another family and had quite a nice time. This was during a deep period when she and her analyst were maintaining contact with each other seven days a week and had been doing so for several weeks. She had been back from the weekend for a day and was concerned that her friends had not yet called her. She was further concerned when she could not reach them, feeling the panic of being out of contact with them. Her husband thought nothing about it and even chanced the comment of, "Well, don't worry about it. They're probably just sick of being with us and need a few days off!" Realistically, she knew that this was the case, but inside she felt a terrible panic because a close and intimate connection was not being sustained.

Her thoughts drifted to a conversation of the previous day regarding her younger brother who was born when she was 18 months old. That conversation centered on the problem of what happened when mother turned to take care of the new baby and how she lost her mother in the process. This particular discussion had been occasioned because for the last two weeks the woman was feeling emotionally shut off from the analyst despite (or as it later turns out, because of) the intense seven-day-a-week contact.

The event that had stimulated the closing down or shutting off had occurred at a Saturday session. When she arrived at her analyst's office she saw another woman whom she did not know in the secretarial portion of the office. Her fantasy was that this special Saturday session was not so special and that the woman was a close friend, or perhaps a date of the analyst, who was waiting for him. She felt the analyst wasn't really emotionally present because he was simply waiting for the time to pass so that he could be with the person of his choice. (This was in fact not the case. The woman was a student doing some work in the office that day. But this piece of information never came to light.) During the two-week interval since, much of the concern had been on the emotional closing down. Although she knew

---

[1]This is a follow-up to the same woman discussed in the third vignette in Chapter 2.

that right now her analyst was more available emotionally to her than ever because of his willingness to provide the possibility of intense contact; nonetheless, it was at this point of greater availability that she found herself cutting off, walling off. There had been much talk about her mother's involvement with her younger brother throughout the years. And then how the situation was no doubt made worse when a sister came along only eighteen months after her brother.

Today, however, she comments that long before her sibling was born there was a third party who she believed had the power to take Mother's attention away, her father. She spoke of her mother's style of relating, which she could remember throughout her childhood. When Mother was angry or felt confronted, she would simply close off in a sort of walled-off, sullen way. She remembers as a child she often did not know what she had done that had made her mother angry. She knew she had done something, but it wasn't clear what because her mother would close off and wouldn't talk. She supplied a piece of new information today. Her mother once told her that in the later phases of pregnancy with her, and into the earliest months of this woman's life, there was extreme marital discord. Now she can imagine that during these early months of life when Father would enter the room or be present, that her mother's overall emotional availability would be suddenly closed off, shut off—as has been her mother's lifelong character style.

In silent, slow tearfulness she then recounted another episode that happened this past week with a close business colleague with whom she frequently gets together to share their mutual concerns and business activities. They had scheduled two meetings during the week that she was very much looking forward to when he called. He said that he had been unexpectedly required to leave town and would be taking a flight out Tuesday afternoon. Was there any way he could get together with her on Tuesday before he left? She had some time and he rearranged his schedule so that a Tuesday meeting could be scheduled. She said, "I tried not to take it personally, but nevertheless I did. As soon as he said he had to cancel the two meetings I was looking forward to, there was no way I could hear that he wanted to be with me and was doing a great deal to rearrange his schedule so that he could meet with me before he left town. It was as though that was all incidental." She experienced a total collapse inside around his canceling the meetings.

She is very tearful now and the sensation is that the relationship will never be the same again. This parallels the sense that she had with her friends today. Because the contact wasn't there exactly when she needed it, she collapses into feeling somehow they would be lost forever. This feeling parallels her sense that the analyst has other concerns with other people and is also lost forever. She experiences a tearful realization that there would never be another person "there for her" in the way and at the times she desperately needs them.

The picture then emerged of her lying in her crib reaching to Mother, but Mother not being able to respond because she was herself emotionally unavailable. She then became aware of painful body sensations. The lower part of her body became tight and stiff as though she were digging her heels in. This seemed like a way of filling out the picture that with the upper part of her body she could reach to her mother, to her analyst, but the lower part of her body was refusing. The analyst commented that what seemed lost forever was the passionate link. Even though she knew with her business colleague, with her friends, with her analyst, that she did have a good relationship and good connections, when third parties seemed to detract attention, the internalized sensation was one of the passion being lost forever. She could feel the cutting off process as "something happening" in her body. This was linked to her historical sense as an infant that when Father would enter the room, Mother might remain physically present, Mother might even be doing her motherly tasks, but somehow the passionate link between Mother and baby would be lost, with her not having any power to restore it.

The analyst's question was whether this seems more like the infant's cutting off the passionate link and finally putting herself to sleep in the face of helplessness, as a way of withdrawing to take care of herself. Or was this the infant identifying with the mother who was traumatizing the infant by being passionately cut off from her relationship with her baby?

At present it seemed like both factors were operating, she said. The analyst made the specific point of labeling her experience *delusional*, making very clear that, in fact, her fears did not reflect social realities. She has many loving relationships, many people who care for her, who are passionately involved with her and she with them. But under certain circumstances what comes crashing down is this horrible, internalized sense that the passionate link is lost and that it is lost forever. While historically the emotional abandonment seems related to the presence of third parties, and while third parties can still serve as a trigger, the most salient feature is the connection that Mother somehow ruptured. For reasons that were not clear to the baby, Mother would suddenly close off, affectively disappear, leaving her in a position of desperate and painful reaching out with no return response. The infant's sense of timelessness and forever was discussed. In infancy it must have seemed as though the passionate link could never be regained. Furthermore, since this was the way that the loss of the passionate link had been internalized, in all subsequent significant relationships whenever there was a significant relationship affected by a third party the internalization would quickly destroy the passionate link and make it seem as though there could never be anything other than the excruciating pain and then the lifelessness that has always been. The question for further examination is how through time this shutting-down mechanism apparently developed in relation to the mother's emotional abandonments in the presence of third parties, and has come to serve as a way of limiting her sense of connection with important people. After all, there is always some third party lurking around to point to as the "cause" of shutting down to relating—just when sustained availability is a possibility.

At the close of the session, she said, "This sounds like terrible news. But somehow I'm feeling very relaxed." Her analyst countered with, "It's not terrible news at all. It's a relief to finally have this more clearly defined than it ever has been.

The bad news is that we still have some working through to do. So there is still pain ahead. But as with frightening and confusing things in the past, you have learned that knowing about them, no matter how painful it may be, is preferred over not knowing about them. Now you can be aware of how fragile the passionate link is and how subject it is to being destroyed internally by the mere presence of a third party. This is a valuable thing to know." She agreed.

12

Sandy: The Development of a Transference Psychosis

Sandy, a 31-year-old woman who for a number of years always had a great deal to tell me—many stories, many interesting vignettes—arrived one day in the waiting room full of stories she was eager to relate. In the waiting room, she suddenly began to feel something else—an intense desire to be very emotionally present this hour. She somehow understood at that moment that the stories she had wanted to tell me would be her way of not allowing herself to be psychically present in the room. She keenly felt the disappointment of letting go of the exciting stories she wanted to tell. She slowly began to sink into a very quiet, frightened place. She had been working for some time on trying to allow herself to be more emotionally present, to be fully alive in the room. She wanted to feel herself and to feel my presence, but she had so many things to talk about this was generally difficult for her to accomplish emotionally. On a few occasions she had had a glimmer of it.

On this particular day as she settled down on the couch, Sandy reported starting to feel chaos. With the internal chaos came tears of fright. I stayed with her fears and was able to support her experiencing the chaos of wanting to remain emotionally present but not knowing how. She was able to clearly differentiate this fear from other kinds of fear she's had before. When I indicated that this frightened, chaotic place was a place that she had been working for a long time to allow herself to experience, the tears came profusely. With relief she said, "You mean it's okay that I'm in this frightened place?" Sandy had interpreted my comments as reassuring her that no matter how frightened and confused she felt at the moment, this was an okay place to be. I pointed out that it was not simply a matter of being okay; the chaos and fear she was feeling for allowing herself to be emotionally present with me were very real at this moment, which she reaffirmed. It held a sense of present reality that was very different from what she would have experienced if she had gone ahead and told the stories she had intended to tell.

For about ten minutes she stayed in a quiet state of fear, making occasional quiet comments about physical sensations and her awareness of troubled breathing. Occasionally I checked in with her to see how she was doing, with her reporting that she was still present and feeling emotionally related to me but frightened. She contrasted this more quiet, tearful, chaotic fear with a number of previous regressive experiences that she has had in which she has felt wildly out of control, terrified, sinking, and falling—in much more urgent and frantic forms. She could see now how those were ways of defending against this place of quiet terror, of allowing herself to be emotionally present with another person. At one point when I checked in with her, she said, "I feel like I'm slipping away." Whereupon I extended my hand and said, "Can you stay? Can you stay here now?" She reached her hand toward mine and for a brief moment the two of us felt that we had retained our emotional connection with one another. Her comments were to the effect that this was the first time in her life anyone had ever invited her to stay with them or ever asked her to remain present.

No sooner than she had said that, she began to close in a little more tightly on my hand. She turned on her side, facing more toward me and, with her other hand, grasped my hand. I had the distinct sense that something had changed from the experience of simply being together from the first moment our hands had met. Gradually it became clear that her presence was leaving the room. Upon inquiry she replied, "I'm slipping away, I can't stop it. Something's happening to remove me from you." She began talking about the stories, the unrealness, and how the way we spent our time today had been more real. But once her emotional presence had started to slip away it was beyond her power to keep herself present in the room anymore. The emotional contact that was real, chaotic, and frightening, had gradually melted into a sense of being together and calm. But that sense in turn set off a retreat. The onset of the retreat was marked by her reaching, grasping, and clinging to me, as if for reassurance. But the very contact itself and the grasping set off a sense of uncontrollable slipping away.

Now I had an opportunity to point out the similarity between the way she was grasping my hand with both of hers, and how sometimes she clings to me physically in a hug toward the end of hours. I said, "This clinging, attaching sense is very different from the real chaos and the ensuing fulfilling moment of contact we had before you began to slip away, when you were able stay for a few intense connected moments when I asked you to."

I likened this clinging, grasping, attaching physical contact, which is reassuring, to the stories that she so often excitedly tells, which are also reassuring to her. But both the stories and the clinging contact have a certain unreal sense in that they do not contain the real terrifying emotions of being with another person in the present, nor do they contain safety and calm. Rather, they seem to mask or foreclose the true terror and difficulty of being together, as well as the comfort that can also be real. Her comment was, "Then those reassuring feelings are not quite real." I agreed that they were a way of not allowing the more real feelings of fear as well as comfort to be experienced. She immediately said, "I now feel ashamed of the way I've been using physical contact because it seems so phony." I asked, "Whose mother is speaking now?" She responded that it was the mother who frightened her, who broke contact with her, who accused her of being somehow bad. I commented that she had been abusively shamed for many things, for being dramatic, phony, and manipulative. But that that is not the case. The fears she felt at being alive, vulnerable, and present today had not been received by her mother. Her real presence, with her genuine needs for love and connection, had been deflected by her early mother, causing her to withdraw and/or to assert herself more frantically (as in clinging or storytelling) in an effort to be received, to feel loved, comforted, and safe.

At the end of the hour Sandy was tempted to reach for the customary goodbye hug. Yet she felt awkward about it, realizing that the hug would never quite be the same again. The reassurance it had held for her was in some sense a false reassurance, in comparison with the moments of presence and contact that were terrifyingly real and so reassuring in a very different sense.

Several months later, as the approach to understanding the organizing transference began to occur, there was a great deal of panic and confusion. In order for the organizing transference to become more visible, seven-day-a-week contact had been maintained for three weeks. The contact included four days of regular sessions and three days of scheduled brief telephone contact or office appointments. After working through some of the difficulties in maintaining contact, there had been a week of fairly good contact. By contact it is meant not merely the loving attachment that she had been able to feel for some time, but an emotionally interactive engagement. She had been pleased that the week had gone well and that she had felt emotionally in contact with me around many important issues. The two days of phone contact came, which happened to be Friday and Saturday, and then a special session was scheduled for Sunday. The contact that had been sustained throughout the week had undergone some shakiness during the two days with only telephone contact. During the Sunday session there was initially some limited but good emotional contact. After a period of time she began to be aware of pulling away, of trying to be close again, and then of pulling away again.

During this delicate period I found myself watching very closely for the exact moment at which Sandy might begin a full-fledged withdrawal. At the moment I began to feel her presence leaving, I reached out my hand and asked, "Could we hold onto each other this way?" At first, she was reluctant because it seemed that she was needing to withdraw. But after a little urging she made hand contact. For a few moments there was a real sense of being together and sharing an experience. I remarked on how difficult it was for two people to be together and to sustain an emotional experience with one another. She shortly reported that she was slowly and silently receding, that she was "withdrawing inside." There was nothing she seemed to be able to do about it, she said. She was pulling away. She was frightened and panicked, but clearly withdrawing. Soon the hands that were held together seemed meaningless and she left the session discouraged, feeling that the weekend disruption had made it impossible for her to sustain the sense of connection, that she was physically constricting and closing off. She stated, "Sometimes I can feel much closer to you when I'm not here. Sharing closeness together is hard to do."

I had the impression that my being present only for phone calls on the weekend days reminded her of the countless times her parents, particularly her early mother, had withdrawn from contact, setting up an intense need to clamor for what she needed. But the clamor was objected to by the parents and she was viewed as spoiled, overly needy, phony, or manipulative. The cycle that had become slowly represented in the analysis began when the child's needs were not responded to. This, in turn, led to increased intensity of demand, which the parents had found disgusting or intrusive. Finally it seems she would retreat into autistic isolation. In many overt ways her parents could be there for her and were able to provide basic physical care. But it seemed they never could enjoy being with her and harshly responded to her frantic expressions of chaos and fear that their flawed parenting set up in her. It was as if their emotional deprivations had set up an intense fear of breakdown, emptiness, and death. Their promise of availability coupled with their emotional unavailability was a betrayal of the child's emotional needs.

By the following day she came in practically bent over double with severe pains in her neck and lower back. She had already been to two doctors that day and received several tentative and potentially dire diagnoses, from possible meningitis, to a severe virus, to a chronic chiropractic condition. For the next three days she was under medical care and stayed at home taking pain pills and other medications. Sessions were held by telephone, with the main discussion being around the intense pain and the withdrawal. While medical possibilities could not be ruled out, we both shared the conviction that the severe pains and somatic constrictions somehow reflected the movement of the analytic work. She was inclined to see the disruption (abandonment) of the weekend as causal. I raised the possibility that the week of good contact followed by the brief Sunday revival of connection seemed causal. That is, contact itself is the feared element because it brings a promise of love, safety, and comfort that cannot ultimately be fulfilled and that reminds her of the abrupt breaches of loving care in her infancy.

The following weekend phone contact was maintained. Some domestic difficulties arose between her and the longtime boyfriend with whom she lived. She made it to her sessions on Monday, Tuesday, and Wednesday, and was very glad to be back. She talked a great deal about what was going on. There was some residual weakness left from the illness the week before, but mostly the focus was on "how on earth am I going to be able to continue to stay in the relationship with Marc!" By Wednesday she had been looking at apartments and was on the verge of moving out. Throughout the relationship this had been a pattern. At various times when there would be difficulties in the relationship, it would seem necessary for her to leave. The fantasy was to go somewhere where she could simply be alone, pull away into herself, and feel closed off, comfortable, and safe.

By the end of the Wednesday hour, while there had been obsessive concerns about her relationship with Marc and about whether to move out or not, there was a certain sense of closure. She said, "I think I'm just not fit to live with anyone because I can't get along with anyone. It's like I just can't relate, I can't stay connected, and when I do, it goes badly. I finally have to withdraw into a safe place where I can feel whole and alive by myself." That night she had a horrible nightmare. She got up in the middle of the night and typed up the dream as follows:

This dream was totally vivid and real. It was happening in the here and now, in the very apartment I live in on this day's date. I couldn't really tell the difference between what was going on in the dream and what was going on in my life. Marc and I are fighting or I'm fighting with him and it's the very fight that we're in right now. I'm in the kitchen trying to talk to him. I'm trying to explain and I'm getting more and more hysterical. I look at him. He has short hair so that he looks quite different. He walks calmly away from me and into the living room. I am hysterical. He is calm. I say, "Do you need me to go to your company picnic with you?" I know that he does. He looks at me calmly and says, "No." He has decided that I shouldn't go with him, that he doesn't need me to go. He's totally calm. His neck in the dream is very different from his neck in real life. I know he doesn't look like that with his hair short. I start going after him, all the while aware that I'm being hysterical. He's still totally calm. He begins walking up the stairs. I go after him, grabbing onto his leg. He proceeds upward, ignoring it. Totally calm. He goes to the study. Then I retreat to my room looking out, aware that there are other people in the house. Everyone in the house is calm except me. I'm crying and hysterical.

All through that last part of the dream there's an overlay of children's Golden Books. I don't know where or how they are there. It's more of an image. When I wake up hysterical I feel the Golden Books symbolic of lifelong struggle. I wake up crying and silently screaming and flailing my arms and my legs and kicking. I am aware, in the aftermath, of the indignity of the whole scene. For whatever reason, whether or not it's my fault, I am the one who is raging and hysterical, with Marc being totally calm. Because he doesn't want to deal with my dependency needs, he is pretending that he doesn't need me. He can't enjoy me and my love for him. It feels like it's symbolic of my whole life's struggle, and that loving has something to do with it. That it's because I love him that I am locked into this. I love him and I want to make the connection with him desperately and no matter what I do it fails. The little voices in my head, both in the dream and now, are saying, 'Yes, but it's because you are so infantile and hysterical and don't know how to connect that you have created this situation.' But the stronger knowledge, both within and during the aftermath of the dream, was that this relationship is set up to perpetuate the indignity, the hysteria, and the frustration of my early life. I make constant and futile attempts to connect, while he remains interested but dispassionate, with the rest of the family in the background listening to my hysteria.

I also wonder whether the short hair and the fact that he looks very different in reality than in the dream is symbolic of the fact that his true self and thoughts are different than I would like to believe they are. That unmasked, he is not who I think he is. It feels like he puts out a lot and is resentful that he doesn't get it back in kind. I don't get or give emotional relatedness on a mature level. The relationship remains in an infantile state emotionally, with me raging and hysterical. The indignity of it all is what seems so powerful in the dream. This seems like a replica of my childhood where all of the necessities were more or less taken care of. There was only a moderate amount of mistreatment and even some semblance of love. But there was an overall emptiness and neglect that was abusive. I am done in by my love, because I do love him as I did love my family. The image of the man with his hair short being so different from my image of him haunts me.

During the remainder of the session the interaction was marked alternately with periods of understanding between us, and moments during which Sandy, in confusion, would say, "You know I don't understand all of this. You know I'm not getting it." At some level things were being processed. But at the level of deeply understanding the dream discussion she did not feel that she really did.

After the dream was associated to in various ways the concern from the previous day reemerged as to whether or not she should get an apartment so as to find a retreat where she could be safe and comfortable. I asked if it would be possible for her to apply the dream to understanding the therapeutic relationship. That is, if the dream were representing a transference situation, what would that look like? She thought for awhile but was not able to connect the dream to the analytic relationship, although as my interpretation unfolded, she understood it. I suggested that I was represented in the dream as her boyfriend. She immediately said, "Yes. It seems like it was your neck and short hair in the dream that I was seeing, not his." I interpreted the dream as a picture of the childhood situation, which was being transferred not only into the relationship with her boyfriend but also into the analysis. I thought that this dream presented a version of her living disconnection.

I recounted the week of connection, the disruption of that connection through the Friday and Saturday phone call days, and how difficult it was to regain the connection on Sunday. I reminded her that even the Sunday connection was nip and tuck until I had reached out and asked her to try to stay present and connected. I recalled that she had, in fact, been able to sustain it. But that in less than ten minutes she had felt herself inexorably being drawn away. She had felt her entire body constricting and herself withdrawing, so that even though hands were in contact, her soul had withdrawn from the interaction. I interpreted that the dream picture represented what was going on in those moments of withdrawal. That, "from an objective standpoint you and I may be able to agree that we were in connection and that then you slowly broke the connection. But the dream picture tells us what your subjective internal process was like. That is, you experienced me not needing you, not enjoying you or your love, and then pulling away from you in much the same way that your parents did. And in the dream as your boyfriend did.

I calmly left you and went off to study for the weekend, oblivious to your needs." The nightmare gives a vivid picture of how the withdrawal happens after contact is achieved.

At this point she remarked that her boyfriend often complained that even when they did have moments of closeness and intimacy, immediately afterward she would start some kind of a fight. I commented that the fights were a cover-up or a defense against this more terrifying, painful, and dangerous contact situation, remembered from earliest childhood. "The Golden Book overlay of the dream suggests that this is the story of your childhood. Golden Books tell the way life is supposed to be. Your Golden Book tells you the way life was and somehow is still 'supposed to' be. There were people in your environment, your mother, your father, and your family who had a great deal they could give you, and they did give you basic physical care. But when it came time for emotional interactions they cruelly turned their backs, leaving you grasping at straws in a wild hysteria and finally withdrawing to your closet for safety. You were always made to believe that problems in relationships were your fault."

It horrified her to think that her withdrawal is her internalized reaction to *the connection* rather than her reaction to the other turning away. That is, she has consciously perceived her becoming hysterical because the other person was not connecting. But the dream, viewed as a transference representation, suggests what happens when, in fact, she does connect. There had been a week of good connection followed by a slight disruption, a strong reconnection, and a pulling away. Within twenty-four hours she was in excruciating physical pain and agony and remained so for several days, being physically traumatized by having made the connection, which was then experienced as traumatizing.

She replied, "Then you really don't think I should get that apartment?" By this time, I was quite clear about the meaning of the moving-out fantasy. I pointed out how in the past, as in the present, the moving-out fantasy has served as an autistic retreat for achieving a means of surviving and gaining a sense of comfort when she cannot safely connect to a person whom she needs.

I had been considering Tustin's (1981, 1986) formulations in attempting to understand her. Tustin thinks that the infant and mother are in a sensuous relationship during pregnancy. During the earliest extrauterine months the physical sensuous relationship optimally continues comfortably until psychological bridges begin to be made between the mother's mind and the child's mind. If the mother cannot maintain the sensuous relationship with the child, or abruptly ruptures it, the child begins engaging in withdrawing autosensuous behaviors. These ideas were presented to the client informally. She interrupted, "You mean the spacing out and withdrawing I do at times?" "Yes, when sensuous connection to your mother was needed but she did not provide it, you retreated to the safety and comfort of self-stimulation." She in fact had physically withdrawn in childhood to her closet and in adulthood to separate apartment-type settings to escape several relationships, feeling—at least briefly—soothed by the aloneness.

This vignette spans perhaps six weeks of intensive contact. The actual time it took to produce the dream picture of the withdrawal was about twelve days. The intervening time was spent in intense physical agony, frenzy, and daily contact. During this period there was no interpersonal emotional connection with me. The contacts were of a frenzied attachment kind. She is correct when she speaks of her love for others, but she was also becoming aware that there is an attachment kind of love and a connection kind of love; in the latter there is an emotional engagement. She is readily able to experience desperate, clinging attachment love, but is limited in being able to experience or to sustain the mutual, emotional engagement kind of love. When she experiences others as not needing her, not enjoying her, abandoning her to their own preoccupations she becomes desperate and clinging. The dream portrays her experience of the other coldly turning his back, unconcerned about her desperation and the autistic retreat that follows the trauma of feeling unresponded to. The entire cycle is internalized and endlessly repeated.

In the discussion following the dream, the focus was on whether her boyfriend would someday be able to interact with her. That could not be predicted yet. I said, "You chose him because he was sufficiently emotionally withdrawn so that you could maintain an attachment with him over a long period of time without this threatening transference from your childhood cropping up to destroy the relationship. As you begin to find a way to be more present and to ask for more emotional connection and emotional interaction, the question remains whether he will be able to evolve with you and develop increasing connectedness as well. At the present you simply don't know the answer, because you've not been able to stay present long enough to allow him to struggle with what he needs to struggle with in the relationship in order to remain fully present."

Following an extended summer vacation break there was much news and settling down for three weeks, with the earlier working through of connection experiences seeming to her to be a long way in the past. After having worked for some months on a creative and complex marketing strategy, Sandy had presented her proposals to colleagues and company officials late one Thursday afternoon. She received an overwhelmingly positive and enthusiastic response. People were interested and asking complicated questions she had had good answers for. People really connected to her in a favorable way. She enjoyed it and took pride in her work. A group took her out for celebration drinks afterward and she felt surrounded by a warm glow.

Within hours doubts and fear began and throughout Friday and Saturday a downward spiral of self-criticism, hopelessness, and despair evolved until she went into a panic and called me at home on Saturday night. I was available to talk for about forty minutes. The panic gradually subsided and the main connecting issues from before the vacation break were brought back into focus. The details of the marketing meeting were reviewed. The admiration, respect, and warm personal connectedness she experienced from her colleagues and her superiors were interpreted by me as causal in the downward spiral. She was reminded that loving connection and self-value are forbidden and dangerous. We felt deeply connected and I alerted her to the danger of a reaction to the good connection she was now achieving with me. I agreed to call her Sunday morning.

During the brief Sunday call several reactions emerged. She was in a mild state of confusion and perplexity. Not wanting to lose the good connection she had experienced the night before, she had pulled out some newspaper articles on childhood development I had written and she spent time reading them and trying to stay in touch with the good experience of our connection. But confusion started as she read, because many of the ideas on the written page seemed to be her own ideas. Had I taken her words and made them into my own without asking permission to do so? Or had the ideas been mine, but with so much interaction had she taken them in and felt them to be her own? She cited several examples, wanting to know whose words they were. I discussed the issues with her, showing her that some of the ideas came from others who were quoted and that both of us had taken in the ideas. Other ideas had clearly been picked up from me, but possibly there were some that came originally from her although examples were not available at the moment. I encouraged a search, indicating that I always wished to obtain permission or to credit what I take in from others whenever possible and appropriate.

Privately, I thought that the content seemed to express the organizing-level uncertainty of "Whose body is this? Whose breast is this?" and heralded disillusionment with the infantile omnipotent wish that usually precedes a breakdown experience (Winnicott 1974). That is, my mind (words) should belong to her, but after the good connection it appeared that I was running away, stealing my (nurturing) self from her and she became confused and frightened. The working-through experience was being resumed after the vacation break but with some new themes: being affirmed sets off a downward spiral, and the confusion of the source of nurturance.

She then presents a screen memory that had arrived earlier in the morning. "I was back at my parents' home. You know how I used to have my closet set up with a small desk and things for me to read and do—my retreat? Well, I had something really important to say and came out of my closet and went to tell my father. Whatever it was, he immediately put it down and humiliated me in the process so I went running back to hide in my closet." The interpretation offered was that the night before she had come out of the safety of the vacation break and permitted a regression precipitated by the gratifying marketing meeting. She had then made successful contact with me Saturday night. But while reading my articles she became agitated and confused about whose words these were. The feeling of being devalued by my differentness or "word theft" was viewed as a transference feeling demanding that she flee from the frightening and humiliating contact back into her closet. The screen memory suggested that the infantile omnipotent possession of the maternal body was abruptly and unempathically broken by her mother's narcissistic preoccupation with her own concerns, causing an autistic retreat. What she thought belonged to her was claimed by her mother, leaving her suddenly frightened and in uncontrollable confusion and retreating into herself. More adverse reactions were anticipated, I warned, as contact was being needed and being found.

By Monday evening Sandy arrived in my office dragging, looking terrible, and barely able to speak. She had been in excruciating pain all day with problems breathing and talking. She felt she was extremely ill and disoriented. Did I think she should go to a doctor? I encouraged medical coverage and also reviewed the events, saying that it has been a strain getting up the courage to begin the deep analytic work again but that last Saturday night it had begun. The total aching body, the gasping for breath, the chest pain, and the near laryngitis all seemed like reactions to the contact—her body was protesting the forbidden pleasures of relating that had been enjoyed. The bioenergetic interpretation of such pains is that they are body memories of early constrictions in the throat and bronchial area. The constrictions, begun in infancy, represent a bodily reaction to deprivation of food and/or air and simultaneously an effort by the life force to assert in the musculature a desire to live. As this desire to be alive in human relationships is revived in the real world and in the analytic transference, the early and painful body memories assert themselves. We were touching that terrifying wall of relating that went back to the original wish to be biologically safe and in control of vitally needed substances. What became somatically internalized was expressed in the screen memory of an abusive rebuff at the hands of a narcissistic father (or crazy mother).

On Tuesday she reported that she had been to see a doctor who thought she had pneumonia. Every bone ached and she could barely talk or make it to session. There were deep heaving sighs on the couch as she expressed the fear that she was dying. She was anticipating being so bad tomorrow she would not be able to come to session. She asked if she should try to make it if at all possible. I affirmed the need to take care of herself and respect her illness and the effects of the antibiotics. I also affirmed the importance of making her analytic session if possible.

I pointed out again how the sequence seen before the summer break had been revived. There was the Thursday triumph, the downward spiral, and the Saturday analytic contact, followed by the losing of the contact with the confusion of whose thoughts were whose, and the screen memory involving total body agony, humiliation, and running terrorized in pain back to her closet after a devaluing contact with the narcissistic father.

Wednesday she was in great pain and distress. There was much talk about the physical symptoms, problems sleeping, and the agonies of the week. I attempted, as on Monday and Tuesday, to contextualize the agony as the body's retreat from fulfilling contact. Agony and retreat were body memories that arose in relation to the analytic contact. But in her illness today, more than in the previous two days, she seemed totally inaccessible in any way to my words. While she listened to attempted interpretations, she could only nod her head. But nothing could be discussed or processed. She reported "slipping into a black void and nothing can stop it."

On Thursday she arrived with a pained facial expression, an antibiotic in hand, and a request for water to take it with. She continued talking in the same vein as the previous days for about ten minutes. Suddenly she asked, "Why are you being so silent?" I responded, "Because I haven't thought of anything to say yet." This enraged her and the remainder of the hour was spent railing at me for being emotionally absent, for being narcissistically preoccupied, and for not empathically "coming after me to rescue me." My instinctive response was to be somewhat defensive to the barrage of accusations. "This always happens. It's happened every time I've really needed you – when I'm slipping into the black void, when I have no way of staying alive, you back away emotionally. You just vanish when I get dependent and regressed and need you. You would let me die." The anger mounted until she bolted out of the room seven minutes early, slamming the door saying she didn't know how she could stay alive (it was not a suicidal threat the way it was said).

I had been struggling not to be defensive, to understand the mounting despair and rage. This type of tirade had been present before but the context had never been so clear as now. But with the hour cut short I didn't get the opportunity to point out that these kinds of rages in the past had tended to be either when she longed for reassuring mergers or on Thursdays before the weekend break. I did not get to say that we could certainly schedule phone contact over the weekend if that would help. Although once or twice I attempted to relate the present rage reaction to events of last weekend, the reaction and the violent accusation of coldness, distance, and narcissistic preoccupation made all possibility of interpersonal contact impossible.

I found myself quite upset by the raging intensity of the hour and the rageful exit, but I had experienced a similar intensity on prior working-through occasions with her so I decided to wait out the reaction rather than to cut it short by intervening with a call. She knew my home number; I knew I would be at home for the three days. So if connection was needed it would be readily available.

In a subsequent consultation I questioned the possible meaning of my seemingly not very helpful role in this difficult situation. It seemed to me upon reflection that, as uncontained as the situation might appear on the surface, the context and previous experience suggested that the ego function of body memory recall was in operation and needed to be heard out.

The Monday session was missed. Again, I believed that contact was possible if needed and so decided to wait. The rageful exit and missed session had a dramatic, manipulative flavor, making the evolving situation all that much more interesting for understanding the unfolding transference sequence. In past understandings of the infantile situation, what I had experienced as the client's pressured manipulations had been discussed at length as an internalized residue of an infant whose needs were abusively ignored to the point of terror and a fear of dying. They had been seen as the historically meaningful manifestation of an infant fearing imminent death through neglect or abandonment and learning to do everything in its power to force people in the environment to respond to its needs, to rescue it from aloneness and psychic death. The muscular constrictions in the chest and throat were further indications of how deeply embedded the desperation was. Although a manipulative flavor was present, what seemed more important on this occasion was the clearly articulated desperation, the despair, the fear of dying, the rage at my perceived emotional abandonment, the wish to be rescued, the fury at my spoken helplessness, which was seen as narcissistic preoccupation, and the "bailing out" when true need is present. Because the sequence had been somewhat experienced previously, because it was being articulated so clearly and forcefully with meaningful transference accusations and body memory, and because I would be readily available should she attempt contact, it again seemed best to wait this out rather than to intervene in the unfolding elaboration of the primitive transference sequence.

Tuesday was spent in anger, silence, and despair. "Why didn't you save me last Thursday? I was dying. You just let me fall off the face of the earth. Why didn't you call Thursday afternoon or over the weekend? When I wasn't here yesterday weren't you worried about me? You knew I was in bad shape. Why didn't you call?" (Note: My calls in the past were always by appointment so there was no precedent for her expecting a call in response to analytic distress.) I tried to remain as present at the feeling level as possible, so as not to become defensive in the face of the barrage of accusation. The session teetered on some empathic engagement around the despair and rupture because of my "narcissistic" inability to stay with her "true need." In one moment of rage near the end of the hour she slipped and called me by her boyfriend's name. She was horrified and redoubled her anger, saying that now I would capitalize on the slip and use it against her.

Wednesday she sat up to confront me on the series of breaches, my brutal and insensitive personality, how I could have handled each event, and how my failings were cold and cruel.

All this occurred as is to be expected in the development and working through of the transference psychosis. The experience of the diabolized parent is strongly authentic, the analyst *becomes* the hated object of infancy (the "psychotic mother") and no capacity for a split-off observing ego or reality testing ego is present at the moment of the experience. As on the previous two days I attempted empathic attunement with the despair and anger, but also continued to bring forth the overarching context of all the events. Sandy insisted the breach was on the previous Thursday when she needed me to be empathically attuned to her despair. I believed that the breach was internal and related to the Saturday night of the previous week when, following a long break, deep contact had been made, which was immediately broken by the confusion of words, the screen memory of father devaluing and humiliating her, and the ensuing painful body memories. I saw the entire round of rageful accusation and painful physical symptoms as the reemergence of an internalized primitive reaction to the treacherousness of interpersonal contact. But an analyst's attempt to be abstract in interpreting themes at the moment the analytic speaker is experiencing infantile concreteness always makes for gaps in the communication.

Unlike the previous session, small parts of my argument gradually did seem to be reluctantly taken in, but only after my patience had worn thin and I was clearly on the verge of anger myself. The countertransference feeling was clearly, "God damn it! I'm here, I'm holding on to you in this regression the best I know how. Why are you accusing me so fiercely—where is your rationality, your sense of human decency? Why do you treat me so badly?" This was, of course, not spoken at the moment because the present priority was clearly with the emergence of the organizing transference. She stated, "I always have to give in, to do it your way. I can never win. It's always been that way. With my parents they were right, I was wrong. They were okay, something was wrong with me. My only choice is to sell out and be false." I did get a chance to point out that despite how badly injured and angry she felt, "we are not in adversarial roles like you were with your parents. We might be in a tough spot at the moment, but winning and losing are not what we are about. We are working together to allow patterns and memories of past sequences of agony to appear so that we can study how your mind operates. The last thing I would want you to do is to sell out, to give in. You've got to hold firm while we get all of this sorted out." We were slightly calmer at the end of the session.

On Thursday she resumed the couch and for half an hour a conversation with more understanding of each other's views was possible. I commented to the effect that I am who I am and that I misbehaved according to my personality, which was one matter. But her *reaction* to shortcomings of my nature provided an opportunity to see the whole sequence as a part of her mental structure. This did not mean that my behavior was being justified or that I, as the analyst, was right and she was wrong, but rather that I had my personal way of responding, which set off primordial rage in her because my personality limitations are reminiscent of those of her parents. This was repeated and then somewhat reluctantly taken in.

I pointed out that the other person's self-preoccupation is always our enemy and has to be dealt with. In every relationship it would be only a matter of time before she found the other person's narcissistic preoccupations that would remind her of traumatic infantile encounters with her parents. Our investigation was into her reactions when she did encounter the other's narcissistic limits. What we have been seeing these two weeks in the unfolding of a mental sequence is *her*, her own personal reactions to others' narcissistic limitations.

She then reported a dream from the night before in which she discovered someone putting her boyfriend's clothes in her closet, where, she protested, they didn't belong. She saw the dream as condensing the childhood retreat from unempathic invasions into the safety of her closet, the transference humiliation and fury she so often experienced with her boyfriend, and the current transference situation with the analyst in which she felt my identity (clothes) an intrusion into her autistically safe place.

On the telephone the next morning she confided, "I'm afraid to tell you this. You know one of the injunctions of my growing up years was 'never tell anyone anything.' I'm afraid I'll lose this if I tell you. That you will somehow interpretively blow it so I don't want you to say anything about it." She explained, "By the time I left your office on Tuesday I realized that I cannot relate to anyone, that I've never been able to, and that there is no hope. Since I don't know how to relate to people, I have to relate to something or die. I thought I might start relating to my body, just trying to be in tune with it and I did. When reaching you is beyond possibility, I can be with myself and, even though it's painful, I can be okay." Respecting her wishes, I only echoed what was said at the time and agreed that staying with her body was of paramount importance. The overall context of the sequence was spoken again and arrangements were made for phone contact the following evening.

After two full days of heavy social demands on her, the next call was again filled with agony, which did not surprise me, given the inevitable strain of the anticipated social events. Sandy wanted to run, withdraw, pick a fight but could remember there was some reason she was not going to do this. She could not remember the reason but she hoped she could stay with it. I chose to remind her that she had been able to stay present Tuesday night because she had chosen to stay connected to a sense of herself, to her body, no matter how painful that might be. The intense social interactions were upsetting enough that she was wishing to retreat to her closet and to soothe herself. Perhaps she could stay in touch with herself. Staying with the painful reactions she was having in her body at present seemed more important than leaving them. Why not curl up in bed for a while? That way she would be by herself, could reduce incoming stimuli, and focus on the physical pains caused by attempting to relate to people. It sounded like a possibility.

The next day the retreat to bed was reported as successful in that by focusing on herself she was able to feel her labored breathing and chest pains slowly diminish into physical calm, thus reconstituting a satisfactory self state. She asked, "Do you think that maybe the breach, instead of that Thursday marketing meeting, was around my reading your newspaper articles and becoming confused Saturday night?" I said, "No, that was when you began feeling the fragmentation, the slipping into traumatic confusion as a result of our connecting on the phone. Connection serves to remind you of when you were once satisfyingly connected to Mother's body and then abruptly lost it. It happened on Thursday at your marketing meeting and set off the downward spiral until you called me and connected again to me on Saturday night. It's the connection that's feared because it was always somehow destroyed by your parents' narcissistic preoccupations. At present it's impossible to feel interpersonal connection without immediately expecting the traumatic and abusive turning away of your parents."

AN ASIDE ON PSYCHOANALYTIC EMPATHY

This vignette further raises an interesting and difficult issue regarding empathy. Kohut and the self psychologists have stressed the importance of selfother attunement—the analyst remaining tuned in to the subjective concerns of the person in analysis. Kernberg and others have sharply criticized this approach (see Hedges 1983b, pp. 269–270), saying that it is relatively easy to formulate an interpretation that agrees with the subjective state of the client. It is more difficult to provide psychoanalytic interpretations that empathize with the broader personality picture, but may be subjectively unpalatable or unpleasant at the moment.

When working the organizing experience this problem often becomes acute, as illustrated in this vignette. One could argue that I was unempathic when I did not respond in an empathic rescuing mode to this woman's despair. When I attempted to stay with what I saw as the broader personality issues, I was accused of being narcissistically preoccupied, out of tune, and wrong. There is always a delicate balance when responding empathically under conditions of accusation. On the one hand the subjective experience of the client has a certain priority or urgency in the immediate setting. But simply going along with the client's subjective demands may mean colluding with the resistance to establishing the painful, helpless, humiliating, rageful infantile transference. Here to have simply rescued the client from reexperiencing the contact-rupturing organizing transference would have been to collude in acting out the resistance. But to hold too firmly to this broader perspective runs the risk of a damaging clash of subjective worlds, which could precipitate a negative therapeutic reaction (Freud 1918, 1923, 1933). The problem of intersubjectivity as seen here involves walking a tightrope between receiving the despairing, manipulative, rageful accusations as the transference object and avoiding defending oneself from the accusations—usually ones that are going to strike home deeply somehow.

Hilton (1994) points out that when we are accused there is a three-part response that arises almost instinctively from most of us: (1) denial—"I didn't do it," (2) defense—"I did the best I could," and (3) blame—"She knows better than this, this accusation is pathological." The real problem, says Hilton, is that an accusation often is aimed, somewhat successfully, at a core wound of the accused, at a blind spot, or Achilles' heel. Until the accused is able to work through the core wound as it is active in the present relationship, it is unlikely that he will be able to give a satisfying response to the accuser who "knows" she is somehow right.

The problem of the core wound of the analyst, at which the accusation is aimed, becomes complex when considering the nature of the organizing experience. With developmentally more advanced symbiotic or borderline experience the fear of the client is abandonment, and an accusation of empathic failure means, "you abandoned me." But with organizing experience the transference is paradoxically comprised of structured terror around the issue of connecting or sustaining an interpersonal connection. That is, it is deeply empathic not to connect. Accusations focusing on the analyst's somehow letting the person down, of empathically failing, arise from the organizing level resistance to experiencing the transference, not from the transference per se. Not until the person in analysis can somehow let go of the accusation or demand, and then permit a lapse into deep yearning, helplessness, and terror, not until the utter sense of breakdown, emptiness, and death can be fully experienced in the here-and-now relationship, can the infantile transference be secured for analysis. Rescue by means of subjective empathic agreement in this situation would have been antitherapeutic.

Thus in an accusation situation involving organizing-level issues, the broadest psychoanalytic empathy would entail being able to navigate between the Scylla of colluding with subjectively valid resistance, and the Charybdis of unwelcome, unpleasant, unempathic transference interpretation. Hilton charts our course: (1) Avoid denial, defensiveness, and blame. (2) Use consultation to work through the core wound the accusation touches in oneself. (3) Show the person that you know how deeply he or she has been wounded by you or by the position you have taken. (4) Provide some reassurance that this particular kind of injury can somehow be averted or softened in the future, that is, that "this won't happen again to me or to someone else." This reassurance may take the form of the analyst's recognizing that there was a technical or empathic misunderstanding or mishandling of the situation by him (the usual Kohutian response). Or in the sort of dilemma presented in this vignette, the interpretation needs to include some reference to the ongoing, overall transference circumstance. Unfortunately, at the moment of organizing transference experiencing, the person is living in a concrete, nonsymbolic world of infantile trauma without his or her usual reality-testing capabilities or ordinary access to symbolic logic, so that sensible and meaningful discussion is virtually impossible.[1] In the example, the dilemma revolves around the problem that "narcissism in others is always a danger. But by our coming to understand your *reaction* to my narcissistic preoccupations as a part of your mental structure, as a sequence of your ongoing mental life, we have a way of working together more effectively to understand how the pattern repeatedly shows up in your life." The client's response was, "Oh, what this all is is a piece of how my mind works? I think maybe I can get hold of that."

Someone may arise here to ask, "But doesn't healing result from the client's feeling the old pain in a new situation in which he or she can be satisfactorily met in a different and more satisfying way in the present? Can't the person feel his or her experience contained in an empathic way so that the experience can be reorganized into a cohesive and meaningful self-structure? If we develop empathic forms that are larger and more containing doesn't the healing that is required occur? Now the

---

[1] I have come to advocate the involvement of a third party when intense or extended working through of the organizing transference is anticipated (Hedges 1994b). A third party case monitor can be available for weekend or vacation contact, can aid in reality testing when the client is lost in concreteness, and can serve to help the analyst with countertransference dilemmas and potential legal or ethical threats.

person is able to be in another place, a place of greater self-containment. Doesn't the analyst's overall containment provide the environment for the development of new personality tools?"

The answer is yes and no. Yes, in that the new and broader canopy of interpersonal containment is needed for more complex representational relating to develop. But merely positively reliving traumatic situations in a more satisfying environment is not enough. In infancy, the first time around, love and containment might have been enough. But after organizing-level extensions have been made and found unsuccessful or painful, a psychological structure is built up that must be dismantled, analyzed, or broken down. A delusion has been created that henceforth makes relating dangerous and terrifying. In analysis the transference can come to include organizing or psychotic elements that revive the early memories of trauma in the form of transference and resistance to the experiencing of transference. In these vignettes we slowly see the transference developing. The analyst is begged to participate in the resistance to remembering the horrors of being rebuffed, humiliated, and sent back into an autistic closet. It would be easy to collude with the resistance by empathizing with the experienced abandonment or by externalizing the accusations of abuse onto others in the past. The resistance can be easily acted out in angry confrontations of parents, family members, and others from one's past who have related traumatically to the person.

"KILL THE BABY":
A COUNTERTRANSFERENCE REGRESSION

What follows is a first person narrative of the countertransference experience that emerged at this point in the ongoing vignette.

The earliest instance of the theme that stimulated my countertransference regression occurred several years ago. I recall a vivid fantasy of this woman about ten feet away facing me in a small subdued crowd, jumping up and down enthusiastically smiling and waving, trying to attract my attention. I reported my fantasy to the client at the time. It was discussed in terms of how she had never felt seen by her parents. In fact, she never felt that she belonged to them, or to anyone else for that matter. She had always felt somehow different, set apart, isolated and separated from others, not really a part of any group or relationship. As a result of our analytic work she now feels that sometimes she "belongs" to Marc, her longtime boyfriend, and at times to me.

Sometime later the theme emerged of her interpersonal intensity. In agonizing over a series of relationships in which for some mysterious reason she felt that people seemed somehow to shun her, to silently ridicule her, to turn their backs quietly on her, to fail to reciprocate her friendly overtures, she worried that she was too intense. *Intense* was a word that seemed to summarize a set of qualities that she felt were perceived by others as intrusive, aggressive, demanding, challenging, complaining, insisting, being pushy, and so forth.

On the one hand she was proud of her assertiveness as a woman and pleased at her ability to make things happen, to express concern for others, to stand up for what is right, and not to be pushed around. But she feared that her intensity drove people away, caused people to be afraid of her, or not to like her. She is a bright woman with keen insight into people and it seemed that perhaps she saw too much, that she knew too much for her own good about what motivated people. It seems she reads people deeply in ways that make them uncomfortable or perhaps provoke them. But despite these intense, somewhat abrasive qualities, she has many friends, is well liked, and is respected for her integrity, vision, and insight.

In the context of an ongoing dialogue about her intensity I had occasion to remark on several occasions how, when she first saw me in the waiting room and sometimes on leaving the office as well, she seemed to take me in, to scrutinize me deeply to the point that I sometimes found it uncomfortable. Over the years I have cultivated a habit in this business of avoiding heavy eye contact, of often averting my eyes so as not to make people feel watched. Limited eye contact with clients now feels natural and comfortable to me, especially with analytic clients who use the couch. But often she would pull for eye contact by staring and then follow up her gaze or scrutiny with questions about how I was, was I okay today, what was I thinking. I found all of this mildly invasive and uncomfortable.

On several occasions she intuited that I was having an off day and commented to that effect. Although I had not perceived any mood irregularities in myself, on two or three occasions when she was upset by what she perceived as my preoccupied mental state I was able to report back to her that later in the day others also had noticed my being somewhat bland, or unresponsive. I reported this to her in the spirit of validating her perceptions of my unconscious moods. I questioned the possible meanings of her extreme sensitivity. The main conclusion we drew was that as a child she was so traumatized by her parents' preoccupied, unavailable, or destructive moods that she routinely surveyed people for "where they might be coming from" at the moment. It seemed some basic survival mechanism was being noted. She needed to know if I was okay, how I was feeling, was I going to be emotionally available to her, was she going to be safe with me today, or were there hidden emotional agendas or dangers?

In time, the question of her interpersonal intensity that seemed to create some discomfort in others was linked to her need to read unconscious moods and motivations. I volunteered how uncomfortable I felt being scrutinized visually and emotionally, but understood her need to check me out each day, although the need was clearly greater on some occasions.

Early in the analysis she began to ask for hugs at the end of sessions. These goodbye hugs began in the context of regressive moments when she felt desperate and was not sure how she could leave or make it to the next day or through the weekend. Afterward on several occasions, I explained my discomfort with the hugs.

She assured me that hugs were human and expressed connection. I explained that while I was not committed to total abstinence of touching like most traditional analysts, I always felt physical contact of any sort needed to be understood, and that I was always uncomfortable with physical contact that had not yet been understood. She thought analysts were phobic of physical contact and had a problem themselves, no doubt fearing overstimulation themselves or sexualization of contact by the client. Hugs at the end of sessions had nothing to do with that, she asserted. They were an ordinary part of human warmth and understanding. During periods in which she felt stronger, hugs at the end of the session could be omitted.

She did, however, experience a series of powerful sessions in which, when she was emotionally pulling away during sessions, I extended my hand and held on to her while struggling to maintain emotional contact with her as well. I later explained what I believed to be a critical and concrete aspect of touch on such occasions, as it served to help keep us together when she was losing her sense of me at the moment. In time I came to sense her desire for hugs and responded accordingly and spontaneously.

Slowly the organizing transference began to be traced or defined in how she was more or less "present" in the room, more or less available for contact. At first she believed she was present and in contact most of the time. But slowly she realized that she was almost never present in an interpersonally emotionally engaging way, and that she often had not the slightest idea of who I was. She said on several occasions, "I can feel so much closer to you when I'm not with you." This was interpreted as how difficult it was to actually establish a sense of deep and meaningful interaction with me in which she could actually feel my presence as a real person separate and different from herself. She had developed a fantasy of me, of who I was, and could carry on a reassuring dialogue with me in my absence. But when it came to knowing who I was, in the sense of being able in the here and now to interact with me, she often felt lost. She felt discouraged by this and gravely disabled.

I was able in time to draw a distinction between her feeling "attached" to me in a safe way and her being "connected" to me—able to feel open and active channels for communication and connection between two real, live, interacting beings. She was at first upset when I applied the attachment-connection distinction to hugs at the end of the hour. She did not like the idea that her reaching out for physical contact stemmed more from an attaching, clinging impulse or need for physical reassurance than from a communicating, connecting interaction. But on several occasions she clearly felt the distinction and then began to limit the hugs to more special occasions, although she clearly did not like my interpreting them as attaching without connecting.

A series of breaches occurred over time in which she felt emotionally unresponded to by me. Her view was that just when she really needed me to be emotionally present I would somehow withdraw. She believed that I could not tolerate neediness or dependency and so would withdraw or disconnect and go to a cold, critical, imperious place. I could indeed feel the abrupt disconnections, her despair, her agony, and her rage at how I wasn't there for her. But I could not see or experience the pattern she believed to be present. To me it seemed her agonies and disconnections came upon the heels of some connection that she had established with me, and I attempted to point this out to her.

After several breaches I learned to note that at the first inklings of rage or of an intense, invasive, or accusatory demeanor on her part I tended to become more silent because I would be puzzled, attentive, and thoughtful—not having any idea where she was coming from, or not understanding the nature or meaning of her manner. That is, my subjective sense was that we had just successfully connected, that I had been present for her. So when her response was distress or rage I was puzzled and pulled back a bit to try to understand what was happening. My caution and increased alertness would then be felt by her as cold withdrawal.

Afterward she would tell me what I should have done or said in these moments that would have been more empathic. However, the empathic response I "should have" given did not occur to me because at that moment I had gone into a more abstract tracking mode trying to figure out what was happening. That is, when I sensed sourness, intensity, or invasiveness I tended to begin reviewing in my head the overall context of the past hours, weeks, or months while listening as carefully as possible for what the present problem was within the overall context of her personality and our interaction. While I was puzzling in this way she might insist on some sort of immediate response from me. Her demand for immediate responsiveness would catch me off balance. It seemed that under these conditions no response I ever gave was satisfactory and her rage would escalate. Although I'm not sure if any response I might have given would have been more helpful or prevented the escalation, her complaint was invariably that I was inappropriately cold and withdrawing.

In quieter times I seemed to be able to show her the connections and disconnections I was tracking and she seemed to understand them. But in the moment she would tense up. She would feel locked into a fight with me over how I would coldly withdraw, think her complaints to be transference, blame her for disconnecting, and see her as "nuts" and myself as okay and right. There had been a series of interactions that were distressing to both of us. We tended to have different views about what was happening. She believed that I always somehow withdrew when she felt needy and she had a bad reaction to it. She accused me of refusing to examine and to acknowledge that my faulty responsiveness made it impossible for her to trust me or to trust her analysis. She feared I was just going to do it again and worried that there was no point in continuing her relationship with me, that I had a basic personality defect and could not keep from rejecting her. It seemed to me that as she would feel something real in the interpersonal connection or in her body in relation to our connection, something internal would occur causing her to feel that I was cold, isolated, critical, withdrawing, skeptical, and disgusted with her for being so dependent and needy.

My overall tracking for some months had been related to the ways in which she could not allow connection or engagement between us to occur and the ways in which she closed it off when it did occur. I could hear her insistence that at these breach moments the disconnecting problem was with me not her. I could see she needed me to give in to her accusations of my inappropriate emotional coldness and withdrawal. If I did not readily accept the blame for emotional withdrawal, this further escalated her distress because I was in effect saying (like her parents always had) that it was all her fault, that I was right and she was sick, excessively needy, bad, wrong, or pathological.

I became especially interested in tracking how she managed to produce these breaches somehow using features of my personality in order to relive the anguish of her infancy and childhood. I considered the possibility that my tracking on a more abstract plane than she wanted to be heard on, could be an intellectualizing defense, a way of avoiding her connecting overtures. Perhaps my intellectualizing defense was activated when (as she claimed) she was most needy. But whether, or to what extent, I was actually being defensive, or my moods made me significantly less available to connect with, I had the distinct impression that she was using features of my personality to accomplish transferentially determined disconnections. I tried on several occasions to suggest this but was met with the firm conviction that there was a narcissistic personality flaw in me that I was trying to blame on her. If I was correct in believing that she ferreted out something in me to stimulate and/or attach organizing transference to, how was I to show her that, without seemingly replicating her parents' crime of "shifting the blame" to her and further enraging her? What was going on and how were we to sort it all out? We were both clear about a history of these disruptions that occurred on the day before weekend or holiday breaks.

The precipitating incident leading to our next distress occurred on a Friday afternoon. The week had gone comfortably with her allowing herself more body feeling than usual. I thought Friday might go well also. I was, however, aware that I was going backpacking and would not be near a phone for forty-eight hours. I might need to tell her this since she often needed to know how I could be reached on weekends. It seemed to me that I was having a good day. I was looking forward to a beautiful weekend in the mountains with close friends with spectacular autumn weather promising.

In the waiting room I felt her penetrating eyes and I averted mine (as I usually do). In the hallway she made a full turn around to take me in again, something she had not done before. I felt closely scrutinized and averted my eyes again. The past couple of months it seemed that she had been aware of watching me in the waiting room since I had made the comment about her intense eyes. On a couple of occasions there had been an exchange of what I took to be knowing smiles as we were both thinking about the eye contact and what it might be about. In an instant, as I was reviewing all of this in my mind and thinking, "It's Friday and she is forcing me to disconnect, to pull back from her intense, intrusive scrutiny. I feel penetrated and knee-jerk withdraw. She knows this about me. With the weekend coming she is attempting to either break a potential connection or prevent one from occurring by using my instinctive withdrawal from her gaze."

In my consulting room, instead of moving to the couch as usual, she turned, faced me, and asked if I was okay. I assured her, "I am, but [and here comes the breach] when you scrutinize me it forces me to withdraw." She was enraged. That's ridiculous. How could she force me to withdraw? There it is again, and I'm blaming her for it. She wants that in writing because no one will believe it otherwise. In attempting to explain further (clearly a mistake in these circumstances) I reminded her of my aversion to her intense stare and commented that if she wanted to connect with me that's certainly not the way to do it. She was further angered. I attempted a few other rationalizations that failed and then became quiet waiting to hear it all out to see if there was some element I could perhaps take hold of. My silence was further enraging. Toward the end of the session she announced that she had a good week, was overjoyed last night, and wrote an exciting poem that she brought, which she had wanted to share with me. She was happy with what was happening to her, with our work, with me, and she came to share it all with me today until I ruined it. Instead of waiting to see where she was coming from, I wrecked the session by disconnecting (she never got to the enjoyment of reading the poem).

Every session the following week she sat up to confront me. I always do this to her, just when she's ready to connect I managed to spoil it somehow. I am an unanalyzed analyst. She listed the times I had failed her and then blamed her for being somehow pathological. I have a deep character flaw that I will never get over, so what's the point of her trying to relate to me? If every time when she is ready to connect I wreck it, what's the use of continuing her analysis? We need an arbitrator, someone who can show me my part in all of this.

My feeble attempts to talk about our overall context, about her intensity, about eye contact, about her using my discomfort at her scrutiny to achieve a disconnection fell on deaf ears. She was on a rageful roll and nothing I could say engaged her in thought about other aspects of what may be happening. Her body was drawn up tight, her eyes piercing, her voice tense and authoritative, her manner confident and strident. I had done it to her again and it had to stop. As she reviewed past incidents that she believed I refused to acknowledge my part in, I repeatedly attempted to correct her, to remind her that I had acknowledged how I had failed to be empathic, but that acknowledgment had not helped. I continued to ask if it is possible for us to notice how she was reacting to my empathic error. Each time she interpreted this as my trying to blame her, to hold her responsible for what I have done wrong.

The attack is amplified on Tuesday with her pulling out all the stops on her anger, dredging up every complaint and flaw in my nature she could think of, and by mid-session Wednesday I was weakened, exasperated, and banging my hands on the arms of my chair almost shouting that I did not say she was a bad person, or that it was her fault, or that my response last Friday was the best one. I only said that we are different people with different ways of thinking and responding. I had a real personality that responded to things she did. She may be using my personal responsiveness for her unconscious purposes. I was angry that she persisted in turning everything I said to mean that I was okay and she wasn't. I was struggling not to defend myself against her harsh attacks, to find some way of validating her feelings. But she still turned my comments into how nuts I think she is, how I think everything is transference, and that I still believe I haven't done anything to deserve her anger and disillusionment.

Toward the end of the session I was able to say as sincerely as I knew how that she was absolutely right that I started last Friday's session badly. She was quieter and, I hoped, listening to what I had to say for the first time. I tried to explain the long-term tracking I am doing. I said that when I felt her gaze and her immediate demand to know if I was okay, I mistakenly responded on the abstract plane I was considering at the moment, rather than waiting to see where she was coming from. She was having a joyous body experience, had written a poem, and wanted to share it with me. A concrete moment of happy sharing was what she wanted. My error, I said, was responding from another plane than the one she was on.

In struggling to explain how, given who I was and our previous discussions about her intense gaze, she could expect me to avert my eyes when she stared at me, I likened it to hugs at the end of the hour that I thought she had previously given an indication of understanding. I explained that if she wanted to interact comfortably with me, neither of these modes would work because they made me uncomfortable. I had shown her I could go along with what she wanted, but if her desire was to achieve a mutually comfortable interpersonal connection, given who I was, those means would not achieve it. This did not not make me right and her wrong; it was merely the way I was. The intensity and physical contact were simply not ways of approaching me that she could count on a favorable response to. She became quiet and thoughtful and left silently. I hoped I had acknowledged the nature of my error, and how it had indeed prevented me from being with her—and how that replicated the numerous times her parents had done just that to her, leaving her isolated and badly damaged as a result. It seemed that she was taking some of this in and she left the session somewhat subdued.

But the next day she arrived utterly devastated. She could see now that I definitely could not be trusted. All along she had believed me. She had hoped that our relationship would be different. She had believed that I could be emotionally honest, but from my response yesterday she could see that there was no hope. No hope for me, no hope for our relationship, no hope for the analysis, and no hope for her. All I could see was "an error in timing." But the fatal flaw remained; I still believed that it was her fault, not mine. Further, I had humiliated her by saying I never wanted hugs, that I didn't like them, that they were all her neediness and nothing I cared for. It simply wasn't true; I had engaged warmly in those hugs, she said. Or if it was true that I hated her need of hugs, then I was dishonest when I had hugged her. I managed not to be defensively corrective of how she turned things today, but only echoed her despair and how this was exactly the despair she has experienced all her life with the emotional dishonesty of her parents. She now had discovered me to be as emotionally dishonest as they had been. The most devastating trauma of her childhood was being repeated in our relationship.

I had encouraged her earlier to go over her concerns with a consultant we both knew. I brought up that possibility again, this time as a suggestion for a way out of her despair. Near the end of the session there was a long silence and slowly tears began to trickle down her cheeks. She was able to whisper, "Betrayal, what a horrible betrayal. To believe someone is emotionally honest and then to find out he hasn't been." As she left I mentioned that I would be home all weekend in case she had anything to tell me.

By Monday she was ill with asthma again. Betrayal was the theme. She reviewed her distresses with me. I was allowed to correct the "error in timing" she spoke of to my view that I was badly out of tune with her by being on a plane of abstraction, tracking long-term themes when she was wanting to have some concrete happiness of the moment together. That seemed better. I was allowed to repeat my belief that we were experiencing being different people, not that I was right and good and that she was wrong and bad. We were struggling in this together but not as adversaries. She agreed but expressed that she felt I was trying to send her away to resolve this with a consultant when she had to work it out with me. I agreed that she had to work it out with me, but pointed out that sometimes a third party can shed helpful light and provide support.

Then I related the consultation I had had last week regarding my work with her. I told her I had come to understand several things more fully. She listened quietly and intently, but gave little response at the time. I reviewed how I had talked about my dilemma with her. I related that I had shared with my consultant how from her perspective it looked adversarial—and finally, despairing and bleak as she experienced the horror of emotional betrayal. I demonstrated with my hands banging the arm of the chair how I had related how angry I had been that she kept misinterpreting me as saying it was all her fault. I showed her my body freeze-frame that had been caught by my consultant of banging the arms of the chair. I quoted the empathic interpretation of my plight given by my consultant; "Mother, I hate you for not being available to me, for not hearing what I have to say, for misinterpreting my love, for not being there when I need response from you. I thought you understood me and now I find you don't." Our work had succeeded in producing a regressive trend in me that stimulated my response to my own organizing mother.[2]

---

[2]I wish to gratefully acknowledge Robert Hilton as serving as my consultant in this difficult work.

Her eyes grew larger, but still she was silent. I felt she grasped that I was telling her about my regression in our situation, my helplessness and anger, about how fragile and pained I had become. I continued talking about my consultation. I relayed how I spoke about how what was happening between her and me was of critical importance. I was tracking the disconnects on one level and she on another and we were not meeting—how frustrating it was for both of us. I mentioned that I had spoken about how I knew somehow she was doing absolutely the right thing in raging at me, but I still could not understand completely what it was all about. I told her I had been sitting in a love seat when the consultant observed another body freeze-frame at the very moment when I was expressing greatest agony about my plight with her. I showed her how I had leaned forward and sideways (toward a fetal position) with my right thumb approaching my mouth. Our session was drawing near an end. She asked a few questions to be sure she understood what I was saying about the oral and fetal body regression I was experiencing. I communicated compassion for both of us in the dilemma we were in and the strength it took on both sides to allow this deep regression to occur at the depth it obviously was. My sharing with her my consultative experience and the depth of regressive stress our work together was stimulating in me seemed to provide some connecting link, though I couldn't tell at the time exactly how I had succeeded in reaching her.

Several hours later she left word for me to call and I reached her mid-evening. She was sobbing and barely able to whisper, her lungs and throat were unbearably tight and in pain. Her whole body ached. She said she was breaking down and began sobbing uncontrollably. She said Marc was there with her, so she was okay, but very frightened and confused. One thing kept running through her mind that she had not told me before. As long as she could remember, whenever her mother was angry, her mother would first scream and yell, but then lapse into a cold, distant, withdrawn silence. Her mother literally would not speak to her for days on end. She was not ever sure exactly what she had done to produce the awful silence in her mother, but it was icy and cruel. It felt like what she gets from me when I withdraw into silence. Then she said, "This other I'm not quite sure about—what broke the cold silence. But it seems like after a week or so something would happen, maybe we would be passing somewhere in the house or something, and our eyes would catch and I'd break down. As soon as I'd break down she'd be okay again. But she would hold out until I broke down. It was so cruel. How could anyone do something so unbelievably cruel to a child—holding out until she broke. And I did. I always did. I always broke first. Like it was a battle to see who could hold out the longest. And she always won—even to this day she wins, I have to speak first."

I told her I thought something had happened when I shared my own helpless regressed distress with her. She agreed. We talked about it several ways. She was calming down now, glad for the talk. It seemed that when she could see my pain, my regression, something broke. But for once it wasn't her. When I told her about my body regression in response to her she knew I was connected to her. She knew I had feelings, and that I wasn't her steely mother, that we weren't in an awful battle over who was most sane. She replied, "Right now I feel a tremendous need to be taken care of, to be physically attended to, to be held, caressed, comforted. Like it's been a horrible trauma and I need comforting." I suggested she ask for physical comfort from Marc tonight. She asked if she could call me early in the morning.

When she called the next morning she told me that Marc held her all night. First one side of her body and then the other would get cold and be in terrible pain. He was glad to be there for her and she reminded herself that, despite her various frustrations with him, whenever she has really needed him he has come through. I commented, "He does care deeply for you and he has the patience of a mother who holds on until things are okay again."

This was not the first traumatic transference repetition with this client nor the last as we worked through this organizing transference. But in the aftermath several interesting things were said. She had lunch with a close friend and laid out the whole story of her distress with me and felt very understood. She realized for the first time that I didn't have to be a perfect person to be her analyst. She expressed concern that she had made me feel so bad. I hastened to tell her that I was fine, that my regression was certainly in relation to her, but that it was as much a part of our work together as was my sharing it with her. I reminded her how mothers must be able to regress in order to be with the distress of the infant, and that we both felt a need to experience this together no matter how distressing the experience might be. She said, "I do know that. But all those things I said about you, you know they are true."

I explained, "That was the worst part, that you know me too well."

"But," she pondered, "I don't know why I said them all to you so meanly. I have to think about that."

I said, "You had to remember, and this is the only way. I know we both wish for pictures and stories that are easy to remember, that aren't so hard on us. It would be wonderful if we could simply and easily agree that you had bad parents. It would be altogether too easy to simply confront them about their shortcomings, their cruelty, their abusiveness, the cumulative strain trauma they caused. But this painful reexperiencing kind of memory is more difficult. This cruel and abusive battle, beginning as it did from earliest infancy can only be remembered as trauma, rage, betrayal, confusion, fear, tightening in the throat and lungs, and cold and pain all over your body. The accusations directed at my shortcomings are for the damage they caused you by being preoccupied with themselves."

We then spoke of how fragile her mother must have been to have been so threatened by the relationship demands of a baby. She had always thought of her mother as cold, calculating, strong, and cruel. Suddenly she understood that it was not so—that her mother was desperately clinging to her own sanity. "She could only hold to the false life that he [her father] offered. She could hide herself safely in that false life with him. If there had ever been a choice, if it were him or me, it would have been, 'kill the baby.' "

The following week her sessions were quiet, her breathing calm and even as she dozed off several times on the couch—almost asleep, thinking, dreaming, silently enjoying being with me and not having to entertain me, knowing that I was enjoying her peace and restfulness. I had the fantasy of being a parent lost in timeless reverie in a rocking chair with the new baby.

THE DELUSION DEFINED

The following Monday there was again a despairing rage. It was pointless to continue her analysis. She now knew that she could not trust me emotionally, that I was fundamentally psychotic like her parents and could never provide her with the environment she needed to continue her analysis. "You would just let me walk!" Meaning that I did not care about what happened to her, that I would simply let her walk out in all of her pain and disillusionment. I assured her I could not prevent her from walking out. But that would be a horrible loss for both of us, even as discouraged as she was with me at the moment. Perhaps it would help if she spent some time going over her problems with me with the consultant I had on several occasions urged her to see.

On Tuesday she wordlessly moved the large wing-back chair she had been sitting in, turned its back to me, and sat in silence the entire session. I could not tell if it was anger or despair she was feeling.

Wednesday she echoed the uselessness of going on with me, the hopelessness of it all, how psychotic I am and how despairing she is. I struggled to stay with her and know how awful it is to feel that there is no one to trust and nowhere to turn. I had occasion to discuss in basic terms a few ideas of Tustin and Klein. It seemed what she had hoped was that I would be able to restore the intrauterine state of physical at-oneness with her mother's body. Again and again when she bumped into boundaries of me or of others she was painfully reminded that Eden cannot be regained, that the lost maternal body is lost forever. We discussed the broadest dimensions of how a baby can be slowly led to realize that Mother's body is separate and that baby will not die, that basic trust is possible even in an imperfect and failing world. In her case it seemed clear that she was abruptly and cruelly forced into the realization that the necessary and longed-for features of her world were not under her control and that she has been enraged and suffering ever since. She said she had to hold onto this rage and she wasn't sure why—that she must not give in. I supported her in this, saying that she should not give in, that she must stay with her intuition. But I was for the first time a bit worried that she might actually attempt to end her work with me.

Thursday she announced that she was mad. She looked more confused than angry. She declared that this situation was impossibly painful and confusing—she could not function, and she didn't know how she would get through the weekend in this shape. Then came the deepest anguish I had ever heard from her, without the slightest hint of manipulative energy to berate me or get me to rescue her from it. "I can't trust you because you're psychotic and will emotionally damage me. But I can't let go of you or I'll die."

There was a brief silence as we both grasped the impact of her powerful words. The truth had finally been spoken and we both immediately recognized this central definition of the internalized emotional situation in which she has lived since infancy. We talked about it, and how significant this definition of her fundamental delusion is. It was like an enormous boil had finally broken and she was flooded with relief. I agreed to call her each day of the weekend.

She immediately and spontaneously connected this central dilemma with the successful business meeting of several months ago that marked the beginning of this lengthy regressive experience. She saw how when her friends and colleagues connected with her she immediately distrusted their sincerity, their warmth, their good will. The distrust was her transference repetition to her terror of connection. A series of other memories immediately tumbled out that could be seen and understood in light of this new Rosetta stone. It was as though a key to understanding everything in her life had finally been spoken. She said, "You kept talking about connecting and disconnecting and I suppose that is what this is, but when I put it into my own words it suddenly makes more sense to me."

I emphasized the importance of her finally being able to state the bind she was in with me: that I am crazy and may damage her but that she can't do without me. I added that at least this second time around maybe I wouldn't be as crazy as her first mother! She smiled. She recalled that some years earlier she had attended a weekend birth regression seminar. In fantasy she had regressed back to the womb. She had a picture of herself as a hard-boiled egg. All the other eggs were enthusiastically jumping up and down and she was hard boiled. I interpreted that this was a picture of her psychic life with the protoplasm hardened from the beginning, prohibiting any emotional growth. She said, "It goes back to before conception. My mother didn't want me to develop at all. It happened even before my father appeared." Some deep tension had been relieved, a way to rethink and reexperience everything was now available. In light of this image I recalled my countertransference fantasy of a few years earlier in which I saw her amidst a group of others enthusiastically jumping up and down wishing to be seen, longing to connect, to grow.

Spontaneously she related this new discovery to a series of distressing situations that have caused her great puzzlement and pain. Now she could see them as somehow arranged by her to prevent contact by experiencing others as untrustworthy or even using the closed-off or defended parts of others' personalities to get them to do things that would prove that she couldn't trust them or relate to them. On the way out she said, "And there really isn't anyone I can trust." I said, "Not in the way you have always wished to—they are crazy and may hurt you, but the problem you are stuck with is that even if you can't totally trust anybody, you do need people to relate to and to feel alive with."

The reader will understand that the fundamental kernel or nucleus of her character structure had been spoken. The turning point in the analysis had been reached. Her infantile trauma had been remembered by being emotionally repeated in the analytic relationship. The internal character structure could now be subjected to a sequence of working through experiences both inside and outside the analytic relationship. The flexibility required for more spontaneous and creative living was then achievable through gaining conscious knowledge and mastery over the somatopsychic structuring of her personality. Psychoanalysis cannot restore us to Eden. But it can serve to permit us increased access to our personal powers for creatively living a more fulfilling life.

13

The Power and Danger
of the Organizing Experience

The voices in this book speak a message that is strong and clear. Infantile traumas of many types have operated in all human beings to a greater or lesser extent since the beginning of time. We now have at our disposal the psychotherapeutic means to respond effectively and transformatively to the deep scars left by infantile abuse, neglect, misunderstanding, and trauma.

But at the same time our psychotherapeutic resources are rapidly coming under the control of vested business and political/governmental interests that threaten to undermine and render ineffective the professional and technical knowledge that has taken more than a century to create.

You have heard seriously abused and damaged people speak their plight and their desperation in these pages. You have seen the thoughtful and caring application of psychoanalytic understanding painstakingly undertaken by dedicated and hard-working psychotherapists. The work and results with the organizing experience presented here are in their nascent stages as new thought systems have emerged to make effective treatment of psychotic constellations in all people at last a possibility.

But even as the knowledge of how to foster deep regressions to organizing-level transference and resistance experiencing increases, and even as knowledge of how to manage the transference psychosis expands, we have become aware of how risky this work is for the psychotherapist who now practices in a litigious society where it is culturally in vogue to feel victimized. The perils of the intimacy of the psychotherapy relationship now include the loss of reality testing and reasoned judgment when the psychotic or organizing transference is at last put into place for successful treatment. Now the therapist is at risk because the treatment produces an uncanny sense of deep psychological merger between the sources of perceived abuse in infancy and the actual person of the therapist as experienced in organizing resistance and transference experiencing.

Today all psychotherapists are seriously at risk, as are all helping professionals, because at the moment of greatest transformational possibility the person's greatest psychic vulnerabilities and scars are exposed in such a way that it may suddenly seem to that person that it is we, the object of the deep emotional transferences and resistances, who are the cause of the pain and suffering brought from the past to be studied in the present.

The danger is that the person falls into a negative therapeutic reaction and immediately or some time later ends treatment, accusing the psychotherapist of misdeeds and malpractice that have caused the very damage that we set out to study and heal in the first place! It is a serious problem of human perception and memory that we have encountered.

At present these treacherous organizing transference and resistance phenomena are so scantily understood, even in the community of practicing therapists, that one therapist after another is succumbing to disastrous charges of misconduct due to beliefs and feelings of the client that have been stimulated effectively by the treatment process but inadvertently aborted into vicious accusations that speak the plight of the person's early infantile experience.

Currently, we have no protection of due process in our licensing boards where administrative law prevails and we are presumed guilty until we can prove ourselves innocent. We have no effective protection even from our own professional ethics committees because the people sitting on these committees are sometimes unethically making judgments on deep psychological processes that their own training and therapy have not prepared them to be knowledgeable about. And we have no effective protection in courts of law because, despite the possibilities of due process, our malpractice insurance companies would rather settle for exorbitant sums of money than have our work properly litigated. And further, though our judicial system in principle guarantees trial by a jury of peers, there are no juries in this land, or judges who have the sophistication to understand the subtleties of resistance and transference analysis of psychotic processes. In short, our situation at present is tragic and dangerous.

If we allow our tradition of professionalism and accumulated wisdom to be activated in the service of cure of the many traumatized and damaged people who live among us, we put ourselves out on a limb that threatens at any moment to break of its own weight with absolutely no safety net to protect us.

We live with a professional and ethical obligation to advance knowledge of the human psyche and to provide the best possible care to traumatized and suffering people. But the social, political, legal, and financial environment in which we must practice our profession has rapidly deteriorated so that we as persons and our profession as a vital branch of human knowledge are in serious jeopardy.

We each must play a part that is appropriate to our talents and assets in speaking and acting against the many forces that threaten the enlightenment of the human soul that has been so painstakingly achieved in recent years. Each of us must act from our deepest professional sense to ensure that those human beings living among us who have suffered so much for so long be given an opportunity to heal, to grow, to transform themselves, and to be allowed to enter the community of humans with dignity and a sense of worth that our society was organized to guarantee. I hope the people who have spoken to you from these pages have inspired you as they have inspired me to stand up and be counted as human beings who believe in working for fair and effective treatment for all who need it.

Appendix

Informed Consent Regarding Limited Physical Contact During Psychotherapy

I, _____ , hereby grant permission to my therapist, _____ to engage in limited forms of physical contact with me as a part of our ongoing psychotherapy process.

I understand that the purpose of therapeutic touching is to actualize for study, in concrete physical forms, certain basic aspects of human contact which I may have been deprived of or which may have been distorted in my personal development.

I understand that the purpose of therapeutic touching is not for gratification of physical longings, nor for providing physical comfort or support. Rather, the specific forms and times of the limited physical therapeutic contact are aimed towards understanding issues around the approach to, the achievement of, the sustaining of, and/or the breaking off of human emotional contact.

I understand that limited forms of physical contact such as handshakes, "A.A. type" hugs, occasional hand holding, and other token physical gestures are not uncommon as a part of the interpersonal process of psychotherapy. However, other forms of touching are more rare and need to be clearly understood by both parties and discussed in terms of their possible meanings.

I understand that many professional psychotherapists believe that physical contact of any sort is inappropriate because it fails to encourage verbalization and symbolization of exactly what meanings might be implicit in the physical touch.

I understand that sexual touching of any type is unethical, illegal, and never a part of professional psychotherapy.

I understand that many aspects of the psychotherapeutic process, including the possible value of limited physical contact, cannot be established as clearly beneficial on a scientific basis. But I also understand that physical contact has many values in human relationships and that to categorically exclude it from the psychotherapeutic relationship may be detrimental to my therapeutic process when the critical focus for study needs to be around concrete and personal experiences of meaningful and sustained interpersonal contact.

I HEREBY AGREE THAT SHOULD I HAVE ANY MISGIVINGS, DOUBTS, OR NEGATIVE REACTIONS to therapeutic physical contact or to the anticipation of such, that I will immediately discuss my concerns with my therapist.

If for any reason I experience concerns which I am reluctant to discuss directly with my therapist, or if I feel unsatisfied with our discussion, I HEREBY AGREE TO SEEK IMMEDIATE THIRD PARTY PROFESSIONAL CONSULTATION FROM A LICENSED PSYCHOTHERAPIST OF MY CHOICE OR ONE WHO IS RECOMMENDED BY MY THERAPIST. This part of the agreement is to ensure that no misunderstandings or uncomfortable feelings arise as a result of physical contact or anticipation of therapeutic physical touching.

I understand that I may at any time choose to discontinue this permission by a mutual exchange of written acknowledgments indicating that permission for therapeutic physical contact is revoked.

I HAVE CAREFULLY READ ALL OF THE ABOVE PROVISIONS AND HAVE DISCUSSED THEM WITH MY THERAPIST. ANY QUESTIONS OR MISGIVINGS I HAVE ARE WRITTEN IN THE SPACE PROVIDED BELOW.

_____   _____

Client or Patient   Date

_____   _____

Therapist or Analyst   Date

ADDITIONAL SPECIFIC REQUESTED PROCEDURES:

Request	Initial	Date

Request	Initial	Date

Request	Initial	Date

SPECIFIC QUESTIONS, MISGIVINGS, AND CONCERNS:

References

Balint, A. (1943). On Identification. *International Journal of Psycho-Analysis* 24:97–107

Bion, W. R. (1962). *Learning from Experience*. New York: Basic Books.

——— (1963). *Elements of Psycho-Analysis*. New York: Basic Books.

——— (1977). *Second Thoughts*. New York: Jason Aronson.

Blanck, G., and Blanck, R. (1974). *Ego Psychology: Theory and Practice*. New York: Columbia University Press.

——— (1979). *Ego Psychology II: Psychoanalytic Developmental Psychology*. New York: Columbia University Press.

Bollas, C. (1979). The transformational object. *International Journal of Psycho-Analysis* 59:97–107.

——— (1982). On the relation to the self as an object. *International Journal of Psycho-Analysis* 63:347–359.

——— (1987). *The Shadow of the Object*. London: Free Association.

——— (1989). *Forces of Destiny: Psychoanalysis and Human Idiom*. London: Free Association.

Bowlby, J. (1969). *Attachment and Loss: Separation Anxiety and Anger*, vol. 1. New York: Basic Books.

Brazelton, T. B., and Barnard, K. E. (1990). *Touch: The Foundation of Experience*. Madison, CT: International Universities Press.

Castaneda, C. (1991). *The Power of Silence*. New York: Washington Square Press.

Ekstein, R., and Motto, R. (1966). *Children of Time and Space, of Action and Impulse*. New York: Appleton Century Crofts.

Ferenczi, S. (1912). Transitory symptom-constructions during the analysis (transitory conversion, substitution, illusion, hallucination, "character-regression," and "expression-displacement"), pp. 193–212. In *First Contributions to Psycho-Analysis*, compiled by John Rickman. New York: Brunner/Mazel, 1952.

―――― (1919). "On the Technique of Psycho-Analysis." In *Further Contributions to the Theory and Technique of Psycho-Analysis*, pp. 177–189. London: Hogarth, 1950.

Fraiberg, S. (1982). Pathological defenses in infancy. *Psychoanalytic Quarterly* 51:612–635.

Freud, A. (1951). Observations on child development. In *Indications for Child Analysis and Other Papers*, pp. 143–162. New York: International Universities Press, 1968.

―――― (1952). The role of bodily illness in the mental life of children. In *Indications for Child Analysis and Other Papers*, pp. 260–279. New York: International Universities Press, 1968.

―――― (1958). Child observation and prediction of development. In *Research at the Hampstead Child-Therapy Clinic and Other Papers*, pp. 102–135. Taken from M. M. R. Khan, *The Privacy of The Self*, p. 57. New York International Universities Press, 1974.

Freud, S. (1895a). Project for a scientific psychology. *Standard Edition* 1:283–388.

―――― (1895b). Studies on Hysteria. *Standard Edition* 2.

―――― (1900). *The Interpretation of Dreams*. New York: Avon Books.

―――― (1911). Case history. *Standard Edition* 12:12–34.

―――― (1918). An infantile neurosis. *Standard Edition*. 17:1–124.

―――― (1920). Beyond the pleasure principle. *Standard Edition* 18:3–64.

―――― (1923). The ego and the id. *Standard Edition* 19:3–68.

―――― (1933). New introductory lectures on psycho-analysis. *Standard Edition* 22:1–184.

Giovacchini, P. L. (1979). *Treatment of Primitive Mental States*. New York: Jason Aronson.

Green, A. (1986). The dead mother. In *On Private Madness*. London: Hogarth Press.

Greenacre, P. (1958). Towards the understanding of the physical nucleus of some defence reactions. *International Journal of Psycho-Analysis* 39:69–76.

―――― (1960). Further notes on fetishism. *Psychoanalytic Study of the Child* 15:191–207 New York: International Universities Press.

Grotstein, J., ed. (1981). *Dare I Disturb the Universe?* Beverly Hills, CA: Caesura.

Hammett, V. B. O. (1961). Delusional transference. *American Journal of Psychotherapy* 15:574–581.

Hare, D. (1983). *Plenty*. New York: Penguin.

Hedges, L. E. (1983a). *A listening perspective for the organizing personality*. Cassette lecture distributed by The Newport Center for Psychoanalytic Studies, 1439 E. Chapman Ave., Orange, California 92666. Presented June 5.

_____ (1983b). *Listening Perspectives in Psychotherapy*. New York: Jason Aronson.

_____ (1992). *Interpreting the Countertransference*. Northvale, NJ: Jason Aronson.

_____ (1994a). *Working the Organizing Experience*. Northvale, NJ: Jason Aronson.

_____ (1994b). *Remembering, Repeating, and Working Through Childhood Trauma*. Northvale, NJ: Jason Aronson.

_____ (In press). *Strategic Emotional Involvement*. Northvale, NJ: Jason Aronson.

Hedges, L. E., and Hulgus, J. (1991). *Working the organizing experience: a cutting edge approach to work with psychotic, schizoid, autistic, and organizing states.* Seminar filmed at Charter Hospital of Mission Viejo, CA, September 20.

Hilton, V. W. (1994). The devil in America: the end of the millennium. *The California Therapist*, vol. 6, issue #1.

Jacobson, E. (1954). The self and object world: vicissitudes of their infantile cathexis and their influence on ideational and affective development. *Psychoanalytic Study of the Child* 9:75–127. New York: International Universities Press.

_____ (1964). *The Self and Object World*. New York: International Universities Press.

Jorgenson, S. (1993). *Inherent Potentials and Their Relation to Psychotic Features*. Dissertation presented to California Graduate Institute.

Kafka, F. (1926). *The Castle*. New York: Schocken Books.

_____ (1937). *The Trial*. New York: Vintage Books.

_____ (1979). *The Basic Kafka*. New York: Pocket Books.

Kaplan, L. (1978). *Oneness and Separateness*. New York: Simon & Schuster.

Kernberg, O. (1975). *Borderline Conditions and Pathological Narcissism*. New York: Jason Aronson.

_____ (1976). *Object Relations Theory and Clinical Psychoanalysis*. New York: Jason Aronson.

_____ (1980a). *Internal World and External Reality*. New York: Jason Aronson.

_____ (1980b). Lecture given at the conference on "The Narcissistic Personality." Los Angeles, October, sponsored by the Los Angeles Psychoanalytic Society and Institute.

Khan, M. M. R. (1963). The concept of cumulative trauma. *Psychoanalytic Study of the Child*, 18:286–306. New York: International Universities Press.

_____ (1974). *The Privacy of the Self: Papers on Psychoanalytic Theory and Technique*. New York: New York University Press.

Klein, M. (1937, revised in 1975). *Love, Guilt and Reparation and Other Works*. New York: Free Press.

_____ (1952). Some theoretical conclusions regarding the emotional life of the infant. In *Developments in Psycho-Analysis*, edited by J. Rivere. London: Hogarth.

_____ (1957). *Envy and Gratitude*. New York: Basic Books.

Kohut, H. (1971). *The Analysis of the Self*. New York: International Universities Press.

_____ (1978). Introspection, empathy, and psychoanalysis: an examination of the relationship between observation and theory. In *The Search for the Self. Selected*

Writings of Heinz Kohut 1950–1978, volume 1, pp. 205–232. New York: International Universities Press.

———— (1981). Summarizing Reflections at UCLA Conference on "Progress in Self Psychology," October 5.

———— (1984). *How Does Analysis Cure?* Chicago: University of Chicago Press.

———— (1991). *The Search for the Self. Selected Writings of Heinz Kohut: 1978–1981, volume 4.* Madison, CT: International Universities Press.

Kosinski, J. (1970). *Being There.* New York: Harcourt, Brace, Jovanovich.

Kris, E. (1951). Some comments and observations on early autoerotic activities. *Psychoanalytic Study of the Child* 6:95–116. New York: International Universities Press.

———— (1956a). The personal myth. *Journal of the American Psychoanalytic Association* 4:653–681.

———— (1956b). The recovery of childhood memories in psychoanalysis. *Psychoanalytic Study of the Child* 11:54–88. New York: International Universities Press.

Lacan, J. (trans. 1977). The function and field of speech and language in psychoanalysis. In *Ecrits: A Selection.* New York: W. W. Norton, 1953.

Little, M. (1958). On delusional transference (transference psychosis). *International Journal of Psycho-Analysis* 39:134–138.

———— (1960). On basic unity. *International Journal of Psycho-Analysis* 41:377–384.

———— (1981). *Transference Neurosis and Transference Psychosis: Toward a Basic Unity.* New York: Jason Aronson.

———— (1990). *Psychotic Anxieties and Containment: A Personal Record of an Analysis with Winnicott.* Northvale, NJ: Jason Aronson.

Lowen, A. (1975). *Bioenergetics.* London: Penguin Books.

Mahler, M. (1968). *On Human Symbiosis and the Vicissitudes of Individuation, vol. 1, Infantile Psychosis.* New York: International Universities Press.

Mahler, M., Pine, F., and Bergman, A. (1975). *The Psychological Birth of the Human Infant: Symbiosis and Individuation.* New York: Basic Books.

McDougall, J. (1989). *Theatres of the Body.* London: Free Association Press.

Milner, M. (1952). Aspects of symbolism in comprehension of the not-self. *International Journal of Psycho-Analysis* 33:181–185.

Reider, N. (1957). Transference psychosis. *Journal of Hillside Hospital,* 6:131–140.

Rosenfeld, H. (1954). Considerations regarding the psychoanalytic approach to acute and chronic schizophrenia. *International Journal of Psycho-Analysis* 35:135–140.

Schafer, R. (1976). *A New Language for Psychoanalysis.* New Haven: Yale University Press.

Searles, H. F. (1960). *The Nonhuman Environment.* New York: International Universities Press.

———— (1979). *Countertransference and Related Subjects. Selected Papers.* New York: International Universities Press.

Spence, D. (1982). *Historical Truth and Narrative Truth.* New York: W. W. Norton.

Sterba, R. F. (1934). The fate of the ego in analytic therapy. *International Journal of Psycho-Analysis* 15:117–126.

Stern, D. N. (1985). *The Interpersonal World of the Infant.* New York: Basic Books.

Stolorow, R., and Atwood, G. (1982). Psychoanalytic phenomenology of the dream. *Annual of Psychoanalysis* 10:205–220.

Strachey, J. (1934). *The Nature of the Therapeutic Action of Psychoanalysis.* International Journal of Psycho-Analysis 50:275–292.

Suskind, P. (1986). *Perfume.* New York: Washington Square Press.

Tausk, V. (1919). On the Origin of the Influencing Machine in Schizophrenia. *Psychoanalytic Quarterly.* 2:519–556.

Tomatis, A. A. (1991). *The Conscious Ear. My Life of Transformation Through Listening.* New York: Station Hill.

Tronick, E., and Cohn, J. (1988). Infant–mother face-to-face communicative interaction: age and gender differences in coordination and the occurrence of miscoordination. *Child Development* 60:85–92.

Tustin, F. (1972). *Autism and Childhood Psychosis.* London: Hogarth.

—— (1981). *Autistic States in Children.* London: Routledge and Kegan Paul.

—— (1985). *Autistic States and Adult Psychopathology: Introductory Remarks and Case Consultation.* Continuing Education Seminars. (Video). Los Angeles, CA.

—— (1986). *Autistic Barriers in Neurotic Patients.* New Haven: Yale University Press.

Wallerstein, R. (1967). Reconstruction and mastery in the transference psychosis. *Journal of the American Psychoanalytic Association* 15(3):551–583.

Winnicott, D. W. (1949a). *Hate in the Countertransference.* International Journal of Psycho-Analysis. 30:69–75.

—— (1949b). Birth memories, birth trauma, and anxiety. In *Through Paediatrics to Psycho-Analysis,* pp. 174–194. New York: Basic Books, 1975.

—— (1952). Psychoses and child care. In *Through Paediatrics to Psycho-Analysis.* pp. 219–228. New York: Basic Books, 1975.

—— (1953). Transitional objects and transitional phenomena: a Study of the first not-me possession. *International Journal of Psycho-Analysis.* 34:89–97.

—— (1960). The theory of the parent–infant relationship. *The Maturational Processes and the Facilitating Environment,* pp. 37–55. New York: International Universities Press, 1965.

—— (1974). Fear of breakdown. *International Review of Psycho-Analysis* 1:103.

Index